KING OF THE GUNRUNNERS

James W. Miller

University Press of Mississippi / Jackson

KING OF THE GUN RUNNERS

How a Philadelphia Fruit Importer
Inspired a Revolution and Provoked
the Spanish-American War

The University Press of Mississippi is the scholarly publishing agency of the Mississippi Institutions of Higher Learning: Alcorn State University, Delta State University, Jackson State University, Mississippi State University, Mississippi University for Women, Mississippi Valley State University, University of Mississippi, and University of Southern Mississippi.

www.upress.state.ms.us

The University Press of Mississippi is a member of the Association of University Presses.

Copyright © 2024 by University Press of Mississippi
All rights reserved
Manufactured in the United States of America
∞

Library of Congress Cataloging-in-Publication Data

Names: Miller, James W., 1948– author.
Title: King of the gunrunners : how a Philadelphia fruit importer inspired a revolution and provoked the Spanish-American war / James W. Miller.
Other titles: How a Philadelphia fruit importer inspired a revolution and provoked the Spanish-American war
Description: Jackson : University Press of Mississippi, [2024] | Includes bibliographical references and index.
Identifiers: LCCN 2023043162 (print) | LCCN 2023043163 (ebook) | ISBN 9781496849908 (hardback) | ISBN 9781496849939 (epub) | ISBN 9781496849946 (epub) | ISBN 9781496849953 (pdf) | ISBN 9781496849960 (pdf)
Subjects: LCSH: Hart, John D. (Fruit importer) | Spanish-American War, 1898—Causes. | Filibusters—United States—19th century. | Illegal arms transfers—United States—19th century.
Classification: LCC E715 .M55 2024 (print) | LCC E715 (ebook) | DDC 973.8/9—dc23/eng/20231010
LC record available at https://lccn.loc.gov/2023043162
LC ebook record available at https://lccn.loc.gov/2023043163

British Library Cataloging-in-Publication Data available

For Jean

CONTENTS

Acknowledgments ix

Prologue xiii

Chapter 1 A Wondrous World 3

Chapter 2 A New Revolution 10

Chapter 3 Scrambling for Ships 18

Chapter 4 The Wealthy and Useful Ker 28

Chapter 5 The Director of Expeditions 37

Chapter 6 A Lesson in Competition 43

Chapter 7 Fully Vested in the Filibuster Business 49

Chapter 8 Not a Man of Patience 56

Chapter 9 "Until Cuba Is Free" 62

Chapter 10 A Clear Victory in Court 71

Chapter 11 Spanish Spies and US Marshals 81

Chapter 12 "Captain Dynamite" Johnny O'Brien 88

Chapter 13 A Quick Indoctrination into Filibuster Protocol 94

Chapter 14 A Booming Reply of "NOT GUILTY!" 101

Chapter 15 "Damfoolitis" 108

Chapter 16 Prosecution or Persecution? 116

Chapter 17 An Ambitious Expedition 123

Chapter 18 A Worst-Case Scenario 131

Chapter 19 Publicity Agent for an Expedition 140

Chapter 20 "You Don't Often See a Man Like Him" 149

Chapter 21 "Justly Convicted" 155

Chapter 22 The *Laurada*'s Last Expedition 162

Chapter 23 Captain Dynamite's Expedition to Havana 168

Chapter 24 Broke and Headed for Prison 177

Chapter 25 The King of the Gunrunners Is Affirmed 184

Chapter 26 Perceived Wrongs and Righteous Rights 193

Chapter 27 The *Maine* Explodes, and Hart Goes to Prison 199

Chapter 28 A Full and Complete Pardon 207

Chapter 29 The Importing Business Had Changed 217

Chapter 30 He Took Up the Cause and Suffered for It 226

    Epilogue 233

    Source Notes 235

    Bibliography 263

    Index 271

ACKNOWLEDGMENTS

Nobody writes a book on an island, even when it's about an island, so I wish to acknowledge those people whose contributions were invaluable during the discovery, research, and writing of this book.

King of the Gunrunners would not have been possible without the encouragement of Rosemary James, proprietress of the William Faulkner Society in New Orleans and director of the Words and Music Literary Festival. Rosemary provided the platform for my work to be "discovered" through the festival and its writing competition, the same service she has afforded scores of talented authors who just needed an opportunity to showcase their work.

Thanks to Dave Cohn, my fellow "comma cop" at the *Baltimore Evening Sun*, for providing much insight and information on John D. Hart's Baltimore connections. Dave helped me humanize the subject, especially after he located Hart's grave at Loudon Park Cemetery. Cemetery records included handwritten letters from Hart's wife Kate and led to succeeding generations of Hart's family. Sharon Holt Neil and Sandra Holt Luty, the great-granddaughters of John and Kate Hart, provided family stories and a trove of photographs from their grandmother Grace, the Harts' youngest daughter. Included are perhaps the only surviving photographs of John and Kate as well as a photograph labeled "the Hart dock" of a bustling Pier 11 in Philadelphia.

Rick Barton, an author and director of the creative writing program at the University of New Orleans, proved far more than a golf buddy and lunch companion. Rick always was supportive and ready to provide comments, criticism, and encouragement, especially over twenty-five-cent martinis at Commander's Palace. Another great friend at UNO, the late Sybil Boudreau of the Earl K. Long Library, helped locate obscure sources and volunteered a vacant microfilm machine when yet another interlibrary loan produced more information.

Deserving of note are the long-forgotten Spanish professors who tried to teach me the language during four semesters of my undergraduate years at the University of Kentucky. My work in their classes merited nothing higher than a C, but the language option saved me from having to take any math courses. Thankfully, the exposure engendered a love of the language, which has matured as I've grown older. When I did come across a troublesome translation of Spanish-language documents, two special people helped me through it. Jay Sequeira of Managua, Nicaragua, my friend and next-door neighbor in New Orleans, was always willing to help in return for a cold beer. When Jay had trouble with the Old Spanish of the 1890s, I relied on Osvaldo Ortega, a Cuban and my son's Spanish teacher at Jesuit High School. Osvaldo would not even take a beer in payment, informing me that he believed helping me was his "duty" as a Cuban.

Many others contributed to my research. Irene Wainwright, archivist in the Louisiana Division at the New Orleans Public Library, opened her Spanish American collection. Ed Richi, curator of printed media at the Delaware Historical Society, found an original letter from John D. Hart printed on the distinctive stationery of the Hart line.

Elizabeth Ballard of the research staff at the Library of Congress in Washington, a childhood friend from Shelbyville, Kentucky, helped me navigate through the wealth of information at the LOC. Anne-Marie Casolina in the Hispanic Reading Room at the LOC introduced me to the writing of George Washington Auxier, which was invaluable in understanding the propaganda efforts of the Cuban revolutionaries. Charles Johnson of the research staff at the National Archives helped me navigate through Coast Guard files that contained accounts of revenue cutters that chased the filibusters.

Natalie Baur, archivist at the University of Miami's Cuban Heritage Collection, offered valuable insight regarding their Tomás Estrada Palma Collection, while Florence M. Turcotte, literary manuscripts archivist at the University of Florida Libraries in Gainesville, provided information on the *Three Friends* from the Napoleon Bonaparte Broward papers.

After I had cobbled together and refined several drafts, fellow authors and friends Jeffrey Marx, Dr. Bill Ellis, and James Nicholson read the manuscript and offered suggestions that strengthened the story. Similar recognition goes to my proprietary focus group, the monthly meeting of the Bible, Book, and Beverage Society at Lakeview Presbyterian Church in New Orleans. The members have been baffled by Bonhoeffer, frustrated by Faulkner, and comforted by local authors, and offered comments, criticism, and a firm insistence that the manuscript deserved publication. Thankfully, that was achieved when Emily Snyder Bandy, acquisitions editor of the University Press of Mississippi, took a special interest and offered a contract with UPM. Emily and the UPM staff have been professional and helpful at patching over any gaps that I might have overlooked.

Finally, but far from last, I would like to thank my family. My wife Jean's patience and encouragement soothed my conscience during the research process and allowed me the hours, days, and months of isolation during the writing, rewriting, and editing process. Special kudos go out to my daughter Lindsay and brother Jerry, who read early drafts and offered suggestions and encouragement. Apologies to my other children, Charles Connor and Layne, when Dad paid far more attention to John D. Hart than to you. I love you all!

—James W. Miller

PROLOGUE

Forty young Cubans fidgeted in the darkness of the tugboat's hold, cursing the order to put out their beloved cigarettes. It was near midnight on February 25, 1896, and the tug *W. J. McCaldin* bounced across the choppy water of New York Harbor toward a rendezvous off Liberty Island. They dared not invite discovery, for the Spanish minister in Washington had spies in every American port and the backing of the US government. The travelers breathed easier as the tug slowed and came alongside the tramp steamer *Bermuda*, whose engines were in motion, her screw revolving, and the chain cable in the hawsehole rattling with the rising anchor. The sound was music to the Cubans, who knew that the *Bermuda* soon would deliver them to the revolution in their homeland.

Suddenly, a crewman on deck shouted a warning. The US revenue cutter *Hudson*, full of federal agents and Pinkerton detectives, was bearing down and was soon upon them. Captain Charles M. Goodwin of the *Hudson* ordered the tug to heave to, but after no response he barked the order to ram the tug. The government boat struck the *W. J. McCaldin* amidships with far more din than damage, but the reverberation was enough to bring the towboat to a meek standstill. When Goodwin ordered the cutter to break off and head for the steamer, the tug made a wild dash for the Battery.

The *Hudson* glided near the *Bermuda*'s portside companion ladder, and US Marshal John McCarthy grabbed hold and swung onto the rungs followed by a haphazard horde of badges and brass buttons. "We are in charge here," McCarthy shouted, his men tumbling over one another onto the deck, raising their shields in one hand and revolvers in the other.

The Cubans on board quickly surrendered, but in the commotion few noticed the *W. J. McCaldin* returning to the scene with a new player in this maritime drama. A tall, stocky man with a thick mustache and wearing a black bowler stood defiantly at the tug's bow like a carved figurehead. His name was John D. Hart, the most notorious target of two nations that, for different reasons, wanted to put him away for good.

John D. Hart grew up in the shipping community of Baltimore before moving his fruit importing business to the larger market of Philadelphia. He soon became the busiest importer of tropical fruit on the Delaware River waterfront, his fleet of steamships carrying a steady stream of succulent bananas, pineapples, and coconuts from the breadbasket of the West Indies to the insatiable American markets. Hart was often heard before he was seen, his thunderous voice echoing along the harbor in protest of perfidy or incompetence, or his perception of either. He tolerated no rebellious acts on his ships, and his actions confirmed he had even less patience for dissent while on land.

Hart's business model was as aggressive as his demeanor, which left him in a constant state of financial difficulty. His insistence on importing unending loads of fruit ignored the laws of supply and demand. A load of fruit that might go unsold because of economic hard times or intense competition was an afterthought for Hart until it ripened into another fiscal crisis.

It was during one such predicament that Hart was approached by Emilio Nuñez, a member of the Cuban Revolutionary Party, a cadre of exiled conspirators in New York whose singular purpose was to liberate the island from four hundred years of Spanish rule. The head of the party, an ambitious writer and orator named José Martí, had launched the current uprising in January 1895 after determining that the final revolution would require material support shipped in from the United States. After several attempts were thwarted by federal authorities, Spanish spies, or incompetence, Nuñez was named conductor of this gunrunner's railway, securing vessels and enlisting pilots from a farrago of American towboat operators, merchant captains, and importers in the burgeoning fruit industry.

At his first meeting with Hart, Nuñez dangled the promise of adventure in the pursuit of a just cause and adequate payment for services rendered. Hart's vessels merely had to evade the federal revenue cutters that guarded every American port, negotiate the hazards of a reluctant sea, and avoid the shot and shell of the Spanish blockade to deliver their cargo at remote inlets and isolated beaches along the Cuban coast. After fulfilling a mission, Hart was free to send his empty ships to the lush plantations of Jamaica, Nicaragua, and Colombia to fill their empty holds with fruit for the lucrative return northward. What could go wrong?

Hart and others who became embroiled in the trade were called "filibusters," derived from the Dutch word *vrijbuiter* for freebooters or pirates. Their deeds inspired the label attached to a political act in Congress, but in the nineteenth century filibusters were both respected and reviled, depending where sentiment fell. Hart's early success at landing expeditions did not go unnoticed by those who were trying to stop him. Spain wanted to halt the flow of arms into rebel hands, while the US government rigidly enforced its neutrality laws, which prohibited citizens from aiding the enemy of a nation with whom the United States was at peace.

The American public was well informed of Hart's adventures through the aggressive tactics of newspaper publishers William Randolph Hearst, Joseph Pulitzer, and others who demanded stories that captivated their paying readers. A boisterous master of ships thumbing his nose at his own government while transporting guns and ammunition to the Cuban insurgents was an irresistible story. The cooperative "Yellow Press" reported and often embellished Hart's exploits as derring-do on the Spanish Main, eliciting visions of hardened buccaneers sailing fearlessly into danger with a brace of pistols in their hands and a cutlass between their teeth.

Hart's experience in New York Harbor on this night was far less romantic. When the *W. J. McCaldin* returned to the scene, Hart leaped from the tug's railing to the *Bermuda*'s ladder and climbed onto the deck, loudly demanding that the officers explain their actions. Marshal McCarthy told Hart the vessel was being seized by the US government and warned him not to interfere or he would be arrested.

"To hell with the United States marshals and their gang!" Hart yelled defiantly, turning to the bewildered Cubans. "Come on here, get up this anchor and let us get out to sea!" Hart raised clenched fists to confirm his command as a half dozen marshals rushed toward him, only to be scattered like a swarm of mosquitoes. Hart was in high dudgeon, running across the deck trying to rally his men while ignoring the pursuing authorities. The agents, though bloodied for their efforts, finally subdued Hart and pinned him to the deck.

Writhing and trying to break free, Hart sputtered his objections to no avail. He was bound and caged in a makeshift brig below until he could be transported to the federal lockup at the foot of Manhattan. His antagonist out of the way, Marshal McCarthy went to work disabling the *Bermuda* as Hart sat below, seething at the federal officers' disrespectful treatment of an American citizen.

The government would win this battle, but its hold on the flamboyant charter master would be brief. John D. Hart was the most visible of a disparate group of mariners between New York and Key West who for nearly three years tormented Spanish authorities, frustrated the US government, and were hailed as heroes by an oppressed people fighting to be free.

KING OF THE GUNRUNNERS

Chapter 1

A WONDROUS WORLD

Johnny Hart was mesmerized as his packet boat eased into a new world that was the Baltimore Basin. Tall masts loomed like a bobbing forest along the wharves, while fishing boats of every size and color dodged larger craft, delivering their loads of oysters, crabs, and rockfish for sale. High overhead, flocks of seagulls carrying the souls of sailors lost at sea cavorted in their aerial gymnastics.

Along the docks, mules hitched to wagons waited as longshoremen unloaded the oceangoing vessels while agents determined the value and destinations of the products. Stevedores maneuvered their spindly cranes to load outgoing commodities such as grain, sugar, cattle, and lumber, for delivery to New York, Philadelphia, and beyond. The shipping support industry encircled the harbor like a sailor's scarf as carpenters, joiners, smiths, coopers, and vendors of sailcloth, cordage, and iron bustled from ship to ship confirming their value to each captain and charter master.

The practical equation of maritime commerce was hypnotic to the young passenger as his boat pulled into its moorings at the South Street wharf.

The year was 1872, seven years past a destructive yet redemptive Civil War in which Baltimore had grown into one of the busiest ports in America. It was a hub of importing, exporting, shipbuilding, and commerce orchestrated by a mercantile class where riches came to fearless men who were more persistent than their competition.

Confederate veteran James H. Hart had returned to the Eastern Shore of Virginia, where his prospects were as predictable as the sunrise over the ocean and sunset over the bay. For a few years, he tried to squeeze what he could from the earth or sea, but after years of struggling he moved his wife, Susan Rayfield Hart, and children Johnny, eleven, Rebecca, ten, and Levi, seven, from drowsy Accomac County to the harborside colossus 120 miles to the north.

While a father saw greater opportunity to provide for his family, his older son would see the move as a pathway to his own ascendancy. Johnny Hart would thrive in the seafaring community through an unquenchable spirit and extreme confidence in his own abilities. As he grew and matured, those qualities would frame a life of audacious triumph, discouraging failure, and a final desperate grasp at redemption.

Jim Hart settled his family at 146 German Street, where they spent their first three years in the new city. Hart's knowledge of the sea fit the opportunity found in a maritime community, and within two years he joined Byrd & Co., a firm that supplied produce to a growing and diverse population. Hart prospered in the buying and selling of fruits and vegetables, and in 1875 he left Byrd and established J. H. Hart & Co., a commission produce agency, at 71 West Pratt Street. Later that year, Jim Hart brought his fourteen-year-old son, Johnny, into the business.

For Johnny Hart, the wharves confirmed his initial impressions and hinted at the mystery and romance of what lay beyond. Dockwallopers cursing in strange languages unloaded exotic cargoes from locations whose names danced on the tongue, like Aspinwall, Baracoa, and Eleuthera. The boy heard tales of tawny maidens luring sailors onto hidden reefs or bloodthirsty corsairs who would cut out your heart over a jape. He shivered as toothless seamen described storms with waves as high as a tenement house, and he clapped as hornpipe chanteys recalled sunken galleons carrying gold from the New World. Johnny Hart spent his early years among these traders, captains, and crews, their lies and truths blending to create a wondrous world that awaited the unafraid.

Johnny Hart did not let the stories interfere with his work at J. H. Hart & Co., and in 1876 Jim Hart reflected a father's satisfaction when he rechristened the company J. H. Hart & Son. The firm enjoyed rapid growth in the early years thanks to an emerging product. In 1878, brothers Robert and Samuel Henry, fruit merchants who had enjoyed modest success importing pineapples from the Bahamas, learned that the banana was a commercial possibility. Captain Lorenzo D. Baker had been shipping the fruit from Jamaica to Boston since 1870, and author Jules Verne in his 1873 book *Around the World in Eighty Days* described the fruit of the banana "as healthy as bread and as succulent as cream." Still, a banana was considered a novelty and a delicacy to all but the wealthy.

The Henry brothers loaded up their small schooner *David I. Taylor* with a general cargo of flour, grits, and fat pork and headed for Port Antonio on the northern coast of Jamaica. Sugar was the major export of the West Indies, and the banana was such an anomaly of trade that Captain Gaskins of the *Taylor*

A fruiter from the West Indies unloads a cargo of bananas at the Baltimore Basin. Library of Congress, Prints and Photographs Division, Detroit Publishing Company Collection, reproduction number LC-D401–18502.

had great difficulty finding locals who would harvest enough bananas to fill his boat. The *Taylor* returned to Baltimore with about three thousand bunches, cut green to survive the eight-day voyage in the ship's hold. When the vessel arrived at Bowley's Wharf, a fragile twenty-foot-wide pier erected on pilings, word spread rapidly of this curiosity from another world. The *Baltimore Sun* reported that "thousands" gathered at the wharf to get a glimpse, and maybe a taste, of this bizarre-looking fruit. Scattered samples littered the deck after they were knocked off bunches being unloaded. Exposed to the sun, they ripened on the trip, and the more curious helped themselves. The first to sample this mysterious delicacy spat out the first few bites. They had not yet learned that a banana must be peeled to be enjoyed.

Wholesale fruit vendors such as Jim Hart caught on more quickly, and they bought the entire load. They priced the bananas at an extravagant fifty cents a dozen, but anybody who could afford it paid. The success experienced by the Henry brothers prompted other Baltimore businessmen to enter the trade. One such entrepreneur was young Alexander Beauregard Bulack, whose family operated the Chesapeake House restaurant at 223 East Pratt Street. With its proximity to the wharves, the Chesapeake House was a favorite meeting place for captains and crews seeking a steady floor and a tankard of ale. The inevitable whirlwind of

These portraits were likely taken shortly after John D. Hart's marriage to Catherine "Kate" Staylor in 1878. Courtesy of Sharon Holt Neil and Sandra Holt Luty, granddaughters of Grace Hart Holt.

tall tales and badinage that blew through the tavern likely inspired Aleck Bulack's fascination with the adventure and opportunity awaiting in the West Indies.

Before he was twenty, Bulack bought the schooner *Bertha Ellen* at a federal marshal's sale and established a regular route to the port of Baracoa, on the northeastern coast of Cuba. By 1880, business had grown so much that Bulack took on nineteen-year-old Johnny Hart as a partner. The relationship possibly stemmed from a mutual interest of their fathers. Jacob Bulack was a rabid secessionist during the Civil War and had offered his restaurant as a rendezvous point for Confederate spies. It is reasonable that in the small harborside community, the elder Bulack made the acquaintance of fruit agent Jim Hart, who had himself participated in the glorious rebellion. Hart's stories of his days as a private with the Twenty-Third Virginia Infantry and the unit's service at Antietam and Gettysburg would have shaped delicious conversation for like-minded souls at the Chesapeake House.

New business opportunity appealed to Johnny Hart, who already had devoted ample attention to his personal life. At age seventeen, Johnny had married Catherine "Kate" Staylor, who was twenty-five, and they wasted little time starting a family. Daughter Ada Lee was born in 1879, nine months and two weeks after the marriage. Now a produce clerk, husband, and father, Johnny Hart was ready to trade the land-based buying of fruit for the ocean-bound transportation of it. At

Bulack's side over the next few years, Hart would learn the importing business while absorbing all he could about the care and maintenance of ships and crews.

Johnny Hart quickly grew into a ship's master well beyond his age. He learned how to buy, charter, and dispatch boats and crews for profit, dictating means, direction, and purpose for every ship that sailed under the Bulack-Hart banner. He relied on his captains to operate the vessels and chart the course, but it was his voyage and his fruit that had to be bought, loaded, and delivered intact to achieve the company's goal of profit. Johnny Hart was master of his ships wherever they sailed, and he made certain all around him knew it.

His authority was reinforced by his imposing presence. Tall at just over six feet, he was broad at the shoulders, and he advanced the notion that he was seldom wrong. The outside world entered through cynical hazel eyes beneath thick, baleful brows, and a broad black mustache drooped beyond the corners of his mouth enhancing an air of severity. He was not afraid of a scrap, and would frequently find himself in the middle of one, often at his own instigation. John D. Hart was becoming a man who traveled amid his own tumult.

Bulack was his counterpoint, as sturdy and solid as a mainmast, often ignored but just as essential. Bulack preferred to remain in the background and identify opportunities in trade while Hart was the partner on the water. Plying the same waters as explorers and fortune hunters before him, or English and Dutch pirates centuries earlier, suited Hart's soulful lust for adventure.

Hart's voyages took him down the East Coast and past the Bahamas, a few score of islands lifting themselves out of the blue waters of the Atlantic. Good food was scarce aboard the fruiters, the ventilation was poor, and accommodations were sparse. Crew members slept in hastily hung hammocks or on the open deck when the moon was full and bright. The ships glided easily in ordinary weather but became sinister as coffins when gales swept the Caribbean or howled about Cape Hatteras. Clad in his oilskins and emboldened by his curiosity, Johnny Hart saw each storm as just another obstacle before arriving in the rich lands of bananas, pineapples, and promise.

The fruit boats passed Cape Maysí at the eastern tip of Cuba and entered the Windward Passage before taking a southwesterly course for Jamaica. Kingston was larger, but for the fruiters the banana capital of Port Antonio was the destination of legend and beauty. Jamaica's rocky northern coastline was pocked with crevices and secluded coves that provided refuge for pirates in a bygone day. The cloud-wreathed heights of Blue Mountain Peak cascaded into a tangle of smaller mountains and knobs carpeted with ferns, flowering trees, and vines. Below sprawled a lush labyrinth of palm-veiled valleys that spilled into the turquoise waters of Port Antonio's twin harbors. For the young man from Accomac County, Port Antonio held the charm and mystery of a world awaiting his discovery.

Ada Lee Hart was the eldest daughter of John and Kate Hart, born in 1879. Courtesy of Sharon Holt Neil and Sandra Holt Luty, granddaughters of Grace Hart Holt.

Laura Hart was the second daughter of John and Kate Hart, born in 1882. Courtesy of Sharon Holt Neil and Sandra Holt Luty, granddaughters of Grace Hart Holt.

When the fruiters docked, the excursion ended and the work began. Hart learned to negotiate the lowest prices while the shrewd fruit agents of the islands haggled to bid the numbers as high as possible. He learned to buy only properly green bananas that would not spoil on the voyage north, and he watched the loading to make certain no overripe pieces of fruit were laced in. Once the deal was made, the loading commenced with laborers toting the fifty- to eighty-pound stems through sweat and good humor.

Each voyage added yet another layer to Johnny Hart's experience and enthusiasm. No sooner had he returned with one load of fruit than he ordered the vessel back to sea for another. As business expanded, so did the family of John and Kate Hart. A son, Walter Jackson Hart, was born on October 16, 1880, and another daughter, Laura, was born on November 19, 1882. The growing family made it prudent for John and Kate to find a place of their own, and in 1882 they moved out of the family home and into their own house at 81 South Paca Street.

As their partnership evolved, Hart learned that Bulack had engaged in an uncharacteristic activity that would influence his own irrevocable course. Perhaps it was over beverages at the Chesapeake House that Johnny Hart learned that Bulack's ships had carried arms to revolutionists in Cuba. Hart was captivated as Bulack told of clandestine voyages in which his ships evaded persistent US customs vessels and then slipped through the Spanish blockade of the island to deliver arms for a price.

Bulack had entered the game late, after Spain had suppressed an extended rebellion of whites and free mulattos on Cuba that lasted from 1868 to 1878, known as the Ten Years' War. Misrule of the island by Spain, taxation without representation, and a realization by the sugar planters that the days of slavery were numbered all encouraged Cuban aspirations toward nationhood.

The Revolutionary Army paused its quest for *Cuba Libre* when Spain agreed to the Pact of Zanjón, giving freedom to the rebel leaders, liberating all slaves who fought with the rebels, and providing representation in the Cortes. But not all rebel leaders were convinced that Spain would keep her promises, and a group of recalcitrant generals, chief among them General Calixto García, started another revolution in 1879 that Bulack helped supply.

Bulack's war was known in Cuba as La Guerra Chiquita, or "the Little War." Such perilous and illegal activities earned Bulack admittance into an exclusive club whose entry fee was courage and whose success was measured in survival.

Whether stated or merely filed away for the future, Hart likely came to the conclusion that if gunrunning had been a profitable sideline for the modest Bulack, it easily could one day tempt his own more adventurous instincts.

Chapter 2

A NEW REVOLUTION

While the guerrilla wars raged on Cuba, US administrations kept a proper distance from the rebels, accepting Madrid's position that the conflict was purely an internal Spanish matter. But in New York a rebel legation called the Cuban Revolutionary Committee spread pro-Cuban propaganda and raised funds from sympathetic Americans for an eventual "final" revolution.

The Cuban revolutionists in the United States were led by a young man who had not fought in the wars and even had appealed to the generals to lay down their arms. José Martí, a writer and orator, had followed the fighting from Spain, Guatemala, and New York, arguing that it would take more than weapons to oust the Spaniards from the island. A well-planned effort supported by the people could succeed, Martí said, but the military elite were not so easily convinced. The generals who had fought so long and gained so little distrusted bold talkers and politicians who had never swung a machete in battle or shot a Spaniard dead. They were convinced that independence could only be achieved by a coup led by professional soldiers.

Martí was only twenty-six when he arrived in New York the first week of 1880 and joined the Cuban Revolutionary Committee. Martí so inspired those around him that he was appointed interim head of the group, but he knew that if his plan for Cuban independence had any hope of succeeding, he had to enlist the old guardians of the Ten Years' War.

José Martí was convinced that a well-planned effort supported by the people could be successful, but the generals who had fought long and gained little were not easily convinced. Courtesy of the Cuban Heritage Collection, University of Miami Libraries, Coral Gables, Florida.

Martí's initial efforts to persuade the two most respected generals—Máximo Gómez and Antonio Maceo—were ignored. Gómez, living in his native Dominican Republic, visited Martí in New York in 1884 to discuss a new revolution, but the warrior's conclusion was that Martí was a big talker who feared an actual war for independence in which politicians would be eclipsed by military men. Maceo, the "Bronze Titan" who controlled the Black *mambises* that totaled nearly half the rebels, found Martí to be unlikable and unreliable. Not surprisingly, Martí did not trust the two generals, suspecting that Gómez and Maceo desired to set themselves up as military dictators after independence was achieved.

The difference between Martí and the generals was more than age. Martí was an idealist who looked at class differences and the racial animosity dividing the Cubans of the immigration and saw a reflection of all that was wrong with Spanish rule in Cuba. The ultimate goal of the revolution was to end such things on the island. The first step must be to end them among the émigrés who constituted 126 Cuban clubs in eighteen cities. Cubans needed something more to unify them than hatred of Spain. To Martí, the words and ideas that could accomplish that were far more important than the guns and ammunition Gómez sought.

One of the veterans who saw the merits of both positions was twenty-four-year-old Emilio Nuñez. Born in 1855 at Sagua la Grande on the northern coast of Santa Clara Province, Nuñez began fighting the Spanish before he was twenty, rising to the rank of colonel toward the end of the Ten Years' War. But the Cuban people were tired of open conflict and refused to support efforts to keep fighting in the Little War. Without popular support, defeat was imminent, and Nuñez was among those who reluctantly surrendered. He was imprisoned at Morro Castle, overlooking Havana Harbor, but he escaped and joined the widespread emigration to the United States. Cuba's northern neighbor appealed to those who sought a new life, free of war and oppression, where a man or woman could determine their own future. But for patriots like Nuñez, America had a more useful purpose—as a staging area where plans for the final revolution could be formulated with little interference and even sympathetic support.

Nuñez joined Martí's Revolutionary Committee and frequently traveled to Cuba to meet with local leaders and monitor Spanish troop strength on the island. His movements began to draw increased attention from federal agents. In 1884, he was arrested on suspicion of organizing filibustering expeditions between the United States and Cuba. Well known to Spanish authorities in Cuba, Nuñez was arrested in the harbor of Sagua la Grande when his schooner was stopped by a Spanish gunboat. He was released after declaring he was merely in his hometown visiting family members.

Outwardly, Nuñez was following a familiar path as an immigrant in America. He settled in Philadelphia, went to work in a cigar factory, and later enrolled in the dental surgery program at the University of Pennsylvania. He graduated in 1889 and practiced briefly before establishing a cigar business, Emilio Nuñez & Co., at 29 South Third Street. His marriage to Dolores Portuondo y Biez produced three sons and a daughter in the first seven years of marriage. For all appearances, Nuñez and his family were living the American dream.

The fruit business was thriving, and in 1883 Jim Hart and Alexander Bulack merged their firms to form J. Hart & Co. The alliance made sense from a business standpoint, joining two enterprises responsible for both supply and demand. Jim Hart had developed buyers and distribution channels for as much fruit as Johnny Hart and Aleck Bulack could bring back from the West Indies. To fill the demand, Hart and Bulack chartered a fleet of schooners, vessels rigged with fore-and-aft sails on two masts and between 100 and 150 feet in length. The boats required fewer crew members, an attractive feature for any enterprise, but their most compelling feature was their speed. Drawing as little as five feet, schooners sailed like a flat rock skipping across water. They could make the trip to Abaco in the Bahamas in less than four days, Baracoa in six, and Port Antonio in seven.

The merger worked to perfection. J. Hart & Co. became one of five major Baltimore importers bringing products from the West Indies and swelling Bowley's Wharf with the popular cargoes. The little *B. A. Wagner*, a fifty-ton schooner, carried the 1883 season's first load of pineapples, delivering 69,000 "pines" from Abaco, while the *Ebeneezer* delivered its loads from Green Turtle Cay. The *Worden and Evans* brought loads from Eleuthera, while the *E. S. Johnson* did the same from Gregorytown. The 1884 season was even more profitable as 35,000 dozen pineapples were delivered in the first two weeks of the season, and 20,000 dozen were afloat and headed for Bowley's Wharf by mid-June.

Through the steady guidance of Jim Hart and the energy and diligence of Johnny Hart and Aleck Bulack, the prosperous 1884 season catapulted J. Hart & Co. to the level of Henry Brothers as princes of Baltimore's fruit importing business.

But fate would intervene to interrupt young Hart's ascent. On September 24, 1884, his father, mentor, and business partner James H. Hart died suddenly at age forty-nine. Shocked and saddened, John and mother Susan asked Bulack to help navigate the unexpected arrangements and named him executor of James's estate. For the price of $86, Bulack arranged the purchase of a 260-square-foot burial plot at Loudon Park Cemetery, located twelve miles south of the harbor in the rolling fields off present-day Wilkens Avenue. An elaborate headstone was created as a fitting epitaph to James's life and revealed the influences of both wife and son. Standing more than nine feet tall from the base to its top, the stone features an *A*-shaped carved upper section topped with a stone urn. The main section boasts the lunette of a ship in full sail, birth and death dates, and the inscription "To my beloved Husband, Capt. Jas. H. Hart."

Grief's intrusion inevitably evolves into a new normality, and twenty-four-year-old John D. Hart returned to the shipping business as his father's successor in sales and distribution. Jim Hart's experience and knowledge doubtless were essential to the firm's success, and now it would be up to his son to take over and help Bulack keep things running.

But even as Hart grieved for his father, John and Kate suffered a dreadful blow the following May 22 with the death of their son Walter, who was not yet five. Walter was laid to rest in the family plot near his grandfather, a small, simple stone commemorating a shortened life. To whatever lingering extent John was affected by the deaths of his father and son or even by his wife's likely melancholy, he threw himself into business at an even more frenetic pace. What would become clear is that John D. Hart began to drift apart from his business partner Bulack and eventually his wife Kate and began to grasp incautiously for something only he would understand.

The Hart-Bulack partnership deteriorated in the years following Jim Hart's death. The studious Bulack pored over bills of lading and orders for more fruit while trying to identify new lines of business such as carrying barbed wire to Jamaica. The ambitious and energetic Hart, however, believed that success came from expansion despite a careless disregard for the expense it took to achieve it.

With the advent of the winter banana season in November 1885, Hart and Bulack bolstered their fleet by chartering sister steamships *Pirate* and *Kenilworth*, based in Glasgow, Scotland. Steamers made from iron and steel were gradually replacing the wooden schooners, and at 247 tons they could carry three times as much cargo. Just as importantly, they were even faster, breaking the seas at thirteen knots.

The additional capacity brought in even more fruit for Bulack and Hart, who wasted no opportunity to trumpet their success. After the *Kenilworth* arrived with a large load of bananas from Bluefields, Nicaragua, Hart carried a large stalk measuring four and a half feet a few blocks up South Street to the *Sun* offices on Baltimore Street. "It was so closely grown with fruit," the *Sun* duly reported, "that it was a load for one man to carry."

The season was not without its perils, however. In an era of rudimentary storm detection and communication, the *Kenilworth* survived a major hurricane off the Florida coast on August 23 and 24 only to find its destination, Jamaica, in shambles.

Trouble continued into the new year. It was nearly half-past eleven on December 31, 1886, and the revelers on Pratt Street were lighting Roman fire amid the pop-pop-pop of pistols and firecrackers. Ignored in the revelry was a trail of heavy smoke pouring out of an upstairs window at Nos. 22 and 24, Bowley's Wharf. The four-story brick building housed the fruit merchant J. Hart & Co.

The flames leaped from the windows and illuminated the night sky as every bell in Baltimore pealed in the beginning of the new year. Some celebrants believed that the conflagration was a part of the merriment, but to Hart and Bulack it heralded a fitting start to what would become another difficult year.

As Hart and Bulack were assessing damage from the fire later that day, a telegram from Captain Sam Hughes arrived with the news that the *Pirate* had run aground in heavy winds at Cape Henry near Norfolk. The steamer bound for Kingston carried one hundred thousand feet of white pine lumber valued at $2,500. Hart telegraphed a salvage company in Norfolk to tow the *Pirate* to port.

Over the next year, the partners tried everything to turn their fortunes around. On May 2, Hart and Bulack were forced to make a deed of trust for the benefit of creditors, a type of prebankruptcy then in practice. Liabilities of J. Hart & Co. were reported at $60,000, while only $25,000 in assets were listed. Hart's solution was to increase volume, and he continued to charter more vessels over the objections of the more practical Bulack. More and more coconuts and bananas came into Baltimore, but demand could not keep up with the supply. Hart ordered one of his ships to load as many bananas as possible, but when thirty thousand bunches sat unsold on Bowley's Wharf, Hart was forced to have them reloaded, taken out to sea, and dumped overboard.

The Hart-Bulack partnership needed a change, and in 1889 the partners agreed upon a radical solution. Hart believed that the negative atmosphere for business in Baltimore was ill suited to his determination and desire for success, so he proposed that Bulack remain in Baltimore and oversee the company's traditional market, while he open an office in Philadelphia.

The move was likely intended to provide Hart with a fresh start in more ways than one. In the previous ten months, John and Kate lost a child at birth, and Hart's mother Susan had followed her husband in death at age fifty-three. Hart was ready to leave grief and failure behind him, and Philadelphia was perfect. It

Written on the back of this family photograph was the note "leaving Hart's dock." John D. Hart's Philadelphia office was at Pier 11 on the Delaware River almost directly under the present-day Benjamin Franklin Bridge. Courtesy of Sharon Holt Neil and Sandra Holt Luty, granddaughters of Grace Hart Holt.

was the third-largest city in the nation with a population exceeding one million, and more people to feed meant more opportunity for profits.

He moved Kate and daughters Laura and Ada to the new city and established an office at Pier 11 at the Race Street wharf, almost directly under the present-day Benjamin Franklin Bridge. The move immediately energized Hart. Surely this was a place that would appreciate his considerable dash and ambition.

John D. Hart's first six months in Philadelphia convinced him that he had made the right decision. His vessels imported 218,367 bunches of bananas compared with 196,495 by his nearest competitor, the locally owned H. U. Howes & Co. Hart appeared to have resurrected his halcyon days when the fruit trade guaranteed riches, and he had convinced any doubters in the small shipping fraternity that he could, indeed, run a profitable business.

But Hart's apparent good fortune only foreshadowed more trouble. The merchants who depended on Hart's cargoes were meeting privately to determine how to recover a bigger share of the lucrative market. Frank W. Stanton, a former

Grace Hart was the third daughter of John and Kate Hart, born in 1891. This photo was taken in Atlantic City, likely in 1900 when her father was running the Shoreham Hotel. Courtesy of Sharon Holt Neil and Sandra Holt Luty, granddaughters of Grace Hart Holt.

Hart employee who had departed over a disagreement with his boss, proposed a combination, or merger, in which the buyers would import their own fruit. The merchants favored the scheme to a man, especially those who were put off by the brash young upstart from Baltimore.

When the newspapers heard about it, they dubbed it "the Fruit War" and sought reaction from the wronged parties. The elder Howes, who had worked with most of the merchants for years and was well aware of business cycles, declined to burn any bridges and refused comment. However, Hart believed that he had been violated and was not shy about voicing his displeasure. "We propose to stay in the business," he told the *Philadelphia Inquirer*. "We will see who can stand it longest."

The *Inquirer* predicted that the upheaval would depress prices to "next to nothing" in the coming spring fruit season, "as there will be no more half measures upon the part of the Baltimore Fruit Co. J. D. Hart has already chartered eight steamers for the early spring shipments, double the usual number."

Hart considered himself under attack, and he was not about to allow a group of landlocked storekeepers depose him. The Merchants Fruit Company struck first, signing away the steamers *Gurly* and *Holguin* after their charter agreements with Hart expired. Unbowed, Hart surveyed lists of available craft and immediately signed charter agreements with a handful of Norwegian ships, expanding his fleet to ten vessels.

Hart's vessels were bringing in more bananas to Philadelphia than all of his competitors combined, but mere dominance was not enough. Hart added even more ships and spared no expense to supply as much product as possible and let demand take care of itself. This precarious approach was vulnerable to falling prices, uncertain availability of labor, and changing consumer tastes. With the merchants publicly working to deny him markets for the seemingly unending glut of bananas, Hart again was stuck with more bananas than he could sell.

That was the final straw for Hart's partner, sitting helpless in Baltimore. Aleck Bulack wanted nothing to do with an unfamiliar market whose merchants potentially could boycott his shipments, and he persuaded Hart to dissolve their partnership. Bulack established the Bulack Fruit Company and left immediately for Honduras to seek new plantations to supply his ships. Hart rechartered the Baltimore Fruit Company in Camden, New Jersey, where wife Kate would welcome another daughter, Grace, into the family in May.

Chapter 3

SCRAMBLING FOR SHIPS

José Martí's quest for Cuban independence picked up momentum in 1891 and 1892 during visits to the vibrant Cuban communities in Tampa and Key West. Exiles had inflated the population of Key West to eighteen thousand residents, which made it the largest city in Florida. Cuban entrepreneurs and tobacco workers had flocked to both cities after the Ten Years' War, taking advantage of American tariffs that gave preferential treatment to Cuban leaf rolled by Americans in place of cigars imported directly from Cuba. Cigar workers in Cuba and Florida had solid radical pedigrees shaped by the anarchist movement, which was strong in Spain and Cuba. To bring them into the fold, Martí altered his message to give more attention to the social demands of Cuban workers.

During meetings with leaders of patriotic clubs, Martí drew up the "Bases y estatutos secretos del Partido Revolucionario Cubano" ("Bases and Secret Statutes of the Cuban Revolutionary Party"). The document became the cornerstone of the Cuban revolutionary movement. Each of the eight articles of the Bases began with the words "The Cuban Revolutionary Party," which suggested more political appeal than the old "committee." The overriding theme: "The Cuban Revolutionary Party is constituted in order to achieve . . . the absolute independence of the island of Cuba."

After his triumphs in Florida, Martí on March 14 issued the first edition of *Patria*, the newspaper that became the official organ of the revolution. Martí and the CRP called for an independent, democratic Cuba committed to racial equality and economic and political justice, although the party's true purpose

Gonzalo de Quesada y Aróstegui, top, and Horatio Rubens had their 1888 City College of New York senior portraits taken in the form of cartes de visite, which they used as business cards after graduation. Photos courtesy of the Archives, City College of New York, CUNY.

was to collect contributions from Cuban émigrés to purchase arms and make other preparations for the revolution.

By April 10, thirty-four clubs from eight émigré colonies had approved the Bases and Statutes. Thirteen clubs were from Key West, seven from New York, five from Tampa, five from Jamaica, and one each from Philadelphia, Boston, Ocala, and New Orleans. Martí was elected delegate, the organization's premier position, and Benjamin Guerra, forty-four, was elected treasurer. Guerra, a native of Puerto Príncipe, was a teenage messenger during the Ten Years' War who moved to the United States with his family afterward. Martí designated his young acolyte, Gonzalo de Quesada y Aróstegui, as secretary. Quesada, twenty-seven, was born in

Havana and came to the United States, where he was educated at the City College of New York and was editor of the school newspaper. Martí later hired Quesada's roommate at CCNY, attorney Horatio Rubens. The twenty-seven-year-old Jewish New Yorker had earned a law degree at the Columbia School of Law and was admitted to the bar in 1891. More importantly, he spoke Spanish fluently and had learned about the political and economic situation in Cuba from experience at his previous job, as chief clerk in the law offices of Elihu Root, corporate counsel for the Sugar Trust.

In the meantime, the activities of the Cuban Revolutionary Party were drawing attention from New York newspapers. The *New York Herald* published a story that characterized the party as a "patriotic society devoted to preparation for the coming revolution." The *Herald* named names and probably filled in some blanks in the Spanish consul's intelligence reports. Its wide net snagged most of those who would bear watching in the years to come, including Martí. "Mr. Marti has an office at No. 40 Broadway," the *Herald* reported. "He is not yet 40 years of age and was less than 20 when he joined the forces of the revolution. He is today perhaps the most widely known orator and writer among the Spanish speaking residents of North and Central America."

Among others mentioned prominently was Emilio Nuñez: "He now resides in Philadelphia where he has a large practice as a dentist. He was one of the first to espouse the cause of the revolution and is ready now anytime to do it again."

Martí's plans for an invasion were progressing in the proper direction, but even the man who was now called "the Apostle" could not control the economic depression that hit the United States in 1893. In February, the Philadelphia and Reading Railway Company declared bankruptcy, and the resulting panic triggered the nation's worst economic depression until the Great Depression nearly four decades later. More than fifteen thousand companies closed, five hundred banks failed, and as many as three million men and women lost their jobs. The resulting hard times ravaged Key West as cigar factories closed, workers were laid off, and labor leaders accused factory owners of using the situation as an excuse to lower salaries.

The economic panic resulted in a serious decline in contributions to the party, which altered the timetable for revolution. Martí issued a stream of declarations and traveled extensively to emphasize the urgency of his message to key constituents, but the situation grew more critical. Owners of cigar factories that had reopened demanded concessions that the workers saw as unfair. Workers went on strike in many factories, which threatened to eliminate the donations Martí needed to fund his revolution. Many workers tithed 10 percent of their wages to the cause, funds that would stop if the crisis was not averted.

The financial panic also had a negative effect on the shipping industry. Less available income reduced the nation's appetite for luxuries such as fresh fruit, but John D. Hart stubbornly continued to import loads of bananas from Port

Antonio and Baracoa. When demand could not keep up with supply, his competitors noticed and adjusted. The new year of 1894 saw Hart lose charter contracts with the *Gurly*, *Holguin*, and *Bernard* to a new company called Quaker City Fruit, which was formed by the Boston Fruit Company. Boston Fruit, which would evolve into the massive United Fruit Company, formed such local companies with an eye toward replicating the monopolies that were dominating other industries. The evolving business model of owning the fields, growing the bananas, and importing them on company vessels threatened to leave independent importers like Hart in a futile race to catch up.

Hart had only two steamers under contract, the *Empress*, commanded by Sam Hughes, and the *Braganza*, commanded by Charles H. Holttum. Business picked up over the summer months, and Hart chartered three additional steamers of Norwegian registry, the *Sif*, the *Leon*, and the *Georg Dumois*. With five vessels in his fleet, Hart demanded that his captains complete more trips to bring in more fruit. No sooner would a vessel unload than the insistent Hart would order the captain to coal up and head back to sea. There was no time for rest on a Hart charter, because the only thing that mattered was how many loads of fruit the vessel delivered.

Every captain did not embrace the policy. After the *Georg Dumois* arrived from Baracoa with a load of bananas, Hart ordered its captain, Johannes Bru, to put back to sea immediately. The captain objected, preferring to give his men at least one night ashore away from the rigors of a voyage. But Hart's charter agreements did not include the captain's approval of either destination or departures, and he demanded that Bru follow orders. When the captain objected again, Hart attacked him with his walking stick, and Bru filed assault charges against Hart.

Two weeks later, the Norwegian vessels stopped sailing under a Hart charter. The timing could have been coincidental, but Hart again found himself scrambling for ships to maintain routes to the profitable honey hole of the West Indies. An examination of daily East Coast shipping reports in the *Baltimore Sun* and *Philadelphia Inquirer* reveals fewer than a handful of arrivals by Hart vessels from Port Antonio during the last four months of 1894, while other lines continued regular commerce.

Hart refused to give up, and he chartered the Danish vessel *Horsa*, which was commanded by an experienced captain named Jacob Henry Jasper Wiborg. The *Horsa* was 210 feet long with a 26-foot beam and a draft of 13 feet when loaded, and her speed was a frisky eleven to twelve knots. With Sam Hughes piloting the *Empress* and Wiborg commanding the *Horsa*, Hart had two solid rocks at the end of 1894 upon which to stand and fight.

Martí realized that independence could not be achieved without support from the United States, especially in the form of ships to carry the invasion force and weapons to the island. He doubtless was aware of failed expeditions in the past, so he delegated the task to an American businessman. Nathaniel Barnett Borden, tall and curly haired, cut a studious figure in his silver-rimmed glasses, but his youthful countenance betrayed a fearless business sense. Only thirty-four, Borden had established N. B. Borden & Co., a successful shipping business, in the port town of Fernandina Beach, Florida, thirty-five miles northeast of Jacksonville on the northwest shore of Amelia Island. He also displayed the combative nature of his father, Thomas J. Borden, a lieutenant colonel in the Sixth Mississippi Regiment during the Civil War.

Borden greeted Martí and fellow conspirator Julio Sanguily at the Florida House Inn on Third Street in Fernandina Beach, where Borden treated them to all the hospitality he could muster. Timing was critical for Martí. The first expeditionary force of the Cuban Revolutionary Party was scheduled to depart for Cuba in January 1895, and Borden was assigned the task of finding three vessels to return the leaders of the final revolution to Cuba. However, Martí cautioned Borden to wait for final approval because he had not yet collected enough money to pay for three ships.

Martí wrote to Eduardo H. Gato, a Key West cigar magnate, and asked for a loan that would ensure the revolution could commence. Martí pledged to repay the loan with contributions to come, but if the revolution should fail, he pledged to repay the money himself. Martí's writing earned about $8,000 per year, most of which had gone into the revolutionary fund. His impassioned plea to Gato affirmed glory to a son of Cuba, but if Gato had reservations, Martí said he would "beg and lick the ground like a dog." Gato sent the money, and in early December, Martí telegraphed Borden in Fernandina that he was "ready for business."

Borden traveled to New York, but he found the task to secure vessels more difficult than he had envisioned. He was unable to find an available steamship on his own, so he approached the small but chatty community of yacht brokers. A week before Christmas, Borden chartered the yacht *Lagonda* for $2,400 per month. Owned by the Reverend William L. Moore of New York, the *Lagonda* was a schooner-rigged wooden steam yacht, 126 feet long with a 19½-foot beam and a draft of 10 feet.

A few days later, Borden made a bid to yacht broker M. Hubbe for the steam yacht *Amadis*, owned by George H. Kimball of Cleveland, the retired chief engineer of the Lake Shore Railroad. The vessel was smaller at one hundred feet in length with an eighteen-foot width and a draft of seven feet. Its stated passenger capacity was nineteen including a crew of ten, far short of the size needed to carry a large party. However, a boat in the slip was worth two at sea, and Borden paid the monthly charter fee of $1,400. Word traveled quickly, and news that a Florida man was trying to hire crews for two ships fanned suspicion and soon was communicated to authorities.

Borden left New York by train for Rockland, Maine, with ten crewmen and Captain John Dahl to meet the *Amadis*. On the train, Borden introduced Dahl to a Mr. Miranda and a Mr. Mantell, aliases that veiled the identities of Cuban revolutionaries Patricio Corona and Manuel Mantilla, who would command the expedition. Dahl and his crew were suspicious, and when the train arrived in Rockland on December 24, the captain and three crewmen refused to let Mantilla or Corona board the *Amadis*. Borden was not accustomed to such interference from employees, so he fired Dahl and the reluctant crewmen on the spot and named first mate David S. Weed captain. He ordered Weed to bring the *Amadis* to Boston, where Borden still was attempting to secure a steamship. However, Weed shared Dahl's suspicions and sent a telegram to owner Kimball that the *Amadis* might be involved with smugglers.

At Boston, Borden was introduced to Gjert Lootz, agent for the 484-ton steamer *Baracoa*, a Norwegian vessel with a crew of sixteen under veteran captain Solomon Clausen. The *Baracoa* epitomized a tramp steamer with aging equipment and simple design, but she was capable of a respectable eleven knots. Borden chartered the *Baracoa* for $2,375.

Borden wired Martí that the ships were ready. The revolution that Martí had so long envisioned was about to begin.

Martí determined that one of the vessels would take on boxes of arms and ammunition that had been delivered to Borden's warehouse in Fernandina. That vessel would sail to Costa Rica and pick up General Antonio Maceo and his brother José and take them to Oriente Province in eastern Cuba. The second vessel also would load at Fernandina, then sail to Key West, where it would pick up 150 men led by Generals Carlos Roloff and Serafín Sánchez and unload them near Santiago at the southeastern end of the island. Martí would board the third vessel at Fernandina and sail to Santo Domingo, where he would pick up Gómez, General Enrique Collazo, and three hundred men. They would be dropped in Camagüey Province in east-central Cuba.

Borden commanded Captain Weed to take the *Amadis* from Boston to Savannah, and when he arrived to wire Borden at Fernandina for instructions. He instructed Captain Griffing of the *Lagonda* to leave New York on January 1 with the same orders. After the *Lagonda* sailed, rumors of its destination reached a reporter for the *New York World*, the aggressive newspaper owned by Joseph Pulitzer. The reporter questioned Hubbe, the broker for the *Amadis*, who voiced his suspicions with one word: "filibusters."

On January 7, editors at the *World* telegraphed T. A. Hall, their stringer in Fernandina, alerting him to watch for two "suspicious crafts," the *Lagonda* and the *Amadis*. Hall immediately showed the dispatch to George L. Baltzell, the collector of customs at Fernandina. Two days later, the *Lagonda* arrived at Borden's wharf at the foot of Dade Street. On January 10, federal agent James Batewell telegraphed his boss, John G. Carlisle, the secretary of the treasury in Washington, that the *Lagonda* and *Amadis* were on "a filibustering expedition."

Carlisle waited two days to alert special agent S. W. Paul in Tampa: "Department advised that steam yacht *Lagonda* and *Amadis* left New York fourth instant on alleged filibustering expedition. Confer with Collector Fernandina and render all possible assistance in preventing violation neutrality laws."

Martí, who was back in New York making final preparations, learned of the problems from the *World* story of January 11. In a lengthy article titled "Off on a Secret Cruise," the newspaper detailed Borden's suspicious activities and concluded: "[T]he general opinion is that the yachts are bound either to Haiti, Honduras or Nicaragua." The stories sufficiently panicked the owners of the vessels, especially when they learned that the companies insuring them had canceled all policies when they suspected the true nature of the voyages.

Borden's problems compounded when Collector Baltzell and reporter Hall boarded the *Lagonda* at Fernandina and began asking questions. Borden invited the visitors on a two-hour trip up the St. Mary's River to take on a supply of fresh water and wash out the boilers, hoping the audacity of the invitation would disarm any suspicions. Borden's dodge appeared to work as Baltzell and Hall saw nothing peculiar. But when they returned to Fernandina, Hall received another telegram from his editors insisting that he watch the "very suspicious" *Lagonda*. That night, a number of heavy boxes were loaded onto the ship as Captain Griffing slept.

The next morning, Griffing discovered the boxes and stormed into Baltzell's office. He surrendered his sailing papers, effectively resigning from command of the vessel. Baltzell quickly deputized the local deputy sheriff, C. B. Higginbotham, a robust thirty-five-year-old lawman who now enjoyed federal authority, to prevent further boarding.

Reverend Moore met with James F. Kilbreth, collector of customs at the Port of New York, to report that the persons who chartered his *Lagonda* were attempting to use it for illegal purposes. Kilbreth telegraphed Baltzell to "detain the *Lagonda* under Sections 5289 and 5290." Those sections were among a list of statutes that constituted the "neutrality laws," which prohibited US citizens from committing or promoting hostilities upon the subjects, citizens, or property of a "sovereign" nation with whom the United States was at peace, such as Spain. That meant that any vessel departing a US port carrying arms and men whose intention was to aid rebels fighting Spain violated the neutrality laws and risked seizure.

Consistent with the government's intention to prevent private citizens from sparking conflict with other nations, the laws effectively created a two-headed monster for every expedition to avoid. First, they had to avoid the fleet of federal revenue cutters guarding US ports, and, if they could get out of the port and into open water, they had to avoid the Spanish blockade of cruisers and gunboats when they arrived on the Cuban coast.

The *Baracoa* arrived at Fernandina at 7:00 a.m. on January 13, 1895, its white steel hull glimmering in the morning sun. Baltzell and his deputy boarded the vessel and searched it but found no contraband. The commotion unnerved Captain Clausen, who told Baltzell that his orders were to get the vessel to Fernandina and await further instructions from Borden. After the authorities boarded the vessel, however, Borden sent word that he had a severe toothache and could not meet with Clausen.

On Monday the fourteenth, the *Florida Times-Union* reported that José Martí, "the Cuban revolutionist lecturer," was in town. The fact that Martí was in Jacksonville solved one mystery: "The arms found on board the *Lagonda* were to be taken to the Cuban patriots."

Martí checked into the Travelers Hotel under an assumed name and summoned expedition leaders Enrique Collazo, José María Rodríguez, and Fernando López de Queralta, the latter an aide to General Roloff. Martí wired his secretary, Quesada, and attorney Rubens in New York to travel immediately to Fernandina, where they were to gather intelligence, recommend a course of action, and then report to Martí in Jacksonville.

That same morning, Baltzell proceeded to the waterfront office of N. B. Borden & Co., where he demanded access to the adjoining warehouse. The clerk on duty refused to comply until Borden was summoned. According to an agent's report, Borden "appeared very much 'rattled,' as if a dynamite bomb had been exploded under him." After regaining his composure, Borden promised to attend to the request as soon as he saw a party off at the train station. When he returned, he was accompanied by an attorney from Baker & Drew, a prominent Fernandina law firm.

In the warehouse, federal officers seized 140 crates containing rifles, pistols, ammunition, sabers, and supplies. The largest lot of rifles had been shipped "directly from the factory of the Remington Arms Company at Ilion, N.Y." Total value of the seizure was estimated between $25,000 and $40,000. Borden pretended to be "very much amused and surprised at the discovery that the boxes contained arms." Surprised or not, he attempted to head off the *Amadis* at Morehead City, North Carolina, where she had put in because of heavy gales, but the vessel already had left port. When she arrived the next day at Tybee Island, Georgia, she was seized by Customs Collector J. F. B. Beckwith. Treasury Special Agent C. A. Macatee searched the boat but found only bags of coal stored on the deck. Beckwith ordered the *Amadis* to proceed up the Savannah River to the Montgomery Street wharf, where she was placed under the custody of Captain J. H. Rogers of the revenue cutter *Boutwell*.

Captain Rogers took a cynical view of the filibustering efforts, as he exhibited in a telegram to Secretary Carlisle. "The impression is there are several Cuban 'generals' and patriotic agitators who are making a fat living out of the revolutionary movement. Cubans all over the country subscribe to funds for such purposes and to keep up the interest it is necessary to make some pretense of starting a revolution once or twice a year. The utter absurdity of hiring two or three small pleasure yachts and loading them with a few hundred rifles to try and crush out the power of Spain in Cuba must be apparent to everyone."

Martí's initial disappointment at the failure of the Fernandina mission was muted by a wave of glowing newspaper stories and support from the Cuban clubs. The expeditions were hailed as the first significant step toward independence, and the participants were considered heroes. Martí told Rubens that the publicity would prove that the revolution was under way, which would generate great optimism and more contributions. Predictably, new donations began coming in from supporters such as the cigar makers in Florida, who were now convinced that this big talker could achieve the long-elusive dream of a free Cuba.

On January 29, he signed the order for a general uprising, then left two days later for Montecristi in the Dominican Republic to meet with Generals Gómez and Collazo to consolidate plans for the invasion. Martí declared that the revolution would begin symbolically on February 24 to coincide with the first carnival celebration. The war officially began that day in the village of Baire at the eastern end of Cuba, announced by the celebratory *grito*—the cry for independence and liberty.

On February 26, Quesada sent a telegram to Fernando Figueredo, a local revolutionary in Tampa, declaring: "The revolution broke out on Sunday. The whole island is in arms. The *Herald* says Martí and Gómez have landed from Mexico. Send this news to Ocala and Key West." It did not matter that Martí and Gómez were still in Montecristi, working diligently to come up with a document, "El Manifiesto de Montecristi," which Martí intended as a message to the Cuban people. Martí and Gómez signed the document on March 25, establishing the principles of "a just war" that opposed the colonial regime and not the individual Spaniard. It also urged understanding and appreciation, and not fear, of the "Negro." The plank for racial solidarity was consistent with Martí's previous writings, but it also was intended to mollify General Maceo and his followers. The revolution would not succeed without the Black rebels, and the Black rebels would not fight without the leadership of Maceo.

But Martí and Gómez continued to debate the unresolved issue of where Martí would view the revolution. Gómez argued that Martí should return to New York, where his planning and motivational skill would be protected. The debate continued until a newly arrived batch of mail and newspapers from New York pushed Martí to a decision. A story in an issue of the party organ *Patria* announced that Martí already had landed in Cuba. The effect of the story was immediate. "It is decided!" Martí cried. "Now I must go to Cuba!"

Late on April 9, in a lively sea and heavy showers, Martí, Gómez, and two companions climbed down the ladder of a German freighter bound for Port Antonio and into a small boat. They rowed toward shore through huge swells that threatened to capsize them, and one wave broke the tiller in Gómez's hands. Providentially, the rain stopped, and two signal lights were spotted on the shore. Martí, Gómez, and the others jumped out into chest-deep water and guided their boat toward the beach, where all fell to their knees and kissed the Cuban soil.

They soon made contact with Maceo, who had arrived on the island two weeks earlier. On May 5, the leaders met, but the generals did not want to discuss the form of a future government and demanded that Martí return to the United States, where he would be more effective generating funds for ammunition and supplies. Martí reluctantly agreed, and arrangements were made for him to sail from the Juragua mines near Santiago, but Martí hesitated. He wanted to engage the enemy, if only one time.

On May 17, Gómez received reports that an enemy convoy was in the vicinity, and he rode out to harass the Spaniards near Dos Ríos. Gómez returned two days later with Spanish forces in hot pursuit. He ordered Martí to remain in camp, but Martí had long awaited this moment. He jumped on a white horse and rode out into the melee with only one man at his side, Colonel Ángel de la Guardia, which translates, ironically, as "Guardian Angel."

A Spanish soldier took aim at the man on the white horse and fired. José Martí fell, mortally wounded. The inspiration, planner, and moral conscience for Cuba's independence was dead at age forty-two, just as the revolution he had planned was beginning.

Chapter 4

THE WEALTHY AND USEFUL KER

John D. Hart's ability to maintain a breakeven business was in dispute, and he was growing desperate. He needed a boost similar to the one he had experienced after his move from Baltimore to Philadelphia.

Hart began looking for another business partner who would provide much-needed financial backing while allowing him to run the company as he saw fit, with few questions asked. It also had become apparent that he needed someone who could protect him from himself. Such a savior appeared toward the end of 1894.

William W. Ker booked passage in September on one of Hart's vessels for himself and his fifteen-year-old son, Robert. Ker was a former Philadelphia assistant district attorney and federal prosecutor who was well known in the city. Hart placed them on the *Braganza*, headed for Baracoa, Cuba. It is unknown whether Ker had done any legal work for Hart prior to that, but after the Kers returned on October 2, Bill Ker became increasingly involved in Hart's affairs.

Tall, gaunt, and balding, Ker had served with the Seventy-Third Regiment Pennsylvania Volunteers in the Civil War, then built a lucrative legal practice representing high-profile clients, which led to a prominent public life in politics. If Ker was looking for a new challenge, the shipping industry of Philadelphia was a convenient place to find it. One of his first transactions with Hart, enabled by his contacts in Washington, was the purchase of the *Empress*, a steamship Hart had been chartering for nearly two years. Built in Middlesbrough, England, in 1864, the *Empress* was substantial at 1,200 tons and 230 feet in length, with a 30-foot beam and a 17-foot draft. Hart's application for American registry required

William W. Ker was invaluable to Hart, not only as a well-connected attorney and investor but as a moderating influence on the volatile charter master. Line drawing from the December 16, 1894, edition of the *Philadelphia Inquirer*.

congressional approval, which the well-connected Ker facilitated with ease. The registry was granted on December 21, 1894, and Hart renamed the vessel the *Laurada* in honor of his two older daughters, Laura and Ada.

With the wealthy and useful Ker on board, Hart set about to restore his proper place among Philadelphia's mercantile elite.

In a common affectation of the day, Ker preferred to be addressed as "Captain" Ker, reflecting the rank he had attained during some of the most brutal fighting of the Civil War. Ker enlisted at age twenty on June 1, 1861, six weeks after war was declared, and spent most of his first year on picket duty in the Shenandoah Valley.

The frustration of routine and inaction soon disappeared for Ker and the Seventy-Third with engagements at the Second Battle of Bull Run, Chancellorsville, and the Battle of Gettysburg in July 1863. The Seventy-Third faced murderous fire from the Louisiana Tigers at East Cemetery Hill at Gettysburg, and when their ammunition ran out, Ker and 232 Union men were captured. They were destined for the Confederate death camp at Andersonville, Georgia, but Ker and about twenty-five others escaped. Ker ultimately joined General William T. Sherman's army on its invasion of the South and was present when Sherman accepted the surrender of General Joseph E. Johnston and all remaining rebel forces.

After the war, the twenty-four-year-old Ker returned to Philadelphia and went to work in his brother's print shop while studying law at night. He was admitted to the bar in 1869 and opened a general practice at 520 Walnut Street. Immersion in Democratic Party politics soon followed, which led to Ker's appointment as district attorney of Philadelphia. He soon drew the attention of former Philadelphia attorney and US Attorney General Benjamin H. Brewster, who brought him to Washington to take the lead on several difficult national cases. Ker returned home with a growing reputation that helped him restore his practice and vault him to prominence. He picked up major clients whose cases were national in scope and kept his name in the public eye.

Ker was at the peak of his career. His bigger cases drew international attention, and the smaller ones became important because of him. Ker's fame was growing so fast that a tugboat, the *William W. Ker*, was built to replace another tug that had been lost at sea. The only notable public arena left to conquer was the seductress of the vainglorious. A run for office.

Ker became a cat's paw in the plan of William Francis Harrity, new chair of the Democratic National Committee. Harrity had run Philadelphia's Democratic machine for nearly a decade, but Congressman William McAleer, who represented the Third District that encompassed Philadelphia, would not bend the knee. Harrity persuaded Ker to run against the one-term incumbent, but the result was a resounding defeat for Ker, who collected only 5,500 votes to McAleer's 15,516.

Embarrassed and feeling disgraced, Ker returned to his legal practice only to find that the high-profile cases that once crowded his personal docket had disappeared. His association with John D. Hart came at an opportune time in his career, although the pair could not be more dissimilar. Hart was gruff and jagged around the social edges but unafraid and resolute in his drive to gather fame and wealth. Ker had accumulated such things, was erudite, worldly, and made a living off the dances of fools. The Hart-Ker association was a confluence of conflicting contradictions, but it quickly matured into a coalition in which the individual qualities of each man nurtured those of the other.

Ker had received a telegram from a specialized concern asking if the Hart line might consider hauling a very different type of cargo. Ker had been contacted by the International Migration Society, which repatriated willing Black Americans back to Africa. The venture needed a ship to take subscribers from Savannah, Georgia, to Liberia. While Hart saw a paying customer, Ker saw a story that likely would be covered by every newspaper in the land. The opportunity to help secure respect for the disadvantaged Black man and woman, for whom Captain Ker had fought bravely, must have whetted his humanist idealism. Ker also knew that every story undoubtedly would name the benevolent principals who provided such a generous opportunity for the downtrodden.

It was a paradox of American society in the 1890s that immigrants from Poland, Russia, Germany, Ireland, China, and elsewhere saw America as their land of opportunity, while some Black citizens born in the United States longed for a return to their ancestral homeland. The vision of returning to Africa was a recurring theme throughout the nineteenth century, ever since the creation of the American Colonization Society (ACS) in 1816 by such notables as Henry Clay, James Monroe, Andrew Jackson, and Daniel Webster. The odd confederation initially aligned northern abolitionists with southern planters, who saw free Blacks as an unsettling influence on their slaves. The ACS secured congressional support to establish the Republic of Liberia during the 1820s, but the ACS's ultimate plan collapsed during the 1830s as the South's economic commitment to slavery overshadowed the moral evils of its "peculiar institution."

The movement was revived in the early 1880s when a group of 118 Blacks from Arkansas sailed from New York aboard two ships, renamed the *Liberia* and the *Monrovia*. Interest grew in the 1890s when cotton prices plummeted and white racism reached its zenith. Liberia posed an attractive alternative, an escape to an all-Black world with an elected Black government that offered American settlers free land. The International Migration Society (IMS) was created in 1894 by four white businessmen from Birmingham, Alabama, who enlisted several prominent Black church leaders to serve as an "advisory board."

By early 1895, the IMS claimed several thousand applicants and made plans to settle those who had paid the forty-dollar fee. Sadly, the IMS paid far more attention to collecting money than to logistical details. A trainload of emigrants arrived in Savannah on March 7 only to find neither ship nor accommodations waiting for them. The IMS agent located a vacant warehouse for the passengers, and they settled down to wait for their ship to arrive. Another small detail left undone, however, was that a ship had not been secured before the travelers began heading for Savannah. Daniel J. Flummer, president of the IMS, searched vainly in New York before learning that an agent in Philadelphia was soliciting business and might be able to help.

Flummer alighted from the train at the newly expanded Broad Street Station and took a carriage directly to Pier 11. He presented his situation to Ker and Hart, and the bud quickly blossomed. A man with a cargo seeking a ship had found a man with a ship needing a cargo. The fortuitous match soon resulted in an agreement to charter the *Horsa*, which would require some refitting in order to carry the two hundred passengers scheduled to depart. The desperate Flummer agreed to pay for the alterations, and work began immediately.

The emigrants in Savannah remained in their temporary accommodations for nearly two weeks, which cost the IMS seventy-five dollars a day to house and feed the party. Finally, Captain Jacob Henry Jasper Wiborg piloted the refurbished *Horsa* out of Philadelphia and headed for Savannah. On board to look out for the partners' interests was Ker's son, aspiring lawyer Herbert P. Ker.

A festive air prevailed as a mixed crowd of several thousand assembled at the Savannah waterfront on Tuesday, March 19, to watch the ship's departure. As the gangplank was pulled up, the travelers began singing hymns, including an old spiritual "I'm Going Home to Africa's Shores."

Departure of the Back-to-Africa Movement ship *Horsa*, bound for Liberia with approximately two hundred passengers, half of them from Jefferson County, Arkansas; March 19, 1895. From the Encyclopedia of Arkansas, https://encyclopediaofarkansas.net/entries/back-to-africa-movement-4/.

Nothing was heard from the voyage for more than three weeks, sparking rumors the ship had sunk. However, on April 12, Hart received a cable from Wiborg that the *Horsa* had landed safely, unloaded its passengers, and was heading for Barbados to pick up a load of fruit.

The safe arrival did not end the problems for the emigrants. A telegraphed message that supposedly was sent to announce the travelers' imminent arrival failed to reach its destination, and Liberia was not prepared to receive the new settlers. Moreover, the emigrants arrived without most of the supplies the IMS had promised. The company had purchased the goods and brought them to the wharf in

Savannah, but after the passengers and their baggage were loaded, space remained for only a fraction of the food and supplies. Liberian government officials found the new settlers temporary housing in vacant buildings in the capital, Monrovia, while the good citizens of the city fed the immigrants from their own tables.

Within a month, the furor died down. The new arrivals were settled on their own land in communities near the capital, and Flummer began talking to Hart about an even larger expedition the following year. By then, however, John D. Hart's vessels would become involved in quite another voyage for human liberty.

The declaration of a new revolution in Cuba triggered rumors that expeditions were being organized in virtually every American port. The new Spanish minister in Washington, Enrique Dupuy de Lôme, was swamped with reports from his consuls of filibuster activity between New York and New Orleans.

Spain's frustration with the United States as a base of gunrunning was fueled by a mottled history of US efforts to gain possession of Cuba. In 1823, President John Quincy Adams predicted an inevitable annexation of Cuba. In 1848, Spain rejected a $100 million offer from President James Polk to purchase the island, and six years later, the administration of President Franklin Pierce launched another effort in the so-called Ostend Manifesto that strongly implied that Cuba was desired as a buffer between Haiti's Black revolutionary history and another that could eventually spread to the American South.

Dupuy de Lôme passed each report of filibustering on to the State Department, which, in turn, alerted the Department of the Treasury, which administered the Revenue Cutter Service, the precursor of the Coast Guard. The revenue cutter *McLane* was dispatched from Tampa to Key West and ordered to use all diligence to prevent filibuster activity. Indeed, the Spanish vice consul in Key West received word that filibusters were gathering at Bahia Honda in the Florida Keys and telegraphed the information to Dupuy de Lôme. The minister alerted the cruiser *Infanta Isabel*, which had been patrolling the Florida Straits for weeks, to head for the Keys.

The Keys were one hundred miles of small inlets and sporadic isles of sand and coral rising out of the shoals. Only a few feet above the sea floor, the islands were barren and largely uninhabitable except for the occasional sponge fishermen and native "conchs." The passages between the outcroppings were narrow and navigable only by light-draft boats, which prevented the intrusion of the larger revenue cutters. Masked by its natural elements, the area was a land of misery and frustration for federal agents but perfectly suitable for smuggling.

Despite the rumors, no expeditions had been executed after the declaration of war, and no significant engagements between the insurgents and Spanish troops had occurred since Martí's death. Weeks of inactivity on the seas and in the battlefield fostered a perception by the generals on the island that the surviving leadership did not know what to do next. "The death of Martí came like a thunderclap from a clear sky," the *New York Herald* reported, characterizing the independence movement as "temporarily paralyzed."

Cuban Revolutionary Party treasurer Benjamin Guerra tried to respond to the generals' pleas by buying the ocean tug *George W. Childs*. Named in honor of the late Philadelphia editor and philanthropist, the *Childs* was not a large vessel at a length of 100 feet with a 20-foot beam, a draft of 9.6 feet, and a gross tonnage of 107.5, but it was available. Preparations were made, commanders for the expedition were chosen, and arms and munitions were ordered and paid for.

The *George W. Childs* secretly slipped away from Key West the night of Wednesday, June 5, 1895, and headed for a remote rendezvous in the Florida Keys. Spanish agents learned of the expedition and informed the Spanish minister in Washington, who sent word to the US State Department. But the message was either ignored or lost in a transition of department leadership. New secretary of state Richard Olney had been on the job exactly three days after Walter Q. Gresham's unexpected death on May 28. Eschewing sympathy, Dupuy de Lôme demanded that the US government stop such illegal shipments and respect its own laws of neutrality. Olney took the protest to President Grover Cleveland, who ordered Navy Secretary Hilary A. Herbert to send the cruiser *Raleigh* from Hampton Roads, Virginia, to Key West to help keep order.

On June 11, the secretary of the treasury instructed collectors of customs and the Revenue Cutter Service to take appropriate measures to prevent the formation of filibustering expeditions to Cuba. The notice put more than two thousand employees of the department and eight revenue cutter vessels in the Atlantic on high alert. Practically all efforts of the fleet were now dedicated to preventing the shipment of arms and other supplies to the Cuban rebels.

The following day, President Cleveland issued a proclamation to the American public in which he affirmed the United States' neutrality in the Cuban affair. Cuba was Spain's business, he said, and he ordered all American citizens to cease efforts to interfere with the affairs of a sovereign nation. Cleveland made it clear that citizens and anyone else within US boundaries must "abstain from every violation of the laws" or be "rigorously prosecuted."

Two days after Cleveland's proclamation, the *New York Herald* ran a full page of nine stories wrapped around a four-column line drawing of the "Ocean Tug *George W. Childs*." A subhead purported to identify "[t]he vessel which carried the latest expedition to Cuba."

Another report later in the week said that the expedition had landed one hundred men, one thousand repeating rifles, three million rounds of ammunition, and $250,000 in gold on the island. The latest story claimed that the intrepid little tug had been chased by Spanish cruisers but had outrun them in its dash for home. It was stimulating reading and wonderful news for the revolution and for Cuban sympathizers in the United States.

The news would have been even better if any of it were true. Gonzalo de Quesada, Martí's disciple and now the Revolutionary Party's chief propagandist, had artfully crafted a story that the newspaper boys lapped up. In reality, the *Childs* became a liability almost as soon as she was purchased. Guerra had ordered Martí's former messenger, Charlie Hernández, the son of a wealthy émigré from Brockton, Massachusetts, to find a ship as soon as possible. Hernández heard about the *George W. Childs* for sale in Philadelphia, but, after seeing the vessel, reported that her hull was rotten in places, her machinery was balky, and no more than fifty men could stand shoulder-to-shoulder on her deck. After bringing aboard the required coal to make the trip to Cuba, little room would be left for arms or ammunition.

Undaunted by Hernández's report, Guerra bought the vessel for the bargain price of $8,000 and ordered repairs to be completed. When Hernández took the *Childs* to sea, water began to seep in from the seams almost immediately, and she put into port at Baltimore.

After minimal repairs were made, the *Childs* sputtered southward at a speed of four knots. She made it to Key West, where she picked up expedition leaders Carlos Roloff and Serafín Sánchez, then headed to Santo Domingo to pick up General José María Rodríguez and his men. During the voyage, the ship was pounded by heavy waves, and the wheelhouse had to be lashed down to prevent it from being washed away. When they finally arrived, Rodríguez and his men patched up the boat, and the general purchased coal with his own money before he and forty-three men joined Roloff and Sánchez and headed for Cuba.

Rough weather continued to batter the *Childs*, and those aboard bailed water all the way to the landing point on Cuba's eastern coast near Cape Lucretia. When they approached land and dropped the only two landing boats into the water, one crashed on the rocks and the other washed away. Hernández aborted the landing and directed the tug back through the Florida Straits.

The expedition put in at Pine Key, about twenty-five miles north of Key West, where the men and cargo were left with Sánchez in command. Hernández took the *Childs* to Key West, where he dropped Rodríguez, while Roloff headed to New York to find another boat. Sánchez and his men would remain on Pine Key for more than a month under the relentless summer sun while trying to stay out of sight of passing American cruisers. It was difficult enough stretching their scant ration of food and water, but the men, who had been anxious to fight the Spanish, spent most of their time battling raging insects and avoiding alligators and poisonous snakes.

On June 29, Roloff registered at the City Hotel in Baltimore as "C. Miller" along with Dr. Joseph J. Luis, who signed in as "John Lucas." They were soon joined by John F. Hudson, a ship's captain who informed them he had found a vessel that would fit their needs. The *James Woodall* was a small wooden steamer of a type known as a "menhaden fisherman," but its cubic measurement of 150 tons burden made it big enough for smuggling.

Hudson said that the ship's owners would take $13,000 for the vessel, but the captain required an additional $2,000 for brokering the deal. Unruffled by the price, Luis pulled a roll of bills out of his pocket, peeled off fifteen $1,000 notes, and handed them to Hudson along with an additional sum to provision the vessel with tin plates, spoons, stores, and 128 tons of coal. Roloff had one more request, that Hudson purchase one hundred pairs of shoes. Roloff then revealed that the *James Woodall* would sail from Baltimore to a remote spot in the Florida Keys where they would pick up men and cargo. The final destination was the southern coast of Cuba.

On July 9, the crew threw off lines, and the little steamer puttered slowly out of Baltimore cleared for Progreso, Mexico. Captain Hudson guided the *Woodall* down the Atlantic coast, and on the eighth day at sea arrived at Pine Key to rescue General Sánchez and the men dropped off by the *Childs*. The celebration was joined by Roloff, Rodríguez, and a number of other volunteers who had taken the sloop *Blanche* from Key West. Roloff, a Polish-born veteran of the Union Army who had fought in the Ten Years' War, commanded the expedition and was accompanied by a pilot named Henry who knew the waters around their destination.

The vessel proceeded up the west coast to Cedar Key, where she picked up more recruits all wearing tiny Cuban flags on their hats. Over the next four hours, they loaded three hundred rifles, 150,000 rounds of ammunition, three hundred machetes, several hundred pounds of dynamite, electrical explosive devices, and dynamite caps. Also taken aboard were five hundred ounces of Dr. Esquinaldo's "infallible balm" for wounds. After the cargo was secure, Captain Hudson ordered the cook to feed the exhausted men, and Roloff rewarded the Pine Key refugees with the new shoes purchased in Baltimore.

On the evening of July 24, the *James Woodall* sat off the southern coast of Santa Clara Province, Cuba. Hudson turned over the helm to Henry, and the skilled pilot guided the vessel to a quiet landing at the Tallabacoa River near Trinidad. When she was close enough to the shore, the engines were stopped, and Roloff ordered the men to drop the narrow surfboats into the water and begin loading them with the precious boxes on board.

Once the cargo was transported to the beach, volunteers moved the arms, ammunition, and supplies inland on carts, proud of their success and full of enthusiasm and patriotic ardor. The news of the first successful expedition quickly circulated throughout the sugar country, providing tangible evidence that the uprising had begun and that Spanish rule would face its most serious challenge.

Chapter 5

THE DIRECTOR OF EXPEDITIONS

Emilio Nuñez was first a soldier, then a dentist, and then owner of a cigar store. But none of his experiences prepared him for his new assignment as the Cuban Revolutionary Party's director of expeditions. Smuggling arms and volunteers to Cuba was the lifeblood of the new revolution, but he did not have a tough act to follow. The Fernandina fiasco was not the first example of the party's inability to assemble ships for expeditions. The *George W. Childs* expedition could have been disastrous, while previous efforts revealed a mishmash of pirates, opportunists, and adventurers, whimsy drowned in a whirlpool of incompetence.

In one early mission, the CRP identified a vessel named the *Rowena* that was lying at Lemon City near the small southern Florida village of Miami. Funds were transferred, and Charlie Hernández again was dispatched from New York to command her. Hernández arrived at Lemon City and directed the *Rowena* to Jacksonville, where a small cargo of rifles, cartridges, and medicine was to be loaded. However, a wire soon arrived at party headquarters from Hernández, saying: "*Rowena* a total wreck off Cape Canaveral; we have no money and no clothes; telegraph instructions."

Nuñez's task went far beyond finding suitable vessels. He then had to convince the ship's owner to assume considerable risk. American sympathy for Cuba did not extend to payment of insurance claims under any number of negative consequences that could occur. If negotiations commenced, they usually ended with Nuñez paying an inflated price for the vessel.

Before she left the dock, a ship released to the Cubans would be subject to constant scrutiny by federal agents or Spanish spies. Word to the Spanish minister could trigger a federal investigation, tying up a commercial ship for months. Once loaded with armaments and volunteers, the vessel had to avoid the US Revenue Cutter Service, which maintained a vigilant watch along the coast. Capture could mean the arrest of the captain, crew, and owner for violating the neutrality laws, and this could further lead to a prison sentence.

Seizure by the federal government became the least of liabilities once the ship was at sea. A ship transporting arms and men to the Cuban rebels had to avoid the Spanish naval blockade that surrounded the island. Discovery came with the very real possibility that the boat would be seized or even sunk and the captain and crew arrested. That could lead to the far more ominous fate of imprisonment in a Cuban cell and possibly execution without a trial. That deadly precedent was established years earlier with the infamous *Virginius* affair.

On the afternoon of October 31, 1873, the side-wheeler *Virginius* steamed about twenty miles off the Cuban coast. Aboard were more than a hundred rebels and a cargo that included five hundred Remington rifles, a large number of swords and revolvers, and a quantity of ammunition, clothing, medicine, and provisions. The passengers and cargo were on their way to join the rebels in the mountains of eastern Cuba.

At about 2:00 p.m., smoke was sighted on the horizon as a Spanish warship came into view. The *Virginius* came about and headed out to sea, and the Spaniard gave chase. By the standards of the day, the *Virginius* was a swift ship, having started life as a Confederate blockade runner. The combined power of her sails and paddle wheels drove her through the water at more than eight knots, a speed that enabled her repeatedly to slip through the Union blockade while smuggling cotton from Mobile, Alabama, to Havana. But her Spanish pursuer, the *Tornado*, was also a former Confederate blockade runner and had been built in the same Scottish shipyard. On this day, she had the advantage of a few knots over her sister ship laden with cargo.

The two vessels rocked and plunged southward through a choppy sea toward the British island of Jamaica. But as the dark outline of the Jamaican coast came into view, the Spanish ship came into cannon range. Her gun fired, sending up a fountain of seawater ahead of the fleeing *Virginius*. The scene aboard the American ship was wild confusion, and the crew hastily began throwing the incriminating cargo over the side. A second shot from the *Tornado* struck the *Virginius*'s smokestack, and the fugitive ship hove to. The captain of the *Virginius* was Joseph Fry, an Annapolis graduate who had fought for the Confederacy. As he waited for the boarding party, he felt confident because his was an American ship with American registry papers and flying the American flag, with an American captain and a crew predominantly of American citizens. Additionally, Captain Fry knew

Photograph of Emilio Nuñez, who organized the expeditions to Cuba with John D. Hart and others. Library of Congress, Prints and Photographs Division, George Grantham Bain Collection, reproduction number LC-DIG-ggbain-06558.

that his ship was in international waters, and, therefore, the Spanish had no legal right to stop and board her.

Fry presented these reasons to Captain Dionisio Castillo of the *Tornado*, who came on deck with a boarding party. Fry handed over his American papers and protested the Spanish action, but Castillo brushed it aside. The Spaniard informed Fry that the *Virginius*'s owner of record was a front for the Cuban revolutionists. That alone violated the ship's American registry and left her subject to seizure. Castillo ordered the American flag flying from the ship's mast hauled down and the Spanish colors raised in its place. The *Virginius* was considered a "pirate ship," and Castillo was taking her and all aboard to the port of Santiago.

When the *Virginius* steamed into the harbor the following afternoon, General Juan Burriel, the Spanish governor of Santiago, quickly demonstrated how filibusters should be treated. A summary court-martial was held, and the passengers and crew of the captured ship were sentenced to death. Over four days, Captain Fry and fifty-two men were lined up in the public square in Santiago and executed by a firing squad. As a further display of Spain's contempt for filibusters, soldiers decapitated the bodies and trampled them with their horses.

John D. Hart was in a foul mood as he walked down South Delaware Avenue to his office at Pier 11. Hart was battling with the owner of a vessel over a lost cargo of bananas that cost him $6,500. It was not a good time for visitors, but his attorney and new partner, William W. Ker, had informed him to expect a visit from a Cuban who would present an interesting proposition. Ker had friends in the Cuban émigré community, including the prominent Portuondo family of cigar manufacturers. One of the Portuondo daughters was married to Emilio Nuñez, whose prominence was lost on Hart but who was very well known to American authorities.

Hart reached the door of his office when he saw a well-dressed man in a dark suit approaching. The man's coal-black, almost shiny hair was slicked back neatly, in contrast to untamed muttonchops that flared out from both cheeks. Hart thought the man looked like an undertaker, but he knew from Ker's description that this was the cigar seller who held the key to riches the Cubans seemed to be throwing at anyone with a boat and a paddle.

Nuñez introduced himself pleasantly, yet with caution. Any American's willingness to help the Cuban cause must have fanned his natural suspicion. Spanish spies were everywhere but especially in Philadelphia. Spanish consul José Congosto and the Pinkerton detectives at his disposal would have liked nothing better than to catch Nuñez and his allies in an incriminating act. The Pinkerton National Detective Agency was under retainer to the Spanish legation in Washington to assist in identifying revolutionists. The agency was founded by Allan Pinkerton, who took credit for foiling a Baltimore plot to assassinate president-elect Abraham Lincoln. But after Pinkerton's death in 1884, the agency under Pinkerton's sons evolved into an organization whose reputation was sullied by their activities as strike breakers and goon squads.

Still, Nuñez needed ships, and Hart had ships he was willing to lease. As they discussed a possible partnership, Nuñez was adamant that the charter master would be required to provide ships and reliable captains and crews on very short notice to load and haul arms, ammunition, medicine, and supplies to Cuba. Secrecy was paramount, and costly mistakes such as those that had occurred with previous foiled expeditions likely would result in Hart's arrest or worse.

Such an enterprise was fraught with danger, but Hart always had dismissed the costs as incidental to the reward. The possibilities of blockades, arrests, or other dangers were secondary to the greater prize. Aleck Bulack had taught him that the purpose of a shipping firm was to make money, so what difference did it make if the cargo were green bananas or armed men?

More important was the prospect that Hart could return to the top of a world that resented his success, had ridiculed him and tried to put him out of business. Once again, he would be standing in the barrel of the foremast, a high perch where he could watch his opponents thrashing in the merciless waves of competition. He would look down with the satisfaction that no longer could they curb his impulses, slow his ascent, or blunt his recaptured success.

Nuñez and Hart reached an understanding. The Cubans would supply the cargo, Hart would assume all risks associated with the voyages, and the charter master would receive $10,000 for each successful expedition. Although other vessels would be secured elsewhere from time to time, in the summer of 1895 John D. Hart became the primary source of ammunition, guns, and supplies to the revolution that would deliver the long-awaited goal of *Cuba Libre*.

Spanish minister Enrique Dupuy de Lôme called on Secretary of State Richard Olney a few days after American Independence Day in 1895 with the intention

As Spain's minister to the United States, Enrique Dupuy de Lôme spent much of his time feeding intelligence on expeditions and the Cuban Revolutionary Party's activities to American officials. Line drawing from the October 10, 1896, edition of the Washington *Evening Star*.

of mending fences. Their first meeting had not gone well coming so soon after the embarrassing news of the *George W. Childs* and *James Woodall* expeditions. Dupuy de Lôme had another reason for the meeting: to make certain that Olney understood the threat to Spanish sovereignty of the Cuban revolutionists who operated under the nose of the US government. In educating the secretary in a congenial manner, Dupuy de Lôme hoped to enlist a willing ally to help curtail this threat to Spain's overseas empire.

Born in Valencia in 1851, Dupuy de Lôme was a lawyer and career diplomat. His early postings included Japan, where his innate curiosity compelled him to tour the country extensively with frequent excursions into China. Dupuy de Lôme served with distinction as first secretary of the Spanish Embassy in Berlin and was well known to German chancellor Otto von Bismarck. At social gatherings, the chancellor liked to ruffle the dark hair of Dupuy de Lôme's young son, delighting at the little "*Schwarz Kopf.*"

He came to the United States in 1883 as chargé d'affaires of the Spanish legation in Washington, a post he held for six months until Juan Valera, the noted realist author and diplomat, was appointed minister. After some months together, Valera described his new assistant in unflattering terms in a letter to his wife. "Dupuy is a smart man and his wife quite the opposite," Valera wrote. "They both suffer delusions of grandeur. He had grown accustomed to being boss and obviously resents my arrival."

Dupuy de Lôme moved on to other posts until he left the diplomatic service in 1891 to enter politics. His growing prominence in Spain's Conservative Party helped him secure an appointment as minister to Washington in 1892. When the Liberals regained power, Dupuy de Lôme was reassigned as special representative to the World's Columbian Exposition in Chicago, which commemorated the four hundredth anniversary of Columbus's discovery of the New World. Well suited to the largely ceremonial position, Dupuy de Lôme and his wife traveled throughout the American West, developing a fondness for the California wine country. Dupuy de Lôme would experience many more opportunities to sample Napa's finest, for reasons of recreation and reinforcement.

Dupuy de Lôme presented Olney with a lengthy report that acknowledged the efforts of US authorities in pursuing the filibusters and offered assistance "in their task of preventing such violation of laws as may prove detrimental to the interests of a friendly nation." The report alleged several threats to Spanish and American harmony, such as regular military drilling at 1777 Broadway in New York, and the existence in Tampa of "quite a number of wretches awaiting an opportunity to sail for the Island and carry with them certain arms, which everybody knows are now stored in the house of the so-styled Colonel Figueredo."

In other words, Dupuy de Lôme pledged the good offices of the Spanish consulate to assist federal authorities, customs officials at American ports, and the US Revenue Cutter Service in helping Spain keep a tight lid on Cuba. Dupuy de Lôme's message: We will help you help us.

"In the first place," Dupuy de Lôme wrote, "there exists in the United States a complete public organization which includes over 150 clubs known as 'Revolutionary Cuban Clubs,' the only expressed object of which is to promote civil war in a part of territory belonging to a friendly nation." Their members were chiefly Cuban immigrants who upon arriving in the United States acquired papers of naturalization with the only purpose of "shielding themselves behind the American flag and transgressing the laws of the very nation of which they have become citizens." The clubs were administered by a central faction in New York that collected funds "for the purchase of vessels, arms, ammunition, and all implements of war necessary to keep up a revolution."

The minister gave the secretary another tip that an important meeting of revolutionist clubs would soon be convened at the Fifth Avenue Hotel in New York. The clubs, he said, would "propose to elect a new organization with hostile intentions toward Spain and which the newspapers will probably call Provisional Government of the Republic of Cuba." Dupuy de Lôme was correct that the meeting would elect a new organization, but he did not realize that it also would change the direction of the revolution away from the vision of José Martí.

Chapter 6

A LESSON IN COMPETITION

The meeting at the Fifth Avenue Hotel was convened to select the ideal man to take over the coalition so delicately forged by Martí. He had to possess the respect of the Cuban émigré community as well as win support of both civilian and military factions on the island. After many conferences and local elections, the convention held in New York on July 10 ratified Tomás Estrada Palma as the logical choice to follow Martí as delegate. Estrada Palma, who had filled the role as interim delegate since Martí's death, possessed none of the Apostle's personal magnetism. But at age sixty-three he was respected, and his elegant white hair and mustache portrayed a quiet dignity that belied a tumultuous life dedicated to wresting his homeland from Spanish rule.

Born the son of a wealthy plantation owner near Bayamo in Oriente Province, Estrada Palma was sent to Spain to study law at the University of Seville. He returned to Cuba to practice just as the cauldron of unrest was about to bubble up. The young lawyer became involved in the movement that led to the Ten Years' War, during which he displayed his legal and strategic acumen. In 1871, he was elected president of the revolutionary government with the primary task of supporting the troops in the field. However, in 1874 he was captured and sent to Spain, where he was imprisoned for the duration of the war. He was released after the treaty of 1878 and traveled to Paris before moving to New York, where he established a school for the sons of Cuban emigrants at Central Valley in Orange County.

Tomás Estrada Palma did not possess the personal magnetism of Martí, but his quiet dignity made him the logical selection to succeed the "Apostle" after Martí's death. Courtesy of the Cuban Heritage Collection, University of Miami Libraries, Coral Gables, Florida.

Estrada Palma also was one of few candidates acceptable to Martí's staff of headstrong disciples who were often at odds. Martí's trusted secretary, Gonzalo de Quesada, did not trust party treasurer Benjamin Guerra, who was close to Estrada Palma. Attorney Horatio Rubens persuaded Quesada to support Estrada Palma as an alternative to General Máximo Gómez, whose supporters preferred a military state. Confirmed in the positions they currently held were Guerra as treasurer, Rubens as general counsel, and Emilio Nuñez as chief of the Department of Expeditions. Quesada was named chargé d'affaires in Washington, and General Carlos Roloff was named minister of war.

Estrada Palma's staff was officially designated the "Cuban Delegation," but it was difficult to avoid a popular appellation borrowed from the Ten Years' War. Under Estrada Palma's stewardship, the Revolutionary Party became better known publicly as "the Junta."

The confirmation of the new party leadership heralded a very different direction for the revolution from the one envisioned by Martí. Having lived for as long as twenty years in a country that imagined itself the pinnacle of modern civilization, Junta leaders began to adopt policies that projected their pro-imperialist vision onto the revolution. Estrada Palma, Quesada, Guerra, and other top Junta leaders who had become US citizens during their exile did not expect to make Cuba a part of the United States but a smaller version of the United States. It did not matter to them that military leaders such as Gómez and Antonio Maceo did not share their enthusiasm for American models of culture and conduct.

Junta leaders believed that all ends could be achieved through support from the United States, which could provide both material and moral aid. The new

Publisher William Randolph Hearst used the Cuban Revolution and the expeditions as sensational stories to attract sympathetic readers to his *New York Journal*. Library of Congress, Prints and Photographs Division, NYWT&S Collection, reproduction number LC-USZ62-68946.

leadership correctly concluded that pressure on Washington would not come from Cuban exiles begging for help but from an angry American citizenry demanding answers from their elected representatives.

Estrada Palma deviated from Martí in another significant way. In speeches, interviews, and articles, Estrada Palma eloquently aligned the Cuban struggle with America's own revolution: "The cause of the present revolution in Cuba, briefly stated, may be said to be taxation without representation, a phrase certainly familiar to American ears and emphasized by the most important event in the history of the nation, the War for Independence."

To spread this message within the United States, Estrada Palma and his staff launched a calculated strategy that included "sympathy meetings," carnivals, theatrical performances, and public speeches. They utilized *Patria*, the party newspaper Martí had founded, to supplement propaganda pamphlets that espoused the patriotic theme of an oppressed people yearning to be free. However, the most effective device to secure this arousal was to blanket newspapers with examples of noble efforts to secure *Cuba Libre*. The popular journalistic trend in the 1890s, particularly among the large newspapers in New York, fit the Junta's strategy hand-in-glove.

New York was a competitive newspaper town in 1895, hosting such publications as the *World*, the *Sun*, the *Herald*, the *Tribune*, and the *Times*. But each was to receive a serious lesson in competition when William Randolph Hearst purchased the *New York Morning Journal* on September 25, 1895. The thirty-year-old Harvard dropout had operated the *San Francisco Examiner* since 1887 after his father took over the paper for a bad debt and succeeded in making it a financial success. His proven formula was to satisfy the base appetites of his readers through sensational methods, ironically copied from the practice popularized by Joseph Pulitzer's *New York World*. Hearst's ambition to surpass Pulitzer in sensationalism, circulation, and power began an intense rivalry between the two papers that influenced an entire industry.

With the players in place to compete for every shred of titillating news, the only element missing was a compelling and ongoing subject on which to compete. The Junta filled the void with tips and leaks to reporters about high-adventure expeditions to Cuba. Tales of gallant captains and swashbuckling crews smuggling arms in the dark of night, gun battles with Spanish warships, and courageous volunteers who risked their lives for liberty was mother's milk to the sharp-elbowed New York press corps.

It was Nuñez's task to organize and execute such expeditions, the descriptions of which Quesada and Rubens would often enhance before regaling reporters with the Cuban patriots' latest exploits. A regular four o'clock afternoon briefing was established for the newspapermen at Rubens's office at 66 Broadway to dispense updates of the conflict. The meeting became known as "the peanut club," because Rubens provided peanuts as refreshments for the attending scribes.

While his aides messaged the press, Estrada Palma worked to supply Gómez and the other generals with the tools of revolution. The delegate established credit with Marcellus Hartley, a prominent manufacturer of guns, bicycles, and sporting goods who would become the Junta's primary source of weaponry. The Hartley & Graham Company of Ilion, New York, had been in business since 1853 and had the weapons market virtually to itself. Hartley and Malcolm Graham bought the Remington Arms Company in 1888 as a symbiotic match to their Union Metallic Cartridge Company of Bridgeport, Connecticut. H&G also owned a half dozen smaller firms that produced items helpful to the insurgents, such as military supplies and camping equipment. The firm's New York office was conveniently located at no. 313 and no. 315 Broadway.

Also easily accessible to Estrada Palma's office at 56 New Street was the firm of Collins & Company of Canton, Connecticut. Founded in 1824, the firm specialized in axes, picks, and knives, but their blade most prized by the Cubans was the machete. Designed for cutting cane, a Collins machete was valued for its durability, sharpness, and light weight, which was essential in close combat.

Once the weapons were secured, they had to be delivered, a task Estrada Palma left to Nuñez. His method to secure ships was to create a precise network to replace Martí's haphazard attempts. Nuñez recruited men he trusted to help plan specialized aspects of the expedition, from armaments to embarkation. He also enlisted a corps of pilots, each of whom knew a section of the Cuban coastline intimately.

Essential to executing the enlistment and delivery of men and arms were local operatives in key locations. Residing at key ports in Florida were such benefactors as José Dolores Poyo, editor of the patriot newspaper *El Yara*, at Key West; veteran Fernando Figueredo at Tampa; and cigar merchant José Alejandro Huau at Jacksonville, who was the most active. His surname pronounced as "Wow" and often described as "the man with the Chinese name," Huau enjoyed great local influence and had a considerable stake in the fight. In January 1869, Huau and his brother-in-law, Henry Fritot, were imprisoned in Morro Castle in Havana for their revolutionary activities. After the war, he established himself in Jacksonville and donated much of his considerable fortune to the fight for independence.

An extension of Huau was his nephew, Alphonse Fritot, who made Jacksonville a center of expeditionary planning. Fritot was imaginative and bold, but practical and cautious. Local politicians and merchants knew him well from his position as a railroad transportation agent, a critical platform from which he arranged deliveries of men and arms by rail. Fritot spoke perfect English, and his pleasing personality had a multitude of uses.

In late July, Dupuy de Lôme traveled to Philadelphia to prod Consul José Congosto about clamping down harder on suspected organizers of filibustering expeditions. The minister was highly critical of Congosto after the *George W. Childs* slipped out of Philadelphia in June and created such negative publicity for Spain. His ire came through clearly when he wondered aloud "how strange it is when every Spanish official is supposed to be on high alert, that happenings of vital interest in Philadelphia should be learned first [in Washington]."

By all accounts, Congosto had his hands full. Edwin S. Gaylor, the Pinkerton superintendent in Philadelphia, acknowledged that Philadelphia was "the center of the greatest insurrectionary activity among Cubans in this country." Leaders in the Cuban community were under constant surveillance by the Pinkertons, including Nuñez, his in-laws in the Portuondo family, and Dr. Juan Guitéras, a professor of pathology at the University of Pennsylvania and president of the Philadelphia Federation of Cuban Clubs.

Dupuy de Lôme's get-tough message must have been uncomfortable for Congosto. The trained physician had held the consulate post in Philadelphia for ten years and enjoyed an active social life. Congosto's good looks were enhanced by a dark Vandyke beard that only added to his elegant appearance. He mixed freely with the barons of Philadelphia society, including members of the Wanamaker, Eakins, Hires, and Cramp families, as well as numerous judges and local officials. He developed many contacts over glasses of Madeira with men and women who would prove to be both friends and rivals. Congosto even served on a committee with Guitéras in 1891 to celebrate the four hundredth anniversary of the first Spanish-funded expedition to the New World by Columbus.

During the summer, Congosto joined the socially prominent who fled the city every weekend for the endless bathing beaches on the Jersey shore known as the Strand. The newspapers issued regular reports on the summer-long gambol of an "impassable barrier of humanity" frolicking in the waves or lounging in row upon row of "beach tents with [their] quota of pretty girls and handsome matrons." Perhaps it was Congosto's influence that prompted the émigré elite to distance themselves from the insurgents after the fighting commenced in Cuba. Questioned by a Philadelphia reporter gathering news of the social scene, several members of the Cuban community denied any sympathy at all with the rebels, declaring their full support for the Spanish government's efforts to maintain control.

Public rejection from their compatriots did not prevent Nuñez, Guitéras, or others from continuing their activities on behalf of the revolution, presumably far from Congosto's summer getaways. However, few of the conspirators' efforts escaped the watchful eyes of the consul's paid informants, a fact Congosto repeated over and over again until Dupuy de Lôme was satisfied and returned to Washington.

Chapter 7

FULLY VESTED IN THE FILIBUSTER BUSINESS

The *Baltimore Sun* was the first to transmit a document of any length by telegraph, a speech by President John Tyler in May 1846. Since that day, the *Sun* was connected to nearly every remote location where a pole could be sunk and a wire strung. The *Sun* gathered news from the far outposts of the globe every night and delivered it to the breakfast tables of Homewood, Towson, and Dundalk the following morning. On one typical August evening in 1895, dispatches were coming in rapidly as beleaguered telegraph operators hovered over their keys. Wearing green eyeshades, pulled low to protect their eyes from the harsh glow of dangling electric bulbs, they transcribed message after message for an editor's eye.

One particular dispatch from Philadelphia drew an operator's attention. Any news from Cuba was inviting, but of special interest were tales of the gunrunners and their expeditions to arm the rebels. The story claimed that the Cuban clubs in Philadelphia had received word that a major expedition had landed in Cuba. The cargo was said to include five hundred Remington rifles and fifty thousand rounds of ammunition.

The name of the vessel was not given, although it was said to belong to owners from Philadelphia and Baltimore, and the captain was identified as "Captain Humes." The night editor realized there wasn't much meat to the story, but it did mention Baltimore, so he instructed the news desk to run it while the maritime desk examined the known clearances and arrivals to deduce the identity of the mystery ship. After a close examination by a deskman familiar with ship traffic that frequented the Baltimore Basin, an updated version was written that would run in the next day's edition. The updated story reported that the date of the ship's clearance, the port of departure, and the similarity to the name of the captain pointed to one vessel that could have made a trip to Cuba. The press for the first time linked John D. Hart's *Laurada* and Captain Sam Hughes to a gunrunning expedition.

It was not reported, but another Hart line vessel delivered an expedition to Cuba a few weeks later. The *Leon*, under the command of Captain Frederick Svanoe, sailed to Nassau and picked up a handful of recruits led by Colonel Francisco Sánchez Echevarría. The *Leon* evaded a Spanish coast patrol before delivering a handful of men, one hundred rifles, and five thousand cartridges to Antonio Maceo's forces at Playa de Nibujón at the eastern tip of the island.

John D. Hart was now fully vested in the filibustering business. He would not confirm his involvement yet publicly, but a comment to a *Sun* reporter on August 7, 1895, aroused suspicion. The charter master announced that after needed repairs were made, the *Laurada* would suspend its Charleston run hauling phosphate rock and reenter the West Indies trade. Hart likely established the alibi so that a sighting of his vessels in Caribbean waters would not raise undue suspicion. However, his news had the opposite effect when the *Leon* returned to Philadelphia with a cargo of bananas from Port Antonio a week after the expedition to Playa de Nibujón.

The pressure of performance had not eased for Spanish consul to Philadelphia José Congosto. Minister Dupuy de Lôme had delivered a clear message during his July visit: shut down Philadelphia to filibustering expeditions or your next posting might be at Ceuta, a Spanish enclave on the northern coast of Africa. Since then, Philadelphia only had enhanced its reputation as the center of insurrectionist activity with the emergence of an unscrupulous fruit peddler named Hart. With the US Revenue Cutter Service concentrating on Florida and the newspaper dogfight in New York scrutinizing any suspicious activity from that port, Philadelphia became the principal target of Spain's intelligence efforts.

Pinkerton superintendent Edwin Gaylor assured Congosto that no vessel could enter or leave Philadelphia without his agents knowing about it, but the consul demanded proof. After more rumors of expeditions leaving Philadelphia and landing unmolested in Cuba, Gaylor reported that an expedition was being organized in Philadelphia and was about to sail. Pinkerton agents had observed about twenty men loading boxes onto the tugboat *Taurus* at a Philadelphia dock on the night of Thursday, August 29. Emilio Nuñez himself was observed handing a large bundle to one of the passengers. Congosto was relieved that the thousands of pesetas spent on hired spies and Pinkertons finally was yielding results.

At midnight, the *Taurus* headed down the Delaware River with orders to meet up with a steamship near Gordon Heights in Wilmington, Delaware. The steamer was to signal with three whistles, the *Taurus* would tie up alongside, and the cargo and volunteers would be transferred. But when the *Taurus* arrived at the rendezvous location, master Thomas H. Nicholson did not see a steamer. He anchored at Penns Grove, New Jersey, across the river from Wilmington, and waited. Before long, a clerk from the Charles Warner Company, which owned the tug, came aboard and ordered the Cubans off the boat because of some "trouble in Wilmington." The anxious young volunteers followed instructions, then went into the town and gathered at the train station.

US Marshal Hewson E. Lannan in Wilmington assembled a dozen local police and two Pinkerton agents, who boarded the tug *Meteor* and headed for Penns Grove. When they arrived, the officers pulled their weapons and carefully approached the train station. Prepared for a gunfight with a heavily armed rabble, the officers saw a group of twenty young men milling about, apparently waiting for a train. Lannan shouted an order to surrender, and the men did so without incident. Those arrested were described as "a fine-looking body of men, well-dressed and with intelligent faces." The group included several businessmen, two physicians, two attorneys, a druggist, and a chemical engineer, all prepared to fight in Cuba.

Officers searching their travel bags found ammunition and pistols, and the tug's deck was littered with machetes. A search of the cargo hold revealed provisions, clothing, and twenty-seven boxes of ammunition. Also confiscated was the mysterious bundle from Nuñez, which authorities opened, finding a pistol, bottles of ink, a book, and numerous letters addressed to General Máximo Gómez, the Cuban military commander.

The prisoners were taken to the federal building in Wilmington, where they were charged with having prepared for a military expedition in violation of the federal neutrality laws and for violating the proclamation of the president.

In Washington, Dupuy de Lôme sent Secretary of State Richard Olney a handwritten note thanking him for the diligence of the American officials, and he provided additional information on several of the participants. The minister deplored "how little regard for the laws have these so-called American citizens and how they obey the President's Proclamation."

Olney's first assistant, Alvey A. Adee, also wrote his boss a note taking credit for the apprehension. Adee was a permanent fixture in the State Department, an expert on departmental routine and protocol and the humorous tutor of political appointees. A whimsical soul with a quacking falsetto voice who was largely unknown to the public, Adee was respected in Washington and throughout the Foreign Service. His chest-thumping memo alleged that the roundup at Wilmington "was in part due to my prompt action" after Dupuy de Lôme arranged a meeting with Congosto.

"He had facts enough but seemed utterly helpless how to use them," Adee said of the consul. "I packed him back to Wilmington to consult the U.S. attorney and swear out a complaint on which a warrant might issue. I notified the Treasury and suggested cooperation to aid the enforcement of our law.... By five o'clock the whole gang was bagged."

Adee signed the note: "Faithfully, A.A.A., Adios."

Adee's actions and those of the federal marshals were further evidence that enforcement of the neutrality laws effectively confirmed the United States as a police force of Spain. The Grover Cleveland administration was determined not to give Spain any reason to complain of lax enforcement of the laws. The *New York Herald* went further when it observed: "Some of the authorities on international law here are inclined to think the administration is even more zealous in preventing warlike supplies from being shipped to Cuba than is necessary under the law. It has been held by State Secretaries from the time of Jefferson that American manufacturers of arms were at perfect liberty to sell them to whomsoever they saw fit and to ship them out of the United States."

Congosto parroted the party line by telling reporters that future military expeditions would be halted and punished by Spain's good friends in the American government: "It may be set up as a defense that it is lawful to carry and to trade in arms, but that cannot be alleged as a cloak for filibustering, especially when so many details prove that the intent of the accused was not so innocent." Despite his words, Congosto seethed that the big fish—the steamship and those who planned the expedition—were still at large. He demanded that the US government take additional steps to seize any steamer in the vicinity with a "suspicious assemblage" on board. The revenue cutter *Hamilton* was immediately dispatched from New York to Wilmington to discourage future expeditions from the port of Philadelphia, although Captain H. T. Blake's initial concern was not armed filibusters. His next telegram to the Treasury Department included the alarming news that only four days of rations remained on board for his crew.

Congosto's paid informants took a few more days before delivering the information he coveted. Warrants were issued for Ralph De Soto, a Wilmington cigar dealer who was believed to have been a principal organizer of the expedition, and for Captain Samuel Hughes, master of the steamer *Laurada* of the John D. Hart line.

Congosto's spies were certain that the *Laurada* was the mystery steamer the *Taurus* had been scheduled to meet, but proving it was another matter. The vessel, distinct for its bright red smokestack, had left Hart's home base at Pier 11 on August 29, ostensibly to pick up fruit at Port Morant in southeastern Jamaica. But as she cruised down the Delaware River, a problem with the machinery compelled Hughes to return to port. The problem was apparently fixed in short order, and the ship set out again, only to run aground mysteriously at a tricky "horseshoe" bend in the river. It was unknown whether the problems were genuine or merely a convenient excuse to vacate the premises after learning the mission had been discovered.

Fully Vested in the Filibuster Business   53

Horatio Rubens's job as the Junta's legal representative ranged from buying vessels to working with Bill Ker at trial. From the Phi Gamma Delta digital directory, 1898 Chapter Rolls and Directory, Upsilon, College of the City of New York.

The evidence against the accused was largely circumstantial, but Junta attorney Horatio Rubens and Bill Ker did not want to leave the verdict to the whims of a jury. They agreed that lead counsel should be well known in the Wilmington area and to potential jurors, so they enlisted Senator George Gray, who had represented Delaware in the US Senate since 1885. At a comparatively modest $5,000 annual salary in 1895, it was not unusual for some US senators to keep their day jobs.

The case was called in US District Court before bewhiskered Judge Leonard Eugene Wales, a seventy-two-year-old veteran jurist who had been appointed by President Chester Arthur in 1884. Gray's opening remarks demanded that the accused Cubans be fully informed of what crime they were accused of having committed. Gray noted that the indictments did not mention which country the defendants were allegedly plotting against, as they merely repeated the language contained in the statutes. If the men were charged with forming a military expedition, Gray argued, it would be necessary to prove which country they were fighting.

The government's case, argued by District Attorney Lewis C. Vandegrift, was rooted in testimony from Pinkerton agents. The agents methodically described the shadowing of the defendants, the loading of the cargo, and Nuñez's handing over the incriminating bundle of letters addressed to Gómez. Judge Wales determined that the letters to Gómez were inadmissible, since the bundle had been opened without proper authority. The government then attempted to link the *Laurada* to the episode, but Captain Hughes testified that he had no filibusters aboard. After a few days in port, he said, the *Laurada* set out on September 3 cleared for Port Antonio and returned to Philadelphia on September 18 with a load of bananas.

His testimony was supported by the esteemed war hero and attorney William W. Ker, testifying as a part owner of the *Laurada*.

Gray was even more adamant on the second day of testimony. He cross-examined the government witnesses with a vindictiveness that surprised his friends but pleased the large audience of Cuban sympathizers. The gallery resembled a tent revival, with the parishioners grumbling at the sinful thrusts of prosecutors while grunting consent at righteous parries from the defense. Hart sat behind the defense table, near several striking young raven-haired women who were members of the Society Hermanas de Martí, the Sisters of Martí Society. Elegant in their finery of the latest styles, they nodded their approval at Gray's every point and smiled sweetly at the jury members at every opportunity.

In Washington, a frustrated Dupuy de Lôme was under no illusions the defendants would be convicted and predicted so in a letter to Olney. "[T]he filibusters of Wilmington, defended by a United States Senator, will be acquitted," he wrote. "Our detectives followed during months the storing of arms in cellars of known rebels to Spain.... [T]hey have been caught in a tug to embark with the arms ready to fight. The cartridge belts were full of shots. [However,] all that seems not to be sufficient proof of conspiracy and violation of the neutrality laws."

Judge Wales's final instructions to the jury on September 23 hinted to observers that an acquittal was likely. The judge cautioned that a guilty verdict would not be justified by such circumstantial evidence as the defendants' suspicious movements on the night of August 29; the mysterious manner in which arms and ammunition were taken on the *Taurus* with the intention of transferring them to an unknown steamer; the defendants' lack of an answer for their actions; and their nationality as Cubans, or the fact that they were in sympathy with an insurrection going on in Cuba. Such circumstantial evidence was the bulk of the prosecution's case.

The judge further instructed the jury that in order to convict, the prosecution must have proved that the defendants formed a military expedition in this country that was intended to move to another country. In order to fall under the definition of a military expedition, the men must have been organized and properly officered. The judge said it was not a military expedition if two or more men decided to go to another country to fight for or against that country, nor was it an offense under the law to merely ship arms.

After the jury retired, Foreman Charles H. Maull asked for an immediate vote. A lone juror was swayed by the government's argument and voted for conviction, but the other eleven men in the room voted for acquittal. That prompted some discussion and review of the facts, but soon the reluctant soul relented. The second vote was unanimous. Barely forty-five minutes after the jury had adjourned, the bailiff poked his head through the courtroom door and announced that the jury had reached a verdict.

Men and women standing in the hallways rushed back into the courtroom, while those who had remained sat up in their stiff-backed chairs. As the twelve jurors filed in, the onlookers craned their necks and inclined their ears toward the bench. When the jury was seated and the bustle of movement silenced, Deputy Clerk Mahaffy asked Foreman Maull: "Gentlemen of the jury, have you agreed upon a verdict?"

"We have," Maull responded.

"What say you, Mr. Foreman?" the clerk asked. "Do you find the defendants at the bar guilty or not guilty?"

Maull responded loudly, "NOT GUILTY," and bedlam broke loose. Hart broke into a wide grin, grasping every hand thrust his way, as men and women cheered wildly, waving handkerchiefs, fans, and newspapers. Others jumped up on chairs and benches, clapping their hands and stomping their feet, while the defendants hugged one another through smiles and grateful tears. Judge Wales did not object to the outpouring of enthusiasm, appearing more like a doting grandfather before he rose and returned unnoticed to his chambers. A disappointed Marshal Lannan sprang in front of the bench and held up his arms attempting to restore decorum, pausing briefly before the crowd resumed cheer after cheer and surrounded the defendants to offer congratulations and sympathy with their cause.

One woman rushed up to Hart and pinned a small Cuban flag on his lapel, while outside supporters wearing buttons proclaiming "*Cuba Libre*" unfurled large Cuban flags and waved them alongside American flags. Word of the decision spread quickly, and a number of prominent Cubans caught trains from Philadelphia to join the celebration. The people of Wilmington, from bicycle clubs and both Democratic and Republican clubs, hastily put together a parade in honor of the acquitted men, and the festivities lasted well into the evening. The *Philadelphia Inquirer* reported: "Never before was such enthusiasm shown in Wilmington over a matter of this kind and the people all seem anxious to show their sympathy for Cuba."

Hart basked in the victory, and Bill Ker hoped that the verdict would serve as a precedent when other expeditions were discovered and other volunteers and vessels were hauled into court. However, he was experienced enough in the vagaries of the legal system to know that similar cases with identical facts would be subject to their own sets of variables. Not all juries would be instructed by sympathetic judges, and not all jurors would interpret testimony the same way. But neither Ker nor his effusive client could fear the future while savoring the joy of the present.

Chapter 8

NOT A MAN OF PATIENCE

A diverse collection of public figures celebrated the Wilmington verdict as a perceived endorsement of Cuban independence. Labor leader Samuel Gompers and wealthy industrialist Andrew Carnegie expressed their satisfaction at the verdict and were joined by numerous senators and governors. More importantly, that support was reflected in increased donations to party headquarters that would enable the fitting out of more expeditions. But new attempts to deliver arms and ammunition to the fighting met an elevated wave of expected resistance.

Pinkerton detectives and other Spanish agents blanketed the wharves, the custom houses, and every dockside tavern where the ale was cold and lips were loose. Every shred of intelligence they gathered was funneled to the Spanish minister in Washington, who forwarded every scrap to Secretary of State Olney. Dupuy de Lôme predicted increased activity from filibusters, an alert that Olney passed on to Secretary of the Treasury John Carlisle.

"The Spanish consuls in Tampa and Key West report great activity in filibustering expeditions ready to start," Olney wrote. "The revenue cutter [*Winona*] has seized at Pine Key the schooner *Lark* [which] is only a small part of a vast plan.... I venture to suggest that the collector at Key West be specially instructed by wire to take special precautions to prevent any violation of the neutrality laws, and to bring to justice any persons engaged in such violations."

The *Winona* had captured the expedition at Matecumbe Key, sixty miles up the Florida Reef, and arrived at Key West four days later with the *Lark* in tow and thirty-two young Cubans aboard. Eduardo H. Gato, the Key West cigar maker

Secretary of State Richard Olney used intelligence from Spanish minister Enrique Dupuy de Lôme to bolster President Grover Cleveland's proclamations warning American citizens against aiding the expeditions. Library of Congress, Prints and Photographs Division, George Grantham Bain Collection, reproduction number LC-DIG-ggbain-05196.

who had befriended José Martí, paid the bond for the men's release and protested the arrests vigorously.

Within days, the cutter *McLane* spotted the small five-ton schooner *Antoinette* near Bahia Honda Key. She had reportedly been seen with the *Lark* a few days earlier, and when the federal boat drew close, the pursuit was on. The *McLane* was an aging, obsolete side-wheeler that saw duty in the Civil War and should have been no match for the schooner. But in attempting to elude the cutter, the *Antoinette* ran aground on a sandbar. Seven Cubans were arrested, including Dr. Juan Antigas of Havana, a prominent physician who also was a star of the Havana baseball nine.

The frequency of captured expeditions raised Emilio Nuñez's suspicions that a spy within the Junta was leaking information. He saw no other conclusion after Spanish agents continued to supply US authorities with accurate and detailed intelligence about when and where expeditions would depart. One suggestion that "Spanish gold" was a potent factor in the treachery was added to rumors that prominent members of the Cuban Revolutionary Party were seen nightly huddling with representatives of Spain.

The leaks from within were never confirmed, but growing dissatisfaction resurrected old stories that the party was torn by internal dissension. Rumors of Guerra's feud with Quesada were revived, with allegations that Estrada Palma sided with the treasurer while Rubens was loyal to his old college chum. The rift widened after a trivial incident during the *Taurus* trial. Quesada and Rubens requested expense money to travel to Wilmington for the trial, but Estrada Palma

General Antonio Maceo leads a charge of the Cuban Liberation Army in this 1898 lithograph. Maceo complained that the expeditions favored Máximo Gómez's troops and that his mostly Black forces had to fight with captured arms. Library of Congress, Prints and Photographs Division, reproduction number LC-DIG-pga-08174.

and Guerra objected. The delegate relented somewhat but offered only fifteen dollars to cover three days of meals and lodging expenses for Quesada and Leon Benoit, Rubens's legal assistant.

Other signs of dissent were coming from the military in the field as the generals flooded the New York office with complaints. General Antonio Maceo claimed that he had sent money to the Junta in May, presumably from the "*zafra* tax," the protection money the insurgents demanded from planters for not burning their fields. When arms and ammunition were slow to arrive at the front, Maceo declared that he would keep the money and send nothing more to New York.

Maceo also complained that he and his mostly Black army were the victims of discrimination by Junta leaders. Maceo complained that expeditions were planned according to favoritism for Gómez's troops in the east and that his actions against the Spanish forces in the west were fought primarily with captured arms. Maceo received no sympathy from the commander in chief. Gómez's army also was running short of ammunition because not a single expedition had landed in Camagüey Province, where Gómez's army was fighting.

The military's dissatisfaction with the party peaked when Enrique Collazo, who had commanded troops aboard the captured *Lark*, charged that the expeditions were mismanaged, were inadequately supplied, and ignored the needs of commanders in the field. Collazo claimed that Gómez ordered him to take the *Lark* expedition to Vuelta Abajo in western Cuba, but the delegation in New York countermanded the order. After complaining to Gómez, the commander in chief sent Collazo to New York to confront Estrada Palma and Nuñez.

The delegate listened to Collazo's complaints and then presented reasons that explained the party's rationale for its expedition strategy. Estrada Palma argued that the New York office, receiving reports from all over the island, was in the best position to target where the need was greatest. Events were occurring rapidly since the declaration of war, and the delegate argued that the party's knowledge of Spanish troop movements helped shape the strategy of supplying arms and ammunition. Estrada Palma also reminded Collazo that Gómez had given José Martí his assurance that any measures determined by the Junta would receive his support. Collazo returned to Tampa to await the next expedition, chastened but not convinced.

John D. Hart was pacing between his desk and the window in his office at Pier 11. He was anxious to dispatch his next expedition, but the *Laurada* had not yet returned from the Jamaican ports with its load of bananas. He knew she had entered the Delaware Bay and was heading to Philadelphia, according to a telegram from the ship watchers at Cape Henlopen, but she had not arrived yet, and the charter master's irritation was palpable. He was not a man of patience, preferring that he alone control all aspects of the decisions he had made. But even as a baseball nine required men with varying skills, the shipping business required trained men at strategic positions. Able seamen who could hand, reef, and steer, led by a captain who could box the compass and who loved his ship more than his children, were essential to the mission. But to Hart, dependence on others was to cede his soul.

Finally, Captain Sam Hughes brought the *Laurada* into the slip, and Hart hurried to the dock with new orders. Hart told the captain to ignore the clearance papers stating that the steamer would clear the next day for a return to Kingston, and then he revealed the true destination.

The *Laurada* departed early on October 18, 1895, and turned north after leaving the Delaware Bay. By evening, she had anchored in the autumn moonlight off Long Island Sound as the lights of two smaller vessels came into view. A signal was passed, and the boats came alongside and tied up to the *Laurada*. One boat carried thirty-two cases of ammunition, while the other carried thirty-four volunteers under Carlos Manuel de Céspedes, nephew of the first president of the provisional republic during the Ten Years' War. After the ammunition and men were aboard, Hughes set a southward course.

A smooth voyage into warmer water was expected at that time of year, but this was not a typical year. A late major hurricane with winds of up to ninety miles an hour slammed into the *Laurada* on October 22 as she sailed between the Bahamas and Florida. Hurricane no. 5 had crossed Cuba and was headed up Florida's east coast when its northwesterly winds raked the sturdy vessel. Hughes fought the elements bravely as the *Laurada*'s bow rose and fell with the thirty-foot waves, perhaps as much for a personal reason as for reasons of the mission. His wife, Margaret, who insisted on accompanying him on as many voyages as possible, was aboard and sharing the turbulent ride. She must have acquitted herself well, for the Cubans later characterized the only woman on board as "young, brave, and intellectual."

Hughes expertly held the ship on a steady course and plowed through the Florida Straits before reaching Baracoa on the northeastern coast of Oriente Province on October 26. He landed Céspedes's expedition without incident and proceeded to Kingston, where reports surfaced of the *Laurada*'s suspicious activity in Cuba. In Washington, a furious Dupuy de Lôme demanded that the British government in Jamaica detain the vessel, but British authorities rejected his pleas, claiming they had no jurisdiction over the American ship. Hughes would not comment on the charges, and the *Laurada* picked up a cargo of fruit and headed home.

The *Laurada* arrived in New York on November 9 and unloaded its cargo at Harbeck's Stores in Brooklyn, but she soon returned to the center of the diplomatic storm. When the vessel departed after midnight November 12, Hughes had not taken out proper clearance papers. Arturo Baldasano, the Spanish consul in New York, protested to the Maritime Exchange that the steamer would only avoid the Custom House if she were on a filibustering expedition. The *Laurada* had departed in such haste that she left behind her first mate, second steward, and three firemen, who were questioned by Baldasano. The complaint was relayed to the Spanish minister, who notified Olney, who forwarded it to Treasury. Secretary Carlisle alerted collectors of customs and the Revenue Cutter Service to find the *Laurada* and seize her.

Hart and Ker were outraged that Dupuy de Lôme had convinced US authorities to seize the *Laurada*. Ker claimed that the Spanish minister's action was a "high-handed piece of work ... one of the schemes resorted to by the Spanish officials to terrorize ship owners ... and prevent anything at all from being carried to Cuba that could in any way aid the insurgents." Ker offered a biased legal opinion that a clearance to leave port was standard practice but not a legal requirement, and it only entailed additional expense. Ker tried to explain the *Laurada*'s whereabouts, saying that she was headed to Charleston, South Carolina, to pick up a cargo of pyrite cinders. After she loaded the cargo, Ker joked, she would then go to Fort Sumter and pick up the cannons left behind during the Union evacuation to see if they could be of use to the insurgents in Cuba.

When the *Laurada* landed in Charleston on the fifteenth, she was immediately seized and Hughes arrested. The charge, however, was not for violating the neutrality laws. The first legal action taken against the *Laurada* was by New York fruit broker John E. Kerr, who claimed that he had chartered the vessel but that it had been co-opted by the Céspedes expedition. The plaintiff claimed that delays resulting from the expedition caused a cargo of bananas to spoil at a loss of $10,000.

After Hart received the news of the *Laurada*'s seizure, federal agents stormed his office at Pier 11 intending to seize another of his vessels. The *Leon* was alleged to be carrying a number of Cubans to Philadelphia for a meeting with Junta leaders on Congress's upcoming consideration of belligerency rights for the revolutionists. Soon after the fighting began, the Cuban Revolutionary Party launched efforts to have the government in Cuba recognized as belligerents. The recognition of independence, belligerency, or insurgency each carries with it certain neutral rights and obligations in international law. As a Spanish protectorate, Cuba had no standing in international relations, and only acknowledgment of their belligerent rights by the US government would put the rebels on an equal footing with Spain as it pertained to equal treatment.

An angry Hart told the US marshal in charge that no Cubans were aboard the *Leon*, and he demanded they leave his office. A search of the vessel at the Race Street wharf supported Hart's protest, revealing only a cargo of oranges, bananas, and coconuts. Hart further protested that allegations against the *Leon* and the *Laurada* were simply part of the Spanish persecution to which his company had been subjected. Hart said he was forced to go to Charleston with $1,500 to bail out Hughes and hire attorneys to represent his interests. The combination of business interruption and legal expenses, he said, might force him to move from Philadelphia to Boston or even back to Baltimore. At the very least, he told reporters, once he was exonerated he was going to ask Congress to reimburse him for damages.

Such tirades made Hart the reporters' best friend, an accessible, authoritative source who had no spigot to control what came out of his mouth. But as legal scrutiny intensified, Hart had to be increasingly aware of what he said publicly, and Ker began to take on the role as spokesman. Whether it was by agreement or simply an evolution of their relationship and circumstances, Hart sank more into the background, while Ker became a combination of lawyer, apologist, and public point man. Hart's temper would continue to flare, with a juicy quote likely to follow, but as much as he could, Bill Ker became the gatekeeper to Hart and his emotions.

Chapter 9

"UNTIL CUBA IS FREE"

The French line steamer *Champagne* glided into New York Harbor as the thickest fog in years was starting to burn off. The voyage from Le Havre had been unpleasant with westerly gales, high seas, and rain, and the thick haze only added to delay her arrival by twenty-four hours. Most of the 142 cabin passengers and 339 from steerage stood on the deck and watched the city materialize through the mist. One saloon passenger stood in the midst of them with a distinct splendor, tall and stout with snowy shocks of a handlebar mustache and thinning hair betrayed by the wisp of floss that plugged a grotesque scar above his nose.

General Calixto García had traveled from Paris at age fifty-six to join the new revolution. García was among the first to take up arms in 1868 when he and 150 men initiated hostilities in the district of Yara in eastern Cuba. His military victories resulted in a peace overture from Spanish officers, but at the talks García and his small force were ambushed. Seeing no escape, García put his pistol under his chin and pulled the trigger. The bullet remarkably went cleanly up and out the top of his nose, leaving a horrible wound, but he survived. After the peace, García initiated another revolution called La Guerra Chiquita, but when that failed, he fled to Paris. Now, his return to New York raised speculation that he would be on the next expedition to Cuba.

A prestigious delegation waited to greet García as the *Champagne* pulled into the dock. Estrada Palma, Nuñez, Quesada, Guerra, and other party members ran onto the deck as soon as the gangplank was lowered. The reunion was a warm one, and García was taken to 239 West Forty-Fourth Street, the home of Dr.

General Calixto García fled to Paris after the Ten Years' War and his own "Little War" failed. His demand to return to Cuba for the final revolution became one of Hart's greatest challenges. Library of Congress, Prints and Photographs Division, reproduction number LC-USZ62-91767.

Mario García Menocal. General García was adamant that he would not enjoy their hospitality for long. "Cuba's cry for help came to me across the ocean, and I have come to help my brothers in their fight for freedom," he told reporters. "My plans have not been determined upon as yet, but I will not remain in New York for any length of time. I expect to start for Cuba in a day or so."

García's public announcement of his intentions prompted Spanish agents and US authorities to increase scrutiny of the general and those around him. Despite García's insistence, Hart and Nuñez used the increased attention on him as an opportunity to plan another expedition that would slip out of American waters while the authorities were occupied.

Small groups of men walked casually along the darkened streets of lower Manhattan. Their dress was varied, some formal and others threadbare and frayed, and many wore a cap or hat of some fashion. The hair on uncovered heads was slicked back, and most of the men wore trim mustaches; all were neat in their own way. Each carried a small bundle that concealed a weapon, ammunition, and personal belongings. They walked from different directions, in and out of the glow of street lamps, destined for the eleventh floor of 56 New Street, headquarters of the Cuban Revolutionary Party.

The forty volunteers were greeted by General Francisco Carrillo, who would command the next expedition. The veteran of the Ten Years' War was arrested with Nuñez in the Little War, but escaped and made it to New York to join the Revolutionary Party's efforts. Nuñez had asked his forty-four-year-old comrade to lead the expedition because he knew that Carrillo wished to return to the fighting. But first, he wanted Carrillo to impress upon these fleas the task before them.

Whether their motive was patriotism or adventure, the volunteers needed to hear from the proven ones who had experienced both the majesty and the pain of war. The general's remarks were effective, greeted with frequent nods of agreement and an occasional tear. After his speech, the volunteers left individually or in small groups with new resolve and instructions to meet at the wharf, where a tugboat was waiting. They did not know the name of the boat because its name, *Cham*, was hidden by a piece of cloth nailed over the nameplate. No lights were visible, and boarding depended on sure feet and patience. After all were aboard, the tug eased away from the dock and slipped unnoticed into the blackness. Below Staten Island, she met a steam barge named the *J. S. T. Stranahan*, which had left the Atlantic dock in Brooklyn loaded with boxes. Carrillo and his men transferred from the tug to the barge and chugged out past Sandy Hook with the appearance of a moonlight cruise down the Jersey shore.

In the predawn twilight, the barge drew close to a steamship lying at anchor three miles off the coast. The steamer's name was painted out, also to hide her identity, and her funnels were repainted from the original red, black, and yellow to black and red. She was flying a white flag as the signal, and the barge ran up its own white flag in confirmation. The disguised steamer was the *Horsa* of the John D. Hart line that had gained widespread attention for its voyage to Liberia in March. The vessel left Philadelphia on November 10, 1895, with clearance papers for Port Antonio under the command of Danish captain Jacob Henry Jasper Wiborg.

General Carrillo handed Wiborg his orders, which directed the captain to take the men and luggage aboard the *Horsa* and look for a "colored man" in the group. He was the pilot who would tell Wiborg where on the Cuban coast to deliver the men and cargo. After the men were aboard, Wiborg ordered his engineer to spare nothing as he charted a southward course.

During the voyage, the young men loitered on deck, some carrying rifles and most carrying machetes hanging from leather or cloth belts. Their varied wardrobes were bonded by small Cuban flags pinned to their lapels or sleeves. For the next four days, they staved off boredom by practicing dry fire with every faux shot into the horizon hitting the heart of an imaginary Spaniard. Carrillo wanted to break the monotony of travel for the men, so he ordered a test fire of a large Hotchkiss cannon that was the showpiece of the dangerous cargo.

The artillery specialists pulled it from its large box, which was stored in one of the surfboats, and the lounging men came alert. Great anticipation settled over the aspiring fighters as they watched the artillerists attach the wheels and prepare the firing mechanism. The cannoneer aimed the barrel toward the open sea and fired. It was a direct hit in every man's imagination as cheers erupted, then faded with the sifting smoke.

The *Horsa* avoided detection until the night of Friday, November 15, when it neared the southern Cuban coast east of Santiago. A steady rain fell as the men hurriedly lowered four small surfboats that would transport them and their cargo ashore. The cannon and boxes of rifles and ammunition were ferried methodically and stacked on the beach. More than two dozen boxes of cartridges remained on the steamer's deck when someone shouted a warning. A masthead light in the distance grew brighter. A Spanish gunboat was closing fast.

Carrillo was greatly agitated at the interruption and demanded that the men retrieve the rest of the boxes. But Captain Wiborg, a veteran of the Danish navy, ordered the general to be content with what ammunition they had unloaded and get the rest of his men into the boats. Wiborg ordered the cutting of tow lines that connected the boats to the ship, and he directed his engineer to open the valves wide. Soon, the *Horsa* was widening the distance from her pursuer on her way to Jamaica. When she was out of sight of the gunboat, Wiborg ordered the remaining boxes of cartridges heaved overboard.

Upon hearing of the landing, the irate Spanish minister in Washington cabled information to Madrid, which relayed an appeal to London. The British government contacted its officials in Jamaica, who were waiting when the *Horsa* eased into the harbor. Wiborg and his crew were detained for questioning, but the captain denied participating in any filibustering activity. He admitted taking Cubans aboard as passengers, but he claimed he did not suspect their motives until they seized the ship and forced him to drop them in Cuba. British authorities could not prove otherwise. They released the *Horsa* on November 21, but not before she took on a load of bananas and charted a northward course.

In Philadelphia, Bill Ker assured Hart that the British government would not hold the *Horsa*, but when questioned by the press, Ker did not mince words about his own government's perceived obeisance to Spain.

"No other government on the face of the earth would do what this government is doing in this matter," Ker fumed to reporters. "Every United States customs officer is turned into a spy to watch for any vessel that might carry aid from this country to Cuba. Our country has gone out of its way to seize vessels without any warrant of the law, and there is nothing in the laws to prevent the carriage of arms and ammunition from Philadelphia to Cuba."

The eminent representative of the Hart line repeated his comments later that week at a massive rally at the Academy of Music. The meeting was scheduled by the Philadelphia Brigade of Pennsylvania Reserves to raise funds for a monument commemorating their fallen comrades at the Battle of Antietam. But the partisan crowd's enthusiasm was easily co-opted by speakers sympathetic to the Cuban cause. Embracing his platform as a Civil War veteran, a former assistant attorney general, and a lifelong Democrat, Ker lampooned the Cleveland administration for its wayward foreign policy and Attorney General Judson Harmon in particular for a recent comment that such rallies for Cuba incited Spain and might even be unconstitutional.

"We are told it is against the law to send our ships to Cuba with anything on board in the shape of a weapon larger than a penknife," Ker agitated before the loud and sympathetic crowd. "Has it come to this, that we must obey the mandates of Spain, that we must go to the Spanish consul and show him our manifest? The time is drawing near when I hope we will have a government that will recognize the belligerency of Cuba, that will emphasize every line, every word and every syllable of the Monroe Doctrine. By some insidious influence, the Spaniards have controlled the powers that be at Washington. These people are watching every vessel that leaves our port, and every inspector in your Custom House is a Spanish spy, not of his own free will but by the orders of his superiors."

The crowd at the Academy of Music was in a white-hot lather by the time Ker spoke his final words. He paused and wiped his right hand back over his high, glistening forehead as beads of sweat dripped from his beard. He inclined forward toward a crowd hungry to be fed further and thrust his flattened palm down hard on the podium like a gunshot. It was a final promise to reluctant ears in Washington as Ker pledged: "We will go on and land arms and ammunition on the coast of Cuba until Cuba is free!"

Ker soon had another reason to denounce the American puppetry in deference to Spain. After the *Horsa* arrived back in Philadelphia on November 27, Hart sent Captain Wiborg to the Custom House to have the vessel cleared for another voyage. However, Collector John R. Read refused to grant clearance papers, on orders from Ellery P. Ingham, the US attorney for the Eastern District of Pennsylvania. Hart telephoned Ker, who took a fast carriage to Ingham's office and demanded to know the reason. Ingham shrugged his shoulders, saying he did not know the reason. He was acting on a direct order from his boss, US Attorney General Harmon, the butt of Ker's diatribe at the Academy of Music rally.

The attorney general was responding to the latest Spanish demand for action after the *Horsa* arrived in Philadelphia. Consul José Congosto contacted the Danish consulate to question Wiborg, a Danish national in command of a Danish flag vessel. Congosto was acting on information provided to British authorities in Jamaica by a disgruntled crew member, fireman Emil Fredericksen. In a sworn affidavit given after the *Horsa* departed Jamaica, Fredericksen claimed that the ship had rendezvoused with a tugboat two miles off the New Jersey coast, where "thirty or forty" men, two large rowboats, and many heavy boxes were taken aboard. After the vessel put to sea, he said, the men broke open the boxes and took out about fifteen rifles, a small "gun on wheels," and some sabers and cartridges. The fireman said the men conducted drills with weapons during the voyage.

Congosto swore out a warrant charging that Wiborg and members of his crew violated the neutrality laws of the United States by transporting a military expedition to Cuba. Wiborg was arrested along with chief mate Jens P. Pedersen and second mate Hans Johansen. Casting his net wider, Congosto also swore out warrants for the arrests of Captain Frederick Svanoe and first mate Ragnan Christiansen of the Hart vessel *Leon*.

At the bail hearing on November 29, Congosto produced another alleged witness to the expedition. Carl Arnston, a Norwegian identified as a fireman on the *Horsa*, claimed that he was aboard when the *Horsa* was disguised, its funnels and nameplate painted over. Conspicuously seated in the gallery, John D. Hart seethed when Arnston claimed that the charter master was aboard the tug that transferred the cargo to the *Horsa* at Barnegat Light, fifteen miles south of Toms River on the Jersey shore. Arnston said Hart offered each crew member $25 to keep their mouths shut.

Ker elicited loud laughter from the courtroom during cross-examination when Arnston admitted that while the *Horsa* was lying at Port Antonio, he was in jail for public intoxication. Ker also called eleven other members of the *Horsa* crew, as well as Hart, all of whom testified that the vessel carried no filibusters. Wiborg and his two mates were bound over on $1,000 bail, and a further hearing was set for December 16.

Cuba was not the most pressing issue that drew the attention of the Cleveland administration, judging by the content of the president's annual message to Congress on December 2, 1895. After commenting on the nation's financial situation, trade issues with Argentina, the safety of Americans in China, the boundary dispute between Great Britain and Venezuela, and the insufficiency of British patrols in restraining British sealing ships in the Bering Sea, the president finally arrived at the question of Cuba.

"Besides deranging the commercial exchanges of the island, of which our country takes the predominant share," he said, "this flagrant condition of hostilities, by arousing sentimental sympathy and inciting adventurous support among our people has entailed earnest effort on the part of this government to enforce obedience to our neutrality laws and to prevent the territory of the United States from being abused as a vantage ground from which to aid those in arms against Spanish sovereignty."

Confirming the lack of sympathy from the American administration were exchanges Estrada Palma had with Olney and Boston sugar magnate Edwin F. Atkins.

Less than a week after Cleveland's address, Estrada Palma addressed a long letter to Olney outlining clearly why the United States should grant rights of belligerency to the revolutionary government. The delegate repeated his position during a meeting with Atkins, who was part owner of the Soledad Plantation, which had been burned by Maceo's army.

Atkins was not impressed with the Cuban's positions relative to American investments on the island and wrote to Olney in advance of a scheduled meeting between Estrada Palma and the secretary. He quoted Estrada Palma as saying: "[T]he Cubans should be recognized as belligerents and . . . as soon as the Government of the United States recognized the Cuban Insurgents as belligerents, an order would go forth from the Insurgent Government directing that the property and interest in Cuba of American citizens . . . should be exempted from the force and effect of all orders directing the destruction of property."

Atkins stressed to Olney that Americans with investments in Cuba believed that protection of US property was a priority of the US government. When Estrada Palma and Quesada visited the secretary, Olney asked if they approved of the insurgents' practice of burning the sugar plantations; Estrada Palma responded that he considered the burnings necessary acts of war. "Well, gentlemen," Olney responded, "there is but one term for such action. We call it arson." With that, he terminated the meeting.

The case of *United States v. the Laurada* and Captain Sam Hughes came before Judge W. H. Brawley in US District Court in Charleston, South Carolina, on December 6. Ker repeated his Wilmington strategy of hiring prominent local counsel by retaining Matthew C. Butler, a former US senator from South Carolina, and prominent attorney J. P. Kennedy Bryan, who later would argue cases before the US Supreme Court.

Hughes and his legal team sat attentively during reading of the indictment, which charged that in late October 1895 the *Laurada* of the Hart line took aboard a company of soldiers and a large quantity of munitions intended for the Cuban insurgents. US District Attorney W. P. Murphy called as witnesses three Spanish seamen and one Austrian, whose testimony had to be translated since none could speak English. Their testimony was virtually identical, suggesting that the witnesses had been well coached. All claimed to have been employed as firemen on the *Laurada* during the voyage in question. All claimed that the vessel left New York about 6:30 p.m. on October 21 and anchored about two miles off the Scotland lightship at the entrance to New York Harbor. All claimed that two tugs approached from the sea and transferred thirty-five men and many boxes of arms and ammunition onto the steamer.

The witnesses testified that the Cubans drilled constantly below decks during the voyage and that one of them admitted he was going to fight for Cuban liberty. The witnesses claimed that the *Laurada* arrived off the Cuban coast on October 27 and anchored about two hundred yards offshore, and the men and ammunition were put into small boats and landed. The witnesses said the steamer departed for Kingston, Jamaica, where it picked up a cargo of bananas. The three Spaniards all claimed that when the *Laurada* arrived back at New York, Captain Hughes refused to pay their wages, and they protested to the Spanish consul. After they left the consulate, Pinkerton detectives approached and offered them two dollars per day plus expenses if they would testify.

Judge Brawley ruled that nothing he heard proved an expedition began within the territory of the United States, but he said sufficient proof existed that an offense might have been committed on the high seas. He ordered Hughes held under bond for trial at the January term of the court.

The second case involving a Hart line steamer, that of *Horsa* Captain Wiborg, was scheduled to resume when the vessel returned to Philadelphia in mid-December. But the expected dates came and went and the *Horsa* did not return until December 27. Soon after the ship docked, Wiborg went to Hart's office to explain that a devastating "norther" had blown steadily for twelve days, wrecked many Jamaican banana plantations, and destroyed most of the fruit. After the winds finally died down, Wiborg attempted to collect a cargo but was unable to procure any more than one-fifth of her usual load.

It was another harsh financial blow for Hart. With the rich banana plantations reduced to a wasteland of broken plants, the Jamaican trade was dead until an entire crop matured in nine to twelve months. Hart had no recourse but to send his steamers farther south, to the islands of Saint Andrews and Providence, off the coast of Nicaragua, to secure full cargoes. But well before he could dispatch vessels and secure new contacts, Wiborg's trial and other expenses would continue to blow like a raging nor'easter.

The hearing resumed at 11:30 a.m. on December 30 before Commissioner James D. Bell. US Attorney Ingham called to the stand Emil Fredericksen, the disgruntled fireman on the *Horsa*. Fredericksen testified that when the *Horsa* left Philadelphia it carried eighty-three passengers, including John D. Hart, corroborating earlier testimony by the ubiquitous Carl Arnston. Fredericksen repeated that the *Horsa* steamed down the New Jersey coast to Barnegat Light, where forty Cubans and many boxes of ammunition came aboard from the barge *Stranahan*. After the men and munitions were loaded, Hart was said to have boarded the barge for a return to Philadelphia, while the steamer proceeded to Cuba. Ker vigorously cross-examined Fredericksen, who admitted he was "employed" by the Spanish consul at $1.50 per day.

In the absence of his own witnesses, Ker resorted to his vast gifts of oration and obfuscation. He vigorously challenged the memories of the government witnesses and claimed that their testimony was tainted because they were being paid by the Spanish consul. The fact that their testimony was nearly verbatim proved beyond a doubt that the witnesses had been schooled on answers that would incriminate the defendants. However, Ker's efforts were not enough to overcome eyewitness testimony under oath. Commissioner Bell ordered Wiborg and mates Pedersen and Johansen held over for trial at the February term of the court.

While Ker fought the public legal battles, Hart was losing the private, financial war. His vessels were docked, the *Leon* undergoing repairs in Wilmington, Delaware, the *Laurada* detained in Charleston, and the *Horsa* held in Philadelphia.

The three captains and several crew members faced trials. Chartering other vessels was impossible because Hart's insurance policies on the seized ships all had been canceled. Standard language in such policies provided for cancellation in the event of "arrest or restraint by princes, rulers, or people."

The lost income was far exceeded by the increase in expenses, the daily costs of maintaining a steamer whether she was hauling cargo or tied to the dock. The Junta was paying some, but not all, of Hart's legal expenses, which would only continue to rise as the cases trudged through the legal system. The filibuster business provided more excitement than Hart ever had experienced as a fruit importer, but excitement was not a commercial commodity.

If he prevailed in court, he would become a financially ruined hero of the Cuban Revolution. If he lost, he could expect to spend considerable time in prison. How much these problems affected his personal life is unknown, but John and Kate Hart separated and took up different residences sometime toward the end of 1895. The deaths of their son in 1885 and newborn in 1888 were doubtlessly sources of lingering sorrow, and the birth of their third daughter, Grace, came in 1890 when Kate was thirty-seven. Subsequent information suggests that Grace needed special care, which could have further strained the marriage.

Whatever the reasons, John moved out of their Camden home and lodged for a period of time at Green's Hotel in the city. Kate moved into a house at 1220 Mount Vernon Street in Philadelphia, which she turned into a boarding house sometime in 1896.

Chapter 10

A CLEAR VICTORY IN COURT

As the revolution entered its second year, news came from Cuba that the cavalry of Máximo Gómez and Antonio Maceo had surrounded the city of Santa Clara, and panicked Spanish troops were throwing up defensive fortifications. Another dispatch on the same action claimed that Spanish forces under Generals Oliver and Palanca had Gómez and Maceo's main force surrounded, and the rebellion soon would be quashed. The contradictory nature of those reports reflected the confusion for the American public in trying to determine which side was winning. Reports from the front on battles, troop movements, and heroic or cowardly actions by the combatants depended entirely on which sources were talking to which American newspapers.

The Spanish government, anxious to minimize the importance of the revolt, instituted a rigid policy in which reports from Madrid or Havana invariably described Spanish victories. Likewise, the Junta propaganda machine tried to counter Spanish claims and arouse the sympathy of the American people by distributing information about the rebels' perceived military successes. The New York newspapers were willing accomplices, since news from Cuba that fit the prevailing model of sensational reporting was readily available at Junta headquarters.

Estrada Palma opened a new front in Washington when he established a "legation" at the Raleigh Hotel. Quesada was appointed first secretary with the dual tasks of forging relationships with the capital press and encouraging support among congressional leaders. Public sentiment was clearly in favor of the

After joining the Cuban Revolutionary Party as Martí's secretary, Gonzalo de Quesada became the Junta's representative in Washington lobbying Congress on Cuba's behalf. Library of Congress, Prints and Photographs Division, George Grantham Bain Collection, reproduction number LC-DIG-ggbain-15482.

Cubans, and Junta leaders hoped sympathetic voters would persuade their elected representatives to enact legislation to help the insurgents.

Quesada used the office as a press center, dispensing to the Washington newspaper corps daily notes and information as well as the occasional inducement. As Quesada wrote to Estrada Palma: "[S]end me the check, because I had to give some money to our friend at the *Star*." The suggestion of payment for good publicity was reinforced in another letter to Estrada Palma in which Quesada complained that the Spanish minister paid the *Washington Post* $2,000 to print a column he'd written. The competitive nature of the New York press corps apparently took on a different meaning for the Washington scribes.

While news from the battlefield was mixed, the filibustering effort orchestrated by Nuñez and Hart won another clear victory in court on January 23, 1896, with the quick acquittal of Sam Hughes in Charleston. Charged in the October expedition of the *Laurada*, Hughes was freed after jurors took one ballot and barely twenty minutes to declare him not guilty. District Attorney W. P. Murphy based his prosecution on the accounts of disgruntled crew members who admitted they were paid by the Spanish consul, but Hughes's attorney spent time educating the jury on the neutrality laws. J. P. Kennedy Bryan presented a definition of the statutes that he artfully condensed into six reasons why the neutrality laws had not been violated and why the jurors had no choice but to find his client innocent:

1. It was not a violation for any person to go abroad to enlist in a foreign army; 2. It was not a violation for an American ship to carry as passengers such

persons and to land them in a foreign country; 3. It was not a violation to carry by ship to a foreign country ammunition or munitions of war intended to be used in a foreign war; 4. It was not a violation to carry on the same ship with such passengers munitions of war to be used by foreign armies; 5. While such volunteers and munitions may face capture by a belligerent foreign power, the acts of carrying and landing such munitions were lawful commerce; and 6. The *Laurada*'s cargo and passengers did not fit the neutrality law's definition of a military expedition, which includes organized infantry, artillery, or cavalry, properly officered and equipped.

Bryan based his arguments on law established four years earlier in the case of the *Itata*, a steamer captured by a party of Chilean insurgents in rebellion against their existing government. In April 1891, insurgents purchased a large quantity of arms and ammunition in New York with the intention of sending them to Chile for use against the regime. The cargo was shipped to California, where the *Itata* was to pick it up. However, the vessel was seized at San Diego after landing to pick up coal and stores. The arms were subsequently transferred to the *Itata* near San Clemente Island and were transported to Chile, where she arrived on June 3.

A federal court ruled that the mere purchase and carriage of arms and warlike stores to a party of insurgents in a foreign country did not constitute a violation of the neutrality laws, especially since such munitions did not constitute a part of the fittings or furnishings of the vessel. The statutes did, however, prohibit the enlistment of men in the United States for the purpose of fighting a country with whom the US is at peace. That would appear to insulate from prosecution expeditions consisting of separate vessels, one or more to carry war matériel, and one or more to carry "workers" headed to another destination for "employment" purposes. Once in international waters (or far enough off the US coast to avoid the watchful eye of the Revenue Cutter Service), the arms and men could be transferred to a larger vessel for the trip to Cuba.

Hart was emboldened by the verdict, which inspired another pronouncement that raised official eyebrows. The day after Hughes was acquitted, Hart announced that all vessels chartered by the Hart Company would henceforth be prepared for any emergencies, including the immediate installation of cannons and Maxim guns on the *Laurada* and the *Horsa*. The news left Collector John Read at the Port of New York skeptical and apparently confused himself about the fine print in the law. "There is no doubt," Read said, "it is a violation of the neutrality laws to carry arms to a country with which this country is at peace."

When informed of Read's comment, Hart dismissed the collector's opinion with a wave of his hand. His captain was free, he was absolved of violating any laws, and the Cuban trade once again shined brightly as the glimmering pearl in Hart's oyster.

General Calixto García had waited more than two months to be taken to Cuba, a delay he could neither explain nor excuse. He had insisted to Estrada Palma that the Revolutionary Party's most important task was to deliver him to the fighting at the earliest possible instant. He had wasted enough time lounging in the decadence of New York while his countrymen were fighting and dying in their besieged homeland.

García's well-known temper was reaching its boiling point, and he demanded to be taken to Cuba immediately. With John D. Hart's vessels grounded by court cases, Nuñez succumbed to the general's demands and sought to purchase any ship he could find. The *James W. Hawkins*, a 130-foot steamer, was available in Baltimore and was purchased in typical Junta fashion, by a "Mr. Tinsley for Mr. Smith of New York." "Mr. Tinsley" paid cash, then aroused suspicion when he mysteriously disappeared. The vessel was taken to the 138th Street pier at Port Morris in the Bronx, and on the night of January 25, 1896, became the center of much activity. Groups of men in pairs and threes appeared and boarded the steamer, while two lighters soon arrived carrying hundreds of boxes of arms and ammunition and long sacks filled with rifles.

Shortly before the boat was to sail, the 118 volunteers already on board were joined by García, his son Carlos, and several other Cuban officers, including seventy-four-year-old General Juan Fernández Ruz, another veteran of the Ten Years' War. Some of the men questioned the condition of the vessel, saying its hull was rotten and its machinery in disrepair, but the anticipation of seeing their homeland blinded them to further concern.

The *Hawkins* departed under fair skies and headed out the East River toward Long Island Sound. But about 3:00 a.m., the wind picked up and a fierce storm overtook them. Wave after wave roared over the deck in rapid succession, and the rolling seas rocked the *Hawkins* to and fro like a paper hat. The waves pounded those on board, stripping their shoes and clothing from their bodies. The constant thrashing opened leaks at the seams and another in the engine room. Crew members manned the pumps diligently, but they could not keep up with the deadly intrusion. They grabbed buckets and bailed for their lives, but the pumps soon choked with coal and water, and the engine room was flooded. The ship was doomed.

García was asleep below decks suffering from a case of seasickness when the storm's fury woke him. He went on deck and saw the sorry state of his men, who already were wailing and mourning their own certain deaths. He began shouting to them, trying to make himself heard over the tumult. He encouraged them that they were on their way to Cuba to die for their country, if necessary, so what difference did it make where they died? "Here we die for Cuba as if we were on the battlefield," García shouted. "It is the same glory that touches us!"

Captain Hall ordered the coal thrown overboard to lighten the vessel, but it did not help. He then ordered the crew to open the hatches and start tossing the very heavy, and very expensive, cargo overboard. First to go was three hundred pounds of dynamite that Hall feared would break loose and blow them all to atoms. The rest of the load followed, including two Hotchkiss guns, 1,400 rifles, and one million rounds of ammunition. The captain ordered distress rockets sent up into the predawn darkness, and soon three schooners responded.

The sea rose inch by inch around the men's ankles, then to their knees and higher. About 11:30 a.m., with the sky as dark as midnight, Hall gave the order to abandon ship. Crew members were frantically trying to remove the lifeboats from their davits, and one boat was useless after a box of cartridges was thrown through the bottom. That left five small boats to save more than 130 passengers and crew. Some men scrambled into the useful boats while others panicked and jumped into the water. Five crew members and at least four volunteers drowned.

The schooner *Helen H. Benedict* arrived first and picked up the first officer, the steward, and twenty-three Cubans. The schooners *Leander V. Beebe* and *Alicia B. Crosby* began picking up other survivors. Captain Harry Denyse of the ocean tug *Fred B. Dalzell* was patrolling the area looking for an easy tow when he saw the *Beebe* flying an inverted American flag, a maritime signal for distress. Denyse steered his tug close and saw García, looking haggard and exhausted on the deck of the *Beebe*. Denyse took Calixto and Carlos García, Ruz, and about seventy "sorry-looking" Cubans on board and agreed to take them back to New York for a price. García agreed and pulled the necessary cash from one of two satchels full of US banknotes that he had strapped to his body.

The *James W. Hawkins* went down around noon, officially seventy-three miles south-southwest of Montauk Point on the eastern end of Long Island. Denyse took the survivors back to New York, dropping them at the foot of Forty-Second Street on the East River. García was exhausted by the ordeal, but his son Carlos's anger overcame his own fatigue as he railed at the utter waste of men and armaments. "We suffered frightfully," the younger García said in a trembling voice to a *New York Herald* reporter. "My father and I were in the icy water for hours.... Somebody has been guilty of a great crime. It was shameful to send such a large body of men and a load of arms out to sea upon such a craft. She was rotten, unseaworthy and virtually a floating coffin."

Published reports put the value of the steamer and lost weapons at $200,000, although the actual price of more than $72,000 still had a significant impact on the party treasury. The greater damage, however, was another long stretch of inactivity and frustration for García before the Junta could mount another attempt to deliver him to Cuba.

The disaster aroused the émigré community in New York, many of whom gathered to confront Estrada Palma at his residence at the Astor House Hotel. The crowd was angry and wanted answers, especially after the news surfaced that García had been warned about the boat's condition before they departed.

Estrada Palma listened to the bitter denunciations and offered to resign, but the crowd did not want a resignation. They wanted results.

Hart and Nuñez recognized the urgency of delivering García to Cuba and met at Nuñez's home in Philadelphia to devise a new plan. Hart knew it was an act of desperation that had compelled the Cubans to purchase a crumbling vessel like the *James W. Hawkins*. The adroit charter master had developed a reputation for being able to spin ships and crew out of sailcloth, a skill that would be necessary to deliver García and quell the unrest. Federal authorities, Spanish spies, and the press were familiar with his current vessels and were watching them diligently. It was time to add a new vessel to the filibuster fleet, unknown to the snoopers, which Hart would inspect personally to ensure her seaworthiness. He soon found just the ship he was looking for, wasting away in New York.

Despite its propaganda claims to the contrary, the Spanish government in Madrid tacitly admitted in mid-January 1896 that the war was not going well when it recalled Captain General Arsenio Martínez Campos as military governor of Cuba. An editorial in *Diario de Marino*, the organ of the Reformist Party, said the Cuban crisis was destroying the business climate in Spain and laid the blame at the polished boots of Martínez Campos. If a respected military leader could not crush the revolution or even secure a stalemated peace, he had to be replaced before the revolution strengthened.

The new governor sailed into Havana Harbor on February 10, 1896, on board the *Alphonse XIII*. At sixty years old, short and stout with hair and beard almost white, the man who walked off the ship presented a kindly appearance to the celebrants. The balconies along the waterfront and near the palace on O'Reilly Street were decorated with ladies in holiday attire who showered their new commander with flowers, many fashioned into the shape of crowns. He was welcomed by the City Council, who presented him with an assurance of loyalty, which was followed by an elaborate procession along streets packed with enthusiastic crowds. Nearly all the bands in the city were strategically placed at key locations along the route to enhance the festive air. The procession arrived at the palace, where the new governor formally took the oath of Captain General over a crucifix and a Bible.

Valeriano Weyler y Nicolau was well known to the insurgents. Born in Majorca of an Irish father and Spanish mother, Weyler's grandfatherly manner belied a menacing reputation he had earned during the Ten Years' War as a brutal commander whose methods bordered on barbarity.

His cruel treatment of prisoners, both men and women, aroused so much resentment and bitterness that his detractors called him "the Butcher." Ironically, the moderate Martínez Campos had been appointed captain general of Cuba in 1876 in response to Weyler's methods. Madrid believed that a civil approach would win hearts and encourage peace, and the war ended with Martínez Campos

Madrid appointed Valeriano Weyler as captain general of Cuba to stop the revolution, but his term became a reign of terror that included concentration camps, poverty, and starvation. Line drawing from the March 17, 1898, edition of the *New York Journal*.

promising reforms and kindness. On his return to Madrid, he was named prime minister, but his efforts to gain approval for his reforms failed in the Cortes.

Madrid's view of the current situation was, indeed, gloomy. The rebel Máximo Gómez had driven his army almost to the gates of Havana, while Antonio Maceo continued to raid through Pinar del Río, and a formidable army led by his brother José moved westward toward the sleepy seaport of Matanzas. If the restrained Martínez Campos allowed the rebels such progress, then perhaps the once-questionable tactics of Weyler now were appropriate to the circumstances. And he wasted no time implementing them.

Among his first acts as governor, Weyler sent dispatches to all parts of the island, addressing every constituency from local governments, business interests, and the military on down to the common people. He declared to all: "My mission is the honorable one of finishing the war." He did not reveal how he would accomplish that other than to pledge "the reforms the Government may think most proper, with the love of a mother to her children."

Weyler's definition of a mother's love was soon revealed to be consistent with his reputation from the previous war. He pledged to meet warfare with methods of war and to show no mercy to spies or those who gave aid and comfort to the revolutionists. He pledged a blockade of Cuba so rigid that further importation of arms and munitions from the United States would be impossible.

The results of Weyler's declarations were soon manifest throughout the island. In the town of Sabanilla, women could leave their homes only at great risk of being attacked by soldiers or undisciplined rabble whom Weyler refused to control. Arrests of "suspects" sympathetic to the rebels were made in every town with a Spanish garrison. A committee consisting of both Spanish and Cuban citizens from Jovellanos in Matanzas Province arrived in Havana to protest the arrest of thirty-five "suspects" in two days. At nearby Hoyo Colorado, Spanish soldiers arrested seventy-nine "suspects" and threw them into prison.

It was apparent that a prediction made by the outgoing captain general was truly prophetic. When Martínez Campos learned the identity of his successor, he remarked: "If Weyler returns to Cuba even the dead will rise from their graves to fight him."

The US courts had not made Weyler's job any easier. The South Carolina decision that absolved John D. Hart's *Laurada* and Captain Sam Hughes of violating US neutrality laws appeared to affirm the critical distinction between an armed expedition and a load of armaments with men aboard to unload them. The former violated the neutrality laws, while the court proclaimed the latter a legal business transaction.

Two days after Weyler's arrival in Havana, Bill Ker boldly announced that Hughes would soon deliver a load of rifles, ammunition, dynamite, and stores to Cuba, and there was nothing the American authorities could do about it. He announced bluntly that Hughes had departed Philadelphia for Wilmington, North Carolina, where he would take command of a ship already loaded with armaments. Ker said the vessel first would head for Charleston and was less than coy when asked about its final destination.

"I would not wonder if she found her way to Cuba," Ker smirked. "The Spanish authorities have done the Hart Company all the injury they can, and we mean to pay them back better than they give us.... We have grown tired of having our ships stopped, our officers arrested and our line libeled by Spaniards, and we propose to give them a new kind of medicine."

As Hughes headed for Wilmington, authorities in Philadelphia were watching some curious activity on board the *Laurada*, docked at Pier 11. About four hundred bunks were being installed, and Pinkerton agents warned Consul Congosto that the ship was being prepared for a massive transport of volunteers headed to Cuba. In reality, Hart had assigned the *Laurada* to take the *Horsa*'s place for another voyage of Blacks wishing to return to Africa. With Hughes headed to Cuba, Hart hired Captain Charles B. Dickman, a US Navy veteran of the Civil War, to master the *Laurada*'s voyage to Liberia.

Separating Hughes from the *Laurada* was sound strategy. The *Laurada* under Hart's notorious Captain Sam Hughes was a combination as famous as Butch

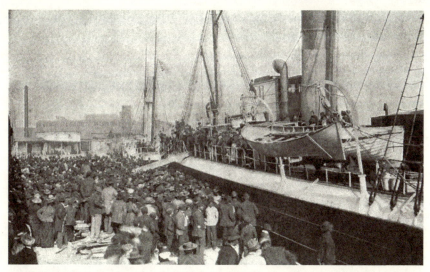

John D. Hart took the *Laurada* out of the "Cuba trade" in March 1896 to carry a voyage of Black emigrants from Savannah, Georgia, to Liberia. Photograph from the March 31, 1896, edition of *Illustrated American Magazine*.

Cassidy and the Sundance Kid soon would become in the American West. The *Laurada*'s every twist and turn with Hughes in command was watched by newspaper reporters, Spanish spies, and the Revenue Cutter Service, who turned equal attention to the ship's owner. It was time to split captain and vessel and let interest drift elsewhere. A voyage of the *Laurada* to Africa and back would keep her out of the public eye for nearly two months while Hughes's talents were devoted to more immediate activities. Separated, the flickering wick of scrutiny could burn down.

Hart shifted Hughes's command to the small steamship *Commodore*, a 178-ton vessel the Junta had bought in August for $13,500. The *Commodore* glided out of Wilmington in the late morning on Thursday, February 13, but Hughes soon noticed he was being followed by the revenue cutter *Colfax*. The captain ignored his unwanted escort until 4:00 p.m. the next day when he arrived at the Consumers Coal Company wharf in Charleston to pick up a load of coal. When the *Commodore* docked at North Central Pier, Hughes spotted two agents posted at the wharf. A second cutter, the *Boutwell*, appeared off the bar, then came into the harbor and anchored within view.

Annoyed at the constant badgering from the Revenue Cutter Service, the press, and curious bystanders, Hughes promptly hung a sign at the gangplank entry announcing "No Admittance." Officers from the US Custom House boarded the vessel anyway and read the manifest, which stated that the *Commodore* was loaded with "arms and ammunition." Forewarned and frustrated at the new interpretation of the neutrality laws, the officials found the papers in order and departed.

But Hughes would not make the voyage. Hart summoned his most reliable captain back to Philadelphia after receiving an urgent, but not unexpected, message from Nuñez. Impatient General Calixto García insisted that he and his troops be taken to Cuba without delay. It was time for the new plan Hart and Nuñez had created to be put into action.

Chapter 11

SPANISH SPIES AND US MARSHALS

The *Bermuda* had been lying idle at Erie Basin off South Brooklyn for a year. At 223 feet in length with a 23-foot beam, the 1,200-ton, two-masted iron screw steamer could easily accommodate General García's party and an arsenal of weapons. Hart closely examined the vessel of British registry and liked what he saw, so he approached the ship brokerage firm of Bennett, Walsh & Co. and bought the *Bermuda* for $22,000.

She was moved from her berth on February 17, 1896, and placed in dry dock at the foot of Pike Street on the East River, where Hart supervised a rapid overhaul. Her bottom was scraped and painted, a new propeller fitted, and the interior renovated to accommodate a large company. Hart hired Captain Lawrence Brabazon from Philadelphia, who, after renovations were completed, guided the *Bermuda* to anchorage off Liberty Island on Saturday, February 22.

Little did Hart or Nuñez realize, but their carefully orchestrated scheme had been discovered. The day the *Bermuda* went into dry dock, Spanish agents received information that Junta treasurer Benjamin Guerra had provided funds for the purchase of a new vessel, information they immediately forwarded to Dupuy de Lôme. The minister alerted Secretary of State Olney, who assigned three deputy marshals to keep the *Bermuda* under surveillance.

On Sunday, the *Bermuda* steamed from Liberty Island to the docks at Communipaw, Jersey City, to have her coal bunkers filled. It became obvious that the *Bermuda* was headed to a tropical destination after another spy discovered that eighty pounds of ice had been put aboard at Pike Street. On Monday morning,

The *Bermuda* was second only to the *Laurada* as John D. Hart's most reliable vessels to deliver armaments and volunteers to Cuba. Line drawing from the March 16, 1896, *New York Tribune*.

spies learned that an unusually large crew had been hired and taken from Pier 7 on the East River by tug to the *Bermuda*. After informants claimed that the steamer was intending to quietly slip out of the harbor that night, the revenue cutter *Chandler* dropped down the bay, between Liberty Island and Robbins Reef, ready to intercept her.

Brabazon entered the Custom House late Monday afternoon and took out clearance papers for Santa Marta, Colombia. By sunset, the *Bermuda* was building up steam. García and his men, who had been kept under constant surveillance since the *Hawkins* shipwreck, were seen Monday walking toward the East River in small groups. The men and arms were to be transported into the bay by three tugs owned by the McCaldin Brothers, a firm operated by the brothers James, William, and Joseph, who themselves had run guns to Haiti in 1888. The tugs *McCaldin Brothers* and *W. J. McCaldin* picked up the men at Pier 4 at 10:00 p.m., while the steam barge *J. S. T. Stranahan* left the foot of King Street in Brooklyn just before midnight with the arms and ammunition.

With a departure imminent, US Marshal John H. McCarthy issued warrants, and the revenue cutters *Chandler* and *Hudson* were alerted. McCarthy and fifteen deputy marshals boarded a swift tug to commence the operation, but they were unexpectedly joined by the Spanish posse. Consul Arturo Baldasano and fifteen Pinkerton detectives climbed aboard the tug, and soon the official contingent was transferred to the *Hudson*.

The federal boat put in behind an empty coal barge, where she lay hidden until the tug *McCaldin Brothers* was spotted heading for the *Bermuda*. Captain Buck Cutler saw the *Hudson* and quickly changed course away from Liberty Island

and toward the Narrows. The cutter gave chase but peeled off at about 10:00 p.m. when Captain Goodwin saw the *W. J. McCaldin*, with every light extinguished, slowly approaching the steamer. The *Bermuda* was belching black smoke and was ready to depart as a Jacob's ladder was let down, and García and about fifty Cubans began clambering aboard even before the ladder was secured. When the last man was on deck, a shout went up that a cutter was fast approaching.

Captain Goodwin ordered the *W. J. McCaldin* to heave to, but when he was ignored, he gave the order to ram the tug. The ninety-five-foot government boat's prow struck her amidships, producing far more din than damage, but the reverberation and the threat brought the tug to a meek standstill. No longer worth the government's time, the tug was allowed to flee, and she made a wild dash for the Battery.

The *Bermuda*'s engines were in motion, her screw revolving, and the chain cable in the hawsehole rattling with the raising anchor. The *Hudson* pulled close on the *Bermuda*'s port side, and Marshal McCarthy jumped on the companion ladder, followed by a haphazard horde of deputies and detectives. "We are in charge here," McCarthy shouted, his men tumbling over one another onto the deck, raising their shields in one hand and revolvers in the other. One British member of the *Bermuda* crew loudly told the officers they could "go to hell," at about the time the *W. J. McCaldin* returned to the scene with a new player in this maritime drama.

A tall, stocky man with thick mustache and bowler stood defiantly at the tug's bow like a carved figurehead. John D. Hart climbed aboard the steamer and loudly demanded that the officers explain their actions. Informed that federal marshals were in charge, Hart yelled: "To hell with the United States marshals and their gang! Come on here, get up this anchor and let us get out to sea!" Hart raised clenched fists to confirm his command, and a half dozen officers leaped on him and were scattered. Hart was in high dudgeon, running across the deck trying to rally his men, but eventually numbers prevailed. A handful of bloodied agents finally subdued the struggling charter master and pinned him to the deck.

Hart was taken below and locked up while McCarthy and his men went after the remaining suspects. Despite his years, García leaped from the deck of the steamer onto the tug *McCaldin Brothers*, which turned and raced toward the Battery. But the *Hudson* had a top speed of eighteen knots and soon overcame the tug off the South Ferry. García was arrested along with another incautious passenger, Junta paymaster Benjamin Guerra.

Marshal McCarthy went to work disabling the *Bermuda*. He disconnected the piston rod, then went about the boat collecting compasses, sextants, chronometer, barometer, marine glass, and charts, all of which he carried on board the *Hudson*. McCarthy also confiscated a bag carrying $4,000 in Spanish coins.

The *Stranahan*, carrying the arms and ammunition, attempted to escape during the confusion, but the *Hudson* crew spotted the steam barge about 3:00 a.m.

passing out of the Narrows. A two-mile chase ensued until the cutter overtook the *Stranahan*. McCarthy went aboard to find a floating armory with forty tons of military gear. Cords of kindling on the deck covered up boxes of cartridges and cases of rifles stamped "Winchester Repeating Arms Company of New Haven." Against the pilot house were six boxes filled with dynamite. McCarthy asked the captain of the vessel what he was doing there. "Waiting for orders," replied Captain Sam Hughes. "Very well," McCarthy said. "I'll give you orders. Follow me to the Barge Office."

Most of the 159 men apprehended were released, but García, Hart, Guerra, Hughes, and Brabazon were arraigned before Commissioner John A. Shields at the Federal Building. García and Hart drew the most attention from the flocking reporters, the former as a leader of the revolution, the latter for his imperious bearing. "He is a tall, well-built man," the *New York Times* reporter wrote of Hart, "who carries himself as if he meant business and would be more likely to act than to talk."

Hart was more cooperative at the arraignment, where he tried to explain his involvement. He acknowledged chartering the vessel and said he had gone to the *Bermuda* to investigate "some trouble," but when he went up the gangway he was attacked by "150 Pinkerton men and marshals on board." Hart's claims elicited much laughter from the deputy marshals in the room.

Hart told an entirely different story to a friendly *Inquirer* reporter after he returned to Philadelphia. Polishing his halo of innocence with every breath, Hart denied anything to do with a proposed military expedition to Cuba. He claimed he had chartered the *Bermuda* for six months from a man named Edward Frau. On the night in question, he took a tug to deliver the steamer's clearance papers to the captain. When he boarded the vessel, he saw "forty-four Pinkerton men and deputy marshals in charge of her."

Hart was free on bond when the Junta received two pieces of good news on the last day of February. Rubens telephoned to say he had negotiated the release of the *Bermuda*, and the $4,000 in Spanish coins would be returned to party headquarters. Rubens also secured the release of the rifles and other military equipment seized on board the *J. S. T. Stranahan*. However, the government did not return the five hundred thousand cartridges or dynamite on grounds that the boxes that held them were not marked with the true nature of their contents.

Victories in the first two federal prosecutions of the neutrality laws had infused the organizers of the filibuster fleet and their defenders with an unrealistic sense of invincibility. The jury in Wilmington, Delaware, had absolved the young Cubans at Penns Grove of wrongdoing, and a massive celebration followed. The jury in Charleston had freed Sam Hughes and the *Laurada* after the defense prepared a systematic argument for their innocence. Bill Ker was so confident the American people shared his indignation against the government's actions that he boasted, "no jury in this country would convict us."

Ker was reminded of the precarious nature of proceedings when the trial of Captain Wiborg and two ship's officers of the *Horsa* resumed in US District Court in Philadelphia. Presiding was Judge William Butler, seventy-three, who was nearing the end of a distinguished career that began in his native West Chester, Pennsylvania. He had served as district attorney in Harrisburg and as presiding judge of the state Court of Common Pleas before he was named to the federal bench by President Rutherford B. Hayes in 1879. Butler tolerated no nonsense in his courtroom and was known for his long and often influential instructions to the jury.

After the prosecution recalled witnesses who had testified in the earlier phase of the trial, Ker surprised government attorneys by calling his client to testify in his own defense. As Wiborg approached the stand, Ker appealed to Judge Butler to clear the courtroom of reporters and observers who could record the witness's testimony. Ker's stated reason was to protect Wiborg, whose testimony could put his life in peril if he ever set foot in a country under Spanish control. Butler declined, saying that a witness who agrees to testify assumes the responsibility of risk.

Wiborg eased into the witness chair, his wide face rimmed with a full salt-and-pepper beard that rested on his ample chest. The captain told the court he had recently received his US citizenship, and he was sensitive to his adopted country's fight for independence, which was not unlike the fight of the Cuban people. He boldly testified that when the voyage began, he had no knowledge he was carrying an expedition to Cuba, but if he had known it he would have done it anyway. He admitted that when the *Horsa* was six miles from the Cuban coast, he was instructed to lower boats so the men could go ashore. The men who climbed into the boats, he said, did not look like soldiers.

Little new testimony was presented, and after Ker offered his closing remarks, he presented Judge Butler a paper containing thirteen points on which the judge should instruct the jury. Butler declined, claiming he did not want to give an essay on the statute.

"The case is in a very narrow compass," the judge responded. "There are but two questions to be considered: whether or not this was a military expedition and did the defendants here in this country undertake to aid that expedition on its way and carry out such undertaking? If these two questions are proven, beyond a doubt, the defendants must be convicted."

Ker approached from another direction, suggesting that a recent case in another US district court might be helpful in framing Butler's instructions to the jury. Ker offered Judge W. H. Brawley's instructions that preceded the jury's decision to absolve Sam Hughes and the *Laurada* on similar charges. Butler, however, responded curtly that he disagreed with Brawley's opinion, and his instructions appeared to confirm it.

"For the purpose of this case," Butler said to the jury, "it is sufficient to say that any combination of men organized to go to Cuba to make war upon its government, provided with arms and ammunition, constitutes a military expedition. It is not necessary that the men shall be drilled, put in uniform, or prepared for efficient service, nor that they shall have been organized as infantry, cavalry, or artillery. It is sufficient that they shall have combined and organized here to go there and make war on a foreign government, and to have provided themselves with the means for doing so."

Ker knew at that moment that his case was lost. Butler's instructions ran counter to the favorable South Carolina decision and confirmed the judge's disapproval of the defendants' activities. The jury adjourned at 3:00 p.m. and took an initial vote of 7 to 5 in favor of conviction. Seven hours and much debate later, an eleventh vote was taken in which all jurors agreed that the actions of Wiborg and his mates, Pedersen and Johansen, violated the neutrality laws as the judge had framed them. The guilty verdict was sealed and read the following morning in Judge Butler's courtroom to great indignation by a crowd heavily favoring acquittal.

Ker protested the verdict loudly while the three prisoners were escorted from the courtroom by US marshals. Butler told defense counsel that he had four days to file any motions he wished before sentencing. Ker quickly filed an application to release the prisoners on bail to allow them to clear up their personal affairs, which Butler granted. Wiborg was released on $3,000 bond and the two mates on $2,000 each.

Afterward, Ker expressed his disappointment, blaming Judge Butler's instructions to the jury. "The judge ... practically directed the jury to convict the defendants," Ker told the assembled reporters. "He told the jury that in his opinion the men and boxes that were taken on board the vessel constituted a military expedition beyond a doubt. That part of the instructions ... cannot be accepted as good law."

Four days later, Judge Butler announced sentence, saying that Wiborg, Pedersen, and Johansen would be fined $3,000 and imprisoned for not less than sixteen months. Ker already had moved well past the sentencing phase and on to planning the ultimate appeal, to the Supreme Court of the United States. Ker argued that the situation in Cuba demanded that the neutrality laws be clarified by the high court. If he could not achieve relief from the Supreme Court, then Hart and anyone similarly charged also faced fines and jail. More importantly, efforts to supply the Cuban rebels would be hampered severely at a critical juncture of the revolution.

But for John D. Hart, the dilemma was more economic than altruistic. Hart's income from the Department of Expeditions depended on his ability to deliver men and ships to Cuba, and he had not done so since the *Horsa* expedition. Nagging interference from Spain's enveloping spy network, supplemented by federal authorities, was making it impossible for Hart to go about his business.

It did not help that his major client leaked secrets like a wormy dhow. The Junta's two most recent attempts to return General Calixto García to Cuba had failed amid charges in the émigré community of betrayals, informants, and simple bungling from all participants. García had nearly drowned in the *Hawkins*'s sinking, and Hart's orchestrated expedition on the *Bermuda* was sabotaged by a web of informants.

It became clear to Hart that a new strategy of delivering expeditions to Cuba was needed, and perhaps new people to implement it. And he knew just the man who could do it.

Chapter 12

"CAPTAIN DYNAMITE" JOHNNY O'BRIEN

John D. Hart stepped off the train at the Jersey City depot and boarded the Communipaw Ferry for the trip into Manhattan. When he arrived at Pier 14 at the mouth of the East River, he hired a carriage that took him to the Stevens House Hotel on Front Street, where he secured a room for two nights.

He had an appointment the morning of March 14, 1896, at the McCaldin Brothers offices at 100 Broad Street, three blocks from the southern tip of Manhattan. He was directed to a small office toward the back of the building. Inside, Hart found a spindly little man, nearly sixty years old, puffing hard on a briar pipe as he shuffled papers on his spare, wooden desk. He had been at the desk since seven in the morning and had spent every minute since in the business of shipping, the warp and woof of New York's economy.

His modest appearance and routine gave no indication of a reputation that Hart knew well. In days gone by, this unpretentious gnome was a notorious confidant of potentates and pretenders and a determined scourge of maritime authority. No man alive knew the West Indies, its perilous tides, hidden inlets, and revolutionary history better than he. If any man could bring a new vision, expertise, and courage to the Junta's mission of supplying the Cuban rebels, it was "Captain Dynamite" Johnny O'Brien.

John O'Brien's parents came from County Longford, Ireland, where they were related to the Sheridans, whose son William would gain distinction as a Union general in the American Civil War. The two families even immigrated to America on the same boat, but while the Sheridans headed inland to Ohio, the O'Briens settled in the old Dry Dock section of New York near the bank of the East River. It was there that Johnny O'Brien took his first voyage, down the birth canal, on April 20, 1837. In a relatively short time, little Johnny began exploring every crack and cleft of the seafaring community.

His father, a farmer in Ireland, became a machinist at George Steer's shipyard, at which the famous yacht *America* was built. It was a time of growth in the shipbuilding industry, and yards such as Webb's, Brown's, Collier's, Mackey's, Westervelt's, and Roosevelt & Joyce's were clustered in the Dry Dock section. The nearby Morgan and Novelty ironworks provided the boilers, while tapering spars crisscrossed the skyline, infusing the love of the water to a wide-eyed boy. Ships were not only creations of wood, iron, and canvas but loyal companions in commerce and exploration. They never refused to go where directed, without argument or evasion, and could provide a man with wealth, adventure, or death, depending on the mood of Mother Ocean. A young man learned to trust his ship and respect the sea as he sailed in search of a fair fight and the spoils of persistence.

Johnny's brother Peter, seven years his senior, operated a ferry across the East River to Greenpoint, Brooklyn, that was little more than a large rowboat equipped with a sail. But it was sufficient to provide an early education for a life on the water. Johnny's earliest lessons taught him how to handle a boat in the tricky and tortuous channel called Hell Gate, which connects Long Island Sound with the East River. At age thirteen, Johnny ran away from home and signed on as cook on the fishing sloop *Albion*, and later studied navigation at the Thom School on Cherry Street, eventually graduating as a ship's pilot.

After the Civil War began, the twenty-four-year-old O'Brien went out as mate and sailing master on the *Deer*, a smart little schooner that purportedly carried a cargo of trade goods from New York to Matamoros, Mexico. Upon their arrival, the owners dismissed the captain, an old square-rigger who could not seem to get the hang of handling a schooner. O'Brien was put in command and soon learned that his cargo was not as harmless as advertised, consisting of munitions intended for the Confederacy. O'Brien unloaded the cargo and guided the *Deer* over the bar and on its way long before ships of the Union blockade realized its importance. The schooner passed a federal cruiser and Captain Johnny waved in recognition, knowing that his discovery might mean a pirouette at the end of a yardarm. But the *Deer* was a light-draft centerboard vessel that sailed like a witch, tempting O'Brien to dare danger. The possibility of a chase invigorated his every cell and infected him with the germ of what would become a lifelong disease.

O'Brien returned to New York and became a master of Hell Gate and Long Island Sound, making runs up to Halifax through calm weather and winter gales. His growing reputation earned him the admiring appellation "Daredevil Johnny."

His admirers said he could sail so close to the rocks he could knock the seaweed off and still slide a sheet of paper in between.

For the next two decades, "Daredevil Johnny" had his share of the toughest piloting jobs in New York, but few sparked his enthusiasm like running the blockade at Matamoros. His appetite for adventure was fed in 1885 when he was hired by Colombian revolutionaries in New York plotting to overthrow President Rafael Núñez. The president's enemies purchased the schooner *City of Mexico* to carry arms and ammunition to the rebels, and the young corsair gained his first experience at dodging customs officials, learning how to violate US neutrality laws without detection or regret.

With revolutions as common in the tropics as late afternoon rain, O'Brien found steady employment. In 1887, he went to work for Marco Aurelio Soto, the former president of Honduras, who launched an unsuccessful effort to regain the presidency. Next he was hired by General Louis Mondestin Florvil Hyppolite, who overthrew the government in Haiti and offered O'Brien the position of admiral in the tiny Haitian navy. O'Brien declined the honor, preferring to keep his anchor raised and glasses up in search of the next opportunity.

Despite O'Brien's reputation as a smuggler and filibuster, a new and lasting nickname came on a comparatively legitimate voyage in 1888. A Cuban merchant with business in Panama purchased sixty tons of dynamite in New York, but he could not find a ship willing to brave the two-week voyage to deliver the explosives to Colón. O'Brien agreed to take on the dangerous task, but he did not disclose the nature of the cargo to the crew.

They left New York in early summer under good weather, but when they entered the Gulf of Mexico a howling northeaster kicked up a savage sea for two days. Captain Johnny felt no great anxiety as they ran before the storm under shortened sail. However, the next day a terrific electrical storm sent rain down in solid sheets, the falling rain picking up the electricity. Each time O'Brien touched metal he felt a shock. Lightning danced around the mastheads, threatening to send a current down into the hold that would send them all to Fiddler's Green, the legendary afterlife of sailors.

If the lightning did not blow them up, O'Brien feared that some of the boxes could break free and shift in the tumult, exploding the dynamite by concussion or friction. That night, he slipped into the hold alone to make certain the load was secure. He could not summon help because the boxes were stamped "dynamite," a discovery that could have set off a mutiny. Singlehandedly and with the ship constantly trying to turn turtle, O'Brien made cushions of canvas strips and stuck them into every open space until the cargo was fast. As if Providence had approved his tactics, the trade winds blew the clouds away, and the vessel reached Colón twelve and a half days after departure. When the crew saw hundreds of boxes of dynamite coming out of the hold, their emotions ranged from heart failure to thoughts of murder.

When the merchant learned that his dangerous cargo had arrived safely in Panama, he decided that "Daredevil Johnny" no longer sufficiently described the skilled and daring captain. From that day forward, Johnny O'Brien was known as "Captain Dynamite."

During O'Brien's numerous trips to Cuba, he developed a strong dislike for the imperious Spanish officials who were in charge at every port. If an opportunity ever came to work for the island's independence, he would consider it, which made the call by John D. Hart fortuitous. O'Brien's memoirs recounted their first meeting.

"Captain," Hart began, "I have called upon you to discuss how we can aid Cuba by bringing General García's expedition there. The recent setbacks and betrayals have produced such an effect upon the Cubans that unless García returns, the skeptical attitude of the contributors will fester, and the morale of the rebels will suffer. I have a good boat, and I am disposed to risk it in the hands of a loyal and able man of resolve, like yourself. The Junta treasury can afford $500 for your services, which may end up costing you your life. But there is glory in the enterprise itself. What is the price of aiding a people struggling to be free?"

O'Brien did not ponder Hart's offer for long. Sailing the same channels, carrying the same cargoes, and dealing with the same bilge rats every day raised barnacles on a stout-hearted man's need for adventure. O'Brien missed the thrill of loading ships in the middle of the night for missions to anywhere and nowhere, outrunning those who chased him and outwitting those yet to avoid. The opportunity to cause trouble for Spanish authorities was reason enough, but at age sixty this might be his last chance to put a favorable wind at his back.

"Mr. Hart, the economic part of your offer does not interest me," O'Brien responded. "I am happy to help the Cubans' cause. You can count on me."

"When will you be ready to start?" Hart asked.

"I am ready now," responded Captain Dynamite.

Captain Johnny O'Brien squinted into a brilliant sunrise on Sunday, March 15, from the deck of John D. Hart's *Bermuda*, sitting off Liberty Island. The temperature was a crisp twenty degrees as he ordered the anchor raised, then guided the steamer through the Narrows. On board were nine enthusiastic Cubans who began to shout, sing, and dance a whirligig in anticipation of their voyage. Hart stood at O'Brien's left to make certain everything was on schedule, and to his right stood first mate Edward Murphy, barely thirty and full of spit and vinegar. A reflection of O'Brien himself at that age, the young Irishman was fond of proclaiming he was "all for excitement and agin' the Government."

O'Brien's plan was to clear the *Bermuda* for Vera Cruz carrying a cargo ostensibly intended for a buyer in Mexico. The shipment included 310 cases of war matériel and four rapid-fire Hotchkiss cannons, larger than any guns currently in the possession of the Cuban insurgents. O'Brien knew that breaking free from New York Harbor would not be easy, so he ordered the crew to spend the night painting the *Bermuda*'s towering red funnel black.

Despite the early hour, a tug hired by the *New York Herald* had staked out the vessel overnight and followed closely behind as the *Bermuda* sailed down the New Jersey shore. The clandestine facelift proved its value when O'Brien saw in the half-light a Spanish man-of-war sitting just outside the three-mile limit. Apparently, the disguised funnel persuaded the Spaniard that this was not the vessel he was looking for. O'Brien soon left the *Herald* tug behind when he pointed the *Bermuda* for Assateague Island off Maryland's Eastern Shore. There, he picked up a load of lumber and eight surfboats and then retraced his route, heading back north.

Meanwhile, a group of seventy-two dark-skinned "southern excursionists" boarded a tug in Philadelphia that took them down the Delaware River. Among them were Emilio Nuñez and a skeptical General García, wondering if the third time was a charm for his attempted return to Cuba. Their presence was no secret, as attested by a boatload of Spanish spies and Pinkertons who trailed closely behind, acting on a tip that the tug would meet up with the *Bermuda* at Cape Henlopen, where the Delaware Bay spills into the Atlantic Ocean.

But good fortune was on the side of the Cubans. A disturbance in the west had moved into the Atlantic region late in the day, creating heavy fog from Hatteras to Cape Cod. The tug's alert pilot sailed straight into the soupy mist, then reversed course and slipped back up the Delaware to Camden. The travelers disembarked and boarded a special Reading Railroad train and headed for Tuckahoe, New Jersey, about eight miles from Great Egg Harbor Bay. They arrived late on the night of March 16 and quietly boarded the steamer *Atlantic City*, lying in her winter berth. During the trip, Nuñez employed all the optimism and persuasive skills he possessed to bolster García's spirits, but to no avail. The old soldier had endured two failures and had little faith that this children's game of hide-and-seek would be any more successful.

The party endured the sleepless night of nervous men until 6:00 a.m., when the *Atlantic City* steamed to Ocean City, New Jersey, and anchored in the channel. All day and into the night the vessel sat, its men trying to be patient amid the specter of Spanish warships and federal revenue cutters materializing at any moment. Finally, in the morning twilight of March 19, five shrill blasts from a steamship whistle roused them to action. The anchor was hastily weighed, and the *Atlantic City* headed for open sea. As she cleared the Great Egg Harbor bar, cheer after cheer went up from the travelers when they sighted the glossy black hull and funnel of the *Bermuda* coming toward them. The vessels came side by side, and the men scrambled on board the steamer as Captain Johnny O'Brien chewed on his briar pipe, his walrus mustache drooping with stoic satisfaction. Beside him, John D. Hart patted the captain's shoulder and nodded in silent approval.

First off the tug was Nuñez, who had determined to accompany the mission. He grasped Hart's extended hand with enthusiasm, then turned to assist García, still grumbling and suspicious of everyone around him. When all were aboard, Hart bade them an uneventful voyage, then boarded the *Atlantic City* for the trip back to Tuckahoe. The *Bermuda* turned southward with a cargo of rifles and armaments and a party of more than eighty compañeros.

As they ventured south, O'Brien examined the engines carefully, surveyed all the bearings, and cleaned the fires. He also gave the firemen a lesson in smokeless stoking to minimize smoke and prevent detection. The wise way to put on coal was to drop a heap inside the furnace door instead of throwing it far back and scattering it. Allowing it to coke, then slicing it up and pushing it back, generated just as much steam but gave off only a thin, white smoke, which was invisible and prevented excess smoke from pouring out of the ship's funnels. His way also saved coal, and O'Brien would sooner spill his own blood than waste a pound of coal.

The *Bermuda* broke the sea briskly toward Cuba, but the general still was in no mood to celebrate. García's skepticism and melancholy only grew as the boat neared its destination. His constant refrain to the captain was: "I never expect to see Cuba again." O'Brien charted a circuitous course for the eastern end of the island to avoid coastwise traffic and wandering warships. They sailed east of the Bahamas and down through Crooked Island Passage, approaching Cuba on the far eastern tip of the island, beyond Cape Maysí.

"Don't worry, General, you are going to get to Cuba this time," O'Brien assured García.

García looked up and replied, mournfully, "That is what they have all told me."

"I never have told you that before, have I?"

"No."

"Then take my word for it," said Captain Dynamite. "This time, we will get you there."

Chapter 13

A QUICK INDOCTRINATION INTO FILIBUSTER PROTOCOL

A sleek, oceangoing tugboat pulled into the harbor at Jacksonville on March 18, 1896, as a reception committee watched. The Spanish consul had local police and port officials in tow, demanding that the captain be arrested. The boat docked, and the captain, standing on the deck in his formal blue uniform, smiled and warmly greeted by name the officers whom he had long known. Then he turned and directed a puzzled look at Collector of Customs Cyrus R. Bisbee.

"Have you been on a filibustering expedition to Cuba?" Bisbee demanded. The captain smiled broadly and shook his head with feigned innocence. He admitted he had taken guns and ammunition to Key West, but the parties who had contracted for them had left by the time he arrived. The story did not ring true to a very agitated Spanish vice consul, Henrico de Maritague, who stood a foot shorter than the husky, mustachioed seaman. But it mattered little since there was nothing he could do but wait until next time.

And there would be many more "next times" for Napoleon Bonaparte Broward, native Floridian, former sheriff of Jacksonville's Duval County, longtime river and ocean pilot, and, for the next two years, the southern counterpart to John D. Hart as a major supplier of arms and men to the Cuban revolution.

Despite his confident, hearty countenance, Broward was a romantic with a vision of Florida as a place where the wilderness is conquered for the working man, not for the benefit of tycoons. His was a state where the poor had a shot

A Quick Indoctrination into Filibuster Protocol   95

This campaign booklet detailed Napoleon B. Broward's experiences as a Cuban filibuster, which propelled him into the governor's chair in 1905. Florida Collection, State Library and Archives of Florida.

at dignity and a decent life, a light shining in the economic and social darkness of the reconstructed Deep South. Broward was a revolutionary, like his great-grandfather François Brouard, and like his namesake, the emperor of France. Years later, as governor of Florida, he would try to overthrow the Bourbons and Yankee industrialists who had reinvented the plantation, called it "progress," and ran a railroad down the middle of it. But he would never have been in the position to do so had he not joined the movement to run the Spanish out of Cuba.

Napoleon Bonaparte Broward Jr. was born on his grandfather's plantation at the mouth of the St. John's River in Duval County on April 19, 1857. He was surrounded by wealth, servants, and family until his father sided with secessionists and raised a company to fight the Yankees. When the Union Army invaded Florida, the Broward plantation was burned, and the former slave owners were cast into an existence they could not abide. Weary of the war's privations and fearful of the future, Napoleon's mother died in 1869, and his grieving father a year later.

Napoleon and brother Montcalm were passed between aunts and uncles and eventually moved in with their mother's brother, Joe Parsons, at Mill Cove, a settlement five miles inland on the St. John's River. Napoleon started as a deckhand on

Uncle Joe's steamboat, and in 1876 he signed on as a mate with Captain David Kemps's towboat *Kate Spencer*. Broward learned the salvage and towing business in voyages up the East Coast to New England and east to Nassau in the Bahamas, but his greatest reward came when he fell in love with Kemps's daughter.

Napoleon and Georgiana Carolinas Kemps were married in January 1883 and moved to Mayport, a fishing and lumber village at the mouth of the St. John's River where Broward enhanced his prospects by securing a lucrative pilot's license. Tragedy intervened in October when Georgiana died while giving birth to Napoleon Bonaparte Broward III, who himself died on December 6. The grieving Broward took solace in the river, where he prospered as the tourist trade flourished in the 1880s.

Broward was an appealing and popular figure in Jacksonville, so it was not surprising when a citizens' group asked him in February 1888 to replace the Duval County sheriff, who had been fired in a scandal. Broward was a prohibitionist and personally observed strict standards of law and morality, which explains his first act in office: to wipe out organized gambling in the county. His work led to convictions and jail sentences for the vice's powerful proprietors, which won Broward statewide attention. He was elected to a full term as sheriff in 1890, his integrity and fair-mindedness guiding him whether his positions were popular or not.

When he found himself on the wrong side in the 1894 election, Broward began to recall fondly his more peaceful days on the water. Undaunted by the political setback, he returned full-time to the shipping and salvage business with Montcalm and business partner George DeCottes. The three friends proceeded to build another boat, one that would be among the most powerful constructed in Florida. The seagoing tug, which they appropriately christened the *Three Friends*, was launched on February 2, 1895, at its home port of Jacksonville.

With a boat for hire, Broward soon was contacted by a man he knew well. José Alejandro Huau was a longtime political ally and a trusted friend in addition to being the Junta's representative in Jacksonville and Emilio Nuñez's scout for available vessels in Florida. Huau appealed to Broward's sense of liberty and fair play in trying to persuade him to lend his new vessel to the Cuban cause. Broward resisted the overtures for a time, but when he could not generate any oceangoing business in Nassau or Key West, he relented. Broward signed a contract with the Junta in February 1896, and Huau contacted Nuñez in New York with the news that he had recruited another reliable captain and vessel.

Broward received a quick indoctrination into filibuster protocol on his first expedition, an ocean rendezvous with two schooners filled with men and armaments. He removed the name boards from the *Three Friends*' pilot house, ordered all lights extinguished, and outlawed the use of cigarettes by crew members. With his new boat shrouded in secrecy, Broward guided the *Three Friends* out

Napoleon Bonaparte Broward's tugboat, the *Three Friends*, became one of the most active vessels transporting weapons and men to the Cuban Revolution. Image #PR10065, Florida Memory Photographic Collection, State Library and Archives of Florida.

of Jacksonville late at night and across the St. John's bar headed for the tangle of a smuggler's paradise, the Florida Keys.

The *Three Friends* arrived at Alligator Key where the schooner *Ardell* sat near a deep coral-walled creek hidden by tall pine trees. Aboard were General Enrique Collazo and fifty-four men from Tampa who hustled aboard the tug. Soon, the schooner *Stephen Mallory* arrived from Cedar Key with an immense load of arms and war matériel. Broward assessed the situation and decided that the *Three Friends* would take the *Mallory* in tow because the tug was too small to carry both the men and a huge cargo that included 1,200 rifles, 750,000 rounds of cartridges, 2,100 machetes, and 400 revolvers. The strategy was sound; a tug towing a disabled schooner presented the innocent appearance of a local boatman at work. When Broward saw a clear horizon, he set out for the designated landing place on the north coast of Cuba, near Cardenas.

The tug arrived along the Cuban coast in darkness, but ship lights in the west drew the attention of the crew. Gunrunning was a new business to most of the men, who feared that every sighting of an unknown steamer's smoke spelled their doom. A searchlight at the bow sweeping the waves made it obvious that the mystery vessel was a Spanish gunboat on the hunt for smugglers. The Spaniard did not see the *Three Friends*, but Broward's Cuban pilot apparently lost his bearings amid the mudbanks and dangerous reefs. When he finally identified the landing point, it was fair abreast a Spanish fort. The insistent General Collazo was at Broward's elbow, shouting threats and giving orders that Broward and his loyal crew ignored.

Two large surfboats were lowered, and the five-hour process to transfer men and arms to shore began in silence. As the first boat slid over the waves and skidded to a stop on the sandy beach, a number of hardened men began filing out of the *espinal*, as the locals called the thorn jungle. Fortunately, they belonged to Antonio Maceo's rebel forces.

The Spanish soldiers in the fort heard the commotion and sent out a party to investigate. By the time the rebels were discovered, most of the men and cargo were ashore, but they soon found themselves in a hornet's nest. The rebels exchanged fire with the Spanish soldiers from a distance, but the battle soon intensified to fighting at close quarters. The rebels swung machetes, and the Spaniards countered with rifle butts as the new arrivals and some crew members were pinned down on the beach, unable to retreat through the heavy surf.

To make matters worse, the snooping cruiser from Cardenas was drawing closer. Broward was faced with the first dilemma in his new life as a filibuster. He did not want to lose his new tug, but neither did he wish to forsake his crew members who had rowed the boats ashore. He told those on board to keep their pistols holstered because the firing would alert more gunboats and instructed his men to get out their axes and lie down under the bulwarks. If the Spaniards on the gunboat tried to board, he told them, then take them as they come over the rail.

Fortunately, hand-to-hand combat was not necessary. As the Spaniards and rebels battled each other in the darkness, Broward's men ran the boats from the beach back into the surf and made it back to the tug safely. The *Three Friends* put on all steam and headed for the open sea with the gunboat firing but fading. The next morning, the tug was sitting safely at Key West.

When word of the successful expedition reached the Junta legation in Washington, Gonzalo de Quesada immediately contacted the friendly press to announce that "the most successful expedition yet fitted out to fight for Cuba" had delivered General Collazo and much-needed weapons to Maceo's forces. To protect Broward's identity, however, Quesada announced that the successful venture had been transported on a vessel named the *José Martí*.

Captain Johnny O'Brien hove to off Inagua Island, just northeast of Cape Maysí, and made his final checks in preparation for landing. Their destination was a little notch in the coast between Points Maraví and Aguacate, five miles west of the Baracoa lighthouse. On board were two Cuban pilots who were supposedly familiar with the coastline and could direct the ship to the landing point. But O'Brien recognized that one pilot was an ignoramus and suspected the other was a spy. They arrived near the Baracoa lighthouse after dark, and the suspicious pilot declared it was the light at Cape Maysí, thirty-five miles from their destination. The second pilot did not disagree.

They did not count on O'Brien's familiarity with the Cuban coastline, which was far more extensive than either pilot's. He knew that the light at Cape Maysí could be seen for eighteen miles, while the smaller one at Baracoa was only an eight-mile light. The two pilots continued to insist the *Bermuda* was headed for Cape Maysí, but O'Brien refused to change course. When the pilots realized they could not influence the captain, the suspected traitor appealed to Nuñez, who, as chief of expeditions, was supreme authority on the ship. The pilot claimed that O'Brien was betraying them, as they had often been betrayed before. If he did not change the course, they all would find themselves in front of a Spanish firing squad.

Nuñez had seen treachery before, and he weighed the pilot's claim carefully as he stared at O'Brien. The little captain's reputation described an incorruptible man in a corrupt business, and he had been recruited by Hart, whom Nuñez had grown to trust implicitly. Nuñez ordered the pilots off the bridge, and when the traitor objected, Captain Dynamite, half a head shorter, gave the Cuban three kicks to the backside. The captain's ability to pull the lying pilot's hide off his bones astonished García and his men. From that moment, Nuñez trusted O'Brien as he did Hart.

Setting a course by the Baracoa lighthouse, O'Brien headed in for the landing with all lights extinguished. The engine-room hatch was covered with tarpaulins, and a canvas covered the binnacle light with a small hole through which just enough of the compass could be seen. O'Brien told Nuñez to order the men to extinguish their cigarettes, under penalty of death, an order that Nuñez readily gave.

The *Bermuda* nestled into the glassy coastal waters about five miles out, halting only when a Spanish gunboat came up from the east, hugging the shore. O'Brien believed that the vessel was probably on course to intercept the *Bermuda* according to the renegade pilot's plan. The second pilot, who was guilty only as a fool, lived close to where the expedition was to be landed. When they eased close inshore, he saw his house, at the foot of Anvil Hill, and whispered excitedly that O'Brien had been correct.

Deep water at that point prevented an anchorage, but it also enabled the vessel to drift in closer to the shore. The odor of steaming forests and rotting vegetation was heavy in the air as first mate Murphy and two men landed to scout the area. Murphy had learned to challenge any threats with "Quien va?" in the island dialect, rather than "Quien vive?" in the more proper Castilian that would likely draw a hail of insurgent bullets. A waving lantern from shore soon signaled that the coast was clear, and García and his staff, in full uniform, piled into the next boat. As he went over the side, García gripped O'Brien's hand with tears in his eyes.

"You kept your word, Captain," he said, shaking with emotion. "The others lied to me, but you didn't. I hope you can continue in our service, for we need you."

After García's party landed on the beach, several hundred rebels appeared out of the brush to help carry the arms into the mountains. However, when they recognized the great García, the inspiration of '68 and one of the spiritual leaders of the current revolution, they bowed, took his hands in theirs, and gave thanks for such a deliverance.

Nuñez was in a hurry to get back to New York with the good news of García's landing. The *Bermuda* landed at Puerto Cortes, Honduras, and Nuñez hitched a ride to New Orleans on a fast little steamer. He was confident it would arrive quickly because the vessel carried the greatly anticipated drawing of the Louisiana lottery, which had been transferred to Honduras in 1893 after Louisiana voters defeated its renewal.

O'Brien remained in Honduras to take on a cargo of bananas, per John D. Hart's standing orders: expeditions came first, bananas second. Waiting for the cargo to be loaded, the captain found a telegraph key and a willing operator and on March 29 sent a cablegram to the charter master. Addressed to the code name "HART" under the Watkins universal shipbrokers code then employed, the message said simply: "*Bermuda* arrived out." The simple words signaled that the mission to deliver General Calixto García to Cuba had been a success.

Chapter 14

A BOOMING REPLY OF "NOT GUILTY!"

The joy at Junta headquarters that greeted the news of General García's arrival in Cuba was matched by the rage the same news provoked at the Spanish legation in Washington. Dupuy de Lôme contacted Secretary of State Olney and demanded that the government seize the *Bermuda* and prosecute anyone associated with the expedition.

On April 10, 1896, ship watchers wired Hart's office that the *Bermuda* had entered the Delaware Bay. Ker sent Hart's bookkeeper, Gratz C. Jordan, out to meet the steamer with a gag order to make no comments about the voyage. When Jordan's tug arrived at the *Bermuda*, he climbed aboard and relayed the message, which was understood immediately by the captain. O'Brien turned the helm over to Ed Murphy and hitched a ride to Chester, Pennsylvania, on a passing tug. Jordan spent the rest of the voyage trying to persuade the crew members to keep quiet.

Ker was standing at the Green Street wharf when the *Bermuda* came into view. Jordan's haggard appearance did not fill the attorney with any confidence that his "no comment" message had been delivered forcefully. Standing amid a gaggle of reporters, Ker shouted loudly through cupped hands, imploring the crew not to make any statements about the voyage. He also directed Murphy to back the ship away from the dock and drop anchor in midstream to discourage the feverish news gatherers and lurking Pinkertons.

The attempt to suppress facts of the mission was moot once the crew members were allowed to leave the ship. Scribes and spies alike descended to glean the latest intelligence, whether incriminating or merely titillating. The Pinkertons questioned eight crew members who presented information that Spanish consul José Congosto believed sufficient to merit prosecution. He forwarded the information to the US attorney's office and swore out warrants for the arrests of Hart, O'Brien, Murphy, and Nuñez, who already was back in Philadelphia.

Deputy marshals appeared at Hart's office to serve the warrants and found him alone. He had just returned from his New York trial where he and Sam Hughes were found not guilty in connection with the *Bermuda*'s first attempt to deliver García. Judge Addison Brown's definition of a military expedition was more in concert with Judge W. H. Brawley's in the dismissal of Hughes's earlier case than Judge William Butler's in the Wiborg conviction. After Brown's instructions, the jury deliberated for only ten minutes before finding the defendants not guilty.

Hart reluctantly accompanied the marshals to Commissioner James Bell's office, where he was met by Ker. Bell gaveled the session to order and asked Hart how he pleaded on the claim that he "began and set on foot and proposed and provided the means for a military expedition."

Hart stood slowly, his face reddened by the frustration of having to repeat the same answer over and over again. He glanced at Ker before emitting a booming reply of "NOT GUILTY!" Ker was even more angry, calling the arrest "an outrageous prosecution. He has just been acquitted in New York, the jury being out less than ten minutes of this very same alleged offense, and yet this Spanish official has a warrant issued against him here. Judge Brown said it was the right of a ship owner to get any cargo that he could. To take a cargo of arms and ammunition to Cuba was legitimate."

Ker filed motions to have the trial moved to New York, where the expedition began, rather than have the case tried in federal court in the Eastern District of Pennsylvania. The learned counsel hoped to plant a seed that would help influence the venue by reminding the press of Judge Butler's recent ruling in the *Horsa* case. He suggested that another filibuster case in Butler's court likely would result in another unjust conviction.

At Junta headquarters, Estrada Palma was exultant over the recent successes of the Department of Expeditions. The *Bermuda* had finally landed García, the *Three Friends* had delivered Collazo to Cardenas, and Nuñez's aide Braulio Peña had commanded a successful expedition on the *Commodore* to Nuevitas.

Estrada Palma was especially delighted that Johnny O'Brien had produced such magnificent results. The delegate insisted that O'Brien formally join the party and help Nuñez and Hart arrange future expeditions. O'Brien knew he could make more money as a pilot, but he felt strongly for the Cuban cause and pledged his services for a modest price: one hundred dollars sent to his wife and children immediately plus another three hundred dollars for each expedition he planned that landed safely.

O'Brien was appointed "navigator" for the Department of Expeditions, which had tightened security under Nuñez's leadership. To combat the persistent Pinkertons, Nuñez hired his own agents who communicated through simple yet effective codes. One code utilized identical pocket dictionaries in which one could look up a code word and then turn to the word in the same position on a subsequent page, which was the true word. The system was flexible, the key was carried in their heads, and the occasional loss of a dictionary revealed no secrets.

Other methods were employed to deter Spanish spies and Pinkertons who covered every port. O'Brien's house in Arlington, New Jersey, was watched night and day by at least two detectives, one from a patch of woods across the street and the other in view of the back door. O'Brien concealed a few powerful bear traps in strategic positions around the outside to discourage close surveillance, but it was not always effective. When one agent peered through a window at night, Mrs. O'Brien took measures into her own hands. The captain's wife was no less volatile than her husband, and she "inadvertently" threw a pot of boiling water out the window onto the head of the severely chastened snooper.

While the *Bermuda* sat under government embargo at the Race Street dock, she became a popular destination for the curious. Families arrived by carriages, businessmen gazed as they strolled along South Delaware Avenue, and small boats floated nearby all with an eye to this tangible symbol of the Cuban struggle. Extra police were summoned to control the men, women, and children who gathered to see the famous vessel and, perhaps subconsciously, believe that a visit to her side would allow them to share in her noble deeds.

Hart smiled with the satisfaction of a proud parent. He accepted pats on the back, fine cigars, and good wishes from engrossed admirers as he related his own significant role. He shook every hand, answered every question, and contributed to the gaiety by deciding to spruce up the *Bermuda*. Her smokestack was repainted black at the top and red below, and a fresh coat of white paint gave her a crisp but rakish appearance. At her bow flew the flag of Great Britain, denoting her registry, and at the stern waved the Stars and Stripes. From one of the masts flew the lone star flag of the would-be Republic of Cuba and from another fluttered the flag of the Hart line, a red heart on a white field framed by sky-blue horizontal trim at the top and bottom. Hart not only changed the *Bermuda*'s appearance, he added muscle—cannons mounted fore and aft and rapid-fire guns placed amidships.

The cranks eyed the activity closely, enthralled at literally watching the paint dry on the J. D. Hart Company's famous ship. Her master stood at the dock, himself admiring her lines and anticipating her next voyage. "She is a goer," Hart told a companion, "and she can show a clean pair of heels if pursued." She would soon get the opportunity. The government released the ship on April 22, and Hart ordered O'Brien to secure clearance papers for Puerto Cortes, Honduras.

But the elation at the March expeditions would disappear in April's failures. The *Bermuda*'s sparkling new attire would not protect her from the most catastrophic landing attempt of the revolution.

No curious admirers were on hand when the *Bermuda* eased out of the Race Street dock and headed down the bay in the early morning hours of April 23. Johnny O'Brien shared the bridge with Captain Edward G. Reilly, who would take the helm when they arrived at Jacksonville. O'Brien's presence was required in federal court to explain the *Bermuda*'s expedition that had delivered García. Reilly would guide his first expedition to Cuba.

Four days after leaving Philadelphia, the *Bermuda* chugged down the St. John's River to the Clyde Docks at the foot of Hogan Street. Her arrival in Jacksonville was well timed. The revenue cutter *Boutwell* had just left port, and a visiting Spanish man-of-war had put to sea earlier. After O'Brien left the boat, a squad of dockhands began loading six eight-oared surfboats and a large number of heavy boxes. In addition to rifles and ammunition, the immense cargo included machetes, Hotchkiss and Gatling guns, dynamite, powder, and torpedoes, all destined for the battlefield. A tug was loosed from her moorings and slipped down to the Alabama Coal Company, where she took in tow a barge heavily laden with coal.

Three train cars of young Cubans under expedition leader Colonel Francisco Leyte Vidal arrived from Tampa and hurried to the dock, just ahead of another company from Fernandina. The second group had come from the north by rail and boarded Napoleon Broward's tug *Kate Spencer*, which took them to the *Bermuda*. The two parties of Cubans found yet another group already on board that included a sprinkling of young Americans.

Such activity could not be kept secret for long. Broward's favorite foil, Spanish vice consul Henrico de Maritague, soon discovered what was happening under his nose and began running around the dock trying to find anyone who would arrest this band of Cuban cutthroats. De Maritague was especially distressed when he discovered that Collector Cyrus Bisbee had found the ship's papers in order. Respected cigar maker José Alejandro Huau was listed as the shipper and the Central American Fruit Company of Honduras as the party to receive the shipment.

A large partisan crowd jeered the little Spaniard's every complaint and gesture, and he retreated to his office to telegraph Dupuy de Lôme in Washington. The minister telegraphed ahead to the consul at Key West to communicate the following orders to the three Spanish men-of-war lying offshore: proceed northward and intercept the *Bermuda*.

The *Bermuda* under Captain Reilly avoided the Spanish ships as she steamed toward Cuba at eleven knots. Making good time over a glassy sea and favorable winds, the vessel skirted the western tip of Cuba, then turned to the southeast, heading for the intended rendezvous at Cape Cruz, due west of Santiago. They arrived off the coast at night, and Reilly ordered all lights extinguished. The blackness was broken by a glimmer of light in the distance. It appeared to flicker at first, but the telltale sweeping motion of a searchlight heralded a Spanish man-of-war.

Reilly ordered the *Bermuda* to reverse course and head out to sea, hoping the menace would soon disappear. At a safe distance from shore, the engineer banked the fires, and the ship sat for two hours before Reilly ordered her back to within a half-mile of the coast. The crew lowered the eight surfboats, into which arms and ammunition were loaded, and about fifty men climbed in. The first boat landed safely with the rest scattered between the sand and the ship. But with startling suddenness, another light appeared along the coast, closer and growing brighter.

Wild excitement broke out among the men strung out between the beach and the *Bermuda*. The boats closest to the steamer spun around as the men tried to return, while the men in the boats nearest land jumped out and swam for shore. The Spanish gunners took aim and fired at the *Bermuda*, missing badly but leaving Reilly with the dilemma of saving his men or his ship. The captain ordered all lines to the surfboats cut and full steam ahead. Some men in the boats jumped out and swam toward the ship, grabbing lines thrown to them by the men on board, but too many were caught halfway between land and the fleeing vessel. Two boats capsized, with boxes and men going overboard amid piteous cries of panic. Dozens fought to stay afloat, grasping at floating boxes or overturned skiffs. The *Bermuda* sped out of sight, heading to Honduras and leaving behind the fading cries of the doomed.

Aboard the steamer, the grief of lost comrades and failure gripped the Cuban officers and more than sixty volunteers who remained. The exact number of dead was never determined, although the toll likely was close to the thirty-seven reported later. The disaster on the *Bermuda* would continue to be debated well beyond the revolution, and Captain Reilly came under much criticism in the Cuban émigré community. The press took up the call, blaming Reilly's lack of nerve for the loss of the men.

Emilio Nuñez's primary directive as chief of expeditions was to deliver armaments and men safely to Cuba, but often the urgency of the need trumped his requirement for extreme care and planning. The failures of the *George W. Childs* and *James W. Hawkins* expeditions were haunting, but Nuñez was thrown into a similar situation in mid-April 1896. General Antonio Maceo's army in the mountains of Pinar del Río was pinned down by a force of well-trained Spanish troops and needed immediate support.

Estrada Palma ordered Nuñez to dispatch relief, but his regular vessels were occupied, funds were short, and Hart was preparing for his upcoming case. After a search for available ships, Nuñez identified the *Competitor*, a wooden-hulled schooner owned by a Señor Pindar at Key West. The Cuban clubs of that city raised the necessary funds, and Nuñez paid the asking price. The schooner was small by filibustering standards at forty-seven tons, seventy-five feet in length, and twenty-nine feet in width with a four-foot draft. To captain the vessel, Nuñez selected Alfredo Laborde, a thirty-nine-year-old New Orleans native and a former deputy sheriff in Tampa. Laborde had transported men and arms to Cuba before, reportedly landing a small expedition of forty men, five hundred rifles, and two hundred thousand rounds of ammunition the previous January. Nuñez assigned Colonel Juan Monzón, a veteran of the Ten Years' War, to command the land forces.

The *Competitor* left Key West at 11:00 p.m. on April 22 with about thirty volunteers and two reporters on board. Dr. Elias Bedia was a correspondent for the *Mosquito* of Key West, and Owen Milton, a native Kansan, was a reporter for the *Florida Times-Union*. The cargo included sixty Remington rifles, forty carbines, sixty thousand cartridges, and two hundred pounds of dynamite.

As the *Competitor* approached Berracos on the northern coast of Pinar del Río, the Spanish gunboat *Mesagera* hove into sight. Colonel Monzón ordered the rest of his men into the boats, and they made for shore with what arms and ammunition they could carry. The *Mesagera* opened fire on the *Competitor* and missed widely but continued firing, with every shot coming closer. Laborde attempted to hoist the American flag, but the halyards became fastened in the topsail, and the flag was entangled in the foresail boom. In their haste to get away, the men left thirty rifles, thirty thousand rounds of ammunition, and several boxes of dynamite on deck. Fearing that the rapidly improving gunner would hit the dynamite, Laborde, his mate William Gildea, and Augustin Quesada of Key West jumped overboard and began swimming ashore. The others remained on board.

Monzón, who was nearly two decades removed from his last skirmish, appeared confused when the gunfire erupted. Although he commanded a small force of well-armed troops, he did not fire on the Spanish boat and instead ordered his men to escape into the underbrush.

Spanish soldiers from the garrison responded quickly and pulled Laborde and Gildea out of the water, but Quesada was not found and was believed to have drowned. The men remaining on the *Competitor*, including Dr. Bedia and Milton, also were arrested and taken to Fort Esperanza. The Spaniards threatened to execute them on the spot and even staged a mock execution. A soldier pushed Dr. Bedia's head down to expose the back of his neck as he raised a machete. The doctor, however, showed great courage as he turned his head and smiled at his would-be executioner. The soldier lowered the blade.

The Spaniards took the captives to Morro Castle in Havana, where US consul general Ramon O. Williams demanded a civil trial. Captain General Valeriano Weyler ignored Williams's plea and ordered a Spanish naval court-martial to convene immediately. The men from the *Competitor* were sentenced to death within the week.

The incident created a furor in the United States and widened the American public's impatience with Spain. Press reports insisted the trial was unfair and the prisoners had been denied counsel. The *New York World* declared: "No fair trial will be found in a Weyler tribunal." The *Tribune* declared that a crisis with Spain was likely, while the *Journal* warned Spain of the readiness of the US fleet: "If Spain disregards the United States in the *Competitor* affair, no one will be sorry to see the fleet turn south." Even the usually conciliatory *Herald* warned: "If the American citizens condemned to death at Havana are executed, it is war between the United States and Spain, and nothing can stop it. The United States must and will protect its citizens."

The State Department protested the summary court-martial, claiming that US citizens were entitled to trial in the civil courts. As a result, cooler heads in Madrid ordered Weyler to postpone execution and forward details of the case to the General Council of War and Marine for review. The Spanish government's action relieved the tension for the time being, and the *Competitor* prisoners eventually would be released.

American indignation over the *Competitor* affair prompted Bill Ker to proclaim that even execution of the prisoners would not stop expeditions from going forward. Ker's comments came not only from his own patriotic convictions but from the fervor he saw from the current generation of ardent young Americans that Cuba was the place to find adventure and glory.

"There is nothing the Spaniards can do that will stop the sending of arms and ammunition to the Cubans," Ker told the *Inquirer*. "It is remarkable how the feeling against Spain has already spread in this country. Men come to this office almost every day and beg and plead to be sent to Cuba or to be given a chance on our vessels.... To go to Cuba seems to have become a mania.... I tell these enthusiastic men of the liability to sickness and death from disease in such a climate, but this does not seem to lessen their anxiety to go or dampen their ardor."

Chapter 15

"DAMFOOLITIS"

The scent of war was strong in the nostrils of young American males. The post–Civil War generation was raised in a time where the settlement of the West limited opportunities for adventure, and athletic games and physical fitness became the accepted outlet for competitive aggression. But baseball, cycling, or football was not always enough to put out the fire that burned within them. The Cuban Revolution filled that void, providing the young hotheads with an opportunity to cultivate their masculine independence in the guise of patriotism. They could go to Cuba and fight for a just cause, similar to what their fathers and uncles had done three decades earlier, then return to the accolades of their fellow citizens. Of this wanderlust, one skeptical editor reduced it to "Damfoolitis."

One of the young guardsmen who approached Ker and Hart was Sergeant William H. Cox of Battery A of the Pennsylvania National Guard. The twenty-three-year-old Cox, and Winchester Dana Osgood, twenty-five, the celebrated halfback of the University of Pennsylvania football team, were among eight enthusiastic volunteers who boarded the Hart line steamer *Commodore* in Charleston the second week of March 1896.

In his second year of military training with the state guard, Cox became the avowed leader of these friends seeking adventure. He had gone to camp as a private, come out a corporal, and was promoted to sergeant without an examination because of his keen mind and skill at marksmanship. Osgood's reputation came from his athletic achievements, which were legion. The Massachusetts native enrolled at Cornell in 1888 and became a star oarsman, football player, track man, and bicycle racer. At five foot nine and 180 pounds, Osgood's quick feet and shifty hips made him an elusive target who escaped injury in those days of liberal rules and brutal tackling. Osgood transferred to Penn in 1893 and starred in games against Harvard and Princeton.

Cox did not tell anyone he was going to Cuba, although he gave his family a hint weeks earlier when he asked his mother if she would object to him joining the patriotic army. Cox was following in the footsteps of his father, a member of the 214th Pennsylvania who fought the rebels under General Winfield Scott Hancock. Osgood also had the military in his blood, his father a US Army captain then stationed in St. Louis.

Their quest for adventure began as a grand time. The moment they boarded the train in Philadelphia, they were beset by Spanish spies looking for greenhorns headed to Cuba. For Osgood, facing Princeton on the gridiron was not nearly as swell as dodging the Pinkertons, who could not have been more obvious if they had worn jerseys with numbers attached. The giddy group was less concerned about being arrested than of falling asleep and waking up with a hot foot, compliments of their mates.

In Charleston, they approached Captain Charles Dickman of the *Commodore*, perhaps after presenting a letter of introduction from the well-known attorney William W. Ker. Scrutinizing the lads, Dickman admitted them on the condition that when they arrived at their destination, the eight of them would unload all the boxes aboard. They agreed, not realizing that the expedition included thirty other volunteers under the command of Nuñez's assistant Braulio Peña and nearly eleven tons of armaments that included 600 rifles, 580,000 rounds of ammunition, and other implements of war.

But soon after departure, the college boys were wondering which gate of Hell they had walked through. Pleasant afternoons of sailing down the Delaware were distant memories as the clouds turned blue-black and the blowing rain came down, as it can in the tropics, battering the iron decks with a rattle and roar and speckling the oily sea with white. For days, they were at the mercy of the elements, frightened, nauseated, and intimidated, but not one would allow his discomfort to diminish the thrill of their mission.

The *Commodore* dropped the adventurers on the east coast of Cuba, near Nuevitas in Camagüey Province. As the captain promised, they were put to work transporting the cargo to shore in two small boats, often wading in water up to their necks. By evening they had unloaded every box, one of which contained a dissembled Hotchkiss mountain cannon. The landing party hid the weapons in the jungle and the next morning set off to find the Cuban forces. For five days, they tramped through squishy sand beaches and muddy swamps, crawling over trunks of dead trees with only their valiant intentions to guide them. Their food was soon gone, and they survived on raw sweet potatoes scavenged from a sympathizer in a small farmhouse.

Finally, the tired troupe ran into a rebel unit commanded by Brigadier General Santana. With news of the ammunition and cannons hidden near the beach, the Pennsylvania college boys and other volunteers were immediately welcomed. Ammunition was a precious commodity and not easily obtained. Prostitutes who entertained Spanish troops in Havana and other cities demanded cartridges in return for their favors, then sent the ammunition to the insurgents. The price of pleasure was one hundred Mauser cartridges for a private, two hundred or more for a noncommissioned officer, and one thousand for an officer. A Spanish soldier's pay was small, and diversions were expensive, but cartridges issued by the government provided an amicable arrangement for all.

The revolution's newly honored guests were treated like princes. They were given fresh meat, although they were not certain of its origin or former species. They also were given hammocks they could tie between two palm trees rather than sleeping on the ground like rank-and-file soldiers. As artillery specialists, Cox and Osgood were appointed *tenientes*, or lieutenants, whose rank came with two horses and a servant.

"Every day we ride to the creek to take a bath," Cox wrote to his parents from the field. "Everywhere we go we ride. Our horses are saddled all the time. They are very small, about the size of our mustangs, but they can go all day long and not get tired."

Cox regaled his parents with the tale of a skirmish in which fifteen of their men surprised and routed a Spanish column. It was great fun, and the young Americans were in their glory. As Cox wrote: "I cannot go on describing these things any more except to say that this is the ideal spot on earth."

Like Cox and Osgood in Philadelphia, young members of Baltimore's "swell set" also heard the siren call of glory. At his office in Washington, Gonzalo de Quesada received an inquiry from two young Baltimore men who wished to join the fight. On March 31, he wrote to Estrada Palma asking: "Is it possible for two distinguished young men from Baltimore to go in Nuñez's next expedition? They have resources, arms and are of excellent families."

The delegate did not immediately respond to Quesada's note because he was tiring of such requests. Young Americans' motives "of fulfilling a spirit of adventure" were not the same as those of the young Cubans. As he wrote to Dr. Ramón Emeterio Betances, the Junta representative in Paris: "Let me tell you that the presence of these gentlemen in the insurgent ranks must not morally or materially influence the course of the revolution. Right here are Cubans waiting, ready to move to Cuba. Not everyone can enroll in the expeditions; in these days I have refused an offer of various Americans because their services are not indispensable to us."

Hearing nothing for nearly a month, the young men visited Quesada again to make a personal plea. Quesada must have been impressed, for he wrote to Estrada Palma on April 24: "Yesterday the Baltimore youth who want to leave were in here and begged me to ask you if they could go to New York."

The delegate relented, and the first week of May, Stuart S. Janney, who had attended Johns Hopkins University, and his friend Osmun Latrobe Jr. told family members they were going on a hunting trip to western Maryland. Their true destination was Florida, where they would begin training for a role in the Cuban fight for independence.

Latrobe, the nephew of former Baltimore mayor Ferdinand C. Latrobe, was employed as a draftsman for an architectural firm, but the lure of battle ran in his blood. His father had experienced the horror of war at Antietam and Fredericksburg as a Confederate Army officer. Osmun Jr. limited his perilous activities to football, but he was a spunky player and not afraid to get his nose bloodied.

But if anyone was suited for war, it was Janney, who stood six feet tall with broad shoulders and a superbly muscled body that befitted his rank as Hopkins's most accomplished athlete. Janney was a star of the lacrosse and football teams and was known as a hard man to get off his feet. He was elected cocaptain of the Hopkins football team in 1894 along with his future brother-in-law, W. Stuart Symington Jr. Off the field, Janney never shied from a scrap. After a local prizefighter insulted one of Janney's friends, the young Baltimorean soon had the bully against a wall, banging his head through a door until several friends intervened.

Janney and Latrobe made their way to Tampa, where they joined other volunteers receiving training as artillery officers. After they were deemed proficient with the big guns, they were shipped along with about seventy other men to the east coast of the state. They boarded the tugs *Kate Spencer* and *Lillian B* with high anticipation for their great adventure in Cuba.

John D. Hart's *Laurada* came to New York from Philadelphia in ballast on Saturday, May 9, and anchored off Liberty Island. Her arrival prompted much excitement at the Spanish consulate, and Consul Arturo Baldasano hurried to the barge office, where he met with US Marshal John H. McCarthy. Word of the *Laurada*'s presence was wired to the Treasury Department in Washington, and orders were flashed back to McCarthy to stop her if it could be determined she was "on filibuster bent." McCarthy could not act on suspicion, so he challenged the consul to come up with the proof.

Baldasano rushed to board a rented tug, which took him to within a few hundred yards of the unmoving *Laurada*. He watched the ship until a launch approached with news that a suspicious steam lighter had put into Pier 11 on the East River and taken on numerous boxes and crates. Baldasano knew that the evidence he sought was within his grasp, so he ordered the tug to make a dash for Pier 11. When he arrived, he spotted the lighter pulling away from the dock, loaded high with an apparent cargo hidden by a tarred canvas cover. The men on the lighter saw the suspicious tug and decided to take her on a chase, steaming down the bay around Governor's Island. Baldasano's boat followed until the lighter tied up at the Atlantic Basin in Brooklyn. Her lights were doused, giving the appearance of a work boat finished for the day. The Spaniard watched the mouth of the basin for a time before ordering his tug to return to the *Laurada*.

Baldasano knew that evil was afoot, but the steamship had not moved from its anchorage. He ordered the tug to make another run to Brooklyn, where the lighter was still tied up. However, as his boat drew closer, Baldasano's hopes fell. The incriminating load had disappeared from her deck. The frustrated consul ordered his tug back to Liberty Island to concentrate on the *Laurada*, realizing the lighter had been an effective decoy. He did not know that nearly four hundred cases of cartridges and dynamite, fifty cases of rifles, and four Gardner rapid-firing guns had been put aboard the *Laurada* earlier.

The *Laurada* was waiting only for an important passenger before she weighed anchor. Watching from the deck of the tug, Baldasano saw the tug *C. P. Raymond* pull alongside the *Laurada*, and the notorious John D. Hart stepped out, accompanied by a tall, elderly Cuban. General Juan Fernández Ruz, at age seventy-four, had survived the ill-fated *Hawkins* shipwreck with Calixto García and was anxious to join his old comrade in Cuba.

On board the steamer, Hart handed Captain Dickman his orders. The tug *Fred B. Dalzell* came alongside to push the *Laurada*'s nose away from the city and toward the Narrows. At 8:30 p.m., Hart left the steamer to Dickman, Ruz, and the crew and returned to the *Dalzell*, which transported him to the Battery. He walked casually over to the Barge Office in time to see Baldasano arrive and run inside. Angrily waving his arms at Marshal McCarthy, the consul demanded he seize the *Laurada* before she escaped.

The revenue cutters *Hudson* and *Chandler* sat at the Barge Office pier, their steam up and ready for a confrontation. But the consul had not given McCarthy the proof he required. Without evidence, he could not recommend an order of seizure. Collector James Kilbreth had cleared the *Laurada* for Port Antonio with papers that claimed a cargo of household goods, mostly bedroom furniture, valued at $163. Baldasano continued ranting, apparently not noticing Hart, who stood quietly in the doorway, amused at the consul's ridicule of him and all enemies of Spain.

"One would think to hear these Spanish talk," Hart said to the officers, "that I was giving Spain more trouble than the entire army of insurgents on the island of Cuba."

A confused, angry, and thoroughly outmaneuvered consul could only watch helplessly as the *Laurada* sailed out of the Narrows. She turned eastward along the southern Long Island coastline and headed to Montauk Point. The tug *Commander* soon arrived from New Haven, pulling two barges carrying a hundred men and additional rifles, ammunition, and dynamite. When the transfer was complete, Captain Dickman charted a course for Cuba.

On May 16, Hart's *Laurada* sat off Nuevas Grandes Cove in Camagüey Province. The small, tortuous inlet, two hundred yards wide in places and navigable only for vessels under twelve-foot draft, looked like a perfect spot for a landing. The cautious Dickman sent a boat out to reconnoiter the spot, and his scouts returned to confirm that it was suitable for a landing and contained brush and rocks to hide the cargo. However, Dickman was skeptical and ordered the ship to return to sea, which generated protests from General Ruz and the other Cubans aboard.

At dawn on May 18, the *Laurada* was about six miles offshore when Dickman ordered the landing to commence. Five boats were loaded with men and cargo, and Ruz was gently helped into the third boat. All was quiet as the small boats set out for land. When Ruz's boat bounced over the final wave and ground into the soft sand, his men assisted the old general to his feet. He stepped out of the boat and reflexively bent to kiss the soil of his homeland, as others had done.

The surfboats were returning to the *Laurada* for the last ten Cubans and the remainder of the cargo when Dickman saw smoke on the horizon. Fearing a Spanish gunboat, the captain declared the expedition ended, and he turned the ship back toward Jacksonville.

The *Laurada* crossed the St. John's bar on May 22, only to be halted at quarantine. With the high incidence of yellow fever and other communicable diseases existing in the tropics, all ships were required to pass a health inspection before being allowed in a US port. Health officers went aboard the *Laurada* and determined she had three sick men aboard, which would require her to remain in quarantine for seven days before entering the port. Dickman protested, pleading he had schedules to meet and could not wait. The ever-helpful Señor Huau volunteered to assist the authorities by going out and talking to the captain.

Huau did as promised and after a short time returned with the knowledge he was seeking. The cigar maker told Collector Bisbee that the *Laurada* would not wait for the quarantine to be lifted and was proceeding to Charleston. He also gleaned another nugget that he chose not to share with the federal officer. The *Laurada* had successfully landed "about nine-tenths" of a massive expedition in Cuba.

Señor Huau proved his value a second time that day after Napoleon Broward was stopped by the revenue cutter *Boutwell* while attempting to leave Jacksonville with a cargo of arms and ammunition. Broward returned the *Three Friends* to the Custom House and appealed to Collector Bisbee that his manifest, which clearly stated he was going to carry munitions of war to Key West, was proper. Bisbee sent a wire to the Treasury Department in Washington, which responded that Broward could proceed on one condition. The *Boutwell* would escort the *Three*

Friends out beyond the three-mile limit to discourage Broward from picking up would-be combatants or other scoundrels who might get the captain in trouble.

Vice consul Henrico de Maritague protested vehemently that to allow the *Three Friends* such freedom violated the US neutrality laws. But Huau, who virtually had taken up residence at the Custom House, intervened with enthusiasm. The cigar maker and the consul went nose-to-nose for a time, shaking their fists at one another and trading colorful insults in Spanish. The bemused Broward finally leaned in, put his arm around the little Spaniard, and said: "That's right. You do your duty, and catch 'em and hang 'em all!"

If the frenzied De Maritague knew the exact composition of Broward's cargo, he might very well have tried to hang the burly captain. Aboard were 1,000 rifles, 525,000 rounds of ammunition, 2 rapid-fire guns with 800 shells, 1,000 dynamite shells, one million dynamite caps, 200 suits of clothes, 200 hammocks, and a ton of medical stores provided by an American wholesale drug company.

The *Boutwell* escorted the *Three Friends* down the river, past the bar, and nine miles into the Atlantic to ensure that she was not meeting another vessel. When darkness fell, the *Three Friends* doubled back toward land and met the tugs *Kate Spencer* and *Lillian B*, which were carrying General Rafael Portuondo and about seventy recruits who had been training in the Florida countryside. Among them were the young Baltimore adventurers Latrobe and Janney, and a twenty-three-year-old reporter for the Key West *Equator-Democrat*, Charles Govin.

The *Three Friends* passed Cape Maysí and sailed around the far eastern tip of Cuba, intending to land at night on May 28. But around 2:00 p.m., the lookout spotted a suspicious trail of smoke on the horizon. Broward raised his glasses and saw a vessel with sailors scurrying around on deck. Men in uniform were watching him in their own glasses, which confirmed that the intruder was a Spanish cruiser bearing down. The *Three Friends* headed for the open sea with the stokers shoveling coal into the furnaces like human pistons. The gunboat began firing shell after shell, but the seagoing tug's speed of better than twelve knots widened the gap as they raced south toward Navassa Island.

On the night of May 29, the *Three Friends* chugged along the coast to the Bay of Baconao, where the landing commenced as dawn was breaking. Two and a half hours later the cargo was ashore, and after another three hours it was hidden from sight. General Portuondo assembled the men and marched them into the interior, where they were met by three thousand soldiers from José Maceo's army and one hundred mules to transport the weapons and supplies.

Maceo's *mambises* gave the young Baltimore gringos a much more suspicious greeting than Cox and Osgood had received from Gómez's army. To the hardened rebels, white men in that part of the country could only mean Spanish spies or fools. During a long interrogation, the officer in charge admired the fraternity pins that Latrobe and Janney naïvely still wore, and he claimed them as the spoils of war. Finally satisfied that these young men were more willing fools than spies, the rebels marched them into the mountains, where they lived for four days on raw sweet potatoes. Janney and Latrobe were soon transferred from Maceo's army to Gómez's army, which employed more white men and American officers.

Wherever they would be assigned, the young Americans were now subject to the whims of war. It no longer mattered whether they had been members of the home guard or college football stars or draftsmen or cyclists or left loving families or sweethearts behind. All that was in a past they freely gave up to accept a future out of their control. The good reasons that motivated them were sensible and soothing to the ear: to fight for independence, to satisfy an aggressive urge for conflict, or merely to engage in a romantic mission that would dazzle their college chums at home. But as they marched through the relentless jungle, such fantasies soon dissolved into the fog of battle and conditions they had never considered. The only motivation that remained as they moved closer to the fighting was to endure and survive.

That message became clear on June 9, when the young reporter Govin, who had landed with Janney and Latrobe, was captured by Spanish soldiers while traveling with a party of insurgents. He showed his US passport and reporter's credentials to the officer in charge, but the officer threw the papers to the ground to show his disdain for Americans. The officer then ordered Govin bound and gagged, and he was hacked to death with machetes.

Chapter 16

PROSECUTION OR PERSECUTION?

Bill Ker had friends in high places, and he was not hesitant to call on them when he needed help. One of these was US Solicitor General Holmes Conrad, a fellow attorney and friend from Ker's days at the Department of Justice. Ker requested that the US Supreme Court expedite its review of the *Horsa* case, persuading Conrad that Judge William Butler's "narrow compass" in instructing the jury defied precedents established in similar cases. It would be the first criminal prosecution under the neutrality laws to come before the high court since the original law's passage in 1794, but, Ker argued, the law must be clarified for future cases.

Conrad, a Virginian and former Confederate officer, agreed and forwarded a motion to the high court. "Constructions of the law announced by the various judges of the United States District Courts have been, since the present insurrection in Cuba . . . not in harmony," Conrad wrote. On the assumption that further prosecutions were likely, Conrad recommended that the court use *Wiborg v. United States* to bring some consistency to application of the law. He said a decision would achieve a twofold purpose: (1) guide officers on the proper interpretation of the law so as to protect undue interference with lawful acts by citizens, and (2) empower officers charged with executing the laws to actively prevent violations and bring offenders to trial. Conrad also noted that Wiborg was the only such case in which the accused had been convicted.

The court took the motion under advisement, then announced it would receive Ker's appeal in the form of a written argument that the justices would review. Ker could not have been happy with a written submission, which lacked the emotion or emphasis of an oral presentation. Bill Ker longed for the latitude to exercise his oracular gymnastics, which he believed gave him a decided advantage in the courtroom. However, he had no choice, so he prepared a succinct argument that the expedition was organized merely to carry munitions of war to Cuba and was not an expedition to wage war. Ker pressed his claim that Judge Butler's instructions all but demanded a guilty verdict for his clients, and he included his thirteen points that Butler had declined to address in his instructions to the jury.

The decision would have serious repercussions, regardless of the verdict. If the lower court was reversed and Wiborg and his mates declared not guilty, expeditions would continue and perhaps increase with little fear of government interference. However, if the court upheld the convictions, it would reverse the traditional argument that such transactions were legal trade. The clandestine smuggling of men and arms to Cuba by filibusters such as Hart would continue as it had, under a cloak of secrecy and threat of prosecution.

Ker received a prompt review, but he did not get the reversal he was seeking. One week after he submitted his written arguments, the Supreme Court sent shock waves through the filibuster fleet when it sustained the lower court's verdict in *Wiborg v. United States*. The ruling affirmed the judgment that John D. Hart's *Horsa* carried a military expedition that violated the neutrality laws and that Captain Wiborg was culpable. Chief Justice Melville Westin Fuller rejected each of Ker's thirteen points alleging that Judge Butler had prejudiced the jury. "From the evidence," the chief justice wrote, "the jury had a right to find that this was a military expedition or enterprise under the statute, and the Court properly instructed them on the subject."

Fuller disagreed with the lower court only when he reversed the verdicts against mates Pedersen and Johansen, whose actions suggested they did not have full knowledge of the mission and were merely following orders. Justice John Marshall Harlan concurred in the reversal of the mates' judgment but disagreed with the majority in the matter of Wiborg's guilt. In his dissenting opinion, Harlan did not believe that the voyage was a military expedition in the meaning of the law, and even if it were, the men and arms being taken on board outside the existing three-mile international limit placed it outside federal jurisdiction.

Harlan's dissent was his second that week, sealing his reputation as "the Great Dissenter" and champion of the underdog. On May 18, 1896, Harlan cast the lone dissenting vote in the case of *Plessy v. Ferguson*, which challenged a Louisiana law that required separation of white and Black passengers on railway cars. Harlan said the law was a "badge of servitude" that degraded Negroes. He prophetically claimed that the court's ruling would become as infamous as its 1857 ruling in the *Dred Scott* case declaring that Negroes, whether enslaved or free, were not citizens and therefore had no standing to sue in federal court. The majority decision in

Plessy established the "separate but equal" doctrine that allowed racial segregation in the United States for more than the next half century.

Wiborg showed little emotion at the decision, expressing gratitude that the court freed his mates, whom he called "good, faithful men." He accepted his own fate with grace, saying "I feel that my conviction is an unjust one, but if this is the law I am willing to submit to it.... If my incarceration will help the course of Cuba in any way it will be the one satisfaction I will have to comfort me during my imprisonment."

Ker, however, was not so resigned to the decision, especially regarding its effect on future attempts to send arms and volunteers to Cuba.

"It will not make a particle of difference," he said after receiving a copy of the ruling by telegraph. "The men who are engaged in that business risk their lives, and the risking of a man's liberty is a trifle compared with the risking of his life. In aiding Cuba, they believe they are performing a patriotic act, a duty to civilization, and they do not fear punishment. They will go right on as if nothing had happened."

The Spanish minister in Washington was elated at the decision, boasting that the conviction came only after the US government acted on the demands of the Spanish legation. Dupuy de Lôme further suggested to Secretary of State Olney that the Cleveland administration could bring the revolt to an end by tightening its neutrality legislation and swiftly enforcing it. The minister urged the administration to convince the American people that Spain was in the right, which would discourage aid to the Cubans. If the revolutionists were certain the United States was unsympathetic, Spain was confident the revolt would collapse.

Ker quickly initiated efforts to secure a presidential pardon for Wiborg, drafting a petition and sending copies to Cuban sympathizers in New York, Washington, and other cities to be signed and returned to his office. Signed petitions began coming in hundreds at a time from the renowned and less so. Every member of the Philadelphia City Council signed the petition, and even Ker's old political rival, Democrat party boss William Francis Harrity, signed it. Other signees included merchants, insurance executives, real estate salesmen, mechanics, and laborers, a reaction that clearly reflected widespread sympathy for the Cuban cause. The publicity given the filibustering expeditions had the American people frenzied to a froth, but President Cleveland was steadfast. He would not pardon Wiborg.

The Supreme Court's decision only contributed to John D. Hart's emotional decline. The charter master's customary resolve was slowly being eroded by the enormous financial burden of lawsuits, seized ships, and constant scrutiny by Spanish spies, the press, and his own government. The breaking point, however, was a tragic accident that occurred a few days before the Supreme Court announced its decision. The *Horsa* was returning to Philadelphia from Jamaica with a load of fruit when a fire broke out in the oil room three hundred miles north of the

Bahamas. The flames quickly spread, and the ship was burned to a shell. Captain C. E. Cook, who had taken Wiborg's place at the helm, reportedly fell overboard and drowned during efforts to extinguish the flames.

Hart was demoralized. He had sustained prosecutions and perceived persecution involving the *Horsa*, the *Laurada*, the *Commodore*, and the *Bermuda*, while a swarm of Spanish spies and informants made it impossible to conduct business, legitimate or otherwise. But Hart's fragile countenance finally broke after hearing of Cook's death. He called Ker at his house at Fourth and Linden Streets in Camden and informed him he had had enough. He said he wanted to move his company out of Philadelphia so he could shrink from the limelight and return to the quiet life of a simple fruit importer. Ker listened patiently, realizing that his most cantankerous client was speaking from emotion and not good business sense.

"My ships will not carry any more men, arms, or ammunition to the West Indies," Hart announced over Ker's objection. "I mean just what I say. I am going to quit the business altogether. I am tired of it. I have done the best I could for the Cubans. Hereafter, I will engage in the regular trade for which the company was established."

Hart traveled to Junta headquarters in New York, where he told Estrada Palma and Nuñez of his decision. The Cubans attempted to talk him out of it, but he appeared steadfast. Hart claimed that the recent trials so far had cost him between $6,000 and $7,000, and he still owed money from litigation resulting from the seizure of his ships and the arrests of himself and their officers.

Hart received more bad news a week later. Warrants were issued for his arrest along with Captain Edward Reilly's in connection with the *Bermuda*'s disastrous expedition in which at least thirty-seven volunteers perished. Fearing the *Bermuda* would be seized, Hart moved her from the Race Street dock in Philadelphia across the river to the Vine Street wharf in Camden, New Jersey, out of the unfriendly jurisdiction of the Pennsylvania courts. That did not, however, end his miseries.

Hart was preparing the *Bermuda* to clear for Port Antonio when he received word that the vessel's British registry had been revoked. Her Majesty's consul Charles Clipperton informed Collector of Customs John R. Read that the vessel's ownership papers stated she was owned by a British subject, but he had contrary information, probably provided by the Spanish legation. Without registry, the *Bermuda* could not clear from any custom house, nor could she take out American papers under the current maritime laws without the approval of Congress. Read ordered a hearing on the matter for the following morning at the Custom House.

Consul José Congosto appeared bright and early, only to find Bill Ker already in attendance and ready for battle. Congosto warned Read that granting clearance papers to the *Bermuda* would allow the vessel to escape federal jurisdiction. Ker objected, saying that Congosto had no right to interfere and that his attendance was merely "a dodge to collect evidence against Mr. Hart."

While Ker and Congosto debated, another problem beset the *Bermuda* at the dock in Camden. US marshals seized the steamship upon a claim from three seaman who said Hart refused to pay them wages that totaled $27.75. As the *Inquirer* reported: "Under ordinary circumstances such a proceeding would attract little attention even in maritime circles, but when it involves . . . the future of a ship the fame of which is now international, speculation and rumor were at once rife throughout the city as to its real meaning."

Hart paid a $250 bond to have the vessel released until the matter was fully adjudicated.

The *Laurada* was expected back in Philadelphia on May 28 after her latest excursion to Cuba, but when she had not arrived a week later, the drumbeats along the Delaware began pounding anew. The modern news platitude that "people want to know" was alive within editorial offices of American newspapers in the final decade of the nineteenth century. Relentless reporters monitored the *Laurada*'s peregrinations as closely as their modern counterparts stalk personalities. A notorious target may be guilty of many things but never of innocence, which was too routine to consider in the contrasting climate of veneration and vilification that enveloped the ships of the filibuster fleet. This time, however, the accused was innocent. The *Laurada*'s whereabouts was no mystery to John D. Hart. He had telegraphed Captain Charles Dickman while the *Laurada* was undergoing repairs in Charleston and ordered him to return to Port Antonio and pick up a load of bananas. After all, bills had to be paid.

"The steamer *Laurada*, of the J. D. Hart line, is expected to return to this city next week," the *Inquirer* reported. "She has become famous in her experience as an aid to the cause of Cuba, and will doubtless attract much public attention on her arrival in view of the many exciting reports that have been circulated about her movements since she left New York on the night of May 9 with a cargo of arms and ammunition and about 100 allies for the insurgents."

When the *Laurada* finally pulled into Philadelphia on June 17, the Race Street dock predictably was festooned like an emperor's feast day. Hundreds of the curious craned their necks and stood on boxes and carriage steps to steal a view of America's most celebrated vessel of liberty since the *Constitution*. Men and boys crowded the docks, jockeying to spy an officer or even crew members who had hung from the ratlines looking for Spanish gunboats. All who were involved were lifted onto an almost divine pedestal by an adoring press and a public sympathetic to Cuban independence.

Captain Dickman, silver haired and distinguished in his dress uniform, waved from the deck, appearing very pleased at the reception. The only element missing was a shower of rose petals tossed upon the waters as the vessel drifted into her berth. The captain graciously declined numerous questions from reporters about delivering men and arms to Cuba, and he denied strongly that his ship had been chased by a Spanish man-of-war. Hart was there to greet his most famous vessel's return and seemed to draw strength from the adulation he and his vessel received from a doting public.

Press accounts of their voyages and court cases framed the filibusters' activities as more tolerated mischief than menace. Violations still were against the law, but the law did not make sense to an American people who demanded liberty for their spiritual cousins to the south. In an atmosphere of great patriotism, enforcement of such laws was repugnant to a public that saw the filibusters engaged in a fight similar to the one their own nation had undertaken successfully more than a century earlier. The filibusters were cloaked in a plausible moral argument that such violations were justified when they defied long-standing infringements upon fundamental rights.

The newspaper located a few blocks away from Hart's expedition headquarters adequately reflected the public's infatuation in an editorial published a few days after the *Laurada*'s return. "When history is written, the expeditions made to Cuba will take on the dignity of the *Mayflower* and her sister ships," intoned the *Inquirer*. "The filibuster is the uncrowned hero of Cuba, and his name is mentioned with a lowering of the head which we give heroes. The early history of every country shows its martyr list, but there is no history that shows a braver one than those who are now filibustering for *Cuba Libre*."

After witnessing the reception the *Laurada* received at the Race Street dock, Hart never again expressed any thoughts of suspending his efforts on behalf of Cuba.

The widespread support of his efforts to aid Cuba bolstered Hart's indignation at what he saw as government harassment. Hart and his contemporaries were viewed favorably when contrasted with a government and its agents who were painted as meddlesome, insensitive bureaucrats working to assist a foreign government the people did not trust. The US government's enforcement of the neutrality laws could be interpreted as a conspiracy against American citizens to further the ambitions of a foreign power.

Despite the widespread support, the government's efforts to uphold its laws continued. Hart, Captain Reilly, and Emilio Nuñez were named in Florida warrants charging they had organized the *Bermuda* expedition that left Jacksonville on April 27 and ended in tragedy. One report described the warrants as "more like persecution than anything else," after Hart and Reilly were arrested at Hart's Pier 11 office.

At his arraignment, Hart verbally assaulted nearly everyone present, from federal marshals to his own attorney. Commissioner W. W. Craig read the charges, and Assistant District Attorney Harvey K. Newitt asked for a continuance until June 26. Ker agreed but noted that Hart had to be in New York on June 22 for a hearing on a previous indictment.

The avalanche of charges and multiple cases was too much for Hart, who stood and glared at the commissioner, his voice shaking with rage. "The US government could not have me in two places at once," he complained loudly. Ker, himself exasperated by the process, snapped at his client: "Let me run this case, and you save your talents for Pier 11!"

"But I want to know by whom I am arrested!" Hart bellowed.

"You are in the hands of the law," Ker said.

"You were taken by a United States marshal," remarked Hewitt.

"Well, if the United States is responsible, that is all I want to know," Hart said, slumping dejectedly into his chair.

A hearing was scheduled and bail was set at $1,000, but Hart rose and declared he would not accept release on bail. He demanded to see if a remedy existed for an American citizen who was arrested on recurring charges that he believed were outrageous. Ker again attempted to quiet Hart, but his client was several emotions beyond silence.

"I have been hounded and persecuted by these people until I can endure it no longer," Hart declared, his hands resting flat on the table in front of him. "I will not sign the bail bond. The arrest is made on a half holiday when many persons who know me are well out of town. I will not ask my friends to go any further for me. I will go to jail and see if I cannot test my rights as an American citizen."

His outburst cheered a gathering of onlookers who shouted encouragement as Ker urged Hart to calm down and sign the bond, but his resolve was granite. His business might further suffer, he said, but he would go to jail and await the outcome. Deputy Marshal Hunt was ordered to accompany Hart to the Eastern Penitentiary in south Philadelphia, known locally as Moyamensing Prison.

Captain Reilly had not said anything during Hart's outburst, but after the charter master was led out of the room, Reilly approached one of the newspaper reporters. He pointed to a statue of Abraham Lincoln that lay on a nearby window sill and remarked quietly: "I wonder how long these outrages would be permitted to go on if he were alive and had the say?"

The week would turn out on a positive note for Hart when Commissioner Craig ordered him discharged in the *Laurada* case. On the same day in Jacksonville, Commissioner Gray ruled that federal prosecutors had not made their case against Hart or Captain Reilly regarding the ill-fated *Bermuda* expedition, and he would not pursue charges. The dismissals were not unexpected, as reflected by the comments of a representative of the US district attorney for Florida who had visited Craig's court.

"It is practically impossible to get a jury together in Florida that would convict any American arrested for rendering aid to the Cuban revolutionists," he said. "It is simply impossible to make a case stick on account of the universal sentiment down there in favor of the Cubans."

Chapter 17

AN AMBITIOUS EXPEDITION

By late summer of 1896 the Spanish minister in Washington was waving the neutrality laws in the face of the US government like Carrie Nation waving her temperance hatchet in front of a saloon. Spain's only chance of halting the troublesome filibustering expeditions was for federal agencies to accelerate enforcement efforts, and Dupuy de Lôme was not shy about calling on his cordial relationship with Secretary of State Richard Olney to get it done.

Olney had assured Dupuy de Lôme that the Grover Cleveland administration wanted to help Spain end the war and would not recognize a state of belligerency for the Cuban rebels. Olney agreed with Spain that the insurgents could not govern the island and feared that Spanish withdrawal might lead to an even bloodier race war. But he was blunt with Dupuy de Lôme that the rebellion appeared to be gaining strength: "It can hardly be questioned that the insurrection . . . is today more formidable than ever and enters upon the second year of its existence with decidedly improved prospects of successful results."

Olney recommended a political solution that would leave Spain "her rights of sovereignty yet secure to the Cubans all such rights and powers of local self-government as they could reasonably ask." The secretary pledged that if Spain would provide political reforms acceptable to the majority of Cubans, the United States would support the reforms. The rebellion would lose its moral force, and with diminishing public support in America, the revolution would end.

But Madrid demanded that Washington first terminate the Junta's ability to operate freely within the United States. Dupuy de Lôme complained to Olney that the Americans were ignoring his steady stream of information on expeditions, vessels, and guilty individuals. Dupuy de Lôme wrote to Olney on July 2: "The facts are so numerous and the situation so unsatisfactory that I feel it is my duty to my government, to you and to myself to call your attention upon the subject. I have to show, at least to my country, that I know what is happening. It seems impossible not to be able to present those continuous attacks to the law."

On July 16, the minister again complained about what he called the "unchecked activity of the law breakers . . . in Philadelphia, Jacksonville and Key West." Two days later, Olney wrote to Cleveland, who was spending the summer months at Gray Gables, his breezy retreat on Cape Cod. "Enclosed please find copies of two more confidential communications from Consul General [Fitzhugh] Lee [in Havana]. I also send a copy of a note just received from Spanish Minister [which] suggested in terms that another Proclamation should be issued, and cited precedents of various Proclamations issued by Presidents during past administrations."

Prodded by Dupuy de Lôme, the secretary suggested that the time was right to issue the new proclamation. Olney sent a previous draft to the president, suggesting that he add one more "whereas," to reflect that recent attempts to launch expeditions "have of late been so numerous as to show that the laws of the United States on the subject are not understood—or something like that." Cleveland approved the proclamation and Olney wrote a new draft, which he sent along for Dupuy de Lôme's review. The Spanish minister responded gratefully in a note dated July 21: "Permit me to present my most sincere thanks for the Proclamation that I have just read. . . . I have wired it to Madrid and I am sure will be fully appreciated."

The new proclamation, released on July 27, targeted both potential offenders and enforcement officers. It included Olney's recommended "whereas," acknowledging that recent events suggested that citizens and enforcement officers might fail to comprehend "the meaning and operation of the neutrality laws." Such persons considering or engaging in illegal transactions, the president warned, "will be vigorously prosecuted."

By no coincidence, the same day Cleveland's proclamation was released, Dupuy de Lôme released a report prepared by legation attorney Calderon Carlisle that named all known expeditions to have departed from the United States since the *Amadis*, *Lagonda*, and *Baracoa* in January 1895. The report included names of vessels, commanding officers of the expeditions, and known outcome of each voyage, whether successful, failed, or resulting in legal action. Carlisle also included transcripts of legal proceedings favorable to Spain, including the Supreme Court's landmark decision in *Wiborg v. United States*. The report, which was printed and distributed throughout Washington, elicited considerable discussion on Capitol Hill. Its stated purpose was to encourage the US government to be more diligent in preventing expeditions, but some believed that its true purpose was to lay grounds for potential claims against the United States in international courts.

The latter was unlikely, since the government's actions so far gave every appearance that the Cleveland administration was in league with Spain. This created such a mood at Junta headquarters that Estrada Palma considered moving out of New York and relocating to a more sympathetic venue outside the United States. But Nuñez and others among the leadership objected, for different reasons. Nuñez believed that the Department of Expeditions' ability to secure weapons and orchestrate the delivery of men and arms from New York, despite legal interference, was an asset that must be exploited. Rubens and Quesada also favored New York, for the reason that proximity and easy access to the sympathetic press corps was critical.

With thoughts of relocation put to rest, the Junta's efforts quickened to a high gallop. On August 10, Estrada Palma ordered Nuñez to plan three new expeditions, which would be funded through a generous contribution by Marta Abreu, a major contributor to the movement who lived in Paris. One expedition would head west to reinforce the army of Antonio Maceo. A second expedition would land in Camagüey and comply with Mrs. Abreu's wishes that it be led by Colonel Rafael Cabrera, an old warrior of the Ten Years' War. The third, targeted for the area of Santiago, would be the most ambitious expedition ever landed in Cuba.

Carefully devised by Hart, Nuñez, and O'Brien, who had taken on greater planning responsibilities while Hart was occupied in court, the latter expedition was designed to produce a multitude of benefits. First, it would revive the rebels' spirits after the battlefield death of José Maceo, Antonio's brother, in July. Second, the perceived strength of the revolution would continue to impress the American public and press. Third and perhaps most important, a large expedition might persuade the lame-duck Cleveland administration to avoid any new adverse policy decisions before the fall elections.

Only one vessel in Hart's fleet was suitable for such an ambitious enterprise: the 1,200-ton *Laurada*, the steamship that had eluded both US revenue cutters and Spanish warships.

Junta attorney Horatio Rubens took the train to Jacksonville, making certain he was seen by Spanish spies. That was not difficult, especially when he consulted openly with José Alejandro Huau and other revolutionists who were under constant surveillance. The presence of a prominent Junta leader conferring with a known supporter of filibusters reinforced the belief that an expedition would soon be sent out on the *Three Friends*.

On August 8, Captain W. F. Kilgore, commanding officer of the cutter *Boutwell*, visited the Custom House in Jacksonville, where he was handed a telegram from Washington. It ordered him: "look out for filibusters." Kilgore's ship was a slow, twin-screw boat built in 1873 and unfit for the nimble work required to chase the filibusters' more agile and faster vessels. Still, Kilgore rode her hard, and over the next two days she ranged up the Georgia coast to St. Simons Island and down the

St. John's River. She stopped twenty-three boats—four schooners and nineteen steamships and tugs—but found no evidence of filibusters.

A day after Kilgore returned to Jacksonville, Spanish vice consul Henrico de Maritague came aboard the *Boutwell* excited with new intelligence that a filibuster expedition would leave that very night. After his fruitless voyage up the coast, Kilgore could not have had much confidence in the consul's information, but, in accordance with his orders, he dutifully instructed his crew they would depart at seven o'clock. An hour later the cutter banked fires, dropped a starboard anchor, and waited. The sailors spent the next three days in routine duties, cleaning decks and washing down spars. Saturday morning, under clear skies and a light southwesterly breeze, sailors were washing the paintwork when at 8:15 a.m. the tug *Three Friends* arrived off Mayport with the schooner *J. S. Hoskins* of Baltimore in tow.

Kilgore hailed Broward and ordered the *Three Friends* to anchor the schooner and come alongside. Kilgore had developed a friendly relationship with Broward over the years, but his demeanor was undoubtedly testy since the nation's press was questioning the Revenue Cutter Service's ability to contain the filibuster vessels. Broward presented Kilgore with the usual protest, claiming he was headed to Key Largo at the top of the Florida Keys to go "wrecking," or looking for boats in distress. Kilgore dispatched two officers to make a thorough search of the vessel, but they found no arms or ammunition. The officers did find an extraordinary amount of coal in the holds and on deck, one more boat than the certificate of inspection specified, and a large quantity of medicine. That was suspicious enough for Kilgore to order the *Three Friends* detained, and he ordered Third Lieutenant Moses Goodrich to go aboard and escort the tug to Jacksonville.

Kilgore took the *Boutwell* on ahead to Jacksonville and telegraphed the Treasury Department for permission to allow the *Three Friends* to leave port. The department granted the release of the tug on one condition: that Broward would pledge to abstain from any filibustering voyages. The captain's reputation in Jacksonville was unimpeachable, but his desire to further the cause of Cuban independence might have prompted a white lie or two along the way. Broward raised his right hand, took the oath, and his boat was released.

With the *Three Friends* drawing attention in Jacksonville and the *Commodore* serving the same purpose at Charleston, Hart, Nuñez, and O'Brien launched the most expensive and most complicated expedition of the war.

On August 6, the *Laurada*, piloted by Captain Ed Murphy, took on five hundred extra tons of coal in Philadelphia and at 5:00 p.m. was cleared for Port Antonio. The *Laurada* proceeded to Christiana River near Wilmington, Delaware, where she met the tug *Martha*. Aboard were Nuñez, General Carlos Roloff (the Junta's minister of war), twenty-eight men, and several cases of dynamite, all of which were loaded aboard the steamer.

The *Dauntless*, usually with "Captain Dynamite" Johnny O'Brien at the helm, participated in more landings than any other expedition vessel. Library of Congress, Prints and Photographs Division, Detroit Publishing Company Collection, reproduction number LC-DIG-det-4a14916.

Hart and his bookkeeper, Gratz Jordan, arrived in another tug with weaponry that had cost the Junta nearly $120,000, their largest order of the revolution, placed with the Winchester company of Bridgeport. The cargo included three thousand rifles, three million rounds of ammunition, three twelve-pound Hotchkiss field guns with six hundred shells, several tons of dynamite, and a large number of machetes. Fully loaded, the *Laurada* headed downriver, past the Delaware breakwater and into open sea.

Meanwhile, Captain Johnny O'Brien left Woodbine, Georgia, a lonely inland station on the Satilla River, in command of a fully laden black-hulled tug named the *Dauntless*. The *Dauntless* was a nearly new 125-foot oceangoing tug with red deck houses and a powerful wheel that could drive her at thirteen knots. She was discovered in Brunswick, Georgia, by Huau's nephew, Alphonse Fritot, whose friend William A. Bisbee wanted to buy her. Bisbee, a street paving contractor and brother of the collector of customs, did not have the $30,000 asking price, so Fritot arranged with Estrada Palma to loan Bisbee the money in exchange for certain services. The mortgage would be reduced by $10,000 for every successful expedition the vessel made to Cuba. Rubens was dispatched with thirty $1,000 bills to complete a quick deal after which Fritot maneuvered a trainload of munitions that was loaded onto the tug at Woodbine.

Captain Dynamite guided the *Dauntless* twenty miles down the river and out to sea, headed for Navassa Island, an uninhabited rock of coral and limestone located two hundred nautical miles south of Santiago. To sailors, Navassa Island was little more than a two-square-mile seabird latrine, but its strategic location made it attractive to pirates, smugglers, and other brigands who had embraced its remote location for more than three centuries. When the *Dauntless* arrived, the *Laurada* was anchored close to the island's thirty-foot cliffs. Half the men and cargo from the steamer were transferred to the *Dauntless* before the next phase of the plan was put into action.

Santiago was Cuba's main harbor for Spanish warships and was full of troops, but O'Brien knew the enemy's habits and practices that made them vulnerable. The war in Cuba was primarily a weekday affair for the Spanish navy. Gunboats that patrolled the coast returned to port by noon on Saturday and lay idle until Monday morning while the officers and crews enjoyed a coveted *vacación*. During this unwatched interval, it was reasonably safe to make a landing at almost any place that was not in plain sight of a Spanish blockhouse.

The *Dauntless* landed in broad daylight on the afternoon of Saturday, August 22, at Santa de Argo Niaco, a little cove twelve miles west of Santiago. She unloaded the men and arms, then returned to the *Laurada* and took on the rest of the cargo, which was landed at the same spot early Monday morning.

Nearly a month after a frazzled Estrada Palma considered moving Junta headquarters from New York, the largest expedition to date had been landed in Cuba without the injury of a man or the loss of a cartridge. The *Dauntless* had paid for herself, but the landing of three cargoes within a week gave the Spanish and American authorities new resolve to somehow seize her or sink her. Such an event would happen only over O'Brien's cold, limp body. If a man could love a bucket of bolts and steel, O'Brien had fallen in love with the *Dauntless*.

Despite the captain's affection and the tug's performance, the *Laurada* received the bulk of attention from the press reporting on the latest expedition. Typical of the praise was this lead from the *Boston Journal*: "The gallant steamship *Laurada* has evaded the agents and warships of two nations, and landed another big expedition on the island of Cuba."

The *Laurada* was treated with far less respect when she proceeded to Port Antonio. She was chased by a Spanish gunboat and blew out three boiler tubes while escaping. When she arrived, British officials seized the steamer, and a search of her deck and hold revealed several rifles that were not listed in the ship's papers. Captain Murphy was arrested and released on a bond of £300. Murphy telegraphed Hart of his arrest, and for his trouble received orders to pick up a load of bananas and bring it home safely.

The *Laurada* passed the breakwater and came up the Delaware River on September 10 to a welcoming committee of diverse source and authority. Collector of the port George F. Townsend had wired the secretary of the treasury's office for instructions. The attorney general's office in Philadelphia was monitoring the steamer's progress in hopes of seizing her when she docked at Race Street. Wilmington district attorney Lewis C. Vandegrift was alerted for any legal action that might ensue, and US Marshal Hewson E. Lannan and his agents were ready for action.

It was a horse race to see who could get to the *Laurada* first, and Hart pulled his own swaybacked nag out of the paddock. Hart dispatched his faithful bookkeeper, Gratz Jordan, to board a tug, go out to the *Laurada*, and unload the cargo onto lighters before the authorities could attach it. The twelve thousand bunches of bananas already had been consigned by Lascelles & Co. of Philadelphia, a transaction that would spoil if the fruit sat for long on a seized ship.

Collector Townsend arrived as the bananas were being unloaded and launched into an animated interrogation of Murphy. The captain was evasive at first but became more cooperative when the collector threatened to have him arrested and the ship seized. That would come the following day when Consul Congosto swore out his customary warrants, and Marshal Lannan arrested Murphy for "setting on foot an expedition against the King of Spain."

Jordan was able to secure the cargo before the *Laurada* anchored at the mouth of the Christiana River at Wilmington, but when the crew was released from duty, government agents and Pinkertons swooped in with offers of money or threats of jail. Six Jamaican crew members agreed to testify in return for $17 a week. The government kept the men in custody and grilled them thoroughly, extracting enough information to merit charges against Roloff, who was arrested in New York as he walked out the door of a cigar factory at 22 Fulton Street.

Murphy's hearing was held on September 19 at the US Circuit Court in Wilmington before Commissioner S. Redmon Smith. Ker again retained Senator George Gray to assist with Murphy's defense, and the prosecution was shared by Vandegrift and Francis Fisher Kane, an assistant district attorney from Philadelphia. One by one, the six witnesses told of their experiences on board the *Laurada*, from her departure on August 5 to her rendezvous with the *Dauntless* at Navassa Island. Witness George Cowley, one of the Jamaicans, testified that he was hired by Hart as a steward on the *Bermuda*. The charter master, seated in the front row of the courtroom directly behind Ker, stared at the witness through piercing eyes.

Glancing at his former boss, Cowley stammered at first but regained his composure. He testified that when the *Laurada* was off Barnegat Light, a steam launch came alongside carrying about two dozen men. He said one of the men was called "general," whom he identified as Roloff, and another man was referred to as "colonel," whom he identified as Nuñez.

But the big fish was yet to come. A warrant was issued later that day for Hart himself, alleging that he had provisioned the *Laurada* before the expedition. Hart appeared in good spirits when he surrendered at the offices of Commissioner Henry R. Edmunds. Depending on his mood of the moment, Hart either recoiled violently or appeared to enjoy the precarious attention at the center of the legal bull's-eye. Ker, who accompanied his client, was not so calm and denounced the "gross persecution" of innocent Americans by the Spanish government.

That point was made exceedingly clear when it was learned that the warrant for Hart's arrest did not come from his local nemesis, Congosto, but directly from the Spanish Minister to the United States, Enrique Dupuy de Lôme in Washington. If a man is measured by his enemies, John D. Hart's importance had risen considerably in the eyes of the Spanish legation.

Prosecutor Kane suggested a hearing for two days later, but Ker demanded a hearing immediately to reduce the likelihood the witnesses could be coached by the Pinkertons about their testimony. The hearing commenced, and a parade of witnesses testified for six hours in the government's attempt to link Hart to the expedition. However, the shipping fraternity closed ranks to protect a colleague.

The first witness was James Smith, agent for the tug *Madeira*, which allegedly took several men out to the *Laurada*. Smith remembered the assignment but could not remember the name of the ship his tug visited. Smith recalled he had sent a bill for the service to Hart, but he did not remember who paid the bill. Another witness, John R. Walker, testified he had supplied coal to the *Laurada*, but he did not recall the quantity. James Burchard, a boat builder, could not remember whether he had sold four surfboats on or about the date the *Laurada* was supposed to have departed. Even Collector of the Port Townsend and Deputy Collector Ayres had no option but to admit that the *Laurada*'s entry and clearance papers were in order.

Seaman Cowley, upon whose claims the warrant was based, denied Ker's allegation that he was being paid by the Spanish authorities to initiate proceedings against Murphy and Hart, although he admitted he was paid by a "detective agency." Ker also questioned Cowley's assertion that he recognized the island of Navassa.

"Do you know where it is?" Ker asked.

The Jamaican raised his chin and responded with certainty: "I know it's in the ocean."

After considering the testimony for a week, Commissioner Edmunds ordered John D. Hart held over on $2,500 bond for an appearance before the grand jury in the November term of the US District Court. It was the worst news Hart and Ker could have received. If indictments were returned, his case would go before Judge William Butler, whose handling of the Wiborg conviction Ker had tried to discredit before the US Supreme Court.

Chapter 18

A WORST-CASE SCENARIO

The American college boys who craved adventure and glory in Cuba had found that and much more by October. Although word would not filter out from the battlefield for months, a major battle at Guáimaro revealed both sides of a thrilling, yet unforgiving, war for the young volunteers. Only five months after the *Three Friends* delivered him to Cuba, Lieutenant Stuart S. Janney, the former Johns Hopkins fraternity man and athlete, was dubbed the "Hero of Guáimaro" after he rescued a companion from almost certain death. However, the same battle also provided the grim reality that war gives no favor to status or privilege.

In mid-October 1896, Generals Gómez and García joined forces and moved upon Guáimaro, in the extreme eastern part of Camagüey Province. The objective was not only strategic but symbolic, as the place where the Revolutionary Army had met in 1869 and created the constitution for a new nation, free from Spanish colonial rule. The combined armies included many young Americans who were brought to Cuba on filibustering expeditions. Janney and his friend Osmun Latrobe were artillery officers with García. Winchester Dana "Win" Osgood, the former Penn football star, commanded Gómez's artillery, and his second in command was Captain Frederick Funston, a University of Kansas dropout and future US general. Another officer in the unit was Osgood's Philadelphia chum, Captain William Cox.

Major Osgood was put in command of the combined battery when the rebels besieged two strongly fortified Spanish forts on October 17 and 18. On the first day of the siege, another American officer, Lieutenant James Devine from Texas,

This image of Baltimore volunteer Stuart S. Janney dragging Lieutenant James Devine to safety first appeared in the November 1910 edition of *Scribner's Magazine*. Library of Congress, Prints and Photographs Division. By permission of the Alfred Bendiner Memorial Collection.

saw a fine saddle horse tethered about two hundred yards from the Cuban lines and five hundred yards from the Spanish blockhouses. The Texan ran out to retrieve the animal when Spanish riflemen opened fire. Devine untied the rope, but the horse, frightened by the gunfire, reared up and began pulling away. Just then, Devine went down, wounded.

Osgood and Funston saw him fall and began running toward him, but Janney was already halfway there. Spanish bullets were whizzing around the lieutenant, their telltale geysers of dust popping up all around him. Janney picked up Devine, threw him over his shoulder, and carried him part of the way back to the Cuban lines. Exposed to heavy fire, Janney reportedly shouted to the Cubans to help him. Not one would venture from behind the safety of the breastworks, so Janney pulled out his pistol, pointed it and threatened to shoot any man who did not help. The reluctant Cubans woke from their slumber and ran out to pull Janney and Devine to safety.

On the second day of the siege, Osgood's battery was ordered to shell several blockhouses. As the sun rose over the low hills, Osgood landed a twelve-pound shell squarely on one blockhouse and kept firing at the others for the next two hours. All the time, Funston remained about forty feet to the front calling the shots. Under steady fire from small arms, Osgood leaned over the gun to adjust the sight and shouted to Funston, "I think that will do." In the next instant, all around him heard a bullet strike flesh with a sickening thud. Osgood slumped over the cannon, shot in the head by a sharpshooter in a church tower 1,100 yards away. Osgood was picked up by his comrades and carried down the hill to the aid station, but the bullet had gone through his brain. He died four hours later.

The death of Osgood was greeted in the United States with the same shock and sorrow as evoked by the death of Corporal Pat Tillman in Afghanistan more than a century later. Both men were star athletes and both put their personal lives aside to fight for freedom. On May 3, 1897, the University of Pennsylvania Athletic Association voted to erect a memorial to Osgood in the recently completed student union building, Houston Hall. The planned memorial was a three-foot plaque inscribed with a picture of Osgood above the family motto "Always to the Front." Osgood would be inducted into the College Football Hall of Fame in 1970, the same posthumous honor that Tillman received in 2010.

Cuba remained on the front pages throughout the fall, but it was not an issue in the American presidential campaign. The Republicans tossed the islanders a bone when they included in the party platform their "best hopes . . . for the full success of [the insurgents'] determined contest for liberty." The Democrats' platform had no more meat on it as it expressed sympathy for the Cubans in "their heroic struggle for liberty and independence."

Having dispensed their platitudes, the two parties turned to the important issue of the campaign, the economy, and the question of free silver versus gold as a monetary standard. Cleveland's agrarian and silverite enemies had gained control of the Democratic Party by 1896 and repudiated his administration and the gold standard. In a rare move, the Democrats abandoned the incumbent and nominated William Jennings Bryan, champion of free silver, at the party convention.

Northern businessmen, however, were not prepared to abandon gold. They put all their resources behind the Republican candidate, former Ohio governor William McKinley, an advocate of the gold standard. McKinley's victory on November 3 was welcomed by the Cuban revolutionists, although they could not know that McKinley's supporters expected four years of sound monetary policy and economic recovery. That did not include a war in Cuba.

The new administration would not take office until March 1897, and the Junta feared that the outgoing administration would ignore Cuba during its lame-duck period. Without fear of American reprisal, Captain General Weyler could be emboldened to deliver a severe stroke against the rebels. Weyler set the stage for such fears when he initiated his most radical action in late October on the eve of the election. His policy of *reconcentrado* ordered all inhabitants of the invaded districts into towns, essentially herding civilians into concentration camps to prevent them from assisting the insurgents. Word of the policy's effects slowly began to leak out of Cuba, sparking rumors of famine, torture, and mass murder. Flying over each camp were said to be flocks of vultures, which the rebels christened "Weyler's chickens."

Weyler was under intense pressure from Madrid to put an end to the revolution. Two prominent newspapers, the *Imparcial* and the *Heraldo*, both condemned his administration and claimed he had done little to suppress the rebellion. Indeed, a war office source said that Weyler's army would not be allowed to return to the Spanish peninsula except as victors.

Weyler's fortunes improved greatly the first week of December when General Antonio Maceo, second in command to Gómez and the spiritual leader of the Black rebels, was killed during a skirmish with Spanish soldiers. Coincidentally, Gómez's son, Lieutenant Francisco Gómez, an aide to Maceo, also was killed in the battle.

Maceo's death occurred on December 7, the same day President Cleveland presented his final message to Congress. The outgoing chief executive defended his Cuba policy and said that the insurgents' failure to establish a revolutionary government gave the United States nothing to recognize. However, he cautioned Spain that the status quo would not long serve American interests: "When the inability of Spain to deal successfully with the insurrection has become manifest and it is demonstrated that her sovereignty is extinct in Cuba for all purposes . . . a situation will be presented in which our obligations to the sovereignty of Spain will be superseded by higher obligations, which we can hardly hesitate to recognize and discharge."

Cleveland's words would prove prophetic. A new year would bring new voices to the debate and new approaches to methods that compounded ongoing problems. Secretary of State Olney met with Dupuy de Lôme in December and assured him that the outgoing administration would not introduce any new policies that would precipitate a conflict for the incoming administration. Olney's assurance was an unveiled message that nothing significant would be done to discourage Spain, nor would actions be taken to encourage the revolution. Thus, while Cubans waited hopefully for positive change that a new administration might bring, they knew that conditions might get worse before they got better.

That appeared to describe John D. Hart's situation two weeks after the election. On November 17, the grand jury in US District Court in Philadelphia returned three indictments against Hart on charges of rendering aid to the insurgents. Ker's worst-case scenario had come true. Hart would go on trial before Judge William Butler in the February session of the court.

Expressions of support for Hart came from many fronts, reflecting the public's sympathy for the rebels and its impatience with its own government's apparent complicity with Spain. On Sunday, November 22, the congregations of several Presbyterian and Baptist churches met at Philadelphia's Fiftieth Baptist Church to express their sympathy for the Cuban cause. The Reverend J. W. Hartpence offered up a prayer urging parishioners to take an active role in providing aid and assistance to Cuba including pressure on elected officials to recognize her

Federal Judge William Butler was not a popular choice to preside at John D. Hart's trial after he officiated at Captain Jacob Henry Jasper Wiborg's conviction of violating the US neutrality laws. From the *Pittsburgh Press*, January 28, 1899, https://www.newspapers.com/image/141833387.

independence. A special prayer was offered that "Captain John D. Hart would be acquitted" at his coming trial and that "Captain Wiborg would be speedily pardoned by the President."

Despite the pleas for divine intervention, Wiborg would remain in prison while Hart's fate would await Bill Ker's rematch with Judge Butler.

The *Laurada* had not participated in the "Cuba trade" since her expedition to Navassa Island in August, and her whereabouts was a mystery. The press and public could only surmise that the noble vessel was once again in service to the Cuban patriots and that she was freely engaged in further expeditions for which she never was caught. Spanish authorities shared the same conviction, but with the fear that such activities could strengthen the resistance and embolden the insurgents. The actual explanation was not so romantic.

Hart, desperate for income and welcoming another opportunity to get the *Laurada* off the front pages, scheduled a world tour of legitimate business activity for the vessel. He put Sam Hughes back in command and gave him a lengthy list of ports to visit and cargoes that would provide Hart with some much-needed income. Hughes was relieved at the routine assignment, and he again took the opportunity to bring his wife, Margaret, along on the trip. However innocent the voyage's intent, the very reputations that both ship and captain had acquired in the Cuba trade would thrust Hughes and the *Laurada* into the middle of an international incident in which the precipitous cargo was not ammunition but oranges.

The *Laurada* cleared Wilmington, Delaware, on October 2 for Halifax, Nova Scotia, where she loaded apples for London. Discharging the cargo there, she picked up a cargo of pitch, then called on Swansea, Wales, for coal. She sailed for Naples, Italy, on November 13, arriving on November 23. After delivering her cargo, she headed for Messina, Sicily, on November 29 to load lemons for J. H. Seward & Sons, a Baltimore fruit dealer. Hughes was to clear Messina for nearby Palermo, where he would load more lemons, and then proceed to Valencia, Spain, to fill up the load with succulent oranges before returning to Baltimore.

Valencia grew the most flavorful oranges in the world, but it was an unfortunate choice of ports. Anti-American sentiment had simmered in Valencia since March, when the US congressional debate over recognizing the belligerent rights of Cuba prompted a violent protest by Spanish students. The American consulate was stoned, and police were called during a tense few days of hostilities. Nine months later, passions against anything American still ran high.

When the famous vessel arrived in Italy, newspapers treated the ship and its captain like conquering heroes. The *Futuro Sociale* of Rome called the *Laurada* a "valiant ship, which amid immeasurable peril, succeeded in eluding the vigilance of the Spanish cruisers and landed on Cuba's shores a strong force of volunteers and a large cargo of ammunition in favor of republican ideas." At Messina, Hughes received a telegram from the president of the Italian Central Committee for the Liberation of Cuba, "in admiration of the noble and valorous achievement of your ship." He also was besieged with dozens of applications from young Italians who wanted to join his crew and fight for Cuban independence. Hughes's claim that his vessel was in Messina on legitimate business disappointed the applicants, some of whom were suspected to be Spanish spies.

R. A. Tucker, manager of J. H. Seward & Sons, cabled his agent in Valencia on December 6 that an American steamer was loading lemons in Messina and would arrive in Valencia around December 15. Agent Wiley Smith Killingsworth, a soft-spoken native of Williston, South Carolina, was instructed to buy three thousand cases of oranges and "insure against delay as steamer can't stay over two days." Whether a deliberate omission or not, Tucker's cable did not mention the name of the vessel. Killingsworth placed the order with his local suppliers then met two British fruit agents at a local *cafetería* for coffee. Killingsworth nearly spewed a mouthful when one of his fellow agents showed him a report in a Liverpool newspaper that the infamous *Laurada* was in Messina loading lemons.

Killingsworth hoped it was a coincidence, but the next morning local and Madrid newspapers confirmed the disturbing truth. The agent knew immediately that any oranges to be picked up in Valencia by the *Laurada* could be detrimental to his health. Killingsworth met with American consul Theodore Mertens, then sent a cable to Tucker: "If steamer loading at Messina is the *Laurada*, don't let her come here. Sure be trouble." The agent received a dismissive reply from the home office:

"*Laurada* is the steamer. Under regular charter to us in our legitimate business. Will sail for Valencia Saturday. There is no reason for trouble. Have fruit engaged."

The news spread rapidly that the notorious American vessel that aided the enemies of Spain soon would sail brazenly into a Spanish port. Already, rumors were rampant that the Junta had sent an operative to Valencia to stir up sentiment against the United States. Killingsworth even heard rumblings that the Spanish government considered him the spy.

The ongoing trouble in Valencia was no secret in the State Department. Less than three months earlier, a regular dispatch from the American military attaché in Madrid included a disturbing report of "discontent, manifested by renewed disorders on the part of the female portion of the population in Valencia, Alicante and at other points. The Carlist or Republican element in the East, in Barcelona and Valencia especially, is responsible for some violations of the public order. The government is much alarmed and many arrests of prominent Republicans have been made in the two cities."

Killingsworth returned to see Consul Mertens, who offered to take him to the civil governor so he could explain his role as an innocent bystander. However, when they arrived, the governor launched a tirade against American intentions and Killingsworth personally. Local authorities knew that Killingsworth was in Valencia for no good, he charged, and the *Laurada* was being sent to embarrass the Spanish government.

The Americans rushed back to the consulate where Killingsworth cabled Messina, attempting to warn the captain of the *Laurada* not to come. After no response came, Killingsworth sent a second cable: "Why don't you answer my cable stating *Laurada* won't come Valencia? Time is an important consideration now. Very great excitement prevails owing to her coming."

Killingsworth attempted to contact the *Laurada* at her second known port, Palermo. "Don't come Valencia, sure meet trouble, probably death. Answer quick you won't come." Again, no response came. After a sleepless night, the frantic agent sent another cable the next morning to Tucker at J. H. Seward & Sons that described the gravity of the situation: "No broker, stevedore or lighterman will touch *Laurada*. Spanish authorities strongly advise keep *Laurada* away. Impossible protect life or property. On no account must *Laurada* enter any Spanish port."

Tucker's response returned him to the depths of despair. "Absurd raising so much fuss over nothing," his manager wrote. "We and our present crew have nothing to do with alleged previous actions aboard *Laurada*. Unable to load elsewhere. We can satisfy Spanish consul at Washington we are not connected in any way with parties averse to Spain."

Tucker cabled the State Department on December 13, asking for the government to provide information, but he received no response. Olney had received Tucker's cable but had forwarded it to Dupuy de Lôme, asking: "Have you any suggestions to make in the matter?" Dupuy de Lôme, who was born in Valencia, responded in typical fashion, claiming that John D. Hart was behind the entire episode. As proof, Dupuy de Lôme avowed that the agent of record for the *Laurada*, John T. Vandiver of Philadelphia, had provided false information that the owner of the vessel was a John J. Molan. Dupuy de Lôme called Molan "a bar room man who lives opposite John Hart & Co., the filibuster agent, [who] is nothing more than a straw man of said Hart, having all of Hart's business in his name to defraud creditors.... The appearance of Molan, and Hart behind him, show plainly the scheme . . . in sending the *Laurada* to Valencia."

After hearing nothing from Olney, Tucker wrote the secretary a letter claiming that his intention was merely to buy oranges and not to foment global turmoil. Tucker's letter, a copy of which he gave to the *Baltimore Sun*, outlined the conditions at Valencia as he knew them from Killingsworth.

"As American citizens and merchants holding a charter of a steamer registered and carrying the American flag," Tucker wrote, "we feel it our duty and our right to ask you in your official capacity to give such directions and orders, as will protect our property under such flag as well as the honor of the nation."

Meanwhile, in Madrid, Spanish authorities were preparing for trouble. The minister of marine, Admiral José María Beranger, ordered the cruiser *Infanta María Teresa* and the gunboat *Vulcana* to Valencia with orders to watch the American vessel when she arrived. Port officials were instructed to avoid trouble and treat the *Laurada* as they would any other merchantman intending to do commerce. In Washington, Dupuy de Lôme called on Olney with the specific intention of discouraging any provocation that might antagonize the pro-Cuban bloc in Congress. Another ugly demonstration against the United States would logically inflame the American public and might lead to increased demands for US intervention on the island.

Olney had his secretary place a telephone call to Tucker, requesting his presence in Washington the following day, although his intentions were unclear. When Tucker arrived in Washington to see the secretary personally, he was told that neither Olney's schedule nor that of his first assistant, W. W. Rockhill, would permit a meeting. Tucker was shuffled off to the chief clerk.

Back in Valencia, Killingsworth was awakened Sunday morning by the hotel manager, who demanded he vacate his room immediately. A mob had gathered outside and was already parading and promising vengeance against the *Laurada* and the American spy inside. Killingsworth fled to the house of a German friend, who hid him for the next two days. When he returned to the American consulate, Mertens gave him the good news that the US minister to Spain, Hannis Taylor, had demanded that the Spanish government protect the *Laurada* and Killingsworth. The agent cabled the news to Tucker at J. H. Seward & Sons, who informed him that the State Department denied Taylor had made such a demand.

Killingsworth was approaching desperation. He was in a country that had grown increasingly hostile, and he was well aware of the "treacherous and hot-blooded nature of the Spaniards." He decided to send one final cable to his firm: "Why don't you answer, *Laurada* won't come to Valencia? Useless, impossible load. I strongly advise not proceed against government decision. Am hiding and being protected for personal safety. Answer quick. Suspense awful."

Aboard the *Laurada*, Captain and Mrs. Sam Hughes were blissfully ignorant of the diplomatic storm swirling in the northwestern Mediterranean. They were enjoying the temperate weather of Messina and the hospitality of US Consul Charles Caughey, a Baltimore native.

Hughes had missed Killingsworth's cables at Messina, but when he arrived at Palermo, the local consul brought him up to date. If the *Laurada* proceeded to Valencia, the Spanish government could confiscate the vessel and probably spoil Captain and Mrs. Hughes's idyllic Mediterranean holiday. Such treatment was a possibility to which Hughes was accustomed in American waters but one he did not wish to entertain with his wife at his side.

Despite the US government's continued assurances that the Spanish government would protect the vessel, Tucker at J. H. Seward & Sons finally heeded the warnings. He cabled a final message to Killingsworth: "Will not send *Laurada* there; will finish loading elsewhere." The *Laurada* was ordered back to Messina to complete the cargo of fruit, then was directed to Gibraltar, where she took on a load of coal for her trip across the Atlantic. She arrived in Baltimore the first week of January, anchoring at the fruit wharves of J. H. Seward & Sons at the foot of Mill Street.

Killingsworth would return to the United States in the next year and eventually run for public office in California. But he always believed that the US government's reluctance to get involved with the *Laurada*'s voyage to Valencia had a dual purpose. His firm's insistence that the voyage be completed was based on assurances from the US government that Spanish authorities would protect John D. Hart's *Laurada*. And if they could not do so?

The seizure or even sinking of the vessel that had done more to carry on the Cuban war than any other would remove a painful thorn from the government's paw, while providing an excuse to intervene. As one Spanish official said to Killingsworth: "The States have for some time been trying to pick a fuss with Spain but didn't want to strike the first blow. Sending the *Laurada* here was for the express purpose of getting Spain to strike the blow."

Chapter 19

PUBLICITY AGENT FOR AN EXPEDITION

During the *Laurada*'s Mediterranean sabbatical, Emilio Nuñez moved the Department of Expeditions base of operations to Jacksonville. John D. Hart was less involved in the day-to-day planning of expeditions, although his court appearances were useful platforms from which to generate ongoing sympathy for Cuba. Bill Ker continued to portray Hart as a symbol of resistance, which reinforced the public's suspicion of Spain and support of the revolution.

Moving expeditionary headquarters to Jacksonville made sense because of proximity to Cuba, but Florida had other practical advantages. Many of the volunteers, both Americans and Cubans, were being trained at camps throughout the state and could be delivered on short notice to expeditions leaving nearby ports. Reluctant judges and a hostile population had made it difficult for the federal government to prosecute alleged violators of the neutrality laws. It also was helpful to have men like José Huau and Napoleon Bonaparte Broward close at hand.

The two were involved in the next expedition, which enlisted other Florida connections. The expedition would leave on Broward's *Three Friends* and would be led by Captain Dynamite Johnny O'Brien, who had come to Jacksonville with Nuñez. But an unaccustomed feature of this expedition would be the presence of its own publicity agent. Ralph Paine, a reporter for William Randolph Hearst's lively *New York Journal* and a native of Jacksonville, was looking for a ride. Paine was on a mission from his flamboyant boss to deliver to the insurgents' commanding general Máximo Gómez a jewel-encrusted sword that cost $2,000. If Paine's mission was successful, Hearst would recover far more value in publicity and newspaper sales.

The son of the Reverend Samuel Delahaye Paine, Ralph Paine had known many of the principals since he was a boy. Convenient among his old acquaintances was José Huau and his nephew, Alphonse Fritot. Paine was confident they would include him on an expedition if he only asked, so he walked into Huau's cigar store at Bay and Main Streets and found the rotund proprietor at his customary seat behind the counter. Paine's childhood memories quickly returned when he spotted a soda fountain in the corner where he had bought many a fizzing drink for a nickel from the genial Cuban.

Paine pitched his case to Huau and was told he did not have long to wait. The next expedition was being planned a few feet away, in the back room of the shop where Nuñez, O'Brien, Fritot, Broward, and O'Brien's engineer, Mike Pagliuchi, were meeting. Pagliuchi was Italian by birth, Cuban by adoption, and for some time an engineering officer in the Argentine navy. He also was O'Brien's official enforcer. Once when two sailors launched into a machete duel, Pagliuchi calmly stepped between them, grabbed both weapons by the blades, and pried the would-be combatants apart before scolding them like a Jesuit headmaster.

The presence of hovering US revenue cutters made operations at Jacksonville difficult, but Broward suggested an opportunity a few leagues to the north. George L. Baltzell, collector of customs at Fernandina, had helped foil Martí's first expeditions of the *Amadis*, *Lagonda*, and *Baracoa* and had since boasted that filibusters never could execute an expedition out of his closely watched port. "They are sending expeditions out of Jacksonville whenever they want to," Baltzell frequently declared, "but I would like to see them try to get one out of Fernandina, by gosh! I'll nail 'em to the cross in a holy minute if they start anything here."

Such words provided a challenge for the conspirators. Broward knew that Baltzell had a weakness for draw poker, so he wired the collector saying he would be in Fernandina that evening and invited him to a game. The *Three Friends* left Jacksonville under Captain Bill Lewis, an accomplished pilot who was one of Broward's most trusted men. The *Three Friends* had a schooner in tow in the guise of legitimate business and reached the bar late in the afternoon. After casting off the schooner, she proceeded up the coast under Lewis, appearing to be looking for more business.

Nuñez had dispatched two boxcars from New York filled with a menu of weapons that included a Hotchkiss twelve-pounder, one thousand rifles, five hundred thousand cartridges, dynamite, and machetes. The cars were intercepted at a siding north of Callahan, Florida, in the distinct Fritot fashion. Their contents were transferred to other cars, and Fritot applied new seals with the same lines and numbers that had been dutifully recorded by Pinkerton detectives when the train left New York. The now-empty cars were run to Jacksonville, where the waiting detectives located them, confirmed the numbers, then proceeded to guard them day and night. The cars that now carried the arms were switched off at Callahan and run over to Yulee, about twelve miles west of Fernandina, where they would sit until claimed.

A few days after meeting with Huau, Paine was instructed to report to a dark side-track at the foot of Julia Street near Fritot's office. Paine boarded a passenger coach that contained about forty young Cubans led by Colonel Rafael Pérez Carbó and Major Rafael Morales, who had suffered a wound during the Ten Years' War that cost his sight in one eye. Paine found the coach in total darkness, all the shades having been pulled. The only light came from cigarettes, which glowed like fireflies amid the rustling mutter of subdued voices.

The locomotive headed north across a flat landscape of pine, palmetto, and sawgrass. When the train arrived at Fernandina, a prearranged signal from Broward told them the poker game that occupied Baltzell was in full swing. Paine peeked out from under the shades and saw a gleam of water reflecting a cloudless sky spangled with stars. The special train was run out on a dock and stopped along a long, creaking trestle. Moored alongside was the large, seagoing tug that loomed tall and spectral against the dusky curtain of night. Lanterns were hung at the gangway, and about thirty dockhands stood ready to hustle the freight into the hold.

As Paine wrote: "The doors of the box-car flew open, the roustabouts jumped like sprinters and a torrent of merchandise flowed into the vessel. Boxes and barrels, bales and crates, they erupted from those cars and the forty-some Cuban patriots spilled out of the passenger coach to help load the ship. The cargo appeared harmless, as the stenciled markings identified the boxes as condensed milk, salted codfish, breakfast bacon and prime lard. But when a case of 'hams' was dropped and smashed, out clattered a dozen Mauser rifles."

At daylight on December 15, 1896, Captain Lewis guided the *Three Friends* out of Fernandina, a satisfied Johnny O'Brien at his side. Back at the poker table, Baltzell was having the night of his life. He had never enjoyed such a winning streak, much of which came with modest hands after the other players folded. When Broward was satisfied his vessel was away, he rose and yawned saying he'd had enough losing for one night, but it was Baltzell's luck that had run out. Heading home for a well-earned rest, he received word that an expedition had just left his port. Baltzell rushed to his office and alerted the revenue cutter *Boutwell*, but it was too late for anything but embarrassment. The cutter pursued the *Three Friends* but could not catch up.

Bad weather forced the tug to anchor inside of Sombrero Light, south of Marathon in the Florida Keys. O'Brien knew that the wind and rain were not the worst threats they faced. Sure enough, as the weather began to clear, the revenue cutters *Newark* and *Raleigh* came into view. Lewis knew the area well and moved

This image of men unloading a boxcar full of weapons for Cuba first appeared in the September 1910 edition of *Scribner's Magazine*. Library of Congress, Prints and Photographs Division. By permission of the Alfred Bendiner Memorial Collection.

farther west, anchoring the low-slung craft behind the leafy curtain of Bahia Honda Key until dark. The two cutters were anchored about a mile apart, but it was sliver enough for a darkened *Three Friends* to slip through undetected. The tug passed Key West, left Dry Tortugas Light over her stern, and steered for the Yucatán Channel to pass around the western end of Cuba.

Paine found his fellow passengers were not all young Cubans radiating the desire to kill Spaniards. One was a student at Harvard, another a distinguished middle-aged consulting engineer from New York. Another, named Jack Gorman, claimed to be an army sharpshooter who had fought in the Indian Wars. But the most interesting, and ultimately useful, passenger was Mike Walsh, a former gunner with the US Navy who had deserted from the battleship *Maine* at Key West because all the navy asked him to do was drill. He joined up to see action, and, by God, action he would see.

Early on the morning of Friday, December 18, the vessel fought a stiff breeze as it passed Cape San Antonio at the western tip of Cuba. Colonel Pérez Carbó opened his sealed orders from the Junta in front of O'Brien, which read simply: "Sail to the mouth of the San Juan River and there await a party of insurgents who will take charge of the cargo." The next morning they stopped about fifteen miles off Cienfuegos, invisible from shore. The Santa Clara Mountains lifted dimly from the sea, and through his powerful glasses O'Brien saw the pass through which the Río San Juan flowed into a small bay. At dark they steamed at full speed toward the mouth of the river. Many of the Cubans aboard had never seen their ancestral homeland and were caught up in the moment. They began singing the Cuban battle hymn of "La Bayamesa" as O'Brien kept a sharp eye out for any music critics in Spanish gunboats.

To guard against unwanted visitors, Major Morales ordered Mike Walsh to set up, oil, and unlimber the twelve-pound Hotchkiss gun on deck. Walsh assembled the piece, adjusted the brake ropes, blocked the wheels by timbers, and anchored it on a platform of cartridge cases. The crew and young Cubans gathered in great anticipation that they soon would see this monster unleash its fury in the face of the enemy. From the shore came flashes of red and white in accordance with the prearranged signal. O'Brien nodded to Pérez Carbó, who ordered his men to begin unloading the bounty. The Cubans swarmed into the hold, joined by some deckhands, while others were stationed at the open hatches. The men below handed the weighty cases, bales, and barrels up to those on deck. Lashed overhead were six wide-bottomed surfboats, which the men pulled down and shoved over the side before filling them with the cargo.

When the tug was within a mile of shore, the ever-vigilant Pagliuchi spotted through his glass a "coaster" showing no lights and sneaking slowly out of the river. O'Brien ordered the engines stopped and put his own glass on the suspicious craft. Convinced she was Spanish, O'Brien ordered the engine room: "Hard-a-port and full speed to sea!" Lewis ordered the crew to the fire room, where they would wield slice-bar and shovel, ramming the coal into the engine as fast as prudence would allow. Fat Jack Dunn, a Broward man and the *Three Friends'* regular engineer, stood at his clamped safety valve near his gasping stokers. The tall funnel glowed red hot, and the needle of the steam gauge twitched to fifty pounds beyond good sense.

The gunboat, in high pursuit, fired a shot that splashed ahead of the tug. Two more shots came no closer, but O'Brien spied two other gunboats about six or seven miles away. They were coming up from the east to cut him off, which made it plain that treachery had infiltrated another mission. Someone who knew where the *Three Friends* was bound had communicated with the enemy, and a trap had been nicely set.

Morales ordered sharpshooter Gorman to gather the riflemen he had been training and stand ready. Then he gave a wink to Walsh to prepare the Hotchkiss for action. The gun was mounted at the aft end, opposite the direction of the

Mike Walsh, an artillery expert who had deserted from the USS *Maine*, added some firepower to Broward's tug, the *Three Friends*. Image #N040909, Florida Memory Photographic Collection, State Library and Archives of Florida.

pursuing Spaniard. But bringing to bear from the bow during a chase meant swinging the ship almost broadside, presenting a tempting target. O'Brien preferred to race for the open sea and get clear of the coast before he allowed Walsh to go for it. But when another Spanish shot came closer, O'Brien relented and nodded his approval to Morales.

Walsh crouched behind his big toy while his mates handed up a shell and shoved at the wheels in response to his commands. He calculated the gunboat to be about nine hundred yards out when he laid his sights and timed the shrapnel fuse. With a jerk of the lanyard, Walsh jumped aside and the gun spat a crimson streak. The field piece recoiled and drove back across the platform of cartridge cases, nearly crushing Walsh against the splintering planks of the deck house. The gunner rose just in time to see the shell go squarely between the short masts of the gunboat. A perfect kick on a football field, the shot threw up a gleaming spray behind the Spaniard.

"Hold her as she is, Cap'n Johnny," roared Walsh, as he leaped to haul the gun back into position. "That one was a sighting shot."

O'Brien held the ship steady to give Walsh a clear range, and he fired again. This time the shrapnel bullets swept the gunboat's deck. It was a clear hit. The gunboat pulled up, Paine wrote, "like a speeding wagon approaching a cliff." She sent up red rockets of distress for a disabled ship requiring assistance, confirming Walsh's hit. One of the other gunboats responded to the signal, but the larger boat kept coming. She was barely within firing range when she lobbed a shell at the *Three Friends* that missed badly.

O'Brien could have stayed and fought, but he did not consider his role in what would become the only naval battle of the Cuban War of Independence.

Choosing discretion over valor, Captain Dynamite, chewing a frayed cigar and rubbing his stubbled chin, gazed astern and said farewell to the Río San Juan. O'Brien ordered the vessel back through the Yucatán Channel under darkness, risking contact with any Spanish craft sent to intercept her. Once clear of Cuba, he made for the interminable labyrinth of mangrove keys off the southern coast of Florida to hide the cargo and drop off the volunteers until he could return.

They stopped on Christmas Day at No Name Key, where they landed the cargo, Mike Walsh, the shootist Gorman, and Major Morales and his volunteers. They left enough provisions to last a week, hoping the company would survive that long battling mosquitoes and sand flies while dodging snakes and alligators. Paine also left his sword for Gómez with Walsh for safekeeping. O'Brien and Colonel Pérez Carbó flagged down a small schooner to take them to Key West, where they caught the *Olivette* to Tampa. There, they boarded a train for Jacksonville, where they would meet with Nuñez to plot the resurrection of the expedition.

Under the steady hand of Fat Jack Dunn and the literary encouragement of Paine, the *Three Friends* limped into Jacksonville, where she was greeted by hundreds of people on the wharf and in river craft. The reception did not stop Collector Cyrus Bisbee from seizing the vessel on instructions from the secretary of the treasury. The *Three Friends* was taken into custody on a warrant that charged O'Brien, Lewis, Dunn, Walsh, Fritot, and even Paine with piracy.

Broward was not at all agitated by the government action against his boat. As he told Paine: "All this pirate stuff will blow itself out. They can't hang anybody, and no grand jury in Jacksonville will return indictments carrying any penalty like that. Shucks, folks would ride 'em out of town on a rail, and they know it."

The reaction to the sea battle off the Río San Juan ranged from indignation to disbelief, but predictable according to the source. Pro-Spain newspapers in Havana vilified the US government for its failure to prevent such expeditions from leaving American ports. Observers along the Florida coast praised O'Brien and skipper Bill Lewis as worthy representatives of the filibuster fleet. Stories cabled to New York about Mike Walsh's assault on the Spanish navy were regarded as reporters' fantasies, probably hatched in a Key West dive. After all, how could a harmless tug fire at a Spanish warship? O'Brien did find it awkward explaining to Broward the ragged gap in the *Three Friends*' bulwark where Walsh's twelve-pounder recoiled with a vengeance while in action.

But the mission was not yet over. With the *Three Friends* well guarded and in need of an overhaul, O'Brien and Nuñez summoned the *Dauntless* to resume the expedition. O'Brien did not want to risk further exposure, so he did not try to contact Paine, who desperately wanted to continue on the mission. O'Brien took the *Dauntless* to No Name Key on New Year's Eve to rescue the cargo and men they had left behind. Because of her draft, the *Dauntless* had to lay three or four miles offshore from the key, which made recovery precarious. Patrolling cruisers and cutters made it necessary to get the cargo aboard quickly, so O'Brien engaged ten little schooners and sloops belonging to friendly "conchs," the locals living on the adjacent keys.

Nuñez was supervising the loading when a white vessel came tearing up from Key West. The conchs took the strange craft to be either a revenue cutter or a Spanish torpedo boat, and they scurried in all directions, taking the arms with them. Two boatloads of Cubans who were just leaving the shore scrambled back to the beach and lost themselves in the mangroves. O'Brien soon realized that the mystery vessel was not a menace but the *Vamoose*, the fast steam yacht chartered by William Randolph Hearst to speed his *Journal* reporters to the action. At the bow, his hands on his hips like a Viking king, stood Paine, ready to resume his adventure. At his side was his accomplice, reporter Ernest W. McCready of the *New York Herald*.

Paine saw the confusion he had caused and directed the *Vamoose* to follow the fleeing flotilla so he could explain things. But the conchs were no friends of authorities and fled among the shoals where no yacht could go. Nuñez was furious, running from one side of the deck to the other and unleashing a multilingual spew of invective while shaking his fist at the interloper. Paine told McCready that he would like Nuñez once he got to know him, but to come aboard and reintroduce himself at this time would be flirting with suicide.

O'Brien was more concerned with reassembling the conchs and retrieving the cargo. He pulled out a whistle he carried to signal all clear, and after several long blasts the locals returned, and the loading resumed. They had lost several valuable hours, and it was dark before the last of the arms were loaded. While Nuñez watched the small boats, Paine and McCready snuck aboard with their own booty, a case of beer for sharpshooter Gorman and a box of cigars for Mike Walsh as thanks for guarding Gómez's jeweled sword.

A southeaster was kicking up a nasty sea, and Nuñez wanted to stay in the lee of the island until next day, but O'Brien recommended they move quickly. The cruiser *Marblehead* and the revenue cutter *McCullough* were in the area, and O'Brien wanted to leave before they were spotted. The *Dauntless* was eight miles off Key West at sunrise, then proceeded around Cape San Antonio at the western end of Cuba.

On the morning of January 3, 1897, they put the cargo and party ashore in Corrientes Bay, an expanse of tranquil water big enough for a fleet. The gleaming white beaches and feathery groves of palms belied the fact there was no sheltered anchorage for the *Dauntless*, but no Spanish gunboats appeared. A steady stream of cargo followed Walsh and his cannon in the first boat to land. The gunner quickly set up the Hotchkiss on the beach, daring any Spaniard to interfere.

Nuñez, who had waived the death penalty but still regarded the reporters with skepticism, approached them and suggested that Pinar del Río was not a good place for them to get off. Antonio Maceo had been killed there, and Gómez was four hundred miles away. There would be little news in Pinar del Río and much trouble in sending it. He recommended they return with the *Dauntless* and try it again on the next expedition. O'Brien said the *Commodore* should be ready to go out again soon. Paine and McCready begrudgingly agreed, and they remained on board.

After the cargo was unloaded, O'Brien and the reporters gave Walsh a hearty wave from the deck and turned the boat toward Jacksonville. They would never see the gunner again, although none would have been surprised to have read that he had captured a sponge boat and bombarded Havana.

As they approached Jacksonville, O'Brien suggested that Paine and McCready disembark before landing to avoid arrest, and the two reporters were put off at a nearby dock. The captain's fears were realized when the tug was stopped by the cutter *Boutwell* at the mouth of the river, and O'Brien, Nuñez, and the crew were detained. The grand jury would investigate the case with great care but again find no evidence to justify indictments. One editorial writer put it this way: "The United States District Attorney of Jacksonville will have to send to Alaska for a jury not absolutely certain to acquit the accused."

Paine was determined to hang around Jacksonville until he could latch on to another expedition. McCready had been recalled to New York by the *Herald*, but Hearst's only pull on Paine was the sword for Gómez. Paine had held onto the jeweled sword, but he realized that delivering it would be difficult. Enter the useful Señor Huau, who again came to Paine's rescue.

Huau sent Hearst's sword to Gómez's wife in Santo Domingo, and she kept it until Spain was driven out of Cuba. Paine later wrote "it is credibly related" that when Gómez examined the splendid sword, he exploded in a turbulent rage: "Those imbeciles in New York, with two thousand dollars to waste! It would have bought shoes for my barefooted men, shirts for their naked backs, cartridges for their useless rifles. Take it away! If the idiot who was sent on the stupid errand had found me in camp, I should have been tempted to stick him in the belly with his wretched gold sword!"

Chapter 20

"YOU DON'T OFTEN SEE A MAN LIKE HIM"

Bill Ker was convinced that the judge's instructions to the jury in the trial of Captain Wiborg prejudiced the jury and led to conviction. The fact that the Supreme Court disagreed did not make Ker's task any easier when he and his current defendant walked into US District Judge William Butler's courtroom on February 16.

Ker's opponent of record in his defense of John D. Hart was federal prosecutor James M. Beck. At forty-five, Beck was a respectful advocate whose ready smile seemed to illuminate his high forehead. He referred to his notes through a pair of pince-nez glasses that hung from a cord dangling from the right lens. Beck and his two assistants had a heavy load on their docket, including cases for counterfeiting and obscenity in the mails and another against the Philadelphia and Reading Railroad for transporting a carload of horses for twenty-eight hours without providing water. But the thirsty horses and obscene mail were all set aside in favor of the filibustering case, which would generate far more publicity for Beck and his office.

The jury did not have to wait long for the parties to begin the thrust and parry of a contentious trial. In his opening statement, Beck informed the jury that the facts of the case were simple, and he introduced into evidence President Cleveland's proclamations that warned American citizens not to breach the neutrality laws. Ker objected immediately on the grounds that neither proclamation referred specifically to a war between Cuba and Spain, but Butler overruled the objection on the grounds that the conflict to which the president's proclamations pertained was well known. He allowed Beck to proceed with his case.

Witness Hosea Horton testified he was sent by his boss to collect a boat that Hart had hired for the expedition. Horton said he did not know Hart but he recognized him from his boss's description, because "you don't often see a man like him." At around 10:00 p.m. on the night in question, Horton arrived at the Gardener's Ditch dock outside of Atlantic City and saw the naphtha launch *Richard K. Fox* next to a sloop with Hart and other men aboard. "Cast off your lines and go to sea. You know the rest," he quoted Hart as telling the men. The witness said Hart saw him and asked sharply, "What business have you to interfere with my business?" Horton said he was merely recovering the launch at the order of his boss, Captain Fleming. "To hell with Captain Fleming," Hart allegedly shouted as he grabbed Horton by the shoulder. "As for you, I will throw you overboard!" Horton said he fled and did not wait around to see where Hart went.

The government continued its case the second day with testimony intended to link Hart to the expedition. Tug owner James Smith testified that several yawl boats of the type used in unloading arms on the beach were put aboard the *Laurada*. Hart's bookkeeper, Gratz Jordan, confirmed that he supervised the taking of supplies on board the vessel. James Anderson, owner of the *Richard K. Fox*, testified that his boat was at Gardener's Ditch chartered for a fishing trip. He said he was among eighteen persons who boarded the vessel and sailed four miles out. Thirteen of the men boarded the *Laurada*, while the other five, including Emilio Nuñez, returned.

Nicholas J. Sooy testified that he knew Captain Hart and saw him at the inlet pavilion at Atlantic City on August 8. Sooy said Hart recognized him and asked him if he could keep his mouth shut in order to make some money. Sooy accompanied Hart to the Pennsylvania Railroad Station, where eighteen men joined them. He said they put to sea and met the *Laurada*. While alongside, a tug came up with a lighter in tow carrying a load of boxes and crates.

Sooy's statement was corroborated by Michael J. McKilleys of Brooklyn, captain of the tug *Dolphin*. McKilleys said he was hired in August to tow a barge from Pier 38 on the East River down the bay. He said he towed the barge as far as Barnegat, New Jersey, where the *Laurada* was anchored. The prosecution then called William J. Bruff of Hartley & Graham, the Junta's source of weapons. Bruff admitted selling $50,000 worth of arms, ammunition, and stores to Luis Espin for delivery to Pier 39 on the East River, on August 8. According to Bruff, Espin, the Junta's purchasing agent for armaments, paid for the items in cash.

George Cowley, the seaman who testified at Hart's arraignment, repeated his earlier claims that many boxes and packages were transferred from the lighter to the *Laurada*. He also said he saw Roloff and Nuñez on board. Nine days after leaving Barnegat, Cowley said, they sighted Navassa Island. He testified that the *Dauntless* came alongside and the cargo was transferred to the tug, which proceeded to Cuba.

On the third day, with Cowley still on the stand, Ker launched into an aggressive cross-examination. Ker questioned Cowley's motivation for testifying, first by asking him how much he was paid as a seaman. His response: $18 per month. "How much do you make as a witness?" The answer: $15 per day. "Who is paying you that amount of money?" The witness replied: "A man at the office of the Pinkerton Detective Agency." Trying to shake the witness's credibility, Ker asked Cowley if he had ever been arrested. Cowley responded that he had been arrested "four or five times," but not once for anything that affected his honesty.

A succession of other witnesses, mostly Jamaican-born seamen like Cowley, repeated similar experiences on the *Laurada*. A thread tying all the government witnesses together, Ker stressed, was the $15 per day stipend each received to tell identical stories, suggesting that the Spanish consul had bought and choreographed their testimony.

Ker called as his first witness James A. Carey, a police officer from Philadelphia's Third District, for his opinion on documents containing Cowley's police record. Judge Butler, however, threw out the records, saying they were not pertinent to the case. He then adjourned for the day.

In Friday's session, Ker continued his questioning of Cowley, who repeated his admission to prior arrests and his willingness to take money for testifying. Satisfied he had discredited the witness, Ker rested the defense's case. Beck presented closing arguments for the government, stating that Hart knew he was taking men and arms on the *Laurada* to aid the Cuban revolution. Ker's co-counsel, John F. Lewis, began the closing argument for the defense, but shortly after his opening comments, Judge Butler interrupted and adjourned the trial for the weekend. He directed all parties to be back in court Monday, Washington's Birthday.

On Monday morning, Hart strolled confidently into a courtroom packed with Cuban sympathizers hoping for an acquittal. They greeted the defendant warmly as he waved like the celebrity he had become. Two surprise visitors to the courtroom were Hart's wife, Kate, and their youngest daughter, Grace, who was six. The Harts were separated, but the presence of Kate and daughter was noted in press reports as a gesture of support for her husband.

Lewis resumed the defense's closing argument, presenting the rationale that had been effective in other courts: the shipping of men and arms, subject to confiscation by the Spanish blockade, did not constitute a military expedition. He argued that the *Laurada* did not carry an organized body of men, only a number of men to load and unload the cargo. No drilling was conducted on the *Laurada*, the men did not wear uniforms, they did not set a watch as a military unit would do, nor were arms distributed. He said that to consider the men on board a military expedition simply because weapons and officers were present would be a travesty of justice.

Lewis also attacked the credibility of the government witnesses, who were paid far more to testify than they would have earned in seamen's wages. None of the testimony, Lewis argued, proved that Hart hired the yawl boats, provisioned the steamer, bought the arms and ammunition, or hired the tug *Dolphin* to carry the cargo. Lewis wrapped up his argument by claiming that Hart was in the business of carrying freight for hire, and the *Laurada* was simply engaged in carrying munitions of war with men to land them, which was a perfectly legitimate enterprise.

Judge Butler took one hour charging the jury, first reviewing the law and explaining what constituted a military expedition under the statute. "Your first inquiry," he told the jurors, "will be: was the expedition which was taken on board the *Laurada*, off Barnegat, and carried to Navassa Island, in sight of Cuba, a military expedition?" Butler reviewed testimony that suggested General Roloff had given orders in the manner of a military organization, then he told the jury: "You must determine whether the men had combined and organized . . . in this country to go to Cuba as a body and fight, or were going as individuals subject to their own wills with intent to volunteer there. If you do not find that they had so combined and organized before leaving this country then they did not constitute a military organization and the defendant must be acquitted."

However, Butler told the jurors, if in their judgment the men did constitute a military organization, then they must determine whether Hart provided the means for their transportation. It was not necessary that he transported them, the judge said, but that he *provided the means* for their transportation, and made that provision in Pennsylvania with knowledge of the character of the expedition and its destination. The judge said the jurors must then determine if Hart made provision for the *Laurada* to transport the men. The *Laurada* was owned by the John D. Hart Company, of which he was president and manager, and it was "uncontradicted" that Hart gave several orders regarding her clearance, bringing supplies aboard and employing her crew.

"That he knew the *Laurada* was going to the point off Barnegat to take the men on board would seem to be clear, if the witnesses are to be believed, and you must determine that," Butler said, "because they testified that he procured the *Fox* and sent them on to a point where they met the *Laurada*. If the latter statement is true, the inference seems irresistible that he knew the *Laurada* was going there for the men."

If the jury believed that Hart was culpable up to that point, the judge said, then they must determine the final question: did Hart know the expedition was a military expedition when he provided the means for its transportation? To satisfy that, the judge said, the government pointed to what it called "suspicious circumstances" regarding the fitting out of the vessel and clearance from Philadelphia to the point off Barnegat. Again, he said the jurors must determine how damning were the circumstances as portrayed by the government.

"In conclusion," Butler said, "if the expedition was a military one, as charged, and the defendant here in Philadelphia provided the means for its transportation with knowledge that it was a military expedition, he is guilty. Otherwise, he is not. He is entitled to the benefit of any reasonable doubt that may exist on a careful and impartial examination of the evidence. If your minds are not fully convinced, he must be acquitted. On the other hand, if your minds are convinced, he must be convicted. No suggestions of prejudice against him or sympathy for him can be allowed to influence your verdict."

Butler's charge to the jury followed the definitions confirmed by the US Supreme Court in *Wiborg v. United States*, but went further. The *Wiborg* decision established that, to secure a conviction, it was not necessary to show that Hart had provided the means for carrying the expedition in question to Cuba. However, Butler said he was guilty in the present trial if he provided the means for any part of its journey with knowledge of its ultimate destination and its unlawful character. The construction made unlawful the expedient of using some point like Navassa Island as a destination for the original expedition and then transferring it to the *Dauntless* for delivery to Cuba.

The instructions seriously narrowed the jury's options as they filed out of the courtroom at 3:45 p.m. to deliberate John D. Hart's future.

Even in the crowded corridors of the Post Office Building, the women of the Society Hermanas de Martí were prominent. Resplendent in their long winter finery with elegant chapeaux in the style of the day, each carried a small Cuban flag. The women, who actively provided relief for the Cuban insurgents, consisted of the doyennes of Philadelphia's Cuban émigré community. Laura Guitéras, daughter of Dr. Juan Guitéras, was president of the society, and she was ably supported by Mrs. Emilio Nuñez, Mrs. Vincent Portuondo, her daughter America, and others.

They were understandably vocal in their support of Hart. The defendant represented a glowing new future for their native land if he and men like him were allowed to continue supplying necessary aid to their patriot warriors. A guilty verdict would mean these men and others might be reluctant to participate in further expeditions. Such a decision could discourage men who would be risking their vessels and possibly facing incarceration and heavy fines. Would a conviction deter men of equal capacity and daring from entering this perilous game?

Their fears and hopes hung in the air as they received word that the jurors were filing in and taking their seats. Spectators who could not crowd into Judge Butler's courtroom pushed toward the door, squeezing into any small opening hoping to hear the words of acquittal. Outside, men stood on the shoulders of other men to peek into the windows and catch a glimpse of an event that surely would dominate the next day's newspapers.

Court Clerk Craig waited until the jurors had taken their seats before he directed them to stand. After a short pause, he drew a deep breath and asked them the anticipated question: "Gentlemen of the jury, have you agreed upon your verdict?"

"We have," responded the foreman, handing over a white envelope as his eleven fellow jurors stood somberly beside him. Craig slowly opened the envelope and took out a folded paper.

"Gentlemen, listen to your verdict as the court has it recorded," Craig said, looking down closely at the opened jury form and the future it would determine. Ker, standing to Hart's left, reached out and gripped his client's arm above the elbow. The clerk hesitated momentarily, then looked up as all eyes watched him and all ears strained for his next word.

"Guilty in the manner and form indicted. So say you all."

The jurymen nodded their confirmation and resumed their seats as a great commotion overtook the courtroom. Cries of protest and shouts of "*Cuba Libre*" and "Death to Spain" rang out as Judge Butler gaveled for order. Hart winced at the verdict and lowered his head as Ker put his right hand on his client's shoulder and whispered in his ear. Ker clearly had not expected a guilty verdict and appeared to one observer as "grievously disappointed." Seated behind them, Kate Hart buried her head into her open hands and began sobbing, as daughter Laura, fifteen, attempted to comfort her. Little Grace sat in her chair looking at her mother and sister.

Deputy Marshal Solomon Foster took Hart by the arm and escorted him from the courtroom to the US marshal's office. They were followed by Kate Hart, her daughters, and a long line of supporters and sympathizers, some furious at the decision and others merely saddened by the perceived injustice.

Ker's associate Lewis made an application for a new trial and requested that his client be released on bail pending the argument on that motion. Lewis stated that Hart's oldest daughter, seventeen-year-old Ada, was lying dangerously ill with typhoid pneumonia at a hospital in Bethlehem, Pennsylvania, and her father's presence would be a great comfort. Lewis's application for bail also said that Hart needed time to settle his personal and business affairs. Immediate imprisonment would ensure his financial ruin.

Butler set Hart's bail at $7,000, pending the disposition of Lewis's motion for a new trial, which would be argued the following week. Ker had said little up until then, but upon hearing the amount of the bond, he stood up and angrily objected. Ker said Butler had released Captain Wiborg, "a stranger," on only $3,000 bond, and to set such an amount for Hart, a well-known businessman in the city, was beyond reason. Butler did not relent, and the amount stood. Unable to raise the money immediately, Hart was ordered to spend the night at Moyamensing Prison.

Chapter 21

"JUSTLY CONVICTED"

Fifteen years in the fruit trade had taught John D. Hart that prosperity and catastrophe walked hand in hand. He had made gambles that paid off, and he had made many more that did not. He had been committed to the fruit importing business, but large combinations such as the Boston Fruit Company were making it impossible for an independent importer to find even one green banana to bring into the country. The fleeting nature of trust was another lesson Hart had learned over the years. He had trusted crewmen who betrayed him and captains who abandoned him, and his own government was another matter altogether. He could not believe that the country he loved would throw him in prison like a common criminal for coming to the aid of another people fighting for the same freedom that Americans had won in revolution.

But Hart also had learned that when sailing into a storm, the captain does not cower only to be blown away. Masters of the sea lean into the gale and allow the wind to steady them until the tempest blows itself out. Hart considered himself the captain of his enterprise, and he even embraced the appellation "Captain Hart" bestowed on him by reporters and headline writers. Life is a test of will and endurance, he knew, and he would not weaken. He would lean into the wind like the captain he was until the gentle breezes of redemption and opportunity returned. After all, a man should be warmed by possibility, not chilled by regret.

In his current condition, Hart needed the emotional support that lawyers, journalists, or worshipful crowds in a courtroom could not provide. He needed the support of the one man whose trust in him had never faltered. They had disagreed in business matters, but that was a time when Hart was drawing all the knowledge that Alexander Beauregard Bulack could spare his friend. Whenever Hart was in trouble, he could rely on the sympathetic ear of his former partner in Baltimore. Hart would be in Baltimore anyway, to settle differences over a suit against the *Laurada* for unpaid repairs made to her machinery. Out on bail until his sentencing, Hart had a short time to tie up the loose ends of business while Ker worked on his appeal. Talking with Bulack would be a comfort.

They met at Bulack's Chesapeake House restaurant over oysters and Pikesville rye whiskey, and for a few hours Hart returned to his old self. No problems existed that could not be bluffed away or diminished by healthy swagger. He told Bulack the filibustering business could have been profitable, and he could count more than $150,000 that passed through his fingers the past two years. But legal fees, high wages to captains and crews, and bribes paid to port collectors in the United States and throughout the West Indies had drained it all to nothing.

"Aleck," Hart said, looking squarely at his friend over another drained glass. "I want you to write something for me. A telegram!" Bulack smiled and pulled out a pen, willing to comply but puzzled at the request.

"Honorable Grover Cleveland, President of the United States," Hart began. "I understand General Fitzhugh Lee has resigned. Am willing to accept position as Consul General of Cuba. Ready to leave at once."

Bulack smiled wanly, knowing that Cleveland's term would end in another week, and at last report Lee was still at his post in Havana. Bulack's thoughts returned to the palmiest days of Hart and Bulack, when the fruit trade was young and gunrunning was an exciting diversion that was considered a virtuous venture if you didn't get caught.

Hart was a dashing businessman whose major fault was the impetuous recklessness that often clouded his good judgment. Even now, with his insistence on sending a telegram to the president, Hart's naïveté clearly clouded the reality of his situation. But he was a friend, and Bulack would send the telegram.

Hart was excited about the possibility of a new trial and what direction he would take when he was free of such encumbrances. He even suggested that Bulack consider a new partnership, but neither man pressed the point. Hart acknowledged he was pinched financially, but he would be back, stronger and more successful than ever. Their meal ended, and the two men parted as the friends they were. Bulack wished his old partner smooth sailing as John D. Hart doffed his bowler and walked into the street, always looking ahead and never behind.

Five days after Grover Cleveland left office, without responding to Bulack's telegram, Hart was back in Judge Butler's court for sentencing. He again was accompanied by Kate and daughters Laura and Grace, appearing as a family supporting one another in the face of adversity.

At 11:00 a.m., Hart rose before Judge Butler, who soberly declared that the convicted man was sentenced to two years in prison and fined $500 plus the costs of the prosecution, which was estimated at just under $5,000. Kate Staylor Hart and her daughters broke down in tears, embracing each other in shock at the sentence. Hart looked at them without emotion, apparently resigned to his fate.

Butler refused to grant a new trial, saying the only debatable question was whether Hart had furnished the *Laurada* knowing at the time she was to carry a military expedition to Cuba to fight against the Spanish government.

"I am sorry to be obliged to sentence you," Butler told Hart. "I believe, however, that you have been justly convicted after a fair and full trial. The offense is a very grave one, involving the nation's honor and the nation's peace. You entered upon it with your eyes wide open as to the consequences. You did it for the unworthy purpose of personal gain. You took the risk for a price, and you must take the consequences."

As Hart was escorted out of the courtroom by a federal marshal, Kate rushed up and put her arms around him. The two held each other tightly until Marshal Reilly put a hand on Hart's shoulder and told him he had to go. Hart looked up, tears welling in his eyes for the first time.

Hart's conviction and sentencing further aroused a public incensed by growing charges of Spanish atrocities on the island. Valeriano Weyler's policy of herding civilians into concentration camps continued to generate rumors of famine, torture, and mass murder. Word of such mayhem only fueled constant pressure from war hawks such as Senator John Tyler Morgan of Alabama, who took the floor of the Senate to deplore the "saturnalia of blood and fire" that Spain had wrought on Cuban civilians.

The most recent outrage was the arrest on February 7 of Dr. Ricardo Ruiz, a Cuban-born, naturalized American citizen, at his home near Havana. A friend and mentor of Emilio Nuñez, Ruiz practiced dentistry in Philadelphia before returning to his home country in 1891 and establishing himself in a fashionable suburb of Havana. Ruiz was imprisoned, accused of having participated in the derailment, capture, and robbery of a passenger train. Ten days after his arrest, Ruiz was found dead in his six-by-eight-foot cell. The *Philadelphia Inquirer* coupled Ruiz's death and Hart's conviction to deplore the Spanish practice of arresting anyone who disagreed with Weyler's policies, while the US government persecuted those who opposed them.

"The Spanish officials on that island have long been a law unto themselves," the *Inquirer* said in an editorial. "They have paid little attention to treaty obligations. They have seized Americans and thrust them into miserable jails without right or reason . . . but we have been too busy protecting Spain to give heed to our own people. We can grab men like Captain Hart and convict them of sending expeditions to Cuba, and we can burn tons and tons of coal under the boilers of our revenue cutters for the purpose of policing our coast and chasing suspected filibusters.... Why this extreme carefulness of the sensitiveness of a little bankrupt nation with a trail of blood extending back through the centuries?"

Ruiz's death swept all other issues off the table in the Senate, and debate intensified on what to do about the worsening Cuban situation. Further rumors alleged violations against "women and little girls" and claimed that Spanish soldiers picked up infants by the feet and hacked them to pieces with machetes. None of this was confirmed, but the salacious reports helped color the issue at hand. Populist senator William V. Allen of Nebraska proposed that American warships be sent to Havana immediately to protect American citizens.

William McKinley took the oath of office on March 4, 1897, but his inaugural address said little to encourage the friends of Cuba. "It has been the policy of the United States since the foundation of the government to cultivate relations of peace and amity with all the nations of the world, and this accords with my conception of our duty now," said the new president. "We have cherished the policy of noninterference with affairs of foreign governments wisely inaugurated by Washington, keeping ourselves free from entanglement, either as allies or foes, content to leave undisturbed with them the settlement of their own domestic concerns. It will be our aim to pursue a firm and dignified foreign policy, which shall be just, impartial, ever watchful of our national honor, and always insisting upon the enforcement of the lawful rights of American citizens everywhere. Our diplomacy should seek nothing more and accept nothing less than is due us. We want no wars of conquest; we must avoid the temptation of territorial aggression. War should never be entered upon until every agency of peace has failed; peace is preferable to war in almost every contingency."

McKinley's lack of commitment was not surprising to Tomás Estrada Palma. He had been informed by a McKinley confidant that the president-elect would give the issue "the cold shoulder." Estrada Palma instructed Gonzalo de Quesada to approach an old ally, Ohio senator John Sherman, to urge McKinley to include sympathetic words for Cuba in his address. But even Sherman, who would become McKinley's secretary of state, could not persuade his new boss to show any departure from the previous administration's policies. At least not yet.

McKinley declared that his administration would follow Cleveland's policy discouraging American citizens from helping the insurgents. That politically correct statement survived only a few hours longer than McKinley's inaugural ball at the Pension Building in Washington. The next day, a rebellious federal judge in Florida created a firestorm when he released a suspected filibuster vessel from government control only days after the US Supreme Court had reversed the judge's similar action in an earlier case.

The *Dauntless* sat at Jacksonville fully loaded with arms and ammunition, but when its owner, William A. Bisbee, requested clearance to sail, the government filed a petition claiming the vessel should be seized and forfeited for filibuster activity. The case came before District Judge James W. Locke, whose earlier decision to release the *Three Friends* had been reversed by the US Supreme Court only four days earlier. The government cited the Supreme Court's ruling in its petition against the *Dauntless*.

But Locke said that what looks, smells, and feels like a filibuster vessel does not make it a filibuster vessel. The judge said the government's fears that the ship might be used to assemble an expedition was not sufficient reason to hold the *Dauntless*. "Apprehensions that the complainant may violate this law, or suspicions that he intends so to do, can furnish no basis for legal action," Locke declared.

The dockside dustup between federal officers and a federal judge had immediate repercussions in the new administration. McKinley called together the cabinet members most involved with the same issues that had bedeviled the Cleveland administration. Sitting at the head of a long table in a swivel armchair with ink, stationery, and books at hand, McKinley used the Cabinet Room as his private office to escape those who waited to see him. Beneath a portrait of Thomas Jefferson and in front of a crowded bookcase, the president sat in a long coat, high collar, and bow tie.

The room was heavy with cigar smoke from McKinley's favorite imported Garcías as he discussed the issue with Secretary of State Sherman, Secretary of the Treasury Lyman Gage, Secretary of the Navy John D. Long, and Attorney General Joseph McKenna. No declarations came out of that meeting nor when McKinley convened his full cabinet two days later, but conflicting interpretations by the lower courts and the Supreme Court's interest in at least two cases clearly influenced the new administration. Free from the encumbrances of precedents and prior commitments to the Spanish minister, McKinley's cabinet could look at the Cuban issue from a fresh perspective, one less inclined than the former administration's to please Spain. It would not come fast enough for the Junta, but it would produce gradual results such as the government's decision not to fight the release of the *Dauntless*.

It did not take long for Dupuy de Lôme to read between the lines. After only two days in office, McKinley's remarks on the rights of American citizens in Cuba prompted the minister to express regret for "the loss of my statesmanlike and scholarly friend Olney."

The *Laurada*, which had become a symbol of Cuban independence, had been kept from Cuba since August by legal and government interference. Several suits for alleged nonpayment of bills, probably fabricated or inspired by the Spanish consul, were settled by the Junta so Nuñez and O'Brien could put the steamship back to work. However, when she appeared ready to sail, her departure was delayed by government inspectors who claimed she was not seaworthy. To further hobble her return to the cause, the government limited her steam-pressure authorization to only seven knots. She was allowed to leave Baltimore only for the purpose of having her boilers rebuilt in Philadelphia.

Incredibly, authorities approached John D. Hart and demanded he sign a statement promising that the steamer would not go to Cuba. On his way to prison with little more to lose, Hart readily signed the waiver, and the *Laurada* prepared to leave Baltimore. However, she would not be heading to Philadelphia. She would be the lynchpin in yet another expedition, and what an expedition it would be!

With New York, Philadelphia, and Florida ports watched constantly, Nuñez and O'Brien composed an elaborate scheme that employed more feints and dodges than a Yale halfback. The mission would involve nine vessels, a shipment of 2,450 rifles, a twelve-pound Hotchkiss gun, 3,000 machetes, 3 tons of dynamite, more than 2,560,000 rounds of ammunition, 3,000 cannonballs, 15,000 cartridges, and 140 cases of medical supplies.

The most anticipated piece of equipment was a Sims-Dudley dynamite gun and 3,000 shells. Appearing like a telescope on wheels, the dynamite gun lofted its shells through the use of compressed air instead of exploding powder. It was comparatively light since the gun tube and projectile did not need to be fabricated from the considerable amounts of heavy steel required in weapons relying on the force of exploding powder. Pneumatic guns were quiet, emitting little more than a *thoomp* when fired, and with no muzzle blast or smoke they could be well hidden at night. The projectiles carried a payload of high explosive in the form of nitrocellulose, also known as "gun cotton" or nitrogelatin. Dynamite was seldom actually used, but the word had taken hold of the public imagination and struck fear in the hearts of the enemy, so the inaccurate sobriquet of "dynamite gun" fit the purpose.

Also included in the expedition was an automatic Colt machine gun, nicknamed the "mowing machine" because it spat out ten rounds per second. The machine gun was donated by a wealthy benefactor, William Astor Chanler, a friend of the Junta who once helped arrange a $30,000 donation from the Tammany Hall political machine. At thirty years of age, Chanler was typical of the wealthy New York adventurer. A Harvard Porcellian Club brother of Theodore Roosevelt and a frequent visitor to Olney's office, Chanler could afford to buy anything, including the thrill of danger. He had climbed Mount Kilimanjaro, been attacked by three thousand African warriors while exploring in Kenya, and later would head west and befriend outlaw Butch Cassidy. Chanler's continued benevolence to the Cuban cause would enable him to achieve one new adventure he had not yet experienced. He wanted to accompany an expedition to Cuba.

The *Laurada* could not carry a huge cargo in her diminished condition, but she could tow a schooner carrying arms and men and rendezvous with another vessel that would take the cargo on to Cuba. The other vessel would be the *Bermuda*, which Nuñez put in the charge of Ed Murphy. Assigning the young captain to another critical mission was a gamble, since he had not gone to sea since the *Commodore* was lost in a January storm in which only Murphy, a steward, and the author Stephen Crane survived. Crane turned the experience into a popular short story titled "The Open Boat," which was published later that year in *Scribner's Magazine*.

Since then, Murphy had been indicted for his role in the *Laurada*'s expedition for which Hart had been convicted. Murphy was currently out on bail, and the only sailing he had done lately was through an ocean of alcohol. However, O'Brien vouched for his former first mate, and Nuñez sent written instructions for Murphy to report for work. His assignment: take the *Bermuda*, with a cargo of coal and Nuñez and Chanler aboard, from New York to Watling's Island, in the Bahamas 250 miles north of Cuba's eastern tip.

Watling's Island was more than just another destination. Christopher Columbus's first landing in the New World was on the island, which he named San Salvador in honor of Christ the Savior. In the seventeenth century, San Salvador was settled by an English colonist, John Watling, for whom the island was renamed after Great Britain declared the Bahamas a crown colony in 1718. Its strategic significance, ironically, was to help control piracy.

Once the *Bermuda* arrived at Watling's Island, Murphy was to wait for the *Laurada* and take aboard a load of weapons and men for delivery to Cuba. Commanding the expedition would be the prominent fugitive General Carlos Roloff. The Junta's minister of war had spent weeks avoiding pursuit after jumping bail in the Baltimore case in which his codefendant, Dr. Joseph J. Luis, would be convicted.

Chapter 22

THE *LAURADA*'S LAST EXPEDITION

The *Laurada* under the command of Sam Hughes cleared from Baltimore on February 26, 1897, and sailed north past Philadelphia to a point below Sandy Hook on the New Jersey shore. Arms and ammunition were brought to New York from Bridgeport, Connecticut, on a commercial steamer, and after dark the cargo was transferred to the three-masted schooner *Donna T. Briggs*. Fifty Cubans were concealed in her hold, and as soon as the transfer was completed, a tug towed the schooner out to meet the *Laurada*.

Pinkerton detectives were watching O'Brien's house in Arlington, New Jersey, and he enlisted his son Fisher to give them the slip. Father and son left the house on February 27 with Fisher carrying a large suitcase. They boarded a ferry at Jersey City for the ride into Manhattan, followed by the detectives. But as the ferry pulled away, the spry O'Brien jumped off and quickly hopped on a ferry headed for Twenty-Third Street. The Pinkertons saw him, but they could not get off the ferry in time, so they focused on Fisher and the travel bag. They assumed O'Brien would not go out of the country without a change of clothes.

After arriving in Manhattan, O'Brien boarded the tug *Josephine B.* and returned to the New Jersey side to pick up a cargo of dynamite and bombs. About two dozen Cubans on board loaded the cargo, but when the tug started down the bay, O'Brien discovered they were being followed. Another tug, loaded with detectives, deputy marshals, customs officers, and Spanish agents, trailed at a distance. O'Brien ordered the *Josephine B.*'s captain to cruise around for a time and then speed for the Atlantic Basin in Brooklyn as if they were going to tie up for the night. Their pursuers followed, then sat out in the bay and watched the mouth of the basin.

The sleuths were unaware that O'Brien had two steam lighters at the basin under waiting orders and banked fires just for such emergencies. The cargo was shifted to the two lighters, and a tarpaulin framework was rigged up on the *Josephine B.* that gave the appearance she was still loaded. O'Brien and the Cubans boarded one of the lighters and waited. After an hour, the *Josephine B.* slipped out of the basin, with every feigned attempt at secrecy. When the tug's captain made certain he was again under anxious eyes, he started off at full speed and headed up the Hudson River with the authorities in hot pursuit.

O'Brien led the lighters out of the basin and down through the Narrows, arriving at Sandy Hook just in time to see the *Donna T. Briggs* tied up to the *Laurada* by a tow line. When the *Josephine B.* pulled alongside the *Laurada*, O'Brien shouted to Captain Hughes: "Throw me a line for my trunk!" O'Brien laughed heartily as the crewmen threw down a ship's rope and hauled up a little cigar box. With Fisher in charge of his father's suitcase, the cigar box filled with pipes and tobacco was the only dunnage O'Brien would carry on the expedition.

Roloff already was on board, along with a handful of experts at blowing things to smithereens. Augustin Agramonte, whose family had long been involved in efforts to break away from Spain, was in charge of a corps of dynamite experts. Emory Fenn, a young American electrical engineer, was in command of a torpedo corps. Other specialists in artillery coddled the boxes holding their large weapons like loving parents caressing their children.

As the men and arms were being transferred, a passing tug captain spotted them. He reported to the authorities that the *Laurada* was tied up alongside a three-masted schooner and a lighter just off Barnegat, New Jersey. The revenue cutter *Manhattan* was dispatched to intercept, but providence again was on the Cubans' side. On its way to Barnegat, the cutter ran into a blinding snowstorm and heavy seas. The delay was all the expedition needed to sneak away safely.

When word leaked, reporters hustled to Pier 11 in Philadelphia to ask John D. Hart about reports the *Laurada* was engaged in yet another illegal enterprise. With a straight face born of resentment at government interference, he positively denied the assertion.

"The steamer went from Baltimore to Hampton Roads the latter of last week," Hart said with the conviction of Sinon. "Her steam power had been cut down from eighty pounds to fifty pounds, and under this pressure she was given a permit to come to Philadelphia for repairs. I know she has left Hampton Roads, because I have received the pilot bill signed by the captain and dated Tuesday. When the *Laurada* arrives at the breakwater she will find orders awaiting to stop at Wilmington, where she will be overhauled by the Harlan & Hollingsworth Company."

The only truth in Hart's statement was that the ship needed repairs. Slowed by the steam-pressure limit, balky machinery, and a schooner in tow, the *Laurada* took a week lumbering toward Watling's Island. However, when she arrived, there was no sign of the *Bermuda*, Nuñez, or the wealthy Chanler. O'Brien discovered later that Captain Murphy was dead drunk when the orders arrived, and he tore them up by mistake.

While the *Laurada* sat waiting for a boat that had not yet left New York, interested observers had time to identify her and make their reports. Officers of the Buckman line steamer *Bowden* knew the *Laurada* well, and when the ship returned to Baltimore they reported that the *Laurada* was anchored at Watling's Island. However, when the *Inquirer* asked Hart about the reports, he amended his earlier statement to say the *Laurada* had no other mission save that of procuring a cargo of fruit to pay for his legal defense.

After waiting a week at Watling's Island, O'Brien gave up on Murphy and suggested they go ahead and make the landing with the *Laurada*. The cargo was transferred from the schooner to the *Laurada*; Hughes's wife, Margaret, who had been aboard the *Laurada* since the Mediterranean trip, was hustled off the boat and put aboard the *Briggs* for a safe return north; and the mission continued.

On Friday, March 18, the *Laurada* anchored at a point about sixty miles north of Cuba. As O'Brien had done before, he waited until the Spanish gunboat crews ran into the large ports on Saturday night for their off-duty frolic, which would last until Monday. With the blockade fleet concentrating more on Cuban rum than invaders, the chances of success multiplied.

The expedition would be landed about one hundred miles west of Cape Maysí at Banes Bay, an inland bay separated from the much larger Nipe Bay by a narrow peninsula. O'Brien knew that three or four Spanish warships would be anchored at Nipe Bay, but that was not the little captain's greatest concern. In order to get from the ocean into Banes Bay, the *Laurada* had to navigate a narrow and perilous channel three miles long in total darkness. Neither O'Brien nor Hughes had ever been through it, and it was too late to find a trusted local pilot for a large steamship. As the sun went down, the two captains shared the bridge on high alert, their only guide a Spanish chart they hoped was accurate. As a precaution, Fenn's experts were sent ashore to mine the mouth of the channel. Fenn's men connected two five-gallon demijohns of nitroglycerin by wires to discourage any curious Spanish gunboats, and a man was left behind to detonate it if necessary.

Unable to see even the bowsprit from the bridge, O'Brien and Hughes relied on dead reckoning to ease their ship slowly through the endless twists and turns. Occasionally, the bow and stem would scrape overhanging branches as they fishtailed around sharp corners. The captains at least were thankful the narrow channel was deep. They entered the bay at daylight, having taken ten hours to travel the three miles. The crew tied hawsers to strong trees on the port side next to an old wharf while O'Brien looked across the bay through his spyglass and saw himself being watched from a small fort that held a detachment of about one hundred Spanish troops. The *Laurada* was flying no flag, and the Spaniards were curious about the origin of this phantom vessel that suddenly appeared out of the morning mist like the ethereal *Flying Dutchman*. A dozen soldiers jumped into a longboat and rowed about halfway across the three-mile bay, but then stopped and rowed back.

Not until the men on board the *Laurada* began to go ashore with their various bundles of rifles and boxes of ammunition did the Spanish garrison realize the nature of commerce that was about to be transacted under their noses. They fired off their guns in a limited display of might, but the shells fell far short of their targets and harmlessly into the water. The soldiers could not summon their warships, because the only pass out of the bay was the channel that the *Laurada* occupied, so they returned to the fort.

A messenger was sent to General Calixto García, who was camped only a few miles away, and soon about three thousand scruffy men arrived in great cheer when they saw the massive cargo piled as high as a royal palm. Much laughter and slapping of backs ensued, and for a day and a night the rebels cheerfully carried the instruments of their survival back into the hills.

Across the bay, the Spaniards remained in the safety of their fort, unwilling to venture out into certain danger. García's men told Roloff that the Spaniards rarely left their fort and made very few attempts to interfere with them. Oriente Province was under such rebel control it was called "Free Cuba."

After the arms were delivered, Roloff and his party joined García's forces and bade the *Laurada* farewell. At first light Monday morning, O'Brien, Hughes, and the crew returned to the narrow channel, wondering how they ever got through it in the dark. At the mouth of the river, Fenn's man was still on duty, and O'Brien hoped he would not blow them up by mistake before they picked him up and fled for open water.

A week later, the *Laurada* crossed the Delaware breakwater, arriving in darkness to elude the revenue cutter *Hamilton*, which was patrolling in the area. The *Laurada* glided slowly up the Delaware River, making no signals but passing close enough to the reporting stations to be identified before arriving at the Harlan & Hollingsworth Shipbuilding Company in Wilmington for overhaul, as John D. Hart had declared.

The two captains left the vessel and headed to the depot, where Hughes boarded a train for Philadelphia and O'Brien one for New York. They fled just in time, for when dawn broke the *Laurada* was swarming with federal officers. US Marshal Hewson E. Lannan acted on a bill drawn up by the inspectors of steam boilers in Philadelphia that claimed the *Laurada* left Baltimore in February on an expired certificate. A few days later, US attorney Lewis Vandegrift unloaded another blunderbuss of charges, including a complaint demanding that the *Laurada* be condemned and forfeited. Vandegrift also prepared a complaint against Hughes, but when the wily captain arrived in Philadelphia, he fetched his wife, and they immediately embarked on that long-awaited trip to her native Ireland he had been promising.

O'Brien's reception at Junta headquarters at 56 New Street was that of a conquering hero. Not only had he delivered much-needed weapons into rebel hands, he learned the mission had the double benefit of antagonizing Captain General Weyler himself. The Spaniard was indignant that the *Laurada* could unload a cargo of war supplies in full view of an impotent Spanish garrison, with a large naval force only a few miles away. But the most gratifying part for O'Brien was that "the Butcher" took it personally. Weyler sent word through a reporter in Havana that one day soon O'Brien would hang from the flagpole at Cabañas, an old fortress in Havana where, frequently during the war, dissenters were lined up against a wall and shot.

O'Brien could not allow Weyler's threat to float unchallenged, so Captain Dynamite sent a message back through the same source: "To show my contempt for you and all who take orders from you, I will make a landing within plain sight of Havana on my next trip to Cuba. I may even land an expedition inside of the harbor and take you away a prisoner. If we should capture you, which is much more likely than you will ever capture me, I will have you chopped up into small pieces and fed to the fires of the *Dauntless*."

After Murphy's drunken episode had prevented the *Bermuda* from linking up with the *Laurada*, the remorseful captain was anxious to restore his dignity. Nuñez scolded him that his insobriety had imperiled a mission and could have cost the lives of men as well as an expensive cargo. He also embarrassed the Junta with such an important donor as Chanler, whose younger brother Winthrop, also a Harvard Porcellian Club member, had been brought into the department by Nuñez.

The chief of expeditions ordered Murphy to take the *Bermuda* to Fernandina and pick up a load of arms and men. It would be difficult, since the revenue cutter *Boutwell* and cruiser *Vesuvius* were closely watching the workboats that normally aided the expeditions, but José Alejandro Huau again came to the rescue. On April 6, Huau arranged with Broward to send the *Three Friends* out the St. Johns River as a decoy while the tug *Kate Spencer* crept into Cumberland Sound north of Fernandina, where she met three barges loaded with three rapid-fire guns and more than two hundred thousand rounds of ammunition. In the early morning she met the *Bermuda*, waiting ten miles off the coast.

After the cargo was transferred, the *Bermuda* proceeded to Cuba, where she landed near Mariel, about fifty miles west of Havana. However, treachery again was afoot. Spies had alerted the Spaniards, who allowed the cargo and men to be landed without interference. As the rebel party was making its way inland,

Spanish soldiers ambushed them and confiscated the entire cargo of weapons. Murphy knew nothing of this, for after the cargo and men were unloaded, he took the *Bermuda* to Port Antonio, Jamaica. Alert authorities promptly arrested their old friend while British marines went aboard the vessel and disabled her. And there she would sit. It would be the *Bermuda*'s final voyage as a filibuster vessel, although Murphy would sit in a Jamaica jail for skipping bail in connection with the *Laurada*'s expedition with the *Dauntless* the previous August.

Chapter 23

CAPTAIN DYNAMITE'S EXPEDITION TO HAVANA

The frequency of ongoing expeditions generated the expected responses from both Washington and Madrid. The legions of Secret Service men, Pinkerton detectives, Treasury agents, and Spanish spies appeared to increase their surveillance proportionately with each new voyage to Cuba.

Spanish agents were thickest in New York, Philadelphia, and Jacksonville, so Nuñez and O'Brien transferred their base of operations to Wilmington, North Carolina. From there, the next expedition would employ sufficient amounts of deception and legerdemain that would make previous efforts appear as simple as parlor tricks. The goal was to divert the attention of the authorities, agents, and spies in one direction so operations could proceed freely in another.

The first stage of the plan was to recover the *Dauntless* and use her as bait to attract the attention of the revenue cutters. The vessel was still free after its March 5, 1897, release by order of Judge Locke, and O'Brien took a train to Jacksonville to claim her. Walking along the wharf, O'Brien made certain all the loudmouths and eavesdroppers saw him, tipping his hat as he climbed aboard the vessel. Other suspicious persons soon came aboard, and the *Dauntless* pulled away from the wharf. When she passed over the St. John's bar, the US cruiser *Vesuvius*, its captain and crew no doubt giddy on rumor and high anticipation, stopped the *Dauntless* to search her. But instead of finding a battalion of Cuban militants on board, they found what resembled a Sunday afternoon picnic cruise.

Aboard was Dr. Joaquín Castillo Duany, second in command of the Junta, along with his wife and Alphonse Fritot and his fiancée. One can imagine linen napkins, fluted glasses, and toasts to the American sailors as the federal boat pulled away in disappointment. Captain Dynamite's decoy cruise fooled the feds and at least temporarily threw them off the trail. When the pleasure cruise ended, Fritot put O'Brien on a private train and sent him back to North Carolina to implement stage two of the plan.

Nuñez chartered an old schooner, the *John D. Long*, with the intention of loading her with arms and having her towed to Cuba by the oceangoing tug *Alexander Jones*. But O'Brien discovered that the *Long* was in such bad shape he decided to swap roles. He ordered the arms loaded on the *Jones* and a large coal supply put on the schooner. With her bunkers practically empty, and taking coal from the schooner, the *Jones* could carry the cargo without any trouble.

However, Fritot sent word that federal agents had learned about the change in operations and were heading to North Carolina to arrest O'Brien. Operations were moved again, this time to Florence, South Carolina, an inland town whose residents sympathized with the Cubans. After failing to uncover anything in two weeks of questioning at Wilmington, the detectives concluded they had been drawn by a false scent and left.

But all was not as it appeared. Fritot had arranged for two carloads of arms and ammunition shipped from New York with Jacksonville as its destination. Fritot knew every junction point in southern Georgia and northern Florida, and he selected one at which the cargo was unhitched and diverted to Wilmington. With virtually all the suspicious parties having departed, the two-car engine ran straight to the dock of the Wilmington & New Bern Railway south of town. The train arrived on the night of May 13 and stopped a few feet from where the *Alexander Jones* waited, Johnny O'Brien standing on its deck.

Transfer of the cargo began, but word came to O'Brien that customs officers were approaching the wharf, and the revenue cutter *Morrill* was docked nearby and getting up steam. Were these coincidences or were their best-laid plans breached by more treachery?

O'Brien ordered the loading stopped, and a small part of the cargo was locked and sealed in one of the railcars. O'Brien took the *Alexander Jones* slowly down the river, passing within sight of the *Morrill*, but the federal boat ignored the familiar tug, which anchored off the bar to wait for the schooner. The *Long* was pulled by a towboat but aroused no suspicions when she passed within hailing distance of the revenue cutter *Colfax*. The towboat cast her off beyond the bar, and O'Brien ordered a line passed to the *Long*. A crippled schooner being towed would not pique official interest, and the vessels headed south down the Florida coast.

The caravan reached Palm Beach and anchored at Damas Key on May 18. A fishing schooner came alongside the *Alexander Jones*, and O'Brien saw a familiar face. Emilio Nuñez accompanied sixty Cubans aboard the vessel, which had sat at anchor for two days before the *Dauntless* came into view. O'Brien, Nuñez, and twenty Cubans went aboard, taking coal from the towed schooner and loading half the cargo of arms.

The *Dauntless* headed through the Bahama Channel and landed in Cuba ten miles east of Nuevitas on the morning of May 21. O'Brien did not wait until dark to unload, fearing the intentions of a Spanish gunboat they had passed earlier in the channel. The next morning, as they were hurrying back to the schooner, they saw the same warship, at the westerly end of the Bahama Channel. She was eight miles away to port, maintaining a leisurely speed of four knots an hour. The *Dauntless* had two new engineers on board, and when they saw the gunboat they began piling on coal in a frantic effort to increase speed. That sent up clouds of thick, black smoke, which drew a sharp rebuke from O'Brien. The captain rang them down to half speed, which terrorized the engineers, but which appeared less menacing to the gunboat.

O'Brien was close enough to Havana that he was overcome by the irresistible urge to make good on his promise to Weyler. His destination, where he would land the balance of the cargo from the *Alexander Jones* and most of the Cubans, was just east of Havana Harbor and scarcely more than three miles from the captain general's palace. Spanish authorities were less concerned with a threat by sea than by land, where the rebels under Colonel Alejandro Rodríguez had surrounded Havana and were carrying the fight up to the gates of the city.

The *Dauntless* arrived off Havana on the evening of May 24 and laid astern a number of merchant steamships waiting to go into the harbor at daylight. When the moon went down, the *Dauntless* steamed slowly up the shore and landed her cargo and party by the illumination from the brilliant lighthouse at Morro Castle, about a mile away. The Morro light flashed on the sentries pacing the walls of nearby Cabañas Fortress, and decent gunnery could have blown the *Dauntless* to pieces. Fortunately, on this night everyone else seemed to be sound asleep.

Unloaded quickly were twenty-three men and most of the cargo, which included 190,000 shots, 450 rifles, machetes, and medicine, but greater care was taken in landing the two thousand pounds of dynamite. The explosives were packed in watertight fifty-pound boxes, little consolation as the surf battered the landing dories against the rocks every time they went ashore. Fearful that the shocks would explode the dynamite, O'Brien ordered the boxes dropped overboard in shallow water, to recover them before daylight after the tide had washed them up on the beach.

But the greatest explosion from the expedition was Weyler's reaction when he learned that Captain Dynamite had made good on his promise to land an expedition "within sight of Morro Castle." The captain general was livid and severely reprimanded his naval chiefs while threatening to court-martial his commanders at Morro, Cabañas, and the shore battery. When news of the episode reached the Spanish minister in Washington, he informed his influential friends in Madrid that the expedition had "made a monkey of Weyler." Dupuy de Lôme said Weyler was unfit to command in Cuba and should be recalled.

Efforts to recognize Cuban belligerency had fallen a few rungs on the ladder of legislative priorities after the presidential campaign the previous summer and fall. But after the McKinley administration took office, Senate hawks renewed the fight, thanks to Gonzalo de Quesada's lobbying efforts. Sympathizers from both parties were major targets, including Democrat firebrand Senator John Tyler Morgan of Alabama and GOP Senator Don Cameron of Pennsylvania. Such efforts had been effective a year earlier when John Sherman, now McKinley's secretary of state, read Estrada Palma's declarations of Spanish atrocities on the Senate floor.

The Senate Foreign Relations Committee appeared favorable to more radical measures after a subcommittee report declared that US citizens on the island were among those driven from their farms and into the towns at Weyler's orders. The committee urged instant action by the executive branch to protect Americans and to aid the rebels. On May 13, McKinley responded by sending Judge William T. Calhoun, an old friend and former congressman from Danville, Illinois, to Cuba to observe conditions in the country and report back.

Two nights later, an enthusiastic audience packed the Columbia Theatre in Washington for a rally to benefit the Cuban cause. General William Henry Browne, president of the Cuban League, called the meeting to order and read a statement from Senator William Chandler (R-NH) that vowed "Congress and the President will soon formally recognize a state of war and Cuban belligerency." This step, said the statement, "cannot fail to insure Cuban independence." Moreover, he urged: "We ought to send a fleet to enter the harbors and an army to land upon the soil of Cuba, first to protect the lives and property of American citizens, and secondly, to stop the atrocious and uncivilized methods of warfare adopted by the Spanish generals."

In the afterglow of the widely reported rally, newly seated Senator William Mason (R-IL) urged the recognition of belligerent rights. The junior senator said recognition would fulfill both Republican party pledges and the broader obligations of "international justice and humanity." At issue was a long-debated resolution by Senator Morgan that declared a state of war existed and recognized both sides as belligerents. The resolution had been kept alive by Morgan, who said the only way to resolve the crisis would be to send a ship of war to Havana.

Opposing the resolution was a bloc led by Senator George F. Hoar of Massachusetts, who said the passage of the Morgan resolution would injure, rather than aid, the cause of the rebels. Hoar's adherents were in sympathy with Cuba but were divided on whether Congress or the executive branch had the exclusive right and responsibility to declare belligerency.

The Senate passed the Morgan resolution on May 20 by a 41 to 14 vote, which the *New York World* said was "mainly significant as a reflection of American sentiment." The *New York Sun* believed that the vote indicated the "almost universal desire of the American people to stop the hellish atrocities." William Randolph Hearst's *Journal* criticized the fourteen senators who voted against the resolution and predicted eventual Cuban independence.

It did not come to a vote, but only because of some political thimblerig by powerful Speaker Thomas B. Reed of Maine. The Republican-dominated House was in a bind. If its members did not show support for the Cuban insurgents, the elected officials defied the overwhelming sentiment of the American public. However, if both houses of Congress passed the resolution and sent it to the president, they would be saying that authority for making such a declaration rested with Congress and not the Executive. Such action would embarrass the new Republican president, who had let it be known he was taking steps that would result in the independence of Cuba. Speaker Reed agreed to place the resolution in a dark corner of his desk while the president worked on his plan.

John D. Hart was following the congressional debates closely. He hoped that a bold move, such as a declaration recognizing the belligerency of Cuba's revolutionary government, would result in a presidential pardon of his impending prison sentence. With such a declaration tied up in politics, Hart jumped at the news that the House resolution also included a $50,000 appropriation for the "Relief of American Citizens" in Cuba.

Hart sent a telegram to Senator Gray, asking him to inform McKinley that he would donate the steamship *Laurada* to carry supplies to the suffering American citizens. McKinley never replied to Hart's spontaneous offer, which W. W. Ker attempted to explain, despite a suggestion of impatience with his loose cannon of a client.

"Captain Hart did not consult me about the matter, and there is no reason why he should," Ker diplomatically told the *Inquirer*. "He attends to such matters himself. His heart is wrapped up in the Cuban cause, and anything he could do to help it he would do.... If the government will accept his offer of the *Laurada*, I have no doubt that he will be willing to go on her himself."

Hart came up with another impulsive idea that landed him in trouble when he determined that the warm Caribbean breezes would be a powerful curative for daughter Ada, seventeen, who had battled illness for several months. She was a seasoned traveler, having taken a voyage to the West Indies on her father's fruiter *Braganza* in 1894 and another on the *Culmore* to Liverpool in 1895. Hart made arrangements for the two of them to take one of his charters, the *Ethelred*, on a two-week cruise to Port Antonio before he began his prison sentence. Spanish agents learned of the plan and hastily telegraphed Havana that Hart, the infamous enemy of Spain, was traveling on the *Ethelred* and must be captured.

When Hart and his daughter were about to step on the gangplank, he was immediately arrested by federal marshals, who were guarding against a flight risk. Hart entrusted Ada into the care of Captain Israel and the first mate, and sent them on, believing that his daughter's health was more important than his presence with her. The *Ethelred*'s cruise to Port Antonio took her around the eastern tip of Cuba, but when the vessel passed Cape Maysí at night a gunboat with no lights appeared and began following the fruiter. After an hour of quiet tailing, the gunboat turned on its searchlight and opened fire. Captain Israel put on all steam and outran his pursuer, making it safely to Jamaica. But he had not escaped the threat.

On the return trip, the *Ethelred* rounded the same cape at almost the same spot when another vessel appeared and gave chase. That boat was larger than the first, and its black hull made it appear even more menacing. For five hours, neither vessel could gain on the other, as frequent plumes of spray erupted each time the Spaniard missed a shot. It appeared the gunboat would chase the *Ethelred* all the way to the Delaware capes, but when another steamship appeared, the cruiser peeled off and chased its new target.

Although Hart was in custody, the system that he, Nuñez, and O'Brien had devised to keep expeditions moving continued apace. The first step was the feint, or rumor of an expedition intended to lead the bloodhounds off the trail. In mid-May an unnamed Junta source informed a friendly reporter that the friends of Cuba would soon hear good news from the island. The reporter asked Bill Ker if he knew whether any expeditions were being planned, but the attorney coyly replied: "I have nothing to say. My instructions now are not to talk, and as a good soldier ought to do, I obey orders." Ker's comment only enhanced the rumor that another big expedition was being sent out from Philadelphia, home port of the notorious *Laurada* and *Bermuda*.

Meanwhile, expedition planners were marshaling one thousand miles south. The well-publicized arrival in Tampa of José Alejandro Huau and William A. Bisbee, owner of the *Dauntless*, shifted attention of the next expedition to Florida's west coast.

Less transparent was the fact that heading in the opposite direction was Huau's nephew Alphonse Fritot aboard a train carrying Cuban Colonel Méndez, thirty compañeros, and two carloads of arms and ammunition. Their destination was Fort Lauderdale, an old trading station twenty-five miles north of Miami. After the train arrived, the cargo and men were placed aboard the *Biscayne*, a coastal stern-wheeler, which steamed to New River Inlet, where it would rendezvous with the *Dauntless*.

Captain Dynamite Johnny O'Brien had taken command of the *Dauntless* in Jacksonville for his first expedition since his successful attack on Weyler's nerves and career track in Havana. Also on board the ocean tug were Nuñez and his aide, José Eliseo Cartaya. The *Dauntless* had not taken on stores, which was the usual confirmation that a vessel would be away for a time, so authorities did not follow her when she left Jacksonville on Thursday night, May 27.

The *Dauntless* arrived off New River on Saturday morning in a relentless southeaster and found the *Biscayne* hunkered down in the inlet. With her shallow draft, the heavily laden vessel dared not leave the inlet in the heavy sea, and the *Dauntless* drew too much water to go into the inlet. The vessels remained in position for two days until the weather eased.

But happenstance, coincidence, and old-fashioned bad luck conspired to sabotage the mission. The *Biscayne* had been spotted by several men innocently vacationing on a sloop lying in the inlet. Those on the stern-wheeler did not realize that one of the vacationers was a special customs inspector from Miami named B. E. Hambleton, who had been chasing filibusters for months. The suspicious Hambleton recognized his good fortune and instructed his friends to remain in the cabin out of sight to await further developments.

On Monday, the *Biscayne* ventured out and sailed close to the mysterious sloop, but Fritot saw no sign of life on board. The stern-wheeler tied up to the *Dauntless*, and coal and provisions were being transferred when a rowboat put out from the sloop and headed for them. Hambleton was seated in the bow with a double-barreled shotgun across his knees, his two friends at the oars. O'Brien was in his room abaft the wheelhouse trying to get some overdue sleep when he heard Fritot shout: "Don't let them come aboard."

Glancing out the window, O'Brien saw the mate trying to shove the rowboat away with a boat hook, but Hambleton stood and raised the shotgun. He climbed over the rail and, pointing his weapon at the men aboard, announced: "In the name of the law I command you to stop putting those arms on this vessel. You are all under arrest." Fritot stepped up behind Hambleton and stuck a revolver in his back. "Do not pay any attention to this person," Fritot instructed the men in Spanish. "He is not going to shoot anyone. Go ahead and load the ship." Trusting Fritot, the men turned back to the cargo without a second glance at the shotgun.

"Where is the captain?" Hambleton angrily inquired, lowering the weapon.

"On the bridge," Fritot replied curtly.

Hambleton started up the gangway leading to the pilot house, but O'Brien raised a big revolver of his own and pointed it between the eyes of the intruder.

"Who the devil are you?" O'Brien demanded, as Hambleton announced his name and rank. "Well, no matter who you are, don't point that gun at anyone on this ship, or you will be shot before you can fire it."

Tom Davis and Charlie Silva, two trusted members of O'Brien's crew, slipped up behind Hambleton and threw him onto the deck. Another crew member grabbed the shotgun and tossed it overboard, while half a dozen men hustled him into his rowboat. Hambleton's intimidated companions rowed back to their sloop and sailed off up New River.

About half the arms and ammunition were on board when Cartaya reported the smoke of a ship coming up from the south. O'Brien was not concerned, suspecting it was the revenue cutter *Winona* coming up from Key West on a scouting trip. The *Winona* could do no more than seven or eight knots an hour, which was only two-thirds the speed of the *Dauntless*. O'Brien thought they had ample time to take on the rest of the cargo.

However, the unknown vessel was coming up much faster than the *Winona* could have. O'Brien stopped the transfer, cut loose from the *Biscayne*, and instructed Silva to take her to Bahia Honda Key and wait for them to return. The last few bundles of rifles and boxes of cartridges were thrown on the deck, and the *Dauntless* headed southeast.

O'Brien soon learned that his pursuer was the cruiser *Marblehead*, one of the fastest ships in her class. Smoke was coming from only one of her two stacks, which meant she had steam up in only two of her four boilers. O'Brien hoped the other boilers were out of commission, because at half-power, the US vessel could not overtake the gunrunner. But the Bahama Bank was seventy-five miles away, and the *Dauntless*'s only chance of escape was to get there first. The shallow sea beyond the bank consisted of uncharted channels known only to the cagiest pilots, and the cruiser would not dare enter such precarious waters.

For an hour it was a match race, with the *Marblehead* eight miles astern and the tug's engine ratcheted up to the last notch. In the meantime, Nuñez was supervising frantic efforts to stow the cargo into the *Dauntless*'s numerous hiding places. A concealed run under the floor and an empty water tank were being stuffed with boxes of munitions and bags of rifles, while other men were tossing boxes and coal-sacks over the side to make it appear they were throwing the incriminating cargo overboard.

On the cruiser, Captain Horace Elmer was toying with the *Dauntless*, but when he fired up his other boilers, the *Marblehead* rapidly closed the gap. She drew to within two miles, then fired a couple of blank cartridges, which O'Brien ignored. But when a solid shot whistled over the Cubans' heads and struck the water square in the tug's path, Nuñez ordered O'Brien to stop, not wanting to take chances with his men.

The *Marblehead* pulled close, and a lieutenant was dispatched in a rowboat to go aboard. The deck was littered with rifle bags and boxes labeled ".43 Caliber," betraying their contents, but no armaments were to be seen. The gruff officer demanded to see the captain, and O'Brien sent out pilot Jim Floyd to answer his questions. Floyd told the lieutenant he was in search of a wreck on the westerly side of the Bahama Bank. The wreck was a big one, which accounted for the number of men on board.

"What are these?" the officer asked, pointing to an empty cartridge box. "Sardines, I suppose?"

"Yes, suh!" agreed the courtly Floyd. "With such a large crew you ought to carry plenty of food."

The lieutenant looked around a few more minutes, then commanded Floyd to accompany him back to the *Marblehead* so Captain Elmer could question the nervous pilot.

"Isn't Captain O'Brien with you?" Elmer asked after Floyd was ushered aboard.

"I don't know. There's a little gray-haired chap aboard who they call Johnny. Perhaps he is Captain O'Brien."

"I guess he is," responded the bemused Elmer.

The *Dauntless* was ordered to follow the *Marblehead* to Key West, where she was turned over to the collector of customs. Two inspectors were sent aboard to search the vessel, but their inspection revealed neither arms nor anything else that suggested a military expedition. Armed guards were sent on board, and the ship was held incommunicado while Washington was contacted. Orders were telegraphed twenty-four hours later to proceed with charges, probably to appease the Spanish minister. O'Brien, Nuñez, Colonel Méndez, Cartaya, and Floyd were hauled before US Commissioner Julius Otto.

Cartaya had many friends in Key West from old relationships, including Otto. He asked quietly how much the bail would be, and Otto replied, "Bail be damned, I am going to turn you all loose as soon as I get a chance." On June 9, Otto fulfilled his pledge and dismissed the case, saying no evidence was given that proved the *Dauntless* or her crew constituted a military expedition against the King of Spain.

The vessel was released, and O'Brien took her back to Bahia Honda to collect the arms they had left behind on the *Biscayne*. Early on the morning of June 18 the *Dauntless* was forty-five miles north-northeast of Key Piedras Light off Cardenas Harbor and pushing hard to make up for lost time. Suddenly, the crown sheet of her boiler blew up in a thunderous explosion. The ship shuddered as if caught in an earthquake, and the men below emerged covered with mud and grease, but nobody was seriously injured. Captain Dynamite, thanking Neptune they were not carrying dynamite, told Nuñez that this expedition would have to wait for a luckier day.

He ordered sail onto the tug and headed due north, arriving two days later at Alligator Reef Light on the Florida coast. The revenue cutter *McLane* performed a useful service when she picked up the crippled vessel and towed her to Jacksonville so the boiler could be repaired. The *Dauntless* went into dry dock, her guilt hidden away in every unseen nook and crawlspace available.

Chapter 24

BROKE AND HEADED FOR PRISON

John D. Hart knew that a prison term was a possibility, but he did not expect an unforeseen event to accelerate the penalty. The man who had paid the bulk of Hart's $7,000 bond that had kept him free decided he wanted his money back. Robert J. Barr, a politician whom Ker had enlisted, held the title piece of paper that made him responsible for the loss of the entire amount should Hart disappear. Hart's intended voyage to Jamaica with his daughter raised suspicions in Barr's mind that his goodwill gesture might be in jeopardy. Hart came smiling into the US Court of Appeals hearing, but it was less the confident smirk of the self-assured than the weak, forced smile of the defeated. He glanced at Barr but said nothing.

Appeals Judge George M. Dallas said that Barr should have understood his responsibility when he put up the money, but he granted the surrender. Fortunately, Jeremiah L. Eldridge, an old river captain and pilot, was accepted along with S. Edgar Trout and John Baizley as sureties to allow Hart to remain free.

However, the bond was merely a holding action in a war that was approaching surrender. From the start of his involvement with the Cubans, Hart believed the pay he received for the expeditions would support his failing fruit importing business. Reality changed that perception as legal costs mounted and the seizure of his vessels sharply reduced his ability to import fruit for sale. Now, with the bulk of expeditions departing from Florida, John D. Hart was broke and likely headed for prison.

"The loss to the Cuban Junta of Captain Hart's services has been a serious one," the *Inquirer* reported. "All the movements connected with the sending of arms and ammunition to the insurgents [are] now confined to Southern ports."

The latest example of Hart's decline came a few days later when District Attorney Lewis Vandegrift in Wilmington, Delaware, asked for an order that would put the *Laurada* up for public sale. Hart was the acknowledged owner of the vessel, yet when the public sale was ordered, US authorities could not find documentation verifying his ownership. Since the vessel went into dry dock at the Harlan & Hollingsworth shipbuilding firm in late March, suits totaling $10,000 had accrued claiming unpaid bills for supplies, coal, piloting, and wages.

Forfeiture proceedings on the *Laurada* began on July 6, 1897, but it was clear that the "Lucky *Laurada*," which was never caught by federal agents or Spanish gunboats, which never failed to deliver a cargo of men and armaments for freedom's fight, which was named for Hart's two older daughters, would never again be of service to the Cuban cause. Her dignified stacks, which once spewed the black smoke of resistance, now were nests for vultures of unpaid bills and neglect.

With the *Bermuda* seized at Port Antonio, the *Three Friends* still in federal custody, and the *Dauntless* incapacitated, Emilio Nuñez was forced to seek other vessels to transport essential armaments and supplies to the fighting. The Cubans also were devoid of two experienced captains, with Sam Hughes still in Ireland with his wife and Ed Murphy in a Jamaican jail for skipping bail. The summer swoon prompted the *Inquirer* to acknowledge that after Hart's conviction, members of the Junta went more than a month without meeting.

The Junta's relative inactivity was more likely because the Cubans were waiting for the new US administration to formulate and announce its policy for the island. McKinley was sympathetic to the Cuban cause and willing to pressure Spain to end the war and the horrors of reconcentration. That attitude reasonably could have been influenced by the relationships his confidants had with members of the Junta. Sherman was a known ally, who, after he was named secretary of state, sent for Gonzalo de Quesada to have a long and careful discussion of the Cuban problem.

McKinley also was impressed by the eloquence and bearing of Quesada. The *Inquirer* went so far as to call Quesada "the brilliant young charge d'affaires, whose flashing eyes attracted long ago the attention of Major McKinley." Quesada had worked hard to build his network, which included Theodore Roosevelt and Senator Henry Cabot Lodge. But perhaps Quesada's most effective confidant within the administration was First Assistant Secretary of State William R. Day. Quesada and Day were in the same social club, and Day introduced Quesada to other friends in government positions. The former judge from Canton, Ohio, would see his influence grow as Sherman's health declined.

Horatio Rubens also maintained ties with another strong McKinley ally, New York attorney Elihu Root, Rubens's boss when corporate counsel for the Sugar Trust. Root was close to the president and would later become his secretary of war.

Relationships alone did not influence the developing US policy over Cuba. The accommodating nonintervention policy of the Cleveland administration was giving way to a more aggressive stance influenced by American shipping and business interests. However, "aggressive" did not mean a demand for independence. More than three hundred US businesses that held interests in Cuba signed a joint statement urging McKinley to end the war, although that did not include independence for what they considered an immature, unstable population.

That view was consistent with the report McKinley received from Judge William T. Calhoun, whom the president had sent to Cuba in May. While Calhoun reported that sufficient justification for the revolution existed, he also wrote that independence threatened to bring class and racial warfare in its wake. That was intolerable to the administration, and to the business interests who wanted to rebuild and expand their commercial relations on the island. Calhoun's report did support the Junta's contention that, with proper military supplies, the rebels would prevail quickly.

Following the receipt of Calhoun's report, the administration began to dictate its solution to Spain. The new policy was evident in the first official note on Cuba that Secretary Sherman sent to Madrid, which accused Spain of the "cruel employment of fire and famine to accomplish by uncertain indirection what the military seems powerless to directly accomplish." Sherman's message charged that Spain was responsible for eventual presidential action by "[t]he inclusion of a thousand or more of our own citizens among the victims of this policy, the wanton destruction of the legitimate investments of Americans to the amount of millions of dollars, and the stoppage of avenues of normal trade. . . . [A]ll these give the President the right of specific remonstrance."

But it was in the instructions to the new minister to Spain, General Stewart L. Woodford, that the administration's new approach to the Cuban question was most clearly evidenced. The former Union general and New York lawyer and politician received a lengthy note from Sherman outlining the position of the new administration, which he was to communicate to the Spanish government. The letter strongly required the end of hostilities and some degree of autonomy to the island while canceling the "measures of unparalleled severity." Otherwise, the United States reserved the right to intervene.

On August 4, Carlos O'Donnell, the Duke of Tetuán and Spain's minister of state, sent a response to Sherman labeling the American position as "exorbitant" and "inaccurate." He said that the "reconcentration" method employed by Weyler was no different from the "scorched earth" policy applied by the secretary's own brother, General William T. Sherman, in his invasion of the South during the American Civil War. O'Donnell said the widespread destruction throughout the island was less the fault of Spain than that of the insurgents. He also stressed that the "reasonable" way of doing things would be for the government in Washington to oppose, "with efficient energy . . . the constant help received by the insurgents from American citizens . . . without whom the insurrection would be totally extinguished."

O'Donnell did not know at the time, but the Cuban problem would not be his concern much longer. Four days after his statement, his boss, Prime Minister Antonio Cánovas del Castillo, was assassinated by an anarchist, and a new government soon would be formed.

Emilio Nuñez was scrambling to find new vessels to keep arms and ammunition flowing to Cuba, even those considered less than traditional. Publisher William Randolph Hearst sent word to Estrada Palma that he would be willing to lease or purchase a vessel he had located in Baltimore that the Cubans could use on their next expedition. Although Hearst likely would attach enough strings to wrap the gift several times, Estrada Palma agreed to send a man to investigate.

Nuñez arrived in Baltimore and was directed to the Columbian Iron Works and Dry Dock at the foot of Martin Street in Locust Point, where he met Simon Lake, a machinist and inventor. Lake escorted Nuñez to the dock, but when they arrived at water's edge, no boat was in sight. Nuñez looked quizzically at Lake, who laughed and said: "Oh, it is there. You merely cannot see it." Suddenly, Nuñez noticed a disturbance a few yards from the dock. Breaking the surface was a cigar-shaped shadow that Nuñez recognized as a submarine.

Lake called his vessel the *Argonaut*. The steel structure measured thirty-nine feet in length and nine feet in width, and it was propelled by a gasoline engine on the surface and electric storage batteries under the water. It had a powerful propeller in the rear, and when it reached the seafloor, it could travel on three wheels. Lake said it could remain submerged for forty hours and travel at a speed of eight knots.

With full black beard and derby, Simon Lake could have walked out of any office on Charles Street, but he was one of a handful of inventors who were competing to obtain the navy's first submarine contract. Lake had been working on designs for the past decade, his inspiration being the *Nautilus*, the futuristic diving vessel in Jules Verne's *Twenty Thousand Leagues under the Sea*, published in 1870. The *Argonaut* was built by William T. Malster, owner of the Columbian Iron Works shipyards. Among the vessels built at the shipyards was the US Navy cruiser *Montgomery*, which was launched in 1891 and within the year would be sent to Cuba. Malster was a nautical engineer and a partner in Lake's enterprise, and in fall 1897 would be elected mayor of Baltimore.

Nuñez examined the submarine and went aboard for a short cruise, but the director of expeditions was not comfortable in the confining atmosphere. He quickly saw the disadvantages of cramped living conditions and a limited ability to carry weapons. Nuñez also was concerned that the vessel appeared sluggish rising to the surface. "Obviously, this invention is still in diapers and is not advisable for Cuba," he wrote to Estrada Palma, who declined Hearst's offer.

Nuñez traveled to Key West to see for himself the damage to the *Dauntless*, when he learned of a possible replacement up the west coast of Florida in Pensacola. During the first week of July, Nuñez chartered the pilot boat *Somers N. Smith*, which would become a worthy addition to the freedom fleet. Joining with the schooner *Donna T. Briggs* from New York, the *Somers N. Smith* would make three landings of men and cargo in a single voyage between September 5 and September 15. Captain Dynamite Johnny O'Brien, José Eliseo Cartaya, and pilot Charlie Silva were in charge of the expedition, which included the usual complement of arms, ammunition, and medical supplies, as well as a half-dozen Cuban officers and forty volunteers.

Word of the *Somers N. Smith* expedition prompted great indignation at the Spanish legation in Washington. Dupuy de Lôme sent a scathing message to Sherman, alleging repeated American failure to stop the filibusters. The minister cited thirteen separate responses from Sherman's office acknowledging tips and rumors of looming expeditions that Dupuy de Lôme had forwarded between July 24 and September 10. The bulk of his complaint chronicled the three-landing voyage executed by the *Somers N. Smith* and *Donna T. Briggs* combination.

"I need not attempt to impress upon your Excellency the gravity of all this," Dupuy de Lôme wrote. "Not only are the so-called neutrality laws a dead letter, since the men engaged in these expeditions have been encamped and drilled . . . and have sailed to the knowledge of everyone how they were going and where they were going, but the sanitary laws so severely enforced elsewhere are suspended in order not to disturb the movements of such notorious transgressors of the law as Nuñez, O'Brien, and Silva, without the authorities apparently having arrived at the knowledge of what is known to all."

Woodford responded by assuring Madrid that McKinley would try and persuade the insurgents to accept autonomy while doing everything in his power to "put an end to agitation and to prevent filibustering." Spain's new minister of foreign affairs, Pío Gullón e Iglesias, said he would submit the information to the cabinet of new prime minister Práxedes Mateo Sagasta along with a desire to end hostilities before January. Gullón did not hesitate to indict the filibustering activity, saying pacification of the island "would have been more rapid if the rebels had not had the succor of filibusters, who under the shelter of the American flag, have contributed to maintain this state of affairs."

On October 22, the president and his cabinet considered Spain's latest protest and agreed to continue patrols of the Florida coast with the navy gunboat *Annapolis*, the cruiser *Montgomery*, and the battleship *Maine*. However, the administration's announcement included a bristling protest of Spain's complaints. Secretary of the Navy John D. Long issued an official statement in which he declared: "Everything possible has been done by this government to discharge the obligations imposed upon it by the neutrality laws. The Navy has maintained a cordon of ships along the coast, especially in Southern waters, where filibusters have shown the greatest activity. The Treasury Department has kept a fleet of revenue cutters on patrol duty."

McKinley attempted to placate Dupuy de Lôme in a private meeting, after which the minister reassured his government of McKinley's opposition to the expeditions. In a cable to Gullón, Dupuy de Lôme said the president "expressed confidence that measures taken by the Spanish government would continue to produce results. He insists that he is opposed to all acts of filibustering, saying that if he had proof of any faults committed by federal employees they would be chastised immediately."

While Dupuy de Lôme was protesting the apparent successes of the filibuster expeditions in Washington, another critical voice from the heart of Cuba was complaining about the Junta's expeditionary failures. The criticism was taken seriously because it came from one who knew the principals well, had himself fought the Spanish on the island, and had experienced firsthand expeditions that had both failed and succeeded.

General Enrique Collazo, a trusted aide of supreme general Gómez, was delivered to Cuba aboard the *Three Friends* on March 18, 1896. But he also was present at Fernandina when the expeditions of the *Amadis*, *Lagonda*, and *Baracoa* were seized by federal officers, an effort Collazo termed "a complete and terrible failure." Collazo later feuded with Estrada Palma after an expedition he commanded aboard the *Lark* was captured.

Collazo found his opportunity on October 10, 1897, when leaders of the revolutionary government convened the prearranged Constituent Assembly at La Yaya in Camagüey Province. The intention of the assembly was to draft a new constitution with definite duties and rights in anticipation of independence. The representatives, many of whom, like Collazo, were officers elected by the various military units, were expected to provide an interim governance and structure of the republic until a definitive constituent assembly could be convened.

However, Collazo saw it as an opportunity to vent old frustrations against Estrada Palma and the party's management of expeditions. He interrupted the assembly's primary work of creating a blueprint for a new government by presenting a report charging that the expedition efforts had been largely bungled.

In the diplomatic manner of unctuous praise followed by scathing criticism, Collazo's report acknowledged that efforts by the New York office had resulted in twenty-four successful expeditions, which he termed as "indisputable proof of the patriotic effort made by our delegation in the United States." But he attached a table to the report that purported to show many more expeditions that failed and others that landed only a portion of the cargo purchased. The report listed specific offenses that Collazo alleged cost the movement time, money, and men.

"It should be necessary to clarify the reasons for these failures," Collazo demanded, along with a full accounting of the original cargoes, their destinations, and what was left on board. He laid blame clearly at the feet of Estrada Palma and Nuñez, both of whom Collazo claimed had failed in "diplomatic and expeditions management."

Collazo's dissent was referred to a committee, which reported its findings at the assembly's October 22 session. Colonel Carlos Manuel de Céspedes, who had come to Cuba on the *Laurada* two years earlier, read the majority opinion of the committee members. Their conclusions were not what Collazo expected. The committee not only declined to censure Estrada Palma or the party's efforts but expressed praise and appreciation for the delegate, his staff, and their efforts to support the revolution. Singled out for recognition were Estrada Palma's attempts to create a subscription of Cuban bonds to fund the revolution, Quesada's lobbying efforts with sympathetic members of the US Congress, and Rubens's legal expertise.

Other members of the assembly stood up to add their own comments. Foreign Secretary Rafael Portuondo, who himself had been landed by the *Three Friends* in Oriente Province on May 30, 1896, challenged Collazo's charges. Representative Ernesto Fonts y Sterling said that Nuñez, as director of expeditions, could not be blamed for the fact that not all the cargo landed. Representative Fernando Freyre recommended that the commission not ask for a vote of censure, but that the assembly approve the Junta's efforts and discard the dissenting opinion.

Clearly chastened, Collazo told the assembly that his intention was not for a vote of censure but merely to point out mistakes that could be instructive for future expeditions. Freyre said that since Collazo had not asked for a vote of no confidence, there was no point in voting at all. He recommended that Collazo's dissent be dismissed. Collazo reluctantly agreed, and the assembly turned its attention to planning the new government.

Chapter 25

THE KING OF THE GUNRUNNERS IS AFFIRMED

John D. Hart sat beside Bill Ker, waiting for the US Court of Appeals proceeding to commence. There was no guarantee the appeals court would be any more receptive than the lower court jury and grant a new trial, but at least Hart's legal engines were well coaled. Bill Ker, Senator George Gray, John F. Lewis, and Horatio Rubens each would take their turn making arguments to the three appeals judges on why their client did not deserve imprisonment.

The night before Hart's appeal, he received an unexpected visit from Emilio Nuñez. They had been good partners. One had ships that carried the implements of freedom to Cuba and the other had the dedication and the means to pay for it all. And isn't success often a combination of passion and resources? Nuñez took a chance interrupting his pursuit of new vessels to come to Philadelphia, but his visit told Hart that the Cuban revolutionists believed that his efforts were worthwhile and appreciated.

The judges entered the room together, and the session was called to order. As lead attorney, Ker spoke first, repeating his argument that the evidence in the first trial was insufficient to have sent the case to the jury. He admitted that the *Laurada* carried arms and munitions of war, but that in itself did not violate the neutrality laws.

Senator Gray argued that evidence presented by the government was as consistent in showing that the *Laurada* merely carried contraband of war as it was in purporting to show that a military expedition was on board. He said "not a scintilla of evidence" showed that Hart did any more than charter his vessel to a party who wished to transport munitions of war, which had been considered a perfectly legal business transaction since the days of Thomas Jefferson.

When Hart's attorneys finished their appeals, the court announced that it would reserve its decision until a later date.

Some good news came two days later when the only man thus far imprisoned for aiding the insurgents was released from the Eastern Penitentiary at Moyamensing. Captain J. H. J. Wiborg walked out through the prison's huge iron doors and into freedom's fresh air at ten o'clock at night before a small group of friends. Wiborg's face, once windburned and rugged, appeared sallow and pale against the plain black civilian suit he wore.

Wiborg was scheduled for parole on November 2, 1897, but he was given an opportunity for early release for good behavior. To gain freedom, he was required to pay a fine and costs of $402. Wiborg declined, saying he was penniless, but Ker and some friends stepped in and paid the fine.

During his incarceration, Wiborg had been visited by a reporter who quoted the captain as saying his treatment was good, but he should never have been sent to such a place because he was innocent of any voluntary crime. "What I did to help free Cuba," Wiborg said, "I did willingly, and I would do it over again, even if I knew that the result was to be as it has been."

A carriage containing three friends sat waiting, and Wiborg stepped inside to warm handshakes and pats on the back. One of the passengers was Peter Thompson, with whose family Wiborg's wife was staying. Mrs. Wiborg arrived from Copenhagen shortly after her husband's imprisonment, on July 6, 1896, and visited him when prison regulations permitted, hoping in vain the movement for his early release would be successful.

Wiborg's carriage pulled up to Thompson's house at no. 46 South Second Street as a petite figure sat watching hopefully at a front window. When her husband stepped from the carriage, Mrs. Wiborg jumped to her feet, and, holding the corners of her long dress, hurried to the pavement. They embraced, and she took his outstretched hand and led him into the house.

While Madrid continued to blame the US government for every successful expedition to Cuba, a jurisdictional squabble between Spanish consuls and federal agents allowed one expedition to escape certain capture. At the center of the controversy was a two-masted schooner of minor renown named the *Silver Heels*. The vessel had been owned by the prominent couple Lorin and Margaret Deland of Kennebunkport, Maine. Deland was a successful businessman but was more widely known as the former head football coach at Harvard who invented the "Deland flying wedge." Deland even wrote a book on gridiron strategy with the prominent coach Walter Camp. Mrs. Deland, herself an accomplished author, achieved great fame with her 1888 book *John Ward, Preacher*.

Built in 1872, the *Silver Heels* was smaller than the chief of expeditions would have preferred, at eighty-seven feet in length with a beam of twenty-five feet and a gross tonnage of only 167. But Emilio Nuñez found the ship available after the Delands sold her to A. F. Cobb of Rockland, Maine, who turned her into a commercial vessel for hire. Nuñez and O'Brien planned to load the *Silver Heels* with a cargo of arms in New York and deliver it to the *Dauntless* at Conception Island in the Bahamas. However, Consul Congosto's relentless Pinkertons in Philadelphia discovered the plan, and the Spanish minister in Washington was notified.

At 3:00 p.m. on Saturday, October 16, Congosto sent US Marshal John McCarthy a telegram, informing him that a "filibustering expedition to Cuba" would soon leave the port of New York. But when McCarthy offered to contact Spanish consul Arturo Baldasano in New York for his help, Congosto and Pinkerton supervisor David C. Thornhill declared that the New York office "did not figure in the matter."

Thornhill's agents learned that the *Silver Heels* would leave after midnight from Pier 39 on the East River. At 10:30 p.m., Congosto appeared at the marshal's office and swore out a warrant for the arrest of "John Doe and Richard Roe," who represented the unknown captain and first mate of the vessel. McCarthy recommended they proceed at once by carriage to Pier 39 with a sufficient force of men. However, the federal officers again were rebuffed by the Philadelphia contingent. Congosto and his agents demanded the arrests be made after the vessel had departed, when the captain and crew would be caught red-handed with the incriminating cargo. Since the Spanish consul and his spies had uncovered the plot, the federal marshals again relented.

McCarthy and eleven federal agents boarded the revenue cutter *Chandler* at the barge office in lower Manhattan, and soon Thornhill and half a dozen Pinkertons appeared and invited themselves aboard. Just past midnight, the authorities received word that the *Silver Heels* had left her dock, and the cutter departed in high pursuit. The Pinkertons directed the cutter up the East River, where their intelligence placed the *Silver Heels*, but no vessel fitting the description was seen.

A lookout reported a distant dark shape in the water, and the seagoing posse took off in hot pursuit. The cutter chased the mystery vessel to a point below the Navy Yard, but when they drew close, they discovered a harmless mud scow. A Pinkerton agent suggested the suspects might be at Staten Island, so the revenue cutter lurched toward that hunch at full speed. Again, they found nothing. Another agent offered the intelligence that a Moran line tug had reportedly towed the *Silver Heels*, so they headed to the Moran wharf at the Atlantic Docks, a tip that proved just as fruitless as the previous ones.

The *Chandler* returned to Pier 39 carrying an increasingly frustrated and weary detachment of US marshals and embarrassed Pinkerton agents. A watchman sitting under a lightbulb greeted them with the news the *Silver Heels* had brushed the pier earlier in the evening but disappeared soon afterward. The authorities questioned two men on a nearby brick schooner who said the same thing. The elusive *Silver Heels* was nowhere to be found.

Unknown to the pursuers, they, too, had been under surveillance. A Cuban agent was watching the *Chandler*'s movements and relayed word when the revenue cutter departed the Battery. To avoid the cutter, the schooner was directed through Hell Gate and into Long Island Sound. Just below Sandy Hook, she met the steam lighter *Lizzie Henderson* and took on arms and ammunition that had been loaded at Bridgeport, Connecticut. By then it was 4:00 a.m., a few hours before the newly renovated *Dauntless* steamed out of Tybee Island, Georgia, toward Conception Island and the intended rendezvous.

The bungled raid prompted much fodder for the following day's editions. The *Tribune* reported that the "alleged filibustering expedition . . . was a myth, founded solely upon Spanish excitability." The *Herald*, "after a thorough investigation," reported: "There is nothing suspicious whatever about the sailing of the *Silver Heels*. She took nothing whatever on board which could be regarded as contraband goods." H. P. Browne, identified as her agent, said the *Silver Heels* was anchored off Red Hook, Brooklyn, with a cargo of coal waiting to sail for Norfolk.

Congosto's finely woven investigation had unraveled into a rag of ridicule. The Spanish government was incensed and blamed the US marshals. That sentiment was echoed by one Madrid newspaper, which faulted the "hypocritical complicity and notorious stupidity of Mr. McKinley's officials."

The *Silver Heels* under Captain Peter Quinlan had avoided the Spanish trap, but unexpected events were about to intervene to threaten the mission. The schooner sailed to Cape May, New Jersey, where she met Johnny O'Brien and Nuñez aboard the tug *P. H. Wise*. It was a terrible night for an expedition as a serious northeast gale heralded a major storm brewing. O'Brien and Nuñez had a lively time of it getting aboard the schooner in the wind and high seas, and after they were on board, a crew member on the tug chopped the towing hawser in two at the bitts. The tug fled to find a safe port, leaving the *Silver Heels* at the mercy of the elements.

O'Brien and Nuñez had fooled Spanish and government agents, but a severe storm was a much more formidable foe. The *Silver Heels* was in the northern feeder bands of Hurricane no. 5, which was ravaging Cuba and heading northward with winds of up to one hundred miles an hour.

The ferocious storm already had caused one catastrophe. The coastal steamer *Triton* was sailing from Havana to Mariel on Cuba's northern coast when she was caught in high winds about eight miles offshore. With two hundred passengers and thirty crew members aboard, the vessel was pushed by high seas into a submerged rock. The impact caused the cargo to shift, and the *Triton* began to sink. A mad scramble ensued for the lifeboats, the first of which capsized when it hit the water, and more than twenty passengers drowned. The second boat was toppled by an enormous wave, and twenty of the twenty-eight passengers on board were washed into the sea. Others grabbed onto planks or other floating debris, but by the time the *Triton* disappeared under the water, more than 150 passengers had been lost.

The same storm was heading straight into the north-south shipping lanes along the East Coast of the United States, but under Captain Quinlan's expert handling, and the likely encouragement of O'Brien and Nuñez, the *Silver Heels* plunged into the gale. As rain constantly pelted everyone aboard, one hard blow after another swept the schooner back north before she would try it again. Finally, Conception Island came into view, and a trip that normally would take five days had taken sixteen to complete. But the *Dauntless* was nowhere to be found.

Only hours earlier, José Eliseo Cartaya had guided the *Dauntless* toward Key West to replenish her empty coal bunkers and larder. After arriving, the tug was held up by orders from Washington to Collector Jefferson Browne. The resourceful Cartaya contacted Browne's deputy collector, Ramón Álvarez, who happened to be a good friend and a local judge. Álvarez arranged for release of the boat on the condition that the *Dauntless* would proceed to her home port of Jacksonville and arrive by a specific day. Cartaya agreed, but made certain that Álvarez allowed time for her to visit Conception Island on the way.

The *Silver Heels* waited for nearly a week until the *Dauntless* hove into sight. The Cubans on the *Dauntless* were transferred to the schooner, which was left in charge of Cartaya and ordered to lay in at Orange Key in the Bahamas. Nuñez and O'Brien went aboard the tug and continued on to Jacksonville to keep faith with Álvarez, but when the *Dauntless* pulled into Jacksonville, the government net was pulled tight. The cruiser *Vesuvius* guarded the front of the city, while the cruiser *Montgomery* and gunboat *Annapolis* patrolled the twenty-mile stretch of river running to the sea. So many government eyes were watching the *Dauntless* that it took two weeks before the tug could slip away to continue her mission.

On November 19, the *Dauntless* displayed all the legitimacy of a workboat in business, leaving for Savannah with the schooner *Jennie Thomas* in tow. After dropping the schooner, the *Dauntless* ran back to the *Silver Heels* at Orange Key to transfer the expedition. Under ordinary conditions, O'Brien and Nuñez would have made two or three trips to transfer the cargo, but so much time had been lost that they decided to put it all aboard at once. The scuppers were awash with the weight of the arms and the landing party, but the sea was smooth as the ship headed for Cuba. On the night of November 28, six weeks after the *Silver Heels* left New York, the *Dauntless* landed the expedition at Cape Lucretia, two miles east of the Banes lighthouse. It was not a secure place for a landing, but the rebels were waiting at that particular spot, and it was too late to make a change. Sure enough, the keepers of the light saw the suspicious activity and signaled to the commander of a Spanish gunboat lying a few miles to the east.

When more than half the cargo was ashore, the gunboat suddenly swung around the point, with every light burning brightly. No time was left to get up the anchor, so O'Brien ordered the rope cable cut in two with an ax, and the *Dauntless* was off. O'Brien took the rest of the cargo back to Jacksonville and hid it at a concealed location to await the next expedition.

The *Silver Heels* expedition threatened what appeared to be an improvement in relations between Madrid and the McKinley administration. The new Spanish leadership headed by the Liberal cabinet under Práxedes Mateo Sagasta had made what it considered a significant concession in its treatment of Cuba. In a letter addressed to Secretary of State Sherman and given to Minister Woodford on October 23, Foreign Minister Pío Gullón pledged that Spain would conduct the war humanely and offer the island autonomy. However, he was adamant that Spain would preserve her sovereignty. To confirm that pledge, Captain General Valeriano Weyler was recalled and replaced by Ramón Blanco y Erenas, who had served the Spanish government in its civil wars and in the Philippines. In a companion move that was partly in reward for his diligence against John D. Hart's scurrilous activities, José Congosto, the Spanish consul in Philadelphia, was recalled and sent to Cuba as secretary general, Blanco's administrative chief of staff.

Although the concessions were fueled by yet another colonial war bubbling up in the Philippine archipelago, Gullón demanded that the United States make two bold moves of its own: (1) stop illegal expeditions from leaving its shores in violation of its own neutrality laws, and (2) stop allowing the Junta in New York to work openly against Spain. The foreign minister challenged McKinley to issue a proclamation stating clearly whether he was ready "to put a stop absolutely and forever to those filibustering expeditions." Gullón said such activities violated "the laws of friendship" and degraded the respect that the US government should command in the discharge of its international engagements. The letter also warned that there must be "no repetition of such lamentable acts as the last expedition of the schooner *Silver Heels*."

But the McKinley State Department did not subscribe to its predecessor's tolerance of Spanish charges. Sherman responded with a detailed analysis that listed every American effort, both at sea and in the courtroom, to curtail the shipping of men and weapons to Cuba. The message said the United States, "inspired by the highest sense of friendly duty, has for the last two years and more endured almost insupportable domestic burdens, poured forth its treasure by millions and employed its armed resources for the full enforcement of its laws and for the prevention and repression of attempted or actual violation thereof by persons within its jurisdiction."

The message claimed the Spanish government "appears to be unaware or heedless" that since June 1895, fifteen American ships of war had patrolled the Florida coast, from Pensacola to Tampa to Key West to Jacksonville. In addition, the Northern Atlantic Station had sent ships to the various Atlantic ports whenever the Spanish minister reported filibustering activities, the sum of whose activities cost the government more than $2 million. "It may be asserted, in short," Sherman continued, "that every vessel of the Navy which could practically be employed in the shallow waters of the Florida coast has been detailed for this work, while for a time two revenue cutters were transferred to the Navy Department to assist."

The secretary said the Treasury Department and the Department of Justice exhibited the same high degree of diligence in efforts through activities of the Revenue Cutter Service and the courts to prosecute offenders. Sherman reviewed a history of US enforcement of the neutrality laws, from 1818 to the case that sent Captain Wiborg of the *Horsa* to prison. All rebutted the Spaniard's charges and praised the diligence of US efforts.

The Sherman message conceded that the only instance of "an alleged culpable expedition" mentioned by Gullón was that of the *Silver Heels*. However, Sherman said that case was known by federal authorities and investigated even before the Spanish legation reported it. In fact, Sherman wrote, the information provided by the US marshal and his deputy suggested that the *Silver Heels* would have been apprehended "but for the officious control of the Spanish agents whose instructions were obeyed in the matter." In light of such "undisputable facts," Sherman wrote, the president believed that the Spanish charges were totally without merit.

Treasury Secretary Lyman Gage presented his own report the first week of December that further rebutted Spanish complaints. Gage went into great detail explaining that the US government was doing everything in its power to stop the shipping of men and arms to Cuba. Gage declared that only three foreign-registered vessels with a significant aggregate of 1,772 tons had avoided American warships and revenue cutters to land successful expeditions. The secretary listed them as the *Leon*, the *Horsa*, and the *Bermuda*. In addition, Gage wrote, one American-registered vessel came into a Cuban port and spent two days unmolested, although Spain knew she was there and did nothing.

In citing the *Laurada*'s expedition to Banes Bay, the four vessels Gage had named were controlled by John D. Hart, thereby indirectly affirming his importance to the Cuban expeditionary effort as well as his reputation as king of the gunrunners.

Despite the attention given her by the Gage report, the *Laurada*'s filibustering days were over. She had sat idle for more than six months, untouched and deteriorating at the wharves of the Harlan & Hollingsworth Shipbuilding Company in Wilmington, Delaware, awaiting a decision whether she would be forfeited for the misdeeds of others. She was a lifeless version of her owner, who was himself helpless and awaiting disposition of his appeal to the US Circuit Court of Appeals.

Still, in the public's mind, the *Laurada* was less a rusting tub of regret than a polished and primped dowager of the deep. People came to see her daily, ogling this once-mighty symbol of freedom that had weathered both bullets and storms in places they could only dream about. If the spirit of Lafayette and John Paul Jones could be embodied in a 1,200-ton bucket of steel and steam, such was the aura that enveloped the *Laurada*. The sightings—real or imagined—had rallied federal authorities and Spanish agents while generating rumors that spawned other rumors. Headlines became exercises in encomia—the "Gallant *Laurada*" or the "Lucky *Laurada*"—that implied the vessel acted independently of human thought or control. All were insufficient to describe the public's infatuation with the ship as a symbol of Cuba's fight for independence.

The less romantic future of the *Laurada* would be determined in the court of Judge Edward G. Bradford II in US District Court in Wilmington. But before he could render a verdict, federal officers again were crawling over her decks. Spanish spies reported that a gang of Cubans intended to seize the *Laurada* and leave immediately for the island. The tipster claimed that twenty Cubans were coming up the Delaware in a tug and would board the steamer, overcome the watchman, then depart downstream for open water. The rumor prompted US Marshal John C. Short to station a dozen men on her decks to keep watch.

Again, the truth was far more mundane. Bill Ker was actively negotiating with a potential buyer who wished to send the *Laurada* to the Klondike gold fields. Ker said the sale would be consummated soon, and the purchase would include a settlement with the government. The resolution was reached on November 27, cleansing the vessel of all legal encumbrances. Judge Bradford released her after a $6,500 bond was paid. Two days later came the announcement that the *Laurada* had been sold to a New York syndicate.

The *Laurada*'s travails with the law were not quite over, however. One William W. Weinert suddenly surfaced to claim he owned a mortgage on the boat after bailing out Hart from some financial troubles. Weinert said he agreed to the sale only because he assumed the steamer would go back into the fruit trade, but he later found out the new owners wanted to send her to Alaska. Not surprisingly, Weinert's dealings with Hart were not memorialized in a written record. As the *Inquirer* reported: "[S]ome interesting facts were developed in connection with the past ownership and management of the famous filibuster, and more are expected."

Finally, on December 18, Judge Bradford released the *Laurada* from all legal complications, freeing her to cruise wherever her new owners decided. The ruling did not persuade the Pinkertons in the employ of the Spanish consulate, however. Several detectives continued watching her long after the ruling.

The day after the *Laurada* was freed, John D. Hart was returned to the Eastern Penitentiary. One of his four bondsmen, "the old pilot" Jeremiah L. Eldridge, notified the court that he desired to be relieved of the security. No one else came forward to provide new security for the bond, and Hart was put back behind bars to await the decision of the Court of Appeals.

Chapter 26

PERCEIVED WRONGS AND RIGHTEOUS RIGHTS

"It was a Wednesday, the morning of January 12 [1898], when the rioting began," recalled Charles M. Pepper, the Havana correspondent of the Washington *Evening Star*. "There was a lull during the midday, but in the afternoon the mob rallied. It made little demonstration, and was content with throwing stones and breaking windows.... It was known that the authorities had been unraveling several supposed conspiracies, and that at all the recent bull-fights extraordinary precautions had been taken to prevent an outbreak. In Spain, the popular uprisings usually begin at the bull ring."

The conflagration in Havana erupted over confusion of who actually ruled Cuba. Spain's new Liberal government of Práxedes Mateo Sagasta strongly opposed the "barbarity" of the previous government's policy in Cuba and sought to replace it with a gentle hand. In October 1897, Sagasta declared he would reverse the policy toward Cuba that Spain had followed since the outbreak of the revolution: "I will fulfill my program, establish autonomy in Cuba and recall Weyler.... The Liberal Party is prepared to grant Cuba all possible self-government, a broad tariff and every concession compatible with inflexible defense of Spanish rule and sovereignty in the West Indies."

That pronouncement triggered an expected response from the Junta that was reflected in a letter General Roloff wrote to Quesada from the battlefield: "We laugh at such offers, for already we see the hour of our liberation at hand. Should

Spain seriously offer us autonomy, it would prove the full extent of her weakness, and we will fight with renewed ardor until she shall recognize our independence."

The weakness of Spain's forces in Cuba were more than a perception. Intelligence from the island claimed that Spanish troops were sapped by illness, disease, malnutrition, and the unremitting tropical heat. In mid-January, acting secretary of state William R. Day asked Consul General Fitzhugh Lee for a status report on Spanish troop strength. Lee responded that as many as thirty thousand of the eighty-five thousand troops on the island were hospitalized by illness; those fit for service were poorly equipped, had no training, had few horses or artillery, and had not been paid for at least eight months. The Junta had heard the same reports, which they took as proof the Spanish army had lost the will and ability to fight. Victory was near, but the only acceptable peace would include full independence, not simply self-government as part of a distant empire.

The new policy went into effect on the first day of the new year 1898. Sagasta established an Autonomist Cabinet that would increase Cuba's representation in the Spanish parliament and enable decisions of home rule. The Autonomist Cabinet believed it was empowered to make decisions for the country's future, yet Captain General Blanco retained the military authority from Madrid to administer the war against the insurgents. The *peninsulares* in Cuba, the Spanish-born loyalists, saw autonomy as a surrender to the insurgents and American meddling. The confusion threw hundreds and perhaps thousands into the streets.

Rioters led by Spanish army officers mobbed three Havana newspapers favoring autonomy. Police dispersed the rioters, who resumed their protest, chanting "Viva España, Viva Weyler, Abajo [Down with] Blanco" and "Abajo la autonomia." The *Philadelphia Inquirer* observed that the "strange political condition that exists in Cuba" could supply "the plot of a comic opera."

None of the rioting was aimed at Americans, probably because Lee had the authority to call in warships if he believed American lives or property were threatened. After the rioting commenced, Lee sent a message to the Havana police warning that even minimal destruction of US property or loss of life would be reason enough for him to call in the navy. That would be the first step toward American intervention.

At 6:00 p.m. on the riot's first day, Captain Charles D. Sigsbee of the battleship *Maine* received a telegram at Key West from Lee containing the words "two dollars," the preestablished code that alerted him to get ready to sail for Havana. If a second telegram from Lee was received containing the code letter "A," the *Maine* was to depart immediately. With high twin smokestacks and sides shining with white paint, the second-class battleship was a potent representative of the might of the new American navy. Sigsbee waited expectantly throughout the evening, but a second telegram did not come.

More rioting occurred during the night and the next day, and Pepper of the *Evening Star* confirmed that members of the Spanish military were among the agitators. "During the days of rioting it was observed that the rioters seemed to be incited by persons not taking part, and the presence of the fraternal spirit between them and the military forces was also manifest. It was a political demonstration of the Army against autonomy, and it served its purpose." Pepper succinctly described the Spanish military's view of autonomy when he wrote: "Autonomy is dead, and the army officers have kicked the corpse."

In Washington, a disappointed Dupuy de Lôme cabled Gullón that the rioting put Cuba back in the American public eye. "The reports from Habana . . . have produced loss of confidence in the future, which had been obtained with so much labor," the minister wrote. "Among the irreconcilable Cubans the occurrence has caused great rejoicing, acting under the direst illusions, and has produced deep disgust among the moderates and those disposed to accommodate differences. For public opinion to be completely tranquil here, it is essential that actions shall be taken which will prevent a repetition of the events just past."

As one of the "irreconcilable Cubans," Quesada in Washington reported Dupuy de Lôme's distress to Estrada Palma at party headquarters in New York, saying: "Dupuy is going around crestfallen with the riots; there is no autonomy."

In Madrid, US Consul General Woodford presented the young ladies of his family to Queen Regent María Cristina on Sunday, January 15. As the reception ended, her majesty asked Woodford to remain. She said she understood he was a personal friend of President McKinley, which he confirmed. She then told the ambassador she had done all that McKinley had asked regarding Cuba, specifically the recall of Weyler and adopting autonomy. Woodford replied candidly: "The mutiny in Havana does not look as if Marshal Blanco can control his own army. If he cannot control his own army, how can he hope to crush the rebels? And besides, I hear every day of mutinies and conspiracies that are threatened here in Madrid."

In his confidential report of the conversation to McKinley, Woodford said the Queen Regent drew herself up and looked every inch a monarch as she said: "I will crush any conspiracy in Spain. Upon this you may rely. I believe that my government will keep peace in Havana and reduce Army officers to obedience. I want your President to keep America from helping the rebellion until the new plan of autonomy has had a fair chance."

The following day, Dupuy de Lôme met with the city editor of the *New York Herald*, William C. Reick, whom he regarded "a person of importance" in Washington. Despite his modest title, Reick was the most influential man at the newspaper after owner James Gordon Bennett Jr. He also was influential in Republican circles and was a confidant of the administration. Historians suggest that Reick came to the Spanish Embassy at the unofficial behest of McKinley to sound out the minister on the sensitive proposal of sending an American ship to Havana.

After Reick left, Dupuy de Lôme fired off a cable to Gullón reporting the conversation:

> He [Reick] told me that in view of recent events the President has stated that, according to information he has received, autonomy in Cuba has come to nothing; that grave disorders are feared in Habana and throughout the island; and that, if the disorders are repeated he had determined to land troops from the war vessels to protect the consulate. He asked me what would be done if that occurred. I told him that it would mean fighting.

Dupuy de Lôme received a sharp response from the foreign minister the next day: "There is neither ground for distrusting the success of autonomy, nor would there ever be any justification for the measures and purposes . . . considered as intolerable. General Blanco today reports that order is completely re-established and yields to his efforts. . . . Your Excellency will endeavor also to speedily make known there, possibly by conference with Day, in order to set the matter clear, that the extreme and inadmissible opinions given to your Excellency by the chief of the *Herald* staff lack even the pretext of reason."

On January 20, Dupuy de Lôme followed orders and met for three-quarters of an hour with Day, who was now in charge of the department because of Sherman's declining physical and mental health. The minister expressed misgivings about the attitude of the United States, which he said was the only thing keeping the insurrection alive. He suggested that McKinley perform a "courageous act of statesmanship" by publicly denouncing the rebels and the Junta and reaffirm his faith in the autonomy policy. Day replied through his drooping red mustache that if Lee needed warships he would have them, and he did not see how Spain could object to the United States exercising its right to protect the lives and property of its citizens.

Dupuy de Lôme asked Day to make certain the president realized that sending naval vessels to Havana would be regarded by Spain as an unfriendly act and that landing American troops anywhere in Cuba would be considered a cause of war. In his report of the meeting to Gullón, Dupuy de Lôme acknowledged: "There is no longer any doubt that the President of the Republic is very much impressed with Lee's statements regarding the failure of autonomy."

As international tension mounted over the Cuba problem, John D. Hart received the news he had dreaded. The US Circuit Court of Appeals voted 2 to 1 to let stand Hart's conviction and sentence for violating the US neutrality laws. The decision so much as left Hart dangling in the middle of the ocean while arrows flew around him between Washington and Madrid. He was not the principal target, but he was clearly the victim of the moment in an evolving irony. He had been convicted and sentenced for violating one country's commitment to protect another country's right to abuse, restrain, and exploit citizens under its control. But now, when events clearly were eroding the foundations of that so-called promise, he was headed to prison.

Judge George M. Dallas said in his majority opinion that the principles established by the Supreme Court in the Wiborg case applied in Hart's case. Thus, he saw the main questions as sufficient proof (1) of the existence of a military expedition under the statute, and (2) of Hart's knowledge of the facts by which a military expedition was formed. Judge Dallas said that District Judge Butler was consistent in his charge to the jury in both the Wiborg and Hart trials, and he dismissed Ker's objection that Butler had influenced the jury by repeatedly stating his opinion during his instructions. Dallas said Butler sufficiently instructed the jury that the verdict was up to their judgment and not his own. The other appellate judge in the majority, District Judge Andrew Kirkpatrick, did not issue a written opinion or comment.

The dissenting opinion came from Judge Marcus W. Acheson, a seventy-year-old jurist appointed to the federal bench in 1880 by President Rutherford Hayes. Judge Acheson based his dissent on historical precedent: "From the very foundation of the government," he wrote, "both before and since the passage of our neutrality laws, the right of citizens of the United States to sell to a belligerent, or to carry to a belligerent arms and munitions of war, subject to the opposing belligerent's right of seizure *in transitu*, and the right of our citizens to transport out of the country, with their own consent, persons who have an intention to enlist in foreign military service, have been firmly and steadily maintained by the executive department, and uniformly upheld by judicial decisions."

Acheson cited more than a dozen precedential decisions, beginning with one made by Thomas Jefferson in 1793, that the mere conveyance of men, arms, and munitions of war did not bring the vessel within the third section of the neutrality act of April 20, 1818. Acheson found no evidence that the men aboard the *Laurada* constituted a military force: "The only thing the men who went on the *Laurada* from Barnegat are shown to have done in respect to the cargo of arms and ammunition was to perform the service of stevedores. There was no evidence that any of these men had enlisted in the United States for military service in Cuba, or that they had even been drilled in military tactics, together or singly. There was no evidence whatever that they had formed or were members of any military organization, nor was there any direct evidence that they were acting in a body for any purpose."

Hart could take little consolation in Judge Acheson's dissent. Hart's only remaining hope was war with Spain. If the United States intervened in Cuba, all perceived wrongs would become righteous rights, and political prisoners would be declared free. Until that time, Hart had thirty days to clear up his affairs before he reported to the Eastern Penitentiary at Moyamensing.

Chapter 27

THE *MAINE* EXPLODES, AND HART GOES TO PRISON

William R. Day invited Enrique Dupuy de Lôme to his State Department office on January 24 on the pretense of a meeting between sovereign nations. The acting secretary of state engaged the Spanish minister on topics of mutual interest and of a personal nature for more than an hour in what until then could be characterized as a cordial exchange. At the end of the meeting, Day informed the minister that President McKinley wished to resume naval visits to Cuba. The visits had been discontinued when the revolution began, but Day said the president wished to resume the friendly gesture in recognition of Spain's successful efforts to pacify Cuba. It was an obvious distortion of the facts, as the administration well knew, and Dupuy de Lôme replied only that it would have been better had the visits never been suspended.

Day immediately conveyed the response to the president, who then called together Day, Navy Secretary John Long, Attorney General Joseph McKenna, and Nelson A. Miles, commanding general of the army. After the meeting, McKinley ordered the cruiser *Montgomery* to touch at the ports of Santiago and Matanzas and the battleship *Maine* to proceed from Key West and sail directly into Havana Harbor. Day communicated the order to the Spanish minister.

Dupuy de Lôme's cable to Madrid that the *Maine* was headed to Havana as "a mark of friendship" generated a less than genial response from the foreign minister. Wrote Gullón: "The attitude of that Government does not completely

The USS *Maine* was dispatched to Havana by President McKinley as a "friendly gesture." Library of Congress, Prints and Photographs Division, George Grantham Bain Collection, reproduction number LC-DIG-ggbain-24268.

satisfy me, because it does not heed your request that the outcome of autonomy be awaited, nor does it publish its unalterable determination to continue in the path of peace." Gullón responded with some diplomatic one-upmanship when he informed his minister: "Wishing to reciprocate such friendly and courteous demonstrations, we shall arrange also that vessels of our squadron may visit the ports of the United States in passing to and from the island of Cuba."

A few days later, the Associated Press in Madrid reported that the Spanish government would dispatch the warship *Vizcaya* to visit American ports. She was described as "a formidable craft, larger, faster and more powerful than the *Maine*." As the *Maine* steamed toward Havana, it was clear to the Junta that a concrete step had been taken that would lead to war. Ricardo Díaz Albertini, Quesada's assistant at the Cuban legation in Washington, reported to Estrada Palma: "I believe the end is approaching."

Compounding the situation were new reports that conditions in Cuba were deteriorating beyond belief. Starvation had spread, and deaths from malnourishment and disease continued at an alarming rate. In Matanzas, burial records showed that 59,000 had died in the province since December, while nearly 100,000 of the remaining 253,000 inhabitants were starving. In Cardenas, 26,000 of 35,000 *reconcentrados* had died, and American aid had not reached the town. The island's total deaths were estimated at between 500,000 and 600,000. Everywhere, women and children were begging for food.

Sentiment for American intervention had been brewing in Congress since the Havana riots. On January 19, Representative Ferdinand Brucker of Michigan had proposed a resolution to recognize Cuban belligerency, but the administration's supporters blocked a vote. It was becoming clear that as Spanish sovereignty in Cuba collapsed, sufficient votes to pass the measure eventually would be collected. Indeed, at a private interview with McKinley, Representative William Alden Smith of Michigan informed the president that Republicans in Congress insisted the party honor its pledge in the party platform with respect to Cuban independence. Only a dramatic move by McKinley now could hold back congressional recognition of Cuban belligerency or independence.

A month earlier, Assistant Navy Secretary Theodore Roosevelt had written to his friend William Astor Chanler: "I do not believe that Cuba can be pacified by autonomy, and I earnestly hope that events will so shape themselves that we must interfere some time in the not distant future." Meanwhile, as Roosevelt reminded Secretary Long that the navy would need a month's warning before war broke out, he was sending out letters on organizing an army unit.

Historians have tended to dismiss Roosevelt's expressions as those of a rabid expansionist and not reflective of the peace-first thinking in the McKinley administration. However, it was obvious the administration was preparing for the growing inevitability of war. On January 12, 1898, Alvey A. Adee, the pro-Spanish State Department expert on Cuban affairs, sent a "confidential" memorandum to Day that advised: "I think it would be well for our squadrons in the Gulf of Mexico to be ready to enter into action immediately since the emergency could arise at any moment."

Thus it was clear that even before the *Maine* left for Havana, a growing feeling existed within the McKinley administration that autonomy had failed and that Spanish rule of Cuba was collapsing. It was clear, too, that if the United States waited too long, the revolutionary forces would emerge victorious, replacing the Spanish regime, a possibility that invited chaos at best or a race war at worst. The moment was arriving for the United States to step in.

Spain's position was not helped when a diplomatic crisis befell none other than the relentless foil of the filibuster fleet, Minister Enrique Dupuy de Lôme. The first week of February, Horatio Rubens informed Estrada Palma that a messenger was on his way to New York with an important document he could use to great advantage. When the messenger arrived, he carried a letter written by Dupuy de Lôme to José Canalejas, editor of the *Heraldo de Madrid* and an unofficial agent for the Sagasta regime. In the letter, Dupuy de Lôme made unflattering personal references about McKinley. In Rubens's translation of the original letter, the minister was quoted as saying the president was "weak and catering to the rabble and a low politician who desires to leave a door open to himself and to stand well with the jingoes of his party."

Rubens obtained the letter from one Gustavo Escoto, "an acquaintance of the private secretary to Canalejas." Assuring himself it was no forgery, Rubens sent the letter to Estrada Palma, who released it to the press. Hearst's *New York Journal*, which had asked and been refused exclusive rights to its publication, was alone permitted to print a facsimile in a February 8 story headlined: "Worst Insult to the United States in Its History."

Dupuy de Lôme knew immediately he was finished. He sent Gullón a message warning that the letter would be released to the public and a day later reported that he confirmed the contents of the letter to Day. "Mr. Day has been to see me to see if the letter was mine," Dupuy de Lôme wrote to Gullón. "I have replied that it was, and that as Minister from Spain, I could say nothing but claiming right to express my opinion privately as with such frequency and less discretion the American agents have done. My position, you will see, can not be what it was before; I do not believe I can continue here."

Gullón accepted Dupuy de Lôme's resignation as publication of the letter catapulted the Spanish minister into a position of notorious prominence. His entire career was draped across the public clothesline and beaten ruthlessly. The scrutiny even revealed a book Dupuy de Lôme allegedly wrote in 1876 that illustrated the author's contempt for America's customs officials, its concept of liberty, and its womanhood. Dupuy de Lôme also had predicted the ultimate partition of the United States into three nations: East, North, and South.

The effect of the letter on the American public was predictable. Beyond their frustration at McKinley's neutral position, people of all parties felt a personal affection for their president. Instead of having "catered to the rabble," as was charged by Dupuy de Lôme, McKinley maintained an attitude that was correct from the standpoint of international law. He had never evinced the slightest public sympathy for the Cubans, and he had exerted all the forces at his command to prevent assistance from reaching the island. He repeatedly declared he "would not be forced into an unholy war" even to influential members of his own party who urged him to intervene and put an end to murder and Spanish brutality within sight of the American flag. Whether or not the American public agreed with their president, they would not stand idly by as he was abused by the diplomatic representative of any foreign power, and least of all by the minister from Spain.

The furor over the Dupuy de Lôme letter lasted less than a week before popular indignation shifted to a far greater assault on America's pride and dignity.

The diplomatic advantage McKinley enjoyed after the Dupuy de Lôme insult could disappear only if Spain had new grounds for protest, such as that provided by another expedition from an American port to Cuba. To guard against such a possibility, the president instructed every federal agency that touched on port authority and enforcement to exercise great care to prevent another filibustering voyage. Estrada Palma, however, was less concerned about McKinley's diplomatic leverage than pressing the revolutionists' growing advantage on the island. With Spain on its heels both diplomatically and militarily, conditions were ripe for another expedition.

Nuñez, Cartaya, and O'Brien took the train for Jacksonville, where they ran into an unusually large force of Spanish spies and Secret Service agents. It was in anticipation of such precautions that one thousand rifles and other war matériel were loaded at Bridgeport and shipped by rail to Tampa. With Alphonse Fritot again orchestrating rail movements, the cargo was transferred to another railcar and sent back to Florida's east coast, where it was dropped at a blind siding at the Florida Central and Peninsular depot in Jacksonville. The car was taken up to Callahan and then switched over to Fernandina, where Nuñez, Cartaya, and O'Brien arrived with a company of men.

On the evening of February 12, the *Dauntless*, in command of Jim Floyd, dropped lazily down the St. Marys River through a thick fog. Under its cover, Floyd stopped the tug at his home and took on a twelve-pound Hotchkiss gun and other arms that had been stored for safekeeping after the *Silver Heels* expedition.

Lustily blowing her foghorn, the revenue cutter *McCullough* was slowly patrolling the mouth of the river looking for the *Dauntless*. The cutter was in the middle of the channel, but Floyd had spent a lifetime on these waters. Running at full speed and showing no lights, Floyd piloted the tug within one hundred feet of the cutter, then cut south toward Fernandina. Sailors who saw her tried to sound the order for battle stations, but the *Dauntless* was quickly lost in the soupy mist, and the *McCullough* did not attempt to follow her. When the tug reached Fernandina, the cargo was quickly loaded, and she fled into the night. The "dynamite" cruiser *Vesuvius*, armed with three fifteen-inch pneumatic gun tubes each fifty-four feet long, left Jacksonville in pursuit. But the ocean tug had too much of a head start and made it to Cuba in three days without incident.

On the afternoon of February 15, the *Dauntless* landed half the arms and men just inside Point Nuevas Grandes in Camagüey Province, at almost the exact spot where she had put an expedition ashore the previous May. The following night, the remainder of the cargo was landed three hundred miles away inside the harbor at Matanzas. Considerable caution was necessary, for the tug went so close to the city that Cartaya pointed out the home of his parents.

General Carlos Rojas, commanding the rebels in that district, had designated an exact landing point halfway between a fort at the mouth of the Canímar River and the lighthouse at the entrance to the harbor. O'Brien took the helm and held the tug steady as she steamed slowly into a broad bay. He brought the tug forward to the landing spot, and through his spyglass saw soldiers at the fort and people moving about the city. They completed a quick and quiet landing, then the vessel returned to Florida waters. Floyd again took the helm and dropped O'Brien,

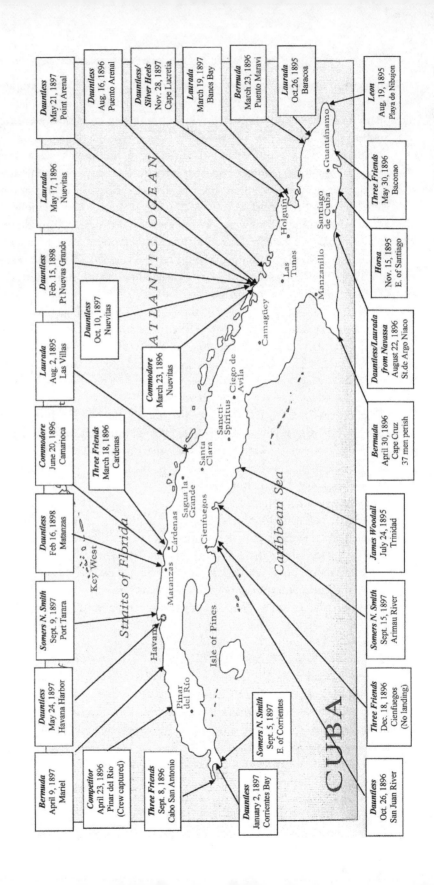

Nuñez, Cartaya, and engineer Mike Pagliuchi ashore at Bahia Honda so they could avoid arrest at Jacksonville.

The *Dauntless* proceeded to Jacksonville with only her regular crew aboard and a story of having been out in search of a wreck. On February 26, the tiny band of filibusters biding their time at Bahia Honda spotted the *City of Key West* on her way from Miami to Key West. They rowed out and were taken on board. Away from other human contact for nearly two weeks, the first thing they asked for was news.

"There is a commission sitting at Havana to investigate that thing, and it looks like war," replied the captain. "What thing?" the travelers asked, in chorus. "You don't know? The *Maine* was blown up ten days ago."

"Our expeditions are ended," remarked Cartaya, the first to express a thought that ran through the minds of every man aboard. No one believed that the Spaniards would make the mistake of blowing up an American battleship, but all knew they would be blamed for it and that an outraged American public would demand immediate intervention. They also knew they had served on probably the final filibuster voyage of Cuba's war for independence.

The sinking of the *Maine* infused a feeling of calamity unmatched in Washington since 1881, when President James A. Garfield was mortally wounded by an assassin at Baltimore and Potomac Station in Washington. Flags drooped from their masts, official functions were canceled, and crowds gathered quietly in front of the White House and the State, War, and Navy Building across the way. At the Hopkins Theater in Chicago, a picture of the *Maine* was cheered for fifteen minutes by a standing crowd. At the Court Street Theater in Buffalo, the actors introduced a new verse about the loss of the battleship that prompted all in attendance to stand and cheer, waving their hats and kerchiefs. Audiences at Manhattan theaters were brought to tears at the playing of "The Star Spangled Banner."

The presumptive court of public opinion in the United States would not wait for the official investigation into the cause of the explosion. The American public was convinced that Spain was guilty, a belief that would be reinforced by the daily press. For at least three years, stories about Cuba's latest revolution had sharpened the patriotic notions of readers who saw a parallel in their own fight for independence more than a century earlier. The public disposition was reinforced by constant stories of the noble filibusters such as John D. Hart who were unjustly persecuted by a government that protected the enemy's interests. Now the news that an American ship had been sunk in Havana Harbor prompted

Previous page: At least thirty expeditions landed armaments, supplies, and volunteers at nearly all parts of Cuba between 1895 and 1898. This image was created by the author and includes the vessel, the date of landing, and the location.

extras of the "Yellow Press," crying treachery and vengeance, supplying the only answer necessary to the vexing question of who and why. The romance of battle, the elixir that had emboldened young Americans like Osgood, Janney, and Latrobe, now intoxicated a nation.

President McKinley was hearing cries for immediate war against Spain from all quarters but especially capitalists with business interests in Cuba. Their investments had suffered during the revolution, and now they had the perfect opportunity to recover their losses. Weyler's policies combined with the rebels' burning of crops had devastated Cuba's economy. The sugar crop of 1897 had fallen to less than 200,000 tons from 1,050,000 tons harvested in 1894, and the tobacco crop of 1897 was less than 50,000 bales, down from 450,000 bales in 1894. The position of the merchant princes was summed up in a message sent to the president by New York attorney and close friend John J. McCook: "As for our interests, for three years we have lost about $100 million a year in commerce, not to speak of the loss to our citizens owning property in Cuba. We have been forced to keep up an expensive patrol, despite which Spain threatens to make claims for breach of neutrality."

True to Cartaya's prediction, the Junta would not send out any more expeditions, preferring to let matters between the United States and Spain take their inevitable course. When those who served in the filibuster fleet resumed the fight for Cuba, they wanted the American flag unfurled and flying over their heads. As O'Brien wrote in his memoirs, "[U]nder [the flag], we found situations as stirring as any we had experienced when we were operating in defiance of a tyrannical law and without any recognized flag. Strange as it may seem, I could see no difference, for the real principle involved seemed to me to have undergone no change."

Tomás Estrada Palma was busy enough denying suggestions from the *New York World* that insurgents might have blown up the *Maine*: "I cannot conceive how a newspaper can allow such . . . to see the light of day, even if its correspondent was idiot enough to send it. It is absolutely absurd, so absolutely untrue that it makes my blood boil." However, the delegate could not resist the hovering reminder that the Cuban fight for independence was grounded in the same love of liberty shared by every American citizen.

"I cannot think that the American people have forgotten the principle laid down in their own Declaration of Independence," he said. "We had to run the blockade to get from these shores and again run the gauntlet in Cuba. Our ships and cargoes were seized, subjected to delay but restored by the slow and costly process of the law. Nevertheless, we never faltered. We always appreciated the fact that the sympathy of the American people was with us."

Chapter 28

A FULL AND COMPLETE PARDON

Eight days after the *Maine* exploded with 266 American sailors going to their deaths, and Cuba's independence drawing closer to reality, John D. Hart gave up his own freedom. He was escorted by his daughters and Bill Ker to the Eastern Penitentiary at Moyamensing on February 23, 1898. As the *Philadelphia Inquirer* reported, Hart was "convicted of no greater crime than that he was active in the interests of a cause which is just now next to the hearts of all patriotic lovers of independence and liberty."

After the Court of Appeals upheld his sentence, Hart was given thirty days to clear up his affairs. But what affairs did he have? His business was ruined, and large trusts were making it impossible for an independent fruit importer to conduct trade. In his prime, Hart's growl sent dock workers and captains alike cowering in fear. But at the prison door, he shook with emotion. Tears ran down his cheeks and into his spindly mustache as he embraced his daughters one by one, not knowing when he would see them again. Most hurtful to Hart was his almost childlike refusal to believe that his country would pursue and prosecute him like a robber or thief. He believed he had engaged in the free enterprise of the capitalist system while benefiting another country's struggle to achieve the same liberty, and wasn't that the very fabric that made this country the greatest in the world? Where was the crime in that?

Hart shook Ker's hand a final time, knowing that his attorney and friend would continue to press his contacts in Washington to persuade the president to grant executive clemency. The final pleasantries ended and the heavy iron doors clanged shut as Hart passed through the entrance of what appeared to be a medieval castle. Dominating the 1400 block of South Tenth Street in Philadelphia, the penitentiary, built sixty years earlier, gave the appearance of a fierce battle between rival architects. The main building was designed in the castellated Gothic style so profound that one could imagine spearmen along the battlements and archers atop the towers. To the right of the main building was an attached wing in the ornate Egyptian Revival style, originally built as a debtor's prison but which now housed only women prisoners.

Hart might have been told that the prison was designed by the same man who later designed the dome of the US Capitol and the Senate and House wings, and that Edgar Allan Poe had served one night there after he was detained for public drunkenness. But Hart was in no mood for a history of jail builders or drunken writers when he was given his simple prison wardrobe and taken to a small cell.

His conviction and sentence called for two years in this nest of thieves, killers, and miscreants. No longer free to make a single decision, he would wear the clothes he was given, eat when and what he was told, and wake when awakened. He believed it was wrong that a man accustomed to the wind and sea spray in his face would be so constricted, but John D. Hart was now anchored to an anguish that had no place in a well-lived life.

With war imminent, the prosecution of pending cases connected with expeditions to Cuba was no longer a priority. The looming American intervention appeared to justify the actions of those who had attempted to supply the insurgents and even affirm their legality under a new application of the neutrality laws. The first reprieve, fittingly, came to the *Laurada*, Hart's most famous vessel.

US District Judge Edward G. Bradford II in Wilmington, Delaware, dismissed the final suit brought for violating the law governing the inspection of marine boilers. Bradford declared the steamer was not forfeited, ruling that if the *Laurada* was guilty, "she is guilty only insofar as the intention of her captain, Sam Hughes, and she could not be guilty unless she was intended as the instrument to commit hostilities. The transportation of the military expedition over a part of its way to Cuba did not constitute hostilities."

The celebrity steamer had been sold to the Boston and Alaska Trading Company and would head for Seattle to carry passengers and equipment to the Klondike gold fields. No longer would her passengers be powered by the dream of independence and come aboard at night from a darkened tug. They would now board peacefully in the light of day, lifted by hopes of riches that would carry them to the riverboats and barges of the Klondike district.

Captain William K. Scott was in command when the *Laurada* left Mills Shipyard in Camden, New Jersey, on March 16. He was familiar with the vessel, having served as purser under both Sam Hughes and Ed Murphy. But he hardly recognized the steamer he now commanded. Her single red smokestack, which had heralded her reputation from afar, was painted white, as were large frame deckhouses built for lodging. Below decks, her machinery and interior were renovated and renewed. The *Laurada* had been completely overhauled for the passenger trade.

The *Laurada* steamed from the shipyard to the Pennsylvania Railroad coaling station at Greenwich Point and took on one thousand tons of coal before heading to Pier 31 at the foot of Green Street. Unlike the expeditions that stole out of port to avoid Spanish spies and American revenue cutters, the *Laurada*'s new assignment would commence with more expectation than fear. Her accustomed cargo of rifles, ammunition, and Hotchkiss guns would be replaced with picks, shovels, and tents. Most of her passengers would speak English and pass the time on board playing whist or anticipating great riches instead of making ready for war.

In seventy days, the *Laurada* would arrive in Seattle. Soon after, she would commence a regular run to New Boston at the mouth of the lower fork of the Yukon River. The nearest Spanish gunboat would be thousands of miles away.

A presidential pardon was John D. Hart's last chance at freedom and redemption. American indignation over the sinking of the *Maine* was speeding the country toward war, and Hart believed it was only a matter of time before he would be released. His offense, punishable in the stifling climate of neutrality, now appeared heroic to those clamoring for the US government to declare war on Spain. Ker, Quesada, and Senator George Gray approached their numerous contacts at the Capitol to push the president for Hart's release. Ker found his champion in his own backyard. Pennsylvania senator Matthew Stanley Quay had so dominated Republican politics in his state that he was popularly known as "Boss" Quay.

The native of Beaver had distinguished himself as a colonel with the 134th Pennsylvania Infantry during the Civil War and been awarded the new Medal of Honor for gallantry at the Battle of Fredericksburg. After the war, Quay entered politics and quickly rose in the Republican Party ranks, from a state legislator to his election to the US Senate in 1886. He was such an effective backroom navigator that President Benjamin Harrison called him the "kingmaker."

If Quay could deliver for the party, Ker surmised, he could deliver enough support to have Hart pardoned. Quay prepared a petition addressed to McKinley that stated: "Your petitioners believe that the requirements of justice have been fully satisfied by the imprisonment already undergone by Captain Hart, and they humbly pray that a pardon may be granted to him." On March 22, Quay carried the petition through the Senate chambers to secure the signatures of every colleague who was present. He pledged to present the signed petition personally to the president.

Meanwhile, other petitions and efforts on Hart's behalf were circulating. William Randolph Hearst posted a "petition to the people" in his *New York Journal* calling for Hart's immediate pardon. Hearst also enlisted Augustus P. Dunlop, a

After the sinking of the USS *Maine*, the Yellow Press plastered its front pages with calls for war, as in this front page of the February 17, 1898, edition of Hearst's *New York Journal*.

prominent drama critic and renowned caricaturist, to rally the theater community to protest Hart's incarceration. David Plough, a Philadelphia fruit dealer who had done business with Hart since 1888 and had become a close friend, made Hart's freedom his primary objective. Plough obtained more than five thousand names on a petition in and around Camden and Trenton.

However, war talk trumped all other topics on Capitol Hill. On March 26, McKinley demanded that Spain cease all hostilities in Cuba. The next day, a naval board of inquiry released its report on the *Maine* disaster claiming the vessel had been sunk by a mine on the port side that triggered explosions in two magazines. The inconclusive findings as to who might have laid such a mine inflamed the public, leaving the powerful suggestion that Spain was to blame.

Behind the scenes, the War Department was mapping Spanish possessions on the island as well as harbors and potential invasion points. On March 30, the Navy Department received a dispatch saying three Spanish warships had left Cartagena, Colombia, westward bound. The flurry of events even compelled the restrained *New York Times* to declare: "War or Peace Monday," depending on Spain's response to McKinley's ultimatum that the Spanish government terminate its presence in Cuba. Spain did not accept the ultimatum in its reply of April 1, and negotiations appeared all but ended.

Quay echoed that sentiment in a speech in the Senate. Just before the reading of McKinley's message, Quay presented a series of resolutions that favored the use of American land and naval forces "to force the Spanish flag from this continent and secure the independence of Cuba." In his own message that followed, McKinley requested authorization from Congress to intervene in Cuba but did not include recognition of the Cuban revolutionary government.

The omission angered many war hawks in Congress, including Representative Hugh Dinsmore of Arkansas. "We talk about liberty," Dinsmore said. "Then let us give the Cubans liberty. We talk about freedom. Let us give to them the right to establish a government which they think will be a free government, and which does not reserve to us, the Government of the United States, the right to say, after it is established, 'Ah, this is not a "stable" government; we can not turn it over to you yet; we must look after this thing.'"

After much debate, the House Foreign Affairs Committee on April 14 sent to the floor a resolution for US intervention to establish "by the free action of the people [of Cuba] a stable and independent government of their own on the island." McKinley favored the resolution, because "intervention" could be interpreted as diplomacy rather than immediate military action.

On April 16, the Senate passed an amendment to its own resolution that would recognize the Cuban republic. Later that day, it passed another amendment, one that would reverberate throughout the next century. Offered by Senator Henry M. Teller of Colorado, it stipulated that the United States "hereby disclaims any disposition or intention to exercise sovereignty, jurisdiction, or control over [Cuba] except for the pacification thereof, and asserts its determination when that is accomplished to leave the government and control of the island to its people."

After more than a week of debate, the House and Senate passed a joint resolution "for the recognition of the independence of the people of Cuba." The resolution demanded that the government of Spain "relinquish its authority and government in the island of Cuba and Cuban waters" and directed the president to use the land and naval forces of the United States to carry these resolutions into effect. However, in final negotiations, the Senate deleted the clause that would have advocated immediate recognition of the Republic of Cuba. The insurgent government that had planned and ignited the rebellion, authorized the expeditions, and directed the war for three years would not be recognized.

McKinley wanted the Cubans to have independence but under American guidance. His administration shared Madrid's belief that the Cubans were not ready for self-government in the partial fear that Cuban soldiers might initiate a racially inspired vendetta against Spanish *peninsulares*, wealthy Creoles, and American interests. Washington was determined to impose order and to protect lives and property.

On April 20, President McKinley signed into law the joint congressional resolution for Cuban intervention. The Spanish naval squadron, which was anchored in the Canary Islands, was ordered to proceed toward Cuba under the command of Admiral Pascual Cervera y Topete. At almost the same instant, Admiral William T. Sampson's Northern Squadron formed up off Key West and headed for Havana. Nothing remained that could stop the collision that would become known as the Spanish-American War.

The sinking of the *Maine* for all practical purposes obviated the rule of neutrality with Spain, thus bringing the US government over to the side of the law's accused violators. Prosecution of all pending indictments for violations of the neutrality laws were dropped, as reflected by the calendar for the May term of the criminal branch of the US Circuit Court of New York, which contained no reference to pending filibuster cases. Although pending indictments still named a galaxy of expedition stars that included Captain Dynamite Johnny O'Brien, Emilio Nuñez, Carlos Roloff, Calixto García, Joaquín Castillo Duany, Captain Charles B. Dickman, and others, the district attorney's office would formally drop all indictments by entering a nolle prosequi in court records indicating it did not wish to pursue the cases.

In a delicious irony, the next expeditions to Cuba now came under the protection of the US government. On May 21, the steamer *Florida* carried an expedition from Port Tampa to Matanzas Province that landed four hundred volunteers, seven thousand rifles, and two million rounds of ammunition. Accompanying the vessel in the unfamiliar role as escorts were the cruiser *Marblehead* and the torpedo boat *Eagle*. The volunteers were dressed in canvas uniforms supplied by the US Army, which also contributed fifteen days of supplies, seventy-five mules, and twenty-five horses. A corps of American engineers also was aboard. The expedition was supervised by José Eliseo Cartaya, Nuñez's capable assistant, and General Julio Sanguily, one of José Martí's original collaborators. Their assignment was to deliver the men and matériel personally to General Máximo Gómez.

The clandestine expeditions of the previous three years that elicited visions of swashbuckling heroes and danger on the high seas had come to an end. Now, each legal expedition under American protection would deliver more men and arms than a dozen secret voyages. Significantly, the ships and captains whom John D. Hart had contributed to the Cuban cause were not forgotten by their most consistent chronicler, the *Philadelphia Inquirer*, which offered its readers a eulogy of sorts:

> With the cessation of these expeditions, it is interesting to know what has become of the vessels and the men who handled them from Philadelphia. The steamers that became famous in this line and the officers who navigated them at the peril of their lives are widely scattered. The *Horsa* was commanded by Captain Wiborg. The ship was partially burned at sea and was towed to New York, where she was rebuilt. Her name was changed, and she is now engaged in a foreign trade. Her commander served a year in the Eastern Penitentiary upon his conviction.
>
> The *Laurada* has gone to the Klondike after all sorts of experiences. Captain Hughes navigated her and twice stood trial for alleged violation of the neutrality laws; once at Charleston, S.C., where the vessel was for a time under seizure by the United States Government, and again at Wilmington, Delaware. In both instances [Hughes] was acquitted, and he is now engaged in less dangerous marine service. The *Bermuda* is lying at Port Antonio as though she were a derelict without an owner or anyone to claim her. Captain Murphy who commanded her was also tried at Wilmington in connection with a voyage of the *Laurada*, and the jury found him not guilty.
>
> The fourth and last of the line, the *Leon*, has disappeared from the list probably with a new name. Captain Svanoe was arrested while in charge of her and was indicted, but as he put it himself before he went away, he "got tired of waiting for trial" and though under bail left this country for his home in Norway.
>
> And the man who was at one time the charter owner of all these vessels—Captain John D. Hart—paces a narrow cell in the Eastern Penitentiary hoping that the efforts of his friends will induce President McKinley to grant him a pardon that he may not have to serve the two years sentence passed upon him by Judge Butler and affirmed by a higher court.

Senator Quay obtained an audience with McKinley on April 21 at which he presented the petition to pardon Hart. The charges that sent the charter master to prison had paled to insignificance with the dramatic shift in the US government's policy. Spain was no longer a sovereign power that commanded American neutrality, so one could reason that laws protecting what no longer existed evaporated as well. But even as the American and Spanish fleets steamed toward confrontation in Cuba, McKinley told Quay he did not have the time to thoroughly investigate Hart's case, although he promised to do so. The United States was no longer neutral in the Cuban question, but John D. Hart was still a prisoner.

Hart had to wait two more weeks before his supporters could divert McKinley's attention from the growing conflict. On May 4, a delegation of congressmen, including William McAleer, James Rankin Young, and Henry Bingham from Pennsylvania and Amos Cummings and George McClellan of New York, met with the president to expedite Hart's pardon. Kate Hart also was at the White House but did not accompany the delegation to meet the president. She awaited his answer in the East Room.

McKinley assured the delegation that Hart would be pardoned, but he refused to provide a date. When they returned to the East Room, Kate was disappointed that her husband would not be released immediately. She diplomatically expressed gratitude to the congressmen, but she could not understand the mysterious holdup. The *Inquirer* editorially asked the same question and suggested the snag might be in the office of the Philadelphia district attorney who had argued the case against Hart. District Attorney James Beck responded that he planned to forward "a petition" to McKinley but had been "unavoidably delayed" for reasons that he would not disclose.

"In this Federal district, there are no cases against filibusters pending," the *Inquirer* said in a May 13 editorial. "The trial and conviction of Captain John D. Hart was the last chapter of that story here. His imprisonment has always been considered an injustice in the light of other rulings in such cases, and if the government at Washington proposed to ignore the cases against other filibusters it is only right that a pardon be extended to Captain Hart. A notable petition requesting executive clemency has gone to the President. Captain Hart is of far more use to the United States as a free man than a prisoner. Why not pardon him at once?"

A week later, on May 19, Hart and Bill Ker sat in the narrow cell at the Eastern Penitentiary, waiting for good news to be delivered. Ker had received a tip that the pardon would be announced that day, and he wanted to be with his client when it arrived. Hart appeared much different from the man who had entered the prison nearly three months earlier. He was noticeably thinner and sported a new beard flecked with gray that gave him the appearance of a man much older than his thirty-seven years.

A handful of newspapermen waited outside the cell area, hoping to write the story announcing freedom for, as one reporter described him, "a man who has probably done more to serve the cause of Cuba than any man alive."

Hart and Ker chatted amiably, confident his ordeal soon would end. Hart presented Ker with a letter he had written to Senator George Gray in which he offered to turn over the *Bermuda* to the US government for use in the war. All he asked was the freedom to man her and the payment of expenses to get her out of Jamaica, where she had been seized more than a year earlier.

"She would make in the end a very valuable boat," Hart wrote. "She is fast and has the latest triple expansion engines. She has two new Scotch boilers, light draught, carries 1,250 tons and is well ventilated as she was specially fitted for the use of the green fruit trade. . . . The *Bermuda* has run away from many Spanish gunboats. Our government can easily man her, and if I am released I can call back the old crew at the government's expense and option."

But Hart's release would not come that day or even that week or the next. Puzzled by the delay, Kate Hart returned to the White House on May 27 and demanded a meeting with the president, which he granted. She knew the pardon was a discretionary decision that only McKinley could make, so her plea for her husband's release was tempered but earnest. McKinley appeared sympathetic but provided no explanation for the delay. He would only give her assurances that her husband would be released "in a few more days."

The Junta's Quesada found the same logjam when he attempted to obtain information on Hart's release. In a letter to Estrada Palma in which he reported a meeting with General Nelson Miles over plans for the invasion, Quesada wrote: "I have not received a response from the Attorney General regarding Hart and his situation. Senator Gray has also spoken to him, however, Mr. Griggs does not appear to be in a hurry."

Attorney General John W. Griggs held the key to Hart's release, as McKinley revealed in a meeting with Quay on May 30. Despite the wide public sentiment to release Hart, including the signatures of seventy-six senators on Quay's petition, the president had instructed Griggs to develop a legal rationale for a pardon that preserved the integrity of the neutrality laws while justifying Hart's immediate release. Griggs was a sagacious lawyer who had resigned as governor of New Jersey to assume the AG position. But Griggs also had a number of other opinions the president expected, and when Kate Hart visited the White House, Griggs was not even in Washington, which delayed the process further.

On June 9, Madrid sources reported that the Spanish garrison at Santiago de Cuba repulsed a fierce attack by the American squadron on Spanish marine and land batteries with heavy losses to the enemy, estimated at 1,500 men. Admiral Sampson's report to Washington on the same battle reported that five US warships had bombarded Caimanera on Guantánamo Bay and Santiago, where the Spanish cruiser *Reina Mercedes* was sunk. Sampson said that American forces sustained no casualties.

On the same day, Attorney General Griggs delivered to McKinley his opinion on the pardon of John D. Hart. As the president had directed, the opinion accomplished the popular result while preserving the integrity of the law. Griggs's opinion dismissed the arguments suggested by Senator Gray and Ker: (1) that war with Spain rendered the reasons for prosecution and imprisonment of Hart moot, and (2) that the dissenting opinion of Appeals Judge Marcus Acheson raised sufficient doubt as to the conviction.

Of the latter, Griggs said Hart was subjected to vigorous prosecution, and Judge Butler was satisfied with his guilt as were two of three judges on the appeals court. Hart was guilty and properly convicted, as the US system only requires a majority to convict, even though one might dissent. Griggs dismissed the war with Spain as a factor, saying that the dignity of the US government, its interest in seeing that statutes of high international importance are not violated with impunity, the country's reputation for good faith and honest purpose, all require that offenders such as Captain Hart should not be let off with merely nominal punishment.

Having said that, Griggs held that while the case affirmed the dignity of prosecution, the prisoner's punishment of time served was sufficient penalty under the circumstances.

"I think it has been made manifest by this time," Griggs wrote, "that the neutrality laws of the United States will be vigorously and severely enforced by the government, and that the punishment already undergone by Captain Hart is adequate under the circumstances to serve as a warning and example and that no harm can come to the administration of justice by his release. His offense is not to be regarded as either justified or condoned. His pardon at this time will imply merely that he has, under the peculiar circumstances of the case, been adequately punished by the imprisonment already undergone."

McKinley signed the official document, attesting that "it has been made to appear to me that the said John D. Hart is a fit object of executive clemency." The language of the document ensured "a full and unconditional pardon."

Chapter 29

THE IMPORTING BUSINESS HAD CHANGED

Kate Hart rushed to the street and ordered the carriage driver to take her to the White House. She had remained in Washington in anticipation of hearing the news of her husband's pardon, and once it came she wished to thank President McKinley personally. The chief executive was in a cabinet meeting when she arrived, but as a token of the good news, McKinley's secretary, John Addison Porter, presented her with the pen with which the president had signed the pardon. Kate was standing on the White House portico when Attorney General Griggs arrived late for the meeting, and upon receiving her thanks, he directed that she be given the official papers to expedite her husband's release.

Accompanying Kate was Augustus Dunlop, the prominent drama critic who had been enlisted by William Randolph Hearst to advocate for the pardon. The publisher saw the pardon as another sensational opportunity for the *New York Journal* to rise above its competitors, which it did when the newspaper proclaimed McKinley's decree as "A *Journal* Victory." With pardon in hand, Kate and Dunlop headed to Union Station, where they boarded a train for Philadelphia. The *Journal* trumpeted the news the following day in typical Hearst fashion with a full-page spread under the headline: "Faithful Wife and *Journal* Representative Convey His Pardon to Brave Captain Hart."

Kate and Dunlop joined Hart's friend David Plough and dozens of well-wishers outside the prison entrance at Moyamensing about 4:00 p.m., June 10,

PARDON AT LAST FOR JOHN D. HART.
A JOURNAL VICTORY.

President Signs the Release of the Noted Filibuster.

Washington, June 9.—President McKinley has signed the pardon of John D. Hart, who is confined in the Pennsylvania Penitentiary under a two year sentence for taking part in a Cuban filibustering expedition.

The papers in the case were brought to the White House to-day by Attorney General Griggs, who signed the recommendation for the pardon. President McKinley was familiar with the facts and at once affixed his signature.

Hart will probably be released to-night. His pardon has been a victory for the Journal, which took up his case and brought it to the attention of the administration.

New York Journal owner William Randolph Hearst was not shy about taking credit for John D. Hart's pardon by President McKinley, as this story from the front page of the June 9, 1898, *Journal* suggests.

1898. Many were waving tiny Cuban flags, and all were in a festive mood. Inside, Warden Michael J. Cassidy received the papers, then sent one of his deputies to fetch the prisoner. Hart was given the dark suit he had worn when he reported 105 days earlier, and he took off his prison uniform and tossed it to one of the guards. It had not been an easy time, locked in a narrow cell, lying on a hard, thin mattress while evoking images of what lay ahead. Probably worst of all was the long ordeal of hope tempered by delay waiting for the pardon to finally come.

After Hart signed the discharge papers, he shook hands with Cassidy and headed toward the long hallway that led to freedom. He swung down the flagging of the yard with as springy a step as when he was rushing around the Delaware Avenue wharves barking orders to seamen and dockhands alike. He appeared sheepish when the iron gate opened and he saw the reception outside. Kate stood in the midst of other faces he recognized and many more he did not, all wreathed in warm smiles.

John D. Hart, again a free man, embraced his wife and warmly greeted those around him.

"I never lost hope," he told the crowd in a halting yet sincere manner. "I knew pardon would come, but it was hard to hear of the splendid work of the Americans in Cuba—the landing of men and arms—just what I did in fact—and lie in prison idle. That is the only thing that was gall and wormwood to me. I felt I was the victim of injustice, but the knowledge of powerful friends working for me kept me happy."

A few days later, while visiting with Ker, Hart sounded less the robust businessman he once was and more like the chastened soul he had become.

"My recent experience has taught me a good many things," he told the *Inquirer*. "I have found out what really constitutes friendship. There were some people who supposed I was possessed of a great deal of money. I did have a good deal two or three years ago, but it is all gone, and I will have to start anew in life. I can do it, too, because I am young and strong and have lost none of my ambition. I am hopeful that I will soon have vessels under my control, and that with strong, steady, hard work, I will be able to recover what I have lost."

But Hart would learn that the world he was walking into was not the same world he had left only months before.

"The Famous *Laurada*" arrived in San Francisco on May 30, 1898, following an easy voyage around Cape Horn. After the United States sent troops to the Philippine Islands, it was reported that the government would put the steamer to use as a transport to carry more troops to Manila. But she was headed for the Klondike, where she would continue to draw the attention of the authorities as well as the curious.

At Victoria, British Columbia, Captain William Scott refused to allow Canadian authorities to inspect the *Laurada* because he attested she had been inspected properly when she left Seattle. The next day she ventured too close to shore at low tide in the Burrard Inlet and cut a huge water main from which Vancouver obtained its water supply from the Coquitlam River. A warrant was sought by authorities, but when the tide rolled back in, the *Laurada* floated free and steamed away.

Most of the news about the ironclad celebrity was less eventful. Her schedule between Seattle and St. Michael, Alaska, was duly published in the *Alaska Mining Record*, while subsequent reports reflected her success as a gold transporter. On one trip from the gold fields to Seattle, the *Laurada* arrived with two hundred passengers and gold dust estimated at $100,000.

Her owner also announced he might add a trip to Honolulu, Japan, or even Vladivostok to her regular runs to Skagway. Still, she was the "famous *Laurada*" in boldface advertisements for her runs, assuring passengers they were boarding a noble and historic vessel. Her fame, however, did not keep her out of trouble. An application for a libel was filed in federal court in Seattle charging that the vessel was involved in illegally transporting 103 cases of whisky, 9 cases of wine, and 20 kegs of beer into Alaska. In order to satisfy the judgment, she was sold by the US marshal to Richard Bell of the Washington and Alaska Steamship Company for $25,100.

By now, the *Laurada*'s reputation had descended from adoration to the butt of humor. The *Tacoma Daily News* editorialized after her most recent trouble: "That it is hard to mend evil ways in old age applies to water craft as well as to people. Now, there is the steamer *Laurada*. She was a filibuster and smuggled arms and other contraband goods into Cuba. . . . She kept the Washington authorities on the jump, arresting her for conduct unbecoming a ship. But at last she tried to reform. She was going to be real good for sure and to take her away from the evil associations, she was sent around the Horn and away up here to Puget Sound. But it was all in vain. She fell into bad habits again and went to smuggling whisky into Alaska as gay and unrepentant as ever. Then she wouldn't pay her debts, and so last Monday she was sold by the United States marshal to satisfy a judgment, and now she will again try to be good."

The *Laurada*'s new owners spruced her up and remodeled the ship to accommodate more passengers. When she sailed into Juneau under the command of Captain Frank W. White, she was welcomed as "the handsome Steamship *Laurada*" whose accommodations were considered "simply grand."

Back on the Alaska route in March 1899, the *Laurada* brought a record haul of gold dust valued at $150,000 from the Klondike. However, trouble again intruded a month later when she was ordered seized, charged with illegally dumping stowaways and paupers at Bella Bella in Canada. The answer for her owners was to avoid Canada, while the Alaska routes continued to be profitable. The *Laurada* picked up the US mail service and added lumber and cattle to her growing list of legal cargoes.

While the glory of riches and adventure captivated most people who traveled to the Yukon, the *Laurada* also carried tales of deprivation and death that reflected the reality of life in the wild. The *Laurada* returned to Seattle in June with a story that more than two hundred men had perished while searching for gold. Fifty men were reported drowned in the Great Slave Lake, twenty died in the rapids of the Mud and Laird Rivers, and at least ten more froze to death. In addition, a large number died of exposure and disease, including scurvy. And one miner, frustrated because his provisions were gone before he reached the Klondike, shot himself in the head.

Other realities were attached to the *Laurada*, which was called a "floating louse cage" by one passenger who objected to the apparently deteriorating accommodations. But all the complaints would soon come to an inglorious end.

On September 12, Captain White piloted the steamer out of Seattle for Cape Nome with a crew of forty-eight officers and men and twenty passengers. She carried a full cargo of general merchandise, fifty tons of lumber, and livestock numbering 130 sheep and 36 head of cattle. She also carried a press and other printing equipment with which George Swinehart intended to establish a newspaper at Cape Nome.

A day out of Seattle, the *Laurada* encountered rough weather, and at six o'clock on the morning of September 13 she was blown by wind and current into shoal water. Captain White guided the vessel back into the open sea as heavy waves broke over her bow again and again. He turned the boat around and chose to take the inside passage down the coast, where the lumber and thirty tons of coal were unloaded to lighten her burden.

She set out again and put in for a day at Dutch Harbor in the Aleutians on September 25, where thirty sheep were landed before the voyage resumed in dismal weather. On September 27, a leak was discovered that widened from the relentless pounding of the sea, and the pumps were barely keeping up with the rising water. Captain White knew his only hope was to reach the Seal Islands, 225 miles north of Dutch Harbor, but heavy seas made landing impossible. Rising water extinguished the fire in the boilers, and at 2:30 p.m. on September 28 Captain White ran the now sinking *Laurada* ashore in the shallow waters of Zapadine Bay, off Saint George Island in the Bering Sea.

The crew and passengers unloaded the livestock and provisions and moved into two small frame houses, used for the storage of seal skins, to await help. The *Laurada*, which had successfully evaded numerous revenue cutters in the Caribbean, drew the friendly attention of a federal cutter when the *Corwin* sighted the distress signal flying from her mast. Captain William J. Herring of the *Corwin* took the passengers and the US mail the vessel carried and returned them to Dutch Harbor. But the "famous" *Laurada*, the "lucky" *Laurada*, the fruit steamer that had given hope to Liberian settlers, Cuban patriots, and her American master, finally had run out of luck.

In early November, the revenue cutter *Bear* returned to Saint George Island on its regular patrol up the coast. The official report from the cutter was that the *Laurada*'s upper works were nearly all gone, and she was deteriorating rapidly. She soon would be consumed by the sea.

John D. Hart stood proudly at the bow as the *Bermuda* passed the Delaware breakwater at the end of July 1898 to undergo repairs at Wilmington. Hart had brought the vessel from Port Antonio, Jamaica, where she had lain quietly at anchor during the Spanish war. Kate's friend, Augustus Dunlop, had intervened on Hart's behalf and persuaded London to free the ship, which still possessed British registry. Hart retrieved the *Bermuda* as the centerpiece of a new empire that would restore the prominence he once enjoyed and believed he greatly deserved.

Under Hart's supervision, the *Bermuda* took on a new look, with its old woodwork replaced and new engines added. No expense was spared for the flagship of the reconstituted J. D. Hart Company. Hart chartered the *Bermuda* to a new enterprise called the West India Trading Company, which sought to revive the fruit trade between Philadelphia and Jamaica.

With it came the opportunity to put such familiar captains as J. H. J. Wiborg, Sam Hughes, and Charles Dickman back to work. Hart gave the dignified Wiborg command of the *Bermuda* and named the younger Hughes his first mate. Hughes's previous command had been a transfer ship that accompanied Admiral William Sampson's fleet when it routed the Spanish fleet at Santiago.

Hart's new venture began with typical optimism, but he soon realized that the importing business had changed markedly in the eighteen months since he had last been an active participant. Industry trends he had seen developing left no room for a struggling independent importer. The wave of the future was consolidation, and the ownership and development of private banana plantations eliminated the expensive layer of fruiters, the middlemen that Hart embodied. At the beginning of the year 1899, as many as 114 companies were engaged in the fruit trade on some scale, most of them inadequately financed or under the management of men who had no practical knowledge of the banana industry.

The future arrived on March 30, 1899, with the chartering of the United Fruit Company under the liberal business laws of New Jersey. At the time, United Fruit controlled 250,000 acres in Colombia, Cuba, Jamaica, the Dominican Republic, Honduras, Nicaragua, and Costa Rica; more than 66,000 acres had producing banana trees.

Bill Ker was skeptical that a fruit trust could be successful and said so: "Such a scheme is as impracticable as the attempts that have been made to corner the grain market from time to time. A company can buy up all the ships it wants to, but it can never control the traffic until it controls the brains and energy of the half a dozen or more men who have shown that they are successes at the business."

Ker's naïveté ignored just such men as A. W. Preston and Minor C. Keith of the Boston Fruit Company who had conceived the combination. Despite Ker's skepticism, the J. D. Hart Company was included in a list of twenty-two "firms, organizations, and persons" engaged in importing bananas into the United States that were bought out or otherwise acquired by United Fruit in 1899.

Bidding the fruit business farewell forever, Hart renamed his new enterprise the Hart Steamship Company, which he envisioned as a passenger and freight line between East Coast ports and the West Indies. He hired Wiborg as superintendent of the fleet and dispatched Hughes to go abroad and secure two more vessels. Outwardly, Hart was as indefatigable as ever, but beneath the veneer existed quite a different man.

Hart's legal and financial problems doubtlessly weighed heavily on his personal life. It was well known that his most famous vessel, the *Laurada*, was named after daughters Laura and Ada, but little else of Hart's personal life was talked about publicly. He was seventeen when he married Kate Staylor, who was eight years older, and little is known of their early relationship other than the documented births of five children and deaths of two. Their separation in 1896 reflected a strained relationship, but Kate's attendance at his trial and her efforts to help secure his pardon suggest a desire at reconciliation. But it was not to be.

The first public hint of problems was a story that appeared on March 1, 1899, appropriately headlined "John D. Hart's Troubles." The focus of his "troubles" was reportedly a contentious support agreement between him and Kate. The article led: "The marital troubles of John D. Hart of filibustering fame were recalled to mind by an order made yesterday by Judge [Abraham] Beitler in Quarter Sessions Court no. 2."

The story said that Hart and "his wife Catharine [sic] separated some time ago, and they have been before the court on a number of occasions to have their difficulties adjusted." On December 23, 1898, an order for $10 per week had been made against Hart, divided between $7 for the support of his wife and $3 for "one of their children." The reference obviously was to Grace, the third daughter who was born in 1890 and would figure into a remarkable incident later that revealed much more of the relationship between John and Kate.

Hart filed to revoke the previous order because the war in Cuba had ruined his business, leaving him without any income. He also made "serious allegations affecting his wife's conduct," claiming she operated a thriving boarding house at 1220 Mount Vernon Street in Philadelphia, had money in the bank, and needed no help from him. Kate denied having money in the bank and countered with charges against him of "brutal treatment."

Judge Beitler discharged Hart's motion for relief and sent them both home.

Four months later, a sensational story appeared that suggested young Grace had been kidnapped. Kate Hart went to the police and reported that her nine-year-old daughter had disappeared from her home, and all attempts to locate her had been futile. The story added that when the couple separated "about two years ago," daughters Ada and Laura went to live with their father, while Grace remained with her mother.

Kate Hart told police that she had sent a message to her estranged husband asking if he had seen Grace. He replied he had not seen her since a previous court proceeding a year earlier. However, when questioned by police, Bill Ker admitted that Grace showed up unannounced at Hart's office at Pier 19 and, with a number of persons present, "threw her arms around his neck and kissed him."

Ker said he had recommended that Hart put his daughter under the care of a physician, and he reported that Grace was "now in a home, not a charitable institution, but one where her care is paid for and . . . where she will be well attended to." Ker also said he expected Kate Hart to contact police and "give unnecessary trouble to the officers."

Hart had placed Grace with a friend, Charles Albany, and his wife. On August 9, Judge Henry McCarthy of Quarter Sessions Court held a hearing and asked Grace which parent she wished to live with. She said her father, and the court awarded custody to Hart. But Kate was not giving up. On February 3, she filed a petition in the Quarter Sessions Court demanding that her husband allow her to see Grace. The public record on the Harts' problems thereafter is silent.

Hart's new business was not going any better than his personal life. In September 1899, he filed a libel against a chartered vessel's owners on a claim for $17,800 in damages over an undelivered cargo. In November, the *Bermuda*, commanded by Sam Hughes, sustained serious damage when it was nearly lost in a hurricane. In December, rumors surfaced that Hart and Hughes might once again be flirting with the filibustering business. Hart was reportedly approached by an agent seeking a vessel to take six hundred men from Baltimore to Lisbon, Portugal, then on to South Africa as volunteers for the Boer army to fight the British. Hart adamantly denied that the *Bermuda* would sail against the country of her birth, and one could almost hear the John D. Hart of old in his denial.

"I am a thorough American, as everyone who knows me at all will testify, and as a thorough American, too good a friend of Great Britain to do a thing to aid any enemies of hers. My sympathies are with the British, and you can wager a whole lot that the *Bermuda*'s owners never even thought of chartering her to carry volunteers to the Boers. Little chance there for an agent of the Boers to get a charter, don't you think? No, sir, the boat will carry no volunteers to South Africa to fight for the Boers. She will be right here in the Delaware, tied up at Pier 19 North, no later than next Wednesday, and Captain Hughes will be in command of her!"

Hart's defiance was not enough for Robert S. Gamble of Kingston, Jamaica, under whose name the British vessel was registered. Although the *Bermuda* was owned jointly by Hart, Ker, and John G. Vogler, a Philadelphia businessman, they could not obtain an American registry without an act of Congress. Familiar with Hart's reputation, Gamble believed that Hart would charter the *Bermuda* to anyone offering a reasonable sum. As the registered owner of the vessel, any liability would fall directly to Gamble, an eventuality he did not wish to entertain.

Through his agents in Philadelphia, Gamble filed an injunction in Common Pleas Court no. 2 against Hart, Ker, and Vogler, as well as Hughes, prohibiting the *Bermuda* from leaving Philadelphia. The court dissolved the injunction on February 8 after Gamble agreed to keep the vessel under his name until the partners could sell it. But after Hart directed Gamble to convey the title of the boat to Joseph H. Smith, Vogler objected, complaining to the British consul that the title was irregular. Hart went back to court asking that Vogler be enjoined from interfering with the transaction because it kept the boat out of commerce.

Once again, legal complications had retarded Hart's attempts to revive his business. Even when cleared from such encumbrances, he could not cover his expenses. Now, with his only vessel tied up by the courts, failure was inevitable.

In March of the new century, Hart announced that the Hart Steamship Company had failed, and he was forced to sell the *Bermuda*. The federal court conducted the sale, at which W. H. Smith, representing the Olga Steamship Company of Jamaica, bought the vessel for $30,750. The price was $2,750 higher than the admiralty surveyor's appraisal, but the additional amount was intended to satisfy all of Hart's pending debts.

Hart expressed hopes of establishing another shipping business, but he could not put together sufficient capital. He returned to Philadelphia a broken man. The recurring despondency he had experienced through the tribulations of court cases, prison, and his personal struggles had returned. Hart tried to relieve the condition with alcohol, but his health only began to suffer further. He had not seen Kate or his children in months.

Hart tried a new line of work, investing what money he had left in the Shoreham Hotel in Atlantic City. The alcohol and the fluctuations in his new business only exacerbated Hart's volatile personality. In one incident, he hired a piano player named Davis Howard to entertain guests. Only fifteen minutes into Howard's first engagement, Hart claimed the music was bad, and he fired Howard. When the piano player refused to leave, Hart threatened to throttle him if he did not vacate the premises. Howard contacted authorities, and Hart was arrested and held under $200 bail. He survived that incident, but the hotel was entering the slow winter season, which did not generate enough business to stay ahead of the ever-present creditors. John D. Hart again was forced to abandon ship.

Chapter 30

HE TOOK UP THE CAUSE AND SUFFERED FOR IT

Sam Hughes stayed on as captain of the *Bermuda* for the new owner and signed on Wiborg as first mate. The two resumed the runs to Jamaica, the first of which in May was reported as the largest cargo of bananas ever delivered to Philadelphia.

But peaceful prosperity was not meant for the vessel with a history of conflict. On her next voyage to Jamaica, the *Bermuda* encountered heavy weather in the Gulf Stream. After the vessel was bounced around for several hours, a bolt of lightning sliced down from the clouds and split the mainmast like kindling. One crew member was seriously injured, but even worse luck was yet to befall the accursed vessel.

Shortly after midnight on June 11, 1900, the *Bermuda* collided with the three-masted schooner *Frank B. Hall* in a dense fog off Winter Quarter Light below Cape Henlopen at the mouth of the Delaware Bay. The schooner was standing on a port tack under a light breeze with Captain Robert G. Moore at the wheel, keeping a sharp lookout and leaning on the foghorn. The fog was so thick that Moore could not see the foresail and was creeping along at two knots when out of the haze came the steamer.

The 1,200-ton *Bermuda* must have appeared like a three-story building roaring out of the mist when she struck the 150-ton *Frank B. Hall* nearly head on. Moore was knocked momentarily from the wheel, and the schooner's bow dipped sharply. She was sinking rapidly. The five crewmen jumped into a lifeboat just as the ship's nose dipped under the water, and she toppled over on her beam ends and sank. The *Bermuda* crew threw a ladder over the side for Moore and his crewmen to climb aboard.

Two days later, Moore filed a libel in US District Court claiming damages of $10,500 for the destruction of his vessel, and a writ was issued to attach the *Bermuda* for the amount of the claim.

A federal marshal served Hughes with the notice that an attachment had been issued for the *Bermuda*. The officer took the vessel into custody, attaching a tiny padlock bearing the seal of the United States to the steamer's rigging. The *Bermuda* was allowed to return to commerce while legal proceedings continued, but it would not be the end of her troubles.

She was leased by the West India Trading Company to haul bananas from the familiar port of Port Antonio. At around noon on August 15, Hughes guided the vessel into Pier 19, near John D. Hart's old office. The *Bermuda* was carrying twenty-five thousand bunches of bananas, a huge load by her standards, and she was moored just above the Vine Street ferry. After she was secured, a squad of stevedores worked until nightfall unloading her. A quarter of the load had been taken off when the stevedores retired, and most of the twenty-seven crewmen returned to their sleeping quarters on the boat. They planned to finish the job the following morning, then head out again for the West Indies.

But there would be no more voyages for the fabled filibuster vessel. About two o'clock on the morning of August 16, quartermaster Charles Anderson was coming down the hatchway when he heard a loud explosion. The *Bermuda* shuddered violently, and the sleeping crewmen awoke and began scrambling past Anderson and onto the deck. Night watchman Charles Hillenbrand heard the noise from his nearby post, and he rushed over to see the boat swaying to and fro and columns of smoke billowing up from the hold.

The *Bermuda* appeared to stabilize, and crew members rushed to clear their bunks before assembling on deck. What they could not see was the water rushing into the hold. The aft end was slowly sinking. Hillenbrand hurried the crew members off the boat as the heavy hawsers mooring it to the wharf snapped under its weight. The vessel lurched downward, the stern going first. As she struck bottom, she slid out beyond the end of the pier and was engulfed by the river. When the *Bermuda* settled, her stern and body were submerged while the bow and forward cabins were raised out of the water at a thirty-degree angle.

The sudden and mysterious demise of a vessel that had experienced the danger and repute of the filibuster trade invited multiple conspiracy theories. One rumor accused Spanish spies of blowing up the vessel in retaliation for her service to the Cuban rebels. Another rumor posited a long-forgotten dynamite torpedo left over from her filibustering days. Until the truth be told, neither the public nor those close to the *Bermuda* would be satisfied with any reason less than equal to her colorful past.

Divers were dispatched by the vessel's owner, the Olga Steamship Company, but their efforts were hampered by swarms of men and boys who swam out and climbed all over the sunken icon. After a police boat finally showed up to drive away the trespassers, divers went down and discovered a hole about one-foot square in the vessel's stern. A powerful explosion had indeed torn through the steel hull, but the hole was more than sixty feet from the boilers and engine, dismissing the theory of an overheated boiler. Jagged edges around the hole were pushed outward, confirming that the explosion had originated from inside the boat and not from a mine or other external cause. The hole was in the vicinity of the coal bunkers, which lent credence to the theory of a hidden mine igniting the coal dust.

Despite the evidence and practical reasons for the explosion, conspiracy theories persisted, including one from an authoritative source. John D. Hart, former master of the *Bermuda*, drew great attention when he suggested that disgruntled crew members had conspired to sink the boat in retaliation for ill treatment and a drop in wages from the charter company.

"The *Bermuda* went down as the result of a mistaken scheme among some of the men aboard the ship," Hart charged from the safety of his home in Atlantic City. He vowed that the truth would be proved once the boat was raised. Even Sam Hughes denied such a claim, saying his own pay was $200 more a month than he ever received from the penurious Hart. He also said the pay of the men had been raised, some had received bonuses, and the food on the boat was better than before.

Proof of any conspiracy or any other reason beyond the spontaneous combustion of coal dust would never be found because the *Bermuda* was not raised immediately. Heavy chains were placed under her hull to be attached to pontoons that would assist in the lifting, but the vessel's weight precluded that effort. The reason for the sinking of the *Bermuda*, much like that of the *Maine*, was never proven conclusively. That left only presumptions, rumors, or such charges as those by the ship's former master that came from either inside information or the ravings of a troubled mind.

John D. Hart moved from Atlantic City back to Philadelphia near the familiar waterfront where he had known great personal pleasure and business success. The weather was unseasonably mild on that autumn Monday, cloudy with temperatures in the mid-forties, which made his noonday walk invigorating. He walked down Vine Street to South Delaware Avenue and his old offices at Pier 19. He had been reluctant to visit the watery grave of the *Bermuda*, which had exploded two months earlier. Now, with a suitable period of mourning past, it was time to pay his respects.

He looked out into the Delaware River and saw the bow of the *Bermuda*, still reaching out to heaven from the murky water. Pity that his favorite, the *Laurada*, was rusting on the bottom somewhere off the icy coast of Alaska.

This is believed to be the last photograph taken of John D. Hart shortly before his death at age thirty-nine. Courtesy of Sharon Holt Neil and Sandra Holt Luty, granddaughters of Grace Hart Holt.

Such high adventure he had enjoyed with all his ships and captains. Hart read recently that the most reliable of them, Sam Hughes, had taken command of a government transport in San Francisco. Such steady work would appeal to Hughes's wife, Margaret. Wiborg was Hughes's first mate on the *Bermuda* when she exploded, and the old Dane might also go west. Hart felt a kinship to Wiborg, whom he had hired in Baltimore and who had also been punished unjustly for aiding the cause of Cuban independence. He and Wiborg deserved rewards after the United States finally intervened, which Hart believed his country should have done all along. Such praise was lavished upon the favorite of the Cubans, Captain Dynamite Johnny O'Brien, who was appointed harbormaster for the new government by Havana's new civil governor, Emilio Nuñez. Young Ed Murphy, headstrong and fearless, was another who deserved credit, but he contracted typhoid fever during the war and went to an early grave.

Hart could do it all again, which is what he told Bill Ker the last time they spoke. He had not heard from his friend and attorney in a while, but together they had weathered all storms and eaten the sweet fruits of success. Others might doubt him, but a man with great resolve who has mastered the sea can plow through any gale. What is a man's life if he cannot face and overcome its dangers with pluck and daring? Hart knew he could do it all again. He was only thirty-nine, still young by most standards, although lately he was feeling every bit the ancient mariner.

Hart walked a way down South Delaware Avenue, but at the corner of Market Street the pain grew worse. He reached out for a rail, like the ones he would grab to steady himself when a thirty-foot wave slammed against the side of the *Laurada* or *Bermuda*. But his grasping hand found only air, nothing to brace himself or prevent himself from going down. His head hit the corner of the hard curb, and he remembered nothing else.

Hart was discovered by passersby, who carried him into a nearby store and alerted police. He was taken to Pennsylvania Hospital, where he experienced convulsions for several hours. When his identity was discovered, police attempted to contact past associates, but none came. John D. Hart died at 3:45 the next morning without regaining consciousness. The blow to his head raised suspicions he had been attacked, but an autopsy by coroner Thomas Dugan discovered no foul play. Doctors said the death was due to apoplexy, which would be renamed "stroke" in years to come.

Just as he died without friends or family by his side, nobody claimed his body when the question was asked. A recent associate from Atlantic City was called who said he would see to arrangements, but no one came. The next day, Kate Hart read in the newspaper that her estranged husband was dead, and she went to claim his remains.

The body she collected from the hospital was a mere shell of the hearty, robust man she knew. She had him brought to her boarding house, where his coffin was adorned with a few bouquets and a wreath, but only a few mourners bothered to pay their respects. Reports of Hart's death were carried in newspapers from coast to coast, most recounting his glorious years as a friend of Cuba but some reporting his recent failures. One account called Hart's life "a pathetic story of a man who abandoned his nearly destitute wife." As the *Inquirer* reported: "Once a popular hero, Captain Hart showed weaknesses in the later years of his life that resulted in the estrangement of most of his more loyal friends."

That so few were present to pay final respects was a sad footnote to an enormous life. Hart was a "thorough American" by his own words who had done much to help the Cuban people throw off the Spanish yoke, yet he died alone. A man who saw himself as a lighter of candles disappeared into the darkness of inattention and neglect. The newspaper that chronicled the heights and depths of his fully lived life provided the only memorial at his death. In a succinct editorial page comment, the *Inquirer* wrote: "There is only this to be said of Captain Hart's death: He took up the cause of the Cubans long before the rest of us, and suffered because he did."

Kate Hart sent John's body back to Baltimore to be buried next to his mother and father and their two children in Section G, Plot no. 150, at Baltimore's Loudon Park Cemetery. His parents' headstones were a tribute to their son's life. Father James's stone featured the lunette of a ship in full sail, while the same space on

This photo of Kate Hart was taken in Philadelphia, likely between her husband's death in 1900 and when she moved to Baltimore in 1905. Courtesy of Sharon Holt Neil and Sandra Holt Luty, granddaughters of Grace Hart Holt.

Mother Susan's stone was adorned by a spray of bananas hanging from a tree. Both included verses lamenting the loss of a loved one.

Like his parents' monuments, John's was also nine feet in height and contained the same cathedral peak and stone lantern on top. But the lunette on John's stone was bare, and the space for a verse was blank. Only his name, the dates of his birth and death, and the barely perceptible inscription "At Rest" provided any information on the man who lay beneath. Perhaps money was tighter for Kate than when John buried his parents at the height of his glory.

A year after John's burial, Kate Hart returned to bury another child in the same plot. Laura, a telephone operator, died of pneumonia on December 3, 1901, at age nineteen. Two years later, Kate's older daughter, Ada, married Laughlin F. McNeill, a building contractor, and remained in Philadelphia the rest of her life. Perhaps to be closer to her husband and three deceased children, Kate Hart moved back to Baltimore in 1905 with daughter Grace, who was fifteen.

It was a tumultuous time in the city, one year after a devastating fire leveled much of the downtown area, including Bowley's Wharf and Bulack's Chesapeake House restaurant. Kate opened a saloon about five blocks west of the burned area, at 678 West Baltimore Street, which she later turned into a boarding house.

Little is known of the remainder of Kate Hart's life except for two revealing clues that suggest she retained strong affection for her late husband. Kate wrote several letters to the cemetery between 1909 and 1920 complaining about the lack of maintenance around her husband's grave. In a neat, flowing script, Kate complained about a two-dollar surcharge the cemetery demanded for additional maintenance, saying: "John D. Hart fixed that lot for it to be kept up, as he knew he could not live always and he wanted no expense on me as his widow after his death." An even more telling indicator of Kate's feelings came later when she began including a parenthetical line into her city directory entry. From 1920 until her death, Catherine Hart was further identified as: "(Widow of John D.)."

In 1922, Kate opened a new boarding house at 106 North Greene Street, where she lived until her death on August 1, 1938. Kate's youngest daughter, by then Mrs. Albert F. Holt, who ran her own boarding house next door at 104 North Greene Street, arranged for Kate to be buried beside her husband in Plot no. 150. Curiously, Grace Hart Holt, who had left her mother at age nine to live with her father, did not erect a stone over her mother's grave, and the grave remains unmarked today. Though the reasons are lost to time, Kate Hart will forever remain as anonymous in death as she was in a life spent with the king of the gunrunners.

EPILOGUE

Despite the unknown struggles that lay ahead, Cuba's fight for independence came to a perceived conclusion with the peace protocol of August 12, 1898. Hostilities were officially suspended, four centuries of Spanish rule was ended, and the anguish of expatriation was over. Years of brooding homesickness and personal sacrifice were vindicated. Convinced that the objectives of the insurrection had been achieved, many Cubans saw no further reason to live anywhere but their homeland. Even as Santiago passed to American control in July, exiles abroad readied themselves to return to the island. In the period immediately following the peace protocol, thousands came home.

Some party members and revolution leaders gradually took their places in the new order. Emilio Nuñez would depart for Cuba soon after the war, eventually becoming civil governor of the Province of Havana and serving as one of thirty-one delegates to the Cuban Constitutional Convention of 1900. That same year, Gonzalo de Quesada became special commissioner of Cuba to the United States and was a member of the Cuban Constitutional Convention in 1901. Tomás Estrada Palma remained in the United States, where he was a citizen, but he would be drafted to become the first president of Cuba in December 1901.

Despite their new roles, Cuban leaders would be confounded trying to interpret the American definition of Cuban independence. If independence for Cuba could be associated with the expulsion of Spain, it appeared that good intentions had yielded good results. President McKinley wanted Cuba to have limited independence but under American guidance. The result was that the Cubans exchanged a vicious and corrupt colonial rule for an overbearing protector that believed it could do a better job than Spain.

To the United States' benefit, Spain had been roundly defeated and removed from the Western Hemisphere, while McKinley's insistent peace negotiations brought the Philippines, Guam, and Puerto Rico under US control. Admiral George Dewey's smashing victory in Manila Bay on May 1, 1898, gave a global dimension to the conflict that emboldened the United States to annex the Hawaiian Islands on July 7.

The war not only heightened American nationalism, it changed American foreign affairs by creating a new diplomatic and political situation and turned attention to expansionism. Americans now were reconsidering the reach of the nation's naval power, foreign trade opportunities, and the Christian mission.

The role John D. Hart and the other filibusters played in this new direction—nourishing a three-year revolution that prompted a short, yet transformative, war—can be debated, ignored, or diminished, but it can't be denied.

SOURCE NOTES

Chapter 1: A Wondrous World

4   *71 West Pratt Street.* Movements of the Hart family were determined from examining annual issues of *Woods' Baltimore City Directory*, digital copies of which can be accessed online from the Rare Books Division, University of Maryland, College Park, Maryland, or from the Enoch Pratt Free Library in Baltimore.

4   *the banana was a commercial possibility. Baltimore Sun*, "Baltimore the First Big Banana Port," October 29, 1911; and Frederick Upton Adams, *Conquest of the Tropics* (New York: Doubleday, Page and Company, 1914), 35.

5   *must be peeled to be enjoyed. Baltimore Sun*, "Baltimore the First Big Banana Port," October 29, 1911.

5   *young Alexander Beauregard Bulack. Baltimore Sun*, "History Made There," February 16, 1906.

6   *his days as a private.* Compiled Service Records of Confederate Soldiers Who Served in Organizations from the State of Virginia, Record Group 109, Catalog ID: 586957, National Archives and Records Administration, Washington, DC, compiled 1903–1927, accessed through www.Fold3.com.

6   *Johnny had married Catherine.* The 1860 Federal Census lists seven-year-old Catherine Staylor in the household of Andrew and Mary Staylor in Baltimore's Eighth Ward. However, the marriage certificate claims that John was twenty-two and Kate twenty when they married on September 4, 1878. Later records suggest that Kate was not shy about fudging her age throughout her life.

7   *past the Bahamas.* The route that Frederick Upton Adams described (*Conquest of the Tropics*, 123–28) would have been the same route that John D. Hart traveled to Port Antonio.

9   *The growing family.* US Census for 1880, Maryland, Baltimore City, Fifteenth Ward, p. 311; Archives of Baltimore City birth records, http://guide.mdsa.net/viewer.cfm?page=birth.

Source Notes

9   *an uncharacteristic activity.* Baltimore Sun, "Baltimore's Part in Cuban Gun Running," May 12, 1912.

9   *aspirations toward nationhood.* G. J. A. O'Toole, *The Spanish War: An American Epic, 1898* (New York: W. W. Norton, 1984), 38–39.

9   *the Little War.* O'Toole, *The Spanish War*, 48.

Chapter 2: A New Revolution

10   *the Cuban Revolutionary Committee.* O'Toole, *The Spanish War*, 39.

10   *a writer and orator.* José Martí's early years with the Revolutionary Party are described by Richard Butler Gray, *José Martí, Cuban Patriot* (Gainesville: University of Florida Press, 1962), 11–16; and O'Toole, *The Spanish War*, 48.

11   *nearly half the rebels.* The word "*mambises*" comes from a Black Spanish officer, Juan Ethninius Mamby, who joined the Dominicans in their fight for independence in 1846. To the Spanish soldiers, the word was a derogatory slur, but the rebels adopted the reference with pride. Jerry A. Sierra, "The War for Cuban Independence," History of Cuba, http://www.historyofcuba.com/history/scaw/scaw1.htm.

11   *126 Cuban clubs in eighteen cities.* Antonio Rafael de la Cova, "Fernandina Filibuster Fiasco: Birth of the 1895 Cuban War of Independence," *Florida Historical Quarterly* 82, no. 1 (Summer 2003): 19.

11   *words and ideas.* O'Toole, *The Spanish War*, 48.

11   *One of the veterans who saw the merits.* Emilio Nuñez's early experiences are taken from the New York Herald, "Cuba Determined to Be Free from Spain," September 13, 1891; and New York Herald, "The Case of Emilio Nuñez," January 29, 1884.

12   *chartered a fleet.* Peter Kemp, ed., *The Oxford Companion to Ships and the Sea* (Oxford: Oxford University Press, 1976), 759. The size and speed of schooners of the type Hart and Bulack secured are described.

13   *a 260-square-foot burial plot.* Records of Loudon Park Cemetery, 3620 Wilkens Avenue, Baltimore, Maryland.

13   *death of their son Walter.* Baltimore Sun, obituaries, May 23, 1885.

13   *chartering sister steamships.* Baltimore Sun, "News the Ships Bring," November 7, 1885.

14   *a large stalk.* Baltimore Sun, "Nicaragua Bananas," November 12, 1886.

14   *Ignored in the revelry.* Baltimore Sun, "Fire among the Fruit," January 1, 1887.

14   *a type of prebankruptcy.* Baltimore Sun, "Business Assignment," May 3, 1887.

14   *dumped overboard.* Baltimore Sun, "Captain Hart Sentenced," March 9, 1897.

15   *the third-largest city.* US Census Office, Census Bulletin, 11th Census, 1890 (Washington, DC: Government Printing Office, 1890).

16   *merchants favored the scheme.* Philadelphia Inquirer, "Fruit Buyers Combine to Resist Monopoly," December 19, 1889.

17   *dissolve their partnership.* Philadelphia Inquirer, "The Baltimore Fruit Company," July 15, 1891.

Chapter 3: Scrambling for Ships

18   *the largest city in Florida.* US Census Office, Census Bulletin, 1890.

18   *solid radical pedigrees.* John Lawrence Tone, *War and Genocide in Cuba, 1895–1898* (Chapel Hill: University of North Carolina Press, 2006), 36.

Source Notes 237

18 *Bases and Secret Statutes.* Philip S. Foner, *The Spanish-Cuban-American War and the Birth of American Imperialism, 1895–1902,* vol. 1, *1895–1898* (New York: Monthly Review Press, 1972), 83–85.
19 *approved the Bases.* C. Neale Ronning, *José Martí and the Émigré Colony in Key West: Leadership and State Formation* (New York: Praeger, 1990), 8.
19 *Martí was elected delegate.* Lillian Guerra, *The Myth of José Martí: Conflicting Nationalisms in Early Twentieth-Century Cuba* (Chapel Hill: University of North Carolina Press, 2005), 44; and Carol A. Preece, "Insurgent Guests: The Cuban Revolutionary Party and Its Activities in the United States, 1892–1898" (PhD diss., Georgetown University, 1976), 57.
20 *Among others mentioned prominently.* New York Herald, "Cuba Determined to Be Free from Spain," September 13, 1891.
20 *the economic depression.* William Jett Lauck, *The Causes of the Panic of 1893* (Boston: Houghton, Mifflin, 1907), 105–10.
20 *cigar factories closed.* Ronning, *José Martí and the Émigré Colony,* 108.
20 *Workers went on strike.* Horatio Rubens, *Liberty: The Story of Cuba* (New York: Brewer, Warren and Putnam, 1932), 16.
21 *replicating the monopolies.* Adams, *Conquest of the Tropics,* 83.
21 *Bru filed assault charges.* Philadelphia Inquirer, "Notes of Cases," August 12, 1894.
21 *the Danish vessel* Horsa. Philadelphia Inquirer, "Hart Had Bought Her," May 22, 1896.
22 *he delegated the task.* De la Cova, "Fernandina Filibuster Fiasco," 18–19.
22 *Borden greeted Martí.* S. W. Paul to John G. Carlisle, January 21, 1895, Records of the Customs Bureau, Special Agents Reports and Correspondence, 1865–1915, Records Group 36, Box 360, National Archives, Washington, DC.
22 *Martí wrote to Eduardo H. Gato.* De la Cova, "Fernandina Filibuster Fiasco," 20; and Rubens, *Liberty: The Story of Cuba,* 69.
22 *chartered the yacht* Lagonda. New York World, "Off on a Secret Cruise," January 11, 1895.
22 *the steam yacht* Amadis. Cleveland Leader, "Chief Engineer George H. Kimball Retires," July 1, 1891; and De la Cova, "Fernandina Filibuster Fiasco," 21.
24 *"a filibustering expedition."* James Batewell to Secretary of the Treasury, January 10–11, 1895, Records of the Customs Bureau, RG 36.
24 *"preventing violation neutrality laws."* John G. Carlisle to S. W. Paul, January 12, 1895, Records of the Customs Bureau, RG 36.
24 *canceled all policies.* De la Cova, "Fernandina Filibuster Fiasco," 26.
24 *Collector Baltzell and reporter Hall boarded.* Columbus (GA) Enquirer, "Is It a Filibuster?," January 13, 1895.
24 *surrendered his sailing papers.* New York Herald, "Still Holding the Lagonda," January 14, 1895.
24 *statutes that constituted the "neutrality laws."* Title LXVII of the Revised Statutes, headed "Neutrality," embraces eleven sections, from 5281 to 5291, applied in various enforcement proceedings, depending upon the circumstances of the particular incident; see *Wiborg v. United States,* US Supreme Court, 163 U.S. 632 (1896), https://casetext.com/case/wiborg-v-united-states.
24 *revenue cutters guarding US ports.* The Revenue Cutter Service was the predecessor of the US Coast Guard, which Congress formalized in 1915 when the Revenue Cutter Service merged with the US Life-Saving Service.
25 *"to be taken to the Cuban patriots."* Florida Times-Union (Jacksonville), January 14, 1895.
25 *travel immediately to Fernandina.* Rubens, *Liberty: The Story of Cuba,* 71–72; and De la Cova, "Fernandina Filibuster Fiasco," 22–23.

25 *demanded access to the adjoining warehouse.* New York Herald, "Captain Clausen's Story," January 21, 1895.
25 *officers seized 140 crates.* S. W. Paul to John G. Carlisle, January 16, 1895, Records of the Customs Bureau, RG 36, Box 360.
25 *seized by Customs Collector J. F. B. Beckwith.* C. A. Macatee to John G. Carlisle, January 15, 1895; and Macatee to Carlisle, January 16, 1895, Records of the Customs Bureau, RG 36, Box 305.
25 *making a fat living.* Captain J. H. Rogers to Secretary of the Treasury, January 12, 1895, Records of the US Coast Guard, Revenue Cutter Service, RG 26, Box 281, National Archives, Washington, DC.
26 *he signed the order.* Tomás Estrada Palma, writing in *The American-Spanish War: A History by the War Leaders* (Norwich, CT: Charles C. Haskell and Son, 1899), 406.
26 *the village of Baire.* Louis A. Pérez Jr., *The War of 1898: The United States and Cuba in History and Historiography* (Chapel Hill: University of North Carolina Press, 1998), 7.
26 *"Now I must go!"* Guerra, *The Myth of José Martí*, 47.
27 *if only one time.* Gonzalo de Quesada and Henry Davenport Northrop, *The War in Cuba; or, The Great Struggle for Freedom* (New York: Liberty Publishing Company, 1896), 82.
27 *"Guardian Angel."* Guerra, *The Myth of José Martí*, 47.

Chapter 4: The Wealthy and Useful Ker

28 *placed them on the* Braganza. Record of Alien Immigrants arriving by steamship, October 2, 1894, provided by the Historical Society of Pennsylvania.
28 *purchase of the* Empress. New York Tribune, September 3, 1895.
28 *the* Empress *was substantial.* Catalogue of the Public Documents of the 53rd Congress and of All Departments for the Government of the United States, for the period March 4, 1893, to June 30, 1895 (Washington, DC: Government Printing Office, 1896), 50.
29 *his first year on picket duty.* See the Seventy-Third Pennsylvania Infantry Soldier Roster in Samuel P. Bates, *History of Pennsylvania Volunteers, 1861–1865*, vol. 2 (Wilmington, NC: Broadfoot Publishing Company, 1994).
29 *invasion of the South.* Philadelphia Inquirer, "They Fought the Tigers," November 29, 1892.
29 *returned to Philadelphia.* New York Times, January 1, 1902.
30 *difficult national cases.* Philadelphia Inquirer, "The Brewster Banquet," January 9, 1882.
30 *the peak of his career.* Philadelphia Inquirer, "The New Pilot Boat," December 6, 1889.
30 *a resounding defeat.* Harrisburg (PA) Patriot, "A Balance Reached," November 19, 1892.
30 *the International Migration Society.* Philip J. Staudenraus, *The African Colonization Movement, 1816–1865* (New York: Columbia University Press, 1961), 23–103.
31 *revived in the early 1880s.* Kenneth C. Barnes, *Journey of Hope: The Back-to-Africa Movement in Arkansas in the Late 1800s* (Chapel Hill: University of North Carolina Press, 2004), 31.
31 *white racism reached its zenith.* Sources disagree on the actual number of lynchings per year, but all agree that the 1890s saw more lynchings of Blacks than any other decade.

Source Notes 239

31   *created in 1894.* Barnes, *Journey of Hope*, 137–38.
31   *the partners' interests.* Memphis *Commercial Appeal*, March 7, 1895.
32   *rumors the ship had sunk.* Philadelphia Inquirer, "The *Horsa* Heard From," April 13, 1895.
33   *a mottled history.* O'Toole, *The Spanish War*, 38–39.
33   *use all diligence.* New York Herald, "No Filibusters from Florida," March 13, 1895.
33   *alerted the cruiser* Infanta Isabel. New York Herald, "Hunting for Filibusters," March 16, 1895.
33   *the surviving leadership did not know what to do.* Enrique Collazo, *Cuba independiente* (1900; Santiago de Cuba: Editorial Oriente, 1981), 171.
34   *"temporarily paralyzed."* New York Herald, "Heavy Blow to Cubans," May 30, 1895.
34   *Guerra tried to respond.* Rubens, *Liberty: The Story of Cuba*, 143–44.
34   *the* Childs *was not a large vessel.* New York Herald, "Safely Landed on Cuban Soil," June 14, 1895.
34   *Dupuy de Lôme demanded.* New York Herald, "Man-of-War for Key West," June 9, 1895.
34   *preventing the shipment of arms.* "Preventing Conveyance of Articles to Cubans," House Document 264, Serial no. 3679, 55th Congress, 2nd Session, 4–5.
34   *or be "rigorously prosecuted."* New York Herald, "Warning Given by the President," June 13, 1895.
34   *a full page of nine stories.* New York Herald, "Safely Landed on Cuban Soil," June 14, 1895.
34   *its dash for home.* Cleveland *Plain Dealer*, "Guns, Gold and Men," June 17, 1895.
35   *if any of it were true.* Philadelphia Inquirer, "The Filibustering Story Doubted," June 14, 1895.
35   *expedition leaders Carlos Roloff and Serafín Sánchez.* General Carlos Roloff Mialofsky, a Polish-born veteran of the Union Army who had fought in the Ten Years' War, was the Cuban Revolutionary Party's minister of war.
35   *bailed water all the way.* Rubens, *Liberty: The Story of Cuba*, 147–48.
35   *avoiding alligators and poisonous snakes.* Collazo, *Cuba independiente*, 171–74, 270.
35   *the City Hotel in Baltimore. Correspondencia diplomática de la Delegación Cubana en Nueva York durante la Guerra de Independencia de 1895 a 1898* (Havana: Archivo Nacional de Cuba, 1946), vol. 5, 180.
36   *one more request.* Justo Carrillo Morales, *Expediciones Cubanas* (Havana: Imprenta P. Fernández, 1936), 57–58. See also Ramiro Guerra y Sánchez, *Historia de la Nación Cubana*, vol. 6, book 5 (Havana: Editorial Historia de la Nación Cubana, 1952), 273; and *Tampa Times*, "Largest and Best-Equipped Ever Landed," August 2, 1895.
36   *Dr. Esquinaldo.* New York Herald, "Filibusters on Cuban Soil," July 31, 1895.
36   *the first successful expedition.* Collazo, *Cuba independiente*, 175.

Chapter 5: The Director of Expeditions

37   *the* Rowena *that was lying at Lemon City.* Rubens, *Liberty: The Story of Cuba*, 143–44.
37   *convince the ship's owner.* Preece, "Insurgent Guests," 38.
38   *the infamous* Virginius *affair.* O'Toole, *The Spanish War*, 39–44.
39   *decapitated the bodies.* Richard H. Bradford, *The Virginius Affair* (Boulder: Colorado Associated University Press, 1980), 52–54.
39   *a lost cargo of bananas.* Philadelphia Inquirer, "Notes of the Courts," May 30, 1895.
40   *under retainer to the Spanish legation.* Charles A. Siringo, *Two Evil Isms: Pinkertonism and Anarchism* (Austin, TX: Steck-Vaughn Company, 1907), 8.

240 Source Notes

41 *enlist a willing ally.* Dupuy de Lôme to Olney, July 7, 1895, Container 28, Reel 10, Richard Olney Papers, Manuscript Division, Library of Congress, Washington, DC.

41 *Dupuy de Lôme was a lawyer.* Carlos García Barrón, "Enrique Dupuy de Lôme and the Spanish American War," *The Americas* 36, no. 1 (July 1979): 39–58.

42 *The report alleged several threats.* The address 1777 Broadway appeared in a story headlined "Drilling to Fight in Cuba" in the August 3, 1895, issue of the *Washington Bee* nearly a month after Dupuy de Lôme's note to Olney. When the *Bee* reporter knocked on the door, he was told that it was a meeting of the Cuban Fencing Club.

Chapter 6: A Lesson in Competition

43 *the logical choice to follow Martí.* New York Herald, "Palma Is Elected," July 11, 1895; *New York Tribune*, "Señor Palma Here," July 13, 1895; and *New York Herald*, "Palma Speaks Up for All Cubans," July 13, 1895.

44 *chief of the Department of Expeditions.* Rafael Rodríguez Altunaga, *El General Emilio Nuñez* (Havana: Sociedad Colombista Panamericana, 1958), 61.

44 *a popular appellation.* Rubens, *Liberty: The Story of Cuba*, 101.

44 *a smaller version of the United States.* George Washington Auxier, "The Propaganda Activities of the Cuban *Junta* in Precipitating the Spanish-American War, 1895–1898," *Hispanic American Historical Review* 19, no. 3 (August 1939): 287–88.

45 *an angry American citizenry.* Lewis L. Gould, *The Spanish-American War and President McKinley* (Lawrence: University Press of Kansas, 1982), 52.

45 *deviated from Martí.* Guerra, *The Myth of José Martí*, 45.

45 *a serious lesson in competition.* Joseph E. Wisan, *The Cuban Crisis as Reflected in the New York Press (1895–1898)* (New York: Octagon Books, 1965), 25.

46 *"the peanut club."* Rubens, *Liberty: The Story of Cuba*, 205.

46 *a prominent manufacturer of guns.* New Haven (CT) Register, "A Great Arms Factory," March 20, 1888; and Collins Company, *A Brief Account of the Development of the Collins Company in the Manufacture of Axes, Machetes and Edge Tools* (Fitzwilliam, NH: Ken Roberts Publishing Company, 1935).

47 *"the man with the Chinese name."* Foner, *The Spanish-Cuban-American War*, 109; and Rubens, *Liberty: The Story of Cuba*, 142.

47 *a center of expeditionary planning.* Rubens, *Liberty: The Story of Cuba*, 150.

47 *clamping down harder.* New York Herald, "Cabinet Talks about Cuba," July 20, 1895.

47 *negative publicity for Spain.* New York Herald, "Safely Landed on Cuban Soil," June 14, 1895.

47 *"the greatest insurrectionary activity."* Philadelphia Inquirer, "Homes of Cubans Closely Watched," March, 25, 1895; and Leland M. Williamson et al., eds., *Prominent and Progressive Pennsylvanians of the Nineteenth Century*, vol. 2 (Philadelphia: Record Publishing Company, 1898), 217.

47 *He mixed freely with the barons.* Philadelphia Inquirer, "Crowds and Cape May," August 3, 1896.

Chapter 7: Fully Vested in the Filibuster Business

48 *a major expedition had landed.* Baltimore Sun, "Baltimore to Cuba," August 2, 1895.

50 *John D. Hart's Laurada.* Baltimore Sun, "That Cuban Expedition," August 3, 1895. The Junta's weekly newspaper *Cuba Libre* reported on August 8 that a huge expedition

Source Notes 241

under the command of General Carlos Roloff had landed in Las Villas Province but did not mention the name of the vessel.

50 *another Hart line vessel.* Preece, "Insurgent Guests," 113–14.
50 *established the alibi.* Baltimore Sun, "News of the Port," August 8, 1895; and New York Herald, "Port of New York Maritime Reports," August 22, 1895.
51 *"trouble in Wilmington."* Philadelphia Inquirer, "The Cubans on Trial," September 19, 1895.
51 *Prepared for a gunfight.* New York Herald, "Cubans Held under the Law," September 1, 1895; and Philadelphia Inquirer, "Arrested as Filibusters," August 31, 1895.
51 *the mysterious bundle from Nuñez.* Letter #11819, August 30, 1895, Entry 148B, Letters Received 1871–1909, Records of the US Coast Guard, Revenue Cutter Service, RG 26, Box 289. See also New York Herald, "The Cubans Acquitted," September 24, 1895.
51 *taken to the federal building.* The US commissioner system, established in 1793, allowed commissioners to conduct initial proceedings in federal criminal cases and to determine bail for federal defendants. The system was superseded by the Federal Magistrates Act of 1968.
51 *a handwritten note.* Dupuy de Lôme to Olney, September 2, 1895, Container 34, Reel 12, Olney Papers.
51 *taking credit for the apprehension.* Adee to the Department of the Treasury, August 30, 1895, Letter #11823, Entry 148B, Records of the US Coast Guard, Revenue Cutter Service, RG 26, Box 289.
51 *A whimsical soul.* Adee to Olney, August 31, 1895, Container 34, Reel 12, Olney Papers; and Margaret Leech, *In the Days of McKinley* (New York: Harper and Brothers, 1959), 152.
52 *"sell them to whomsoever they saw fit."* New York Herald, September 24, 1895.
52 *"a cloak for filibustering."* Philadelphia Inquirer, "May Be Indicted," September 3, 1895.
52 *only four days of rations remained.* Captain H. T. Blake to Secretary of the Treasury, August 30, 1895, Letter #11825, Records of the US Coast Guard, Revenue Cutter Service, RG 26.
52 *a principal organizer of the expedition.* New York Herald, "Another Cuban Suspect," September 12, 1895.
52 *proving it was another matter.* New York Herald, "Debate about Arms," September 2, 1895.
53 *lead counsel should be well known.* US Senate, "Senate Salaries (1789 to Present)," https://www.senate.gov/senators/SenateSalariesSince1789.htm.
53 *the accused Cubans.* Philadelphia Inquirer, "Gray's Defense of Cubans," September 20, 1895; and Philadelphia Inquirer, "The Cubans on Trial," September 19, 1895.
54 *under no illusions.* Dupuy de Lôme to Olney, September 20, 1895, Container 36, Reel 13, Olney Papers.
54 *an immediate vote.* Philadelphia Inquirer, "The Cubans Acquitted," September 24, 1895.

Chapter 8: Not a Man of Patience

56 *A diverse collection of public figures.* See Philip Foner's analysis of widespread support in the United States for the Cuban Revolution in his chapter "The American People and Cuban Independence," *The Spanish-Cuban-American War*, 163–76.
56 *predicted increased activity.* Olney to Secretary of the Treasury, September 18, 1895, Container 36, Reel 13, Olney Papers.

242 Source Notes

56   *captured the expedition.* Captain C. A. Abbey to Secretary of the Treasury, September 18, 1895, Log of the Revenue Cutter *Winona*, Entry 148B, Records of the US Coast Guard, Revenue Cutter Service, RG 26, Box 289; and *New York Herald*, "Cubans under Bond," September 19, 1895.
57   *a star of the Havana baseball nine.* Roberto González Echevarría, *The Pride of Havana: A History of Cuban Baseball* (New York: Oxford University Press, 1999), 99; and *New York Herald*, "Prize Crew and Cubans on Board," September 21, 1895.
57   *captured expeditions raised Emilio Nuñez's suspicions.* Lyman J. Gage, *Annual Report of the Secretary of the Treasury on the State of the Finances for the Year 1897, to the 55th Congress* (Washington, DC: Government Printing Office, 1897), lviii
57   *internal dissension.* Philadelphia Inquirer, "Split among Cubans," September 27, 1895.
58   *send nothing more to New York.* Preece, "Insurgent Guests," 145.
58   *not a single expedition had landed.* Foner, *The Spanish-Cuban-American War*, 83–85; *New York Herald*, "Gómez's Army in Distress," September 24, 1895; and Preece, "Insurgent Guests," 113–17.
58   *expeditions were mismanaged.* Collazo, *Cuba independiente*, 273–76.
59   *pacing between his desk and the window.* New York Herald, "Aid for Cuba's Cause," November 1, 1895.
59   *A late major hurricane.* Carrillo Morales, *Expediciones Cubanas*, 84; and *New York Tribune*, "Notice to Mariners," July 26, 1895. In June 1895, the US Weather Bureau instituted a flag system intended to warn vessels headed toward a suspected hurricane. Dubbed "the hurricane signal," the bureau adopted two red flags with black squares at the center, flying one above the other, to be displayed at all Weather Bureau stations and on steamship and steamboat lines along the Florida and Gulf of Mexico coasts. Hurricane tracking information from National Hurricane Center, National Oceanic and Atmospheric Administration, Hurricane Tracking Chart, 1895: https://www.aoml.noaa.gov/hrd/Landsea/Partagas/1894-1897/1895.pdf.
60   *suspicious activity in Cuba.* New York Tribune, "Report of an Expedition Confirmed," October 31, 1895.
60   *center of the diplomatic storm.* New York Times, "The *Laurada* Slips Away," November 14, 1895. See also the Associated Press dispatch in the *Chicago Inter-Ocean*, "Think She Is a Filibuster," November 14, 1895.
60   *go to Fort Sumter.* Philadelphia Inquirer, "*Laurada* Not a Pirate," November 16, 1895.
61   *caused a cargo of bananas to spoil.* Charlotte Observer, "Right after the *Laurada*," November 16, 1895. In maritime law, a plaintiff's grievance or lawsuit is termed a "libel" (*Webster's New College Dictionary*).
61   *recognized as belligerents.* New York Herald, "Seeking Recognition," March 30, 1895.
61   *certain neutral rights and obligations.* Elbert J. Benton, *International Law and Diplomacy of the Spanish-American War*, Albert Shaw Lectures on Diplomatic History (Baltimore: Johns Hopkins University Press, 1908), 35.
61   *part of the Spanish persecution.* Philadelphia Inquirer, "*Laurada* Has Been Seized," November 17, 1895.

Chapter 9: "Until Cuba Is Free"

62   *glided into New York Harbor.* New York Herald, "Belated by the Storms," November 19, 1895.
62   *a grotesque scar.* Rubens, *Liberty: The Story of Cuba*, 192.

Source Notes 243

62 *A prestigious delegation.* García Menocal's activities during this period would lay the groundwork for a career in government and politics that would culminate in his election as president of Cuba in 1912.

63 *"I expect to start for Cuba."* New York Herald, "The Junta Strengthened," November 19, 1895.

63 *Their dress was varied.* New York Herald, "Cuba Determined to Be Free from Spain," September 13, 1891; and New York Herald, "Bolt in the Cuban Junta," August 18, 1895.

64 *meet at the wharf.* Testimony of Albanus Falkenberg and Arthur V. Hazlett, Wiborg v. United States, no. 986.

64 *he charted a southward course.* Wiborg v. United States, no. 986; and Carrillo Morales, Expediciones Cubanas, 64, 66.

65 *they seized the ship.* Philadelphia Inquirer, "The Horsa in the Toils," November 20, 1895.

65 *"Every United States customs officer is turned into a spy."* New York Herald, "Spies, He Calls Them," November 21, 1895.

66 *"watching every vessel."* Philadelphia Inquirer, "Freedom for Cuba Must Be Secured," November 22, 1895.

66 *The crowd at the Academy of Music.* Ker's comments did not upstage the keynote speaker, Gov. Claude Matthews of Indiana, who said that "no greater crimes in Christian civilization" could be found than those created by Spanish misrule in Cuba. Matthews's speech received widespread coverage, including stories in the November 22, 1895, editions of the Philadelphia Inquirer, New York Times, and New York Herald.

66 *transporting a military expedition.* Baltimore Sun, "Alleged Filibusters Arrested," November 29, 1895; and Brooklyn Daily Eagle, "Horsa's Crew as Witnesses," November 29, 1895.

67 *$25 to keep their mouths shut.* Testimony of Carl Arnston, Wiborg v. United States, no. 986. Newspapers covering the hearing reported the sum Hart was supposed to have received from the Cubans as anywhere from $12,000 to $25,000, although Junta records examined by Carol Preece ("Insurgent Guests") put the figure at $5,158.

67 *bound over on $1,000 bail.* New York Herald, "Captain Wiborg Held," November 30, 1895.

67 *the president's annual message.* New York Times, "Sound and Impressive," December 4, 1895.

67 *Estrada Palma addressed a long letter.* Foner, The Spanish-Cuban-American War, 182.

67 *Atkins was not impressed.* E. F. Atkins to Olney, December 17, 1895, Container 39, Reel 14, Olney Papers.

68 *"We call it arson."* O'Toole, The Spanish War, 64.

68 *repeated his Wilmington strategy.* Records and Briefs of the US Supreme Court, October Term 1906 (Washington, DC: Judd and Detweiler, 1907), 14.

68 *none could speak English.* Charlotte Observer, "Trying the Laurada's Crew," December 7, 1895.

68 *the Cubans drilled constantly.* Charlotte Observer, "The Laurada Guilty of Offense on the High Seas," December 10, 1895.

69 *a devastating "norther."* New York Herald, "A Secret Gets Out," December 28, 1895.

70 *not a commercial commodity.* Philadelphia Inquirer, "Laurada Not a Pirate," November 16, 1895.

70 *John and Kate Hart separated.* Gopsill's 1896 Philadelphia City Directory, published in March, listed John D. Hart's residence as Green's Hotel, while Kate Hart's residence was 1220 Mount Vernon Street, 834.

Chapter 10: A Clear Victory in Court

71 *contradictory nature.* New York Herald, "Cubans Still Loyal," December 14, 1895.
71 *newspapers were willing accomplices.* Wisan, *The Cuban Crisis*, 47.
71 *a "legation" at the Raleigh Hotel.* Auxier, "The Propaganda Activities of the Cuban Junta," 288.
72 *"money to our friend at the Star."* Quesada to Estrada Palma, April 21, 1896, *Correspondencia diplomática de la Delegación Cubana en Nueva York*, vol. 5, 60; and Quesada to Estrada Palma, December 2, 1896, vol. 5, 81.
72 *another clear victory.* Columbia (SC) *State*, "Charleston for Cuba," January 24, 1896.
73 *the case of the* Itata. New York Times, "The *Itata*'s Cargo," June 7, 1891.
73 *did not constitute a violation.* George Breckenridge Davis, *The Elements of International Law* (New York: Harper and Brothers, 1903), 410–11; and *United States v. the Itata*, Circuit Court of Appeals, Ninth Circuit, May 8, 1893, no. 45.
73 *emboldened by the verdict.* Baltimore Sun, "Steamers to Be Armed," January 25, 1896.
74 *succumbed to the general's demands.* Boston Journal, "All at the Bottom; Vast Quantity of Rifles and Cartridges Bound for Cuba," January 29, 1896.
74 *its hull was rotten.* Collazo, *Cuba independiente*, 278.
74 *a fierce storm overtook them.* New York Herald, "Hapless Fate of Filibusters," January 29, 1896.
74 *"Here we die for Cuba."* Rodríguez Altunaga, *El General Emilio Nuñez*, 64.
75 *three schooners responded.* New York Herald, "Hapless Fate of Filibusters," January 29, 1896.
75 *value of the steamer and lost weapons.* Carol Preece's information from Junta records in Havana put the costs of García's expedition aboard the *Hawkins* at $72,817; Preece, "Insurgent Guests."
76 *add a new vessel to the filibuster fleet.* Nuñez to Estrada Palma, January 29, 1896, Documento no. 40, Carta no. 17-701, in Rodríguez Altunaga, *El General Emilio Nuñez*, 273.
76 *the war was not going well.* O'Toole, *The Spanish War*, 56.
76 *The new governor.* Quesada and Northrop, *The War in Cuba*, 87–88.
76 *his detractors called him "the Butcher."* New York Herald, "Campos's Work in Cuba," January 18, 1896.
77 *"the love of a mother to her children."* New York Herald, "No Mercy in Weyler's Plans," January 21, 1896.
78 *"the dead will rise from their graves."* Quesada and Northrop, *The War in Cuba*, 95.
78 *nothing the American authorities could do.* Philadelphia Inquirer, "Off for Cuba Laden with Arms," February 13, 1896.
78 *"we mean to pay them back."* Charleston (SC) *Evening Post*, "The Mystery of the *Commodore*," February 17, 1896.
78 *a massive transport of volunteers.* Philadelphia Inquirer, "Maritime Notes," February 22, 1896.
79 *the small steamship* Commodore. Preece, "Insurgent Guests," appendix, CRP Expenses.
79 *A second cutter, the* Boutwell. Charlotte Observer, "Cuban Arms at Wilmington," September 20, 1895.
79 *a sign at the gangplank.* Columbia (SC) *State*, "The Steamer *Commodore*," February 16, 1896.

Source Notes   245

Chapter 11: Spanish Spies and US Marshals

81 *the* Bermuda *for $22,000*. Preece, "Insurgent Guests," appendix, CRP Expenses.
81 *Her bottom was scraped and painted.* New York Times, "Captured in the Bay," February 26, 1896.
82 *McCarthy issued warrants.* New York Herald, "Cubans Foiled; Ships Seized," February 26, 1896.
83 *belching black smoke.* New York Herald, "The Prisoners Arraigned," February 26, 1896.
83 *stood defiantly at the tug's bow.* New York World, "Cuba Sorely Hurt," February 26, 1896.
84 *a floating armory.* New York Herald, "General García in Custody," February 26, 1896; and Philadelphia Inquirer, "Both Home on Bail," February 28, 1896.
84 *"more likely to act than to talk."* New York Times, "Captured in the Bay," February 26, 1896.
84 *an entirely different story.* Philadelphia Inquirer, "The *Bermuda* Released," March 1, 1896.
84 *two pieces of good news.* New York Herald, "The *Bermuda* Free," March 4, 1896.
85 *the precarious nature of proceedings.* Biographical Directory of Federal Judges, Federal Judicial Center, https://www.fjc.gov/search/site/Biographical%20Directory%20of%20Federal%20Judges.
85 *his adopted country's fight for independence.* Philadelphia Inquirer, "Captain Wiborg as a Bold Witness," February 27, 1896.
85 *"a very narrow compass."* Philadelphia Inquirer, "Horsa's Men Guilty," February 29, 1896.

Chapter 12: "Captain Dynamite" Johnny O'Brien

88 *a notorious confidant.* New York Herald-Tribune, "The *Bermuda* Puts to Sea," March 16, 1896.
89 *took his first voyage.* Horace Smith, *A Captain Unafraid: The Strange Adventures of Dynamite Johnny O'Brien* (New York: Harper and Brothers, 1912), 6–9.
89 *munitions intended for the Confederacy.* Rodman L. Underwood, *Waters of Discord: The Union Blockade of Texas during the Civil War* (Jefferson, NC: McFarland, 2003), 200.
89 *"Daredevil Johnny."* Herminio Portell Vilá, "John O'Brien, el Capitán Dinamita," in *Vidas de la unidad americana: Veinte y cinco biografías de americanos ilustres* (Havana: Editorial Minerva, 1944), 353–67.
90 *a new and lasting nickname.* Smith, *A Captain Unafraid*, 47–53.
91 *"You can count on me."* Smith, *A Captain Unafraid*, 80.
91 *first mate Edward Murphy.* Baltimore Sun, "The *Bermuda* Sails," March 16, 1896.
91 *clear the* Bermuda *for Vera Cruz.* New York Herald, "The *Bermuda*'s Romantic Log," April 10, 1896.
92 *Spanish spies and Pinkertons.* Quesada and Northrop, *The War in Cuba*, 110–13.
93 *no mood to celebrate.* Smith, *A Captain Unafraid*, 86–93.

Chapter 13: A Quick Indoctrination into Filibuster Protocol

94 *Napoleon Bonaparte Broward.* Joe Knetsch and Nick Wynne, *Florida in the Spanish-American War* (Charleston SC: History Press, 2011), 58.

246 Source Notes

94   *a romantic with a vision.* Diane Roberts, *Dream State: Eight Generations of Swamp Lawyers, Conquistadors, Confederate Daughters, Banana Republicans, and Other Florida Wildlife* (New York: Free Press, 2004), 169–72.
95   *plantation was burned.* Samuel Proctor, "Napoleon B. Broward: The Years to the Governorship," *Florida Historical Quarterly* 26, no. 2 (October 1947): 120.
96   *took solace in the river.* Gene M. Burnett. *Florida's Past: People and Events that Shaped the State* (Sarasota, FL: Pineapple Press, 1988), 11.
96   *christened the Three Friends.* Proctor, "Napoleon B. Broward"; and Napoleon B. Broward Correspondence, Legal and Business Papers, 1879–1900, University of Florida Libraries, Gainesville, Florida.
96   *a contract with the Junta.* Napoleon B. Broward, "Autobiography, Platform, Letter and Short Story of the Steamer 'Three Friends,' and a Filibustering Trip to Cuba," booklet, 1904, Florida Memory, State Library and Archives of Florida, http://www.florida memory.com/items/show/346219, 28–31.
96   *indoctrination into filibuster protocol.* Ralph D. Paine, *Roads of Adventure* (Boston: Houghton, Mifflin, 1922), 177–80; and Broward, "Autobiography, Platform, Letter."
97   *Collazo and fifty-four men.* Quesada and Northrop, *The War in Cuba*, 162; and *New York Herald*, "Collazo Now in Cuba," March 19, 1896.
98   *the thorn jungle.* Felix Oswald, "A Guerilla Eden," *North American Review* 162, no. 472 (March 1896): 380.
98   *The rebels swung machetes.* Paine, *Roads of Adventure*, 178; and *New York Herald*, "Collazo Now in Cuba," March 19, 1896.
98   *final checks in preparation for landing.* Smith, *A Captain Unafraid*, 87–91.
99   *A waving lantern from shore.* R. George Reno, "Operating an 'Underground' Route to Cuba," *Cosmopolitan*, August 1899, 435.
100 *sent a cablegram.* Boston Herald, "*Bermuda* Arrived Out," March 30, 1896.

Chapter 14: A Booming Reply of "NOT GUILTY!"

101 *make no comments.* Brooklyn Daily Eagle, "The *Bermuda* Trial," April 9, 1896; and *New York Herald*, "The *Bermuda* Is Back," April 11, 1896.
102 *Scribes and spies alike.* Philadelphia Inquirer, "Arrests to Be Made," April 15, 1896.
102 *found not guilty.* New York Herald, "Verdict of Acquittal," April 11, 1896.
102 *"NOT GUILTY!"* Philadelphia Inquirer, "Arrests to Be Made," April 15, 1896.
102 *he felt strongly for the Cuban cause.* Smith, *A Captain Unafraid*, 100–107.
103 *a pot of boiling water.* Smith, *A Captain Unafraid*, 100–107.
103 *a popular destination.* Philadelphia Inquirer, "The *Bermuda* Docked," April 27, 1896.
104 *O'Brien shared the bridge.* Philadelphia Inquirer, "Captain Ker Says the *Bermuda* Has Not Been Loaded with War Material," April 28, 1896.
104 *Three train cars of young Cubans.* Tampa Tribune, "Cleared with Cubans," April 29, 1896. The number of men aboard this expedition was reported as anywhere between 125 and 400, but later events put the number closer to 100.
105 *piteous cries of panic.* Philadelphia Inquirer, "That Famous Voyage," June 19, 1896; and Philadelphia Inquirer, "Thirty-Seven Brave Men Lost by a Filibustering Steamer," July 2, 1899.
105 *Reilly's lack of nerve.* Philadelphia Inquirer, "Awaiting *Bermuda*," May 16, 1896.

105 *primary directive as chief of expeditions.* Rodríguez Altunaga, *El General Emilio Nuñez,* 67; *New York Herald-Tribune,* "Severe Blow to the Rebels," April 30, 1896; and Estrada Palma to Ulpiano Dellunde, *Correspondencia diplomática de la Delegación Cubana en Nueva York,* vol. 1, 34.
106 *New Orleans native.* New Orleans *Picayune,* "Happenings in the Cuban Country," January 20, 1896.
106 *The* Mesagera *opened fire.* New Orleans *Picayune,* "Trial by Court-Martial Begun in Havana," May 9, 1896; *Philadelphia Inquirer,* "Sentenced to Death," May 10, 1896; Rodríguez Altunaga, *El General Emilio Nuñez,* 68; and Charleston (SC) *News and Courier,* "Capture of the *Competitor,*" May 26, 1896.
107 *Press reports insisted the trial was unfair.* Wisan, *The Cuban Crisis,* 149–50.
107 *"feeling against Spain has already spread."* Philadelphia Inquirer, "Another Expedition," May 10, 1896.

Chapter 15: "Damfoolitis"

108 *"Damfoolitis."* Charles H. Brown, *The Correspondents' War: Journalists in the Spanish-American War* (New York: Charles Scribner's Sons, 1967), 66.
108 *the avowed leader.* Philadelphia Inquirer, "Cox Went to Cuba," April 8, 1896.
109 *quick feet and shifty hips.* Springfield (MA) *Republican,* ". . . Major Osgood," December 5, 1896.
109 *In Charleston, they approached.* New York Herald, "More Filibusters Land," March 24, 1896.
109 *on the east coast of Cuba.* Philadelphia Inquirer, "Cox Writes from Cuba," April 22, 1896.
110 *an amicable arrangement for all.* Charles Johnson Post, *The Little War of Private Post: An Artist Soldier's Memoir of the Spanish-American War* (Lincoln: University of Nebraska Press, 1999), 202.
110 *"we ride to the creek."* Philadelphia Inquirer, "Cox Writes from Cuba," April 22, 1896.
110 *Baltimore's "swell set."* Quesada to Dr. Joaquin Castillo Duany, March 31, 1896, *Correspondencia diplomática de la Delegación Cubana en Nueva York,* vol. 5, 52.
110 *he was tiring of such requests.* Estrada Palma made these points in two letters to Ramón Emeterio Betances: on June 26, 1896, *Correspondencia diplomática de la Delegación Cubana en Nueva York,* vol. 1, 56; and on September 11, 1896, vol. 1, 78.
111 *"the Baltimore youth."* Quesada to Estrada Palma, April 24, 1896, *Correspondencia diplomática de la Delegación Cubana en Nueva York,* vol. 5, 61.
111 *a spunky player.* Baltimore Sun, "A Foot-Ball Association," April 5, 1894.
111 *never shied from a scrap.* Baltimore Sun, "Hero of Guáimaro," March 31, 1897.
111 *training as artillery officers.* Baltimore Sun, "Volunteers for Cuba," May 16, 1896.
111 *Hart's* Laurada *came to New York.* New York Herald, "Off to Help the Cubans," May 11, 1896.
112 *an important passenger.* New Haven (CT) Register, "Off with Arms for Cuba," May 11, 1896. Carol Preece includes an entry of $10,480.52 for May 1896 titled "Fernández Ruz expedition"; Preece, "Insurgent Guests," appendix, CRP Expenses.
112 *"One would think."* Philadelphia Inquirer, "The *Laurada* Gone," May 11, 1896.
113 *a perfect spot for a landing.* Navigation of the Gulf of Mexico and Caribbean Sea, vol. 1, 5th ed. (Washington, DC: Government Printing Office, 1901), 166.
113 *Dickman was skeptical.* Guerra y Sánchez, *Historia de la Nación Cubana,* 304–5.

248 Source Notes

113   *halted at quarantine.* Charlotte Observer, "The *Laurada*'s Safe Return," May 23, 1896.
114   *Henrico de Maritague protested.* Philadelphia Inquirer, "Turned On Her Guns," May 23, 1896; and Rubens, *Liberty: The Story of Cuba*, 553.
114   *The* Boutwell *escorted the* Three Friends. Baltimore Sun, "The *Three Friends* Escorted to Seas," May 25, 1896; and Baltimore Sun, "Landed in Cuba," June 2, 1896. See also Brown, *The Correspondents' War*, 65.
114   *headed for the open sea.* Baltimore Sun, "Hero of Guáimaro," March 31, 1897.
114   *the landing commenced.* Guerra y Sánchez, *Historia de la Nación Cubana*, 306; and Tone, *War and Genocide in Cuba*, 179.
114   *a much more suspicious greeting.* Baltimore Sun, "Baltimoreans in Cuba," February 3, 1897.
115   *more willing fools than spies.* Baltimore Sun, "Fighting for Cuba," August 18, 1896.
115   *hacked to death with machetes.* New York World, "Want Govin Avenged," August 18, 1896.

Chapter 16: Prosecution or Persecution?

116   *friends in high places.* New York Tribune, notes, May 5, 1896.
117   *the Supreme Court sent shock waves.* Wiborg v. United States.
117   Horsa *carried a military expedition.* Philadelphia Inquirer, "Wiborg Decision," May 26, 1896.
117   *"the Great Dissenter."* Plessy v. Ferguson, US Supreme Court, 163 U.S. 537 (1896).
118   *Wiborg showed little emotion.* Philadelphia Inquirer, "Wiborg Decision," May 26, 1896.
118   *The Spanish minister in Washington was elated.* New York Tribune, "Spaniards Elated," May 27, 1896.
118   *The minister urged the administration.* Dupuy de Lôme to Olney, June 14, 1896, *Foreign Relations of the United States, 1897* (Washington, DC: Government Printing Office, 1897), 544–48.
118   *a presidential pardon for Wiborg.* Philadelphia Inquirer, "Wiborg Decision," May 26, 1896; Philadelphia Inquirer, "Wiborg's Sentence," May 27, 1896; and Philadelphia Inquirer, "Urging His Pardon," May 28, 1896.
118   *a tragic accident.* Philadelphia Inquirer, "The *Horsa* Burns," May 21, 1896.
119   *Hart was demoralized.* Philadelphia Inquirer, "Hart Gives It Up," May 22, 1896.
119   *told Estrada Palma and Nuñez.* Philadelphia Inquirer, "Only One Anxiety," May 24, 1896.
119   *more bad news.* Philadelphia Inquirer, "*Bermuda* Disappears," June 2, 1896.
119   *"a dodge to collect evidence."* Philadelphia Inquirer, "The *Bermuda* Muddle," June 3, 1896.
120   *another problem.* Philadelphia Inquirer, "The *Bermuda* Released," June 10, 1896.
120   *drumbeats along the Delaware.* Philadelphia Inquirer, "*Bermuda*-*Laurada*," May 31, 1896.
120   *"She has become famous."* Philadelphia Inquirer, "The *Laurada* Coming," June 13, 1896.
120   *America's most celebrated vessel.* Philadelphia Inquirer, "*Laurada* Docked," June 18, 1896.
121   *"the uncrowned hero of Cuba."* Philadelphia Inquirer, "Cuba's Thirteen Brave Pilgrim Fathers," June 21, 1896.
121   *"more like persecution."* Philadelphia Inquirer, "Hart Goes to Jail," June 14, 1896.
122   *"can endure it no longer."* Philadelphia Inquirer, "Hart Goes to Jail," June 14, 1896.
122   *a positive note for Hart.* New York Herald-Tribune, "J. D. Hart and Companions Dismissed," July 11, 1896; and Philadelphia Inquirer, "Captain Hart Is Free," July 11, 1896.

Chapter 17: An Ambitious Expedition

123   *administration wanted to help.* Olney to De Lôme, April 4, 1896, *Foreign Relations of the United States, 1897*, 540–44.

123   *a political solution.* John L. Offner, *An Unwanted War: The Diplomacy of the United States and Spain over Cuba, 1895–1898* (Chapel Hill: University of North Carolina Press, 1992), 26–27.

123   *the Junta's ability to operate.* Dupuy de Lôme to Olney, July 2, 1896, Container 56, Reel 20, Olney Papers.

124   *"activity of the law breakers."* Dupuy de Lôme to Olney, July 16, 1896, Container 57, Reel 21, Olney Papers.

124   *"Consul General [Fitzhugh] Lee."* Fitzhugh Lee, a former Confederate general and nephew of Robert E. Lee, was named US consul general in Havana in April 1896.

124   *"precedents of various Proclamations."* Olney to Cleveland, July 18, 1896, Container 57, Reel 21, Olney Papers.

124   *one more "whereas."* Dupuy de Lôme to Olney, July 21, 1896, Container 57, Reel 21, Olney Papers.

124   *"will be vigorously prosecuted."* Copy of Presidential Proclamation, July 27, 1896, Container 58, Reel 21, Olney Papers.

124   *all known expeditions.* Calderon Carlisle, *Report to the Spanish Legation* [. . .] (Washington, DC: n.p., 1896).

124   *grounds for potential claims.* Tampa Tribune, "Spain Has a Poor Case," August 21, 1896.

125   *in league with Spain.* Smith, *A Captain Unafraid*, 109.

125   *a generous contribution.* Guerra y Sánchez, *Historia de la Nación Cubana*, 313.

125   *"look out for filibusters."* Gage, *Annual Report of the Secretary of the Treasury*.

126   *no evidence of filibusters.* Logs of Revenue Steamer *Boutwell*, August 10, 1896, Records of the US Coast Guard, Revenue Cutter Service, RG 26; and *Philadelphia Inquirer*, "Officials on Guard," August 15, 1896.

126   *press was questioning the Revenue Cutter Service.* Joseph Wisan writes that the press had declared all of Florida a Cuban refuge and that US revenue cutter vessels were eluded continually by fleet filibusters; *The Cuban Crisis*, 143.

126   *suspicious enough.* Logs of Revenue Steamer *Boutwell*, August 10, 1896, Records of the US Coast Guard, Revenue Cutter Service, RG 26.

126   *a white lie or two.* Tampa Tribune, "Out of the Service," August 21, 1896.

126   *cleared for Port Antonio.* Baltimore Sun, "The *Laurada* Sails Again," August 7, 1896.

127   *their largest order of the revolution.* Preece, "Insurgent Guests," appendix, CRP Expenses, July–September 1896. A line item labeled "Combined expedition of *Dauntless* and *Laurada*" included an entry for August of $103,115.73 and another for September of $16,478.98.

127   *black-hulled tug named the* Dauntless. Smith, *A Captain Unafraid*, 110.

127   *thirty $1,000 bills.* Rubens, *Liberty: The Story of Cuba*, 159.

128   *a weekday affair.* Smith, *A Captain Unafraid*, 127.

128   *the largest expedition to date.* Philadelphia Inquirer, "The *Laurada* Got There," August 27, 1896.

128   *"The gallant steamship* Laurada.*"* Boston Journal, "She Lands," August 26, 1896.

128   *released on a bond.* Columbia (SC) State, "Captain Murphy Convicted," October 21, 1896.

129   *It was a horse race.* Philadelphia Inquirer, "Excitement over *Laurada*'s Entrance," September 11, 1896.

250 Source Notes

129 *his customary warrants.* Philadelphia Inquirer, "Captain Murphy Held," September 13, 1896.
129 *offers of money or threats of jail.* New York World, "General Roloff Arrested," September 18, 1896.
129 *Murphy's hearing.* Charleston (SC) News and Courier, "Trial of Gen. Roloff," September 23, 1896.
129 *big fish was yet to come.* Philadelphia Inquirer, "Still More Trouble for John D. Hart," October 1, 1896.
130 *the worst news.* Philadelphia Inquirer, "Hart Held for Trial," October 17, 1896.

Chapter 18: A Worst-Case Scenario

132 *Spanish riflemen opened fire.* Frederick Funston, *Memories of Two Wars: Cuban and Philippine Experiences* (New York: Charles Scribner's Sons, 1911), 74–76.
132 *Janney was already halfway there.* Baltimore Sun, "Hero of Guáimaro," March 31, 1897; and Baltimore Sun, "Janney Was the Hero," April 6, 1897. The story of Janney threatening the Cubans is exciting, but Frederick Funston claims that he and Osgood ran out to help Janney pull Devine to safety (*Memories of Two Wars*, 76). Both accounts confirm Janney's bravery.
132 *"I think that will do."* Funston, *Memories of Two Wars*, 78; and Philadelphia Inquirer, "Half-Back Osgood Is Still Fighting," November 19, 1896.
133 *"Always to the Front."* New York Herald-Tribune, in notes, May 3, 1897.
133 *the American presidential campaign.* O'Toole, *The Spanish War*, 73.
133 *free silver versus gold.* Philadelphia Inquirer, "Heavy Firing at Sea and in the Senate," December 16, 1896.
134 *pressure from Madrid.* New Orleans Picayune, "De Lôme Will Await the Ides of March," December 21, 1896.
134 *higher obligations.* New York Herald-Tribune, "The President's Message," December 8, 1896.
134 *conditions might get worse.* Philadelphia Inquirer, "Action on Cuba Will Be Delayed," December 18, 1896.
134 *support for Hart.* Philadelphia Inquirer, "Prayers for Cuba," November 23, 1896.
135 *an international incident.* Baltimore Sun, "*Laurada* at Baltimore," February 1, 1897.
136 *an unfortunate choice of ports.* Lexington (KY) Morning Herald, "Olney and De Lôme," December 13, 1896.
136 *"noble and valorous achievement."* Baltimore Sun, "*Laurada* at Baltimore," February 1, 1897.
136 *in Messina loading lemons.* Columbia (SC) State, "Troubles Abroad," May 30, 1897.
137 *trouble in Valencia was no secret.* Captain J. H. H. Peshine, Thirteenth Infantry, Military Attaché, US Legation, Madrid, Spain, to Olney, September 15, 1896, Memorandum on Cuban Affairs no. 27, Container 61, Reel 22, Olney Papers.
137 *"The government is much alarmed."* R. A. Tucker to Olney, December 13, 1896, Container 68, Reel 24, Olney Papers.
137 *"Have you any suggestions."* Olney to Dupuy de Lôme, December 14, 1896, Container 68, Reel 24, Olney Papers.
138 *intention was merely to buy oranges.* Baltimore Sun, "Plea for *Laurada*," December 15, 1896.

138   *"protect our property."* R. A. Tucker to Olney, December 14, 1896, Container 68, Reel 24, Olney Papers.
138   *preparing for trouble.* Baltimore Sun, "Laurada Barred Out," December 14, 1896.
139   *"Why don't you answer."* Columbia (SC) State, "Troubles Abroad," May 30, 1897.
139   *ignorant of the diplomatic storm.* Baltimore Sun, "Laurada at Baltimore," February 1, 1897.
139   *missed Killingsworth's cables.* Baltimore Sun, "Captain Hughes' Dilemma," December 14, 1896.
139   *"Will not send* Laurada *there."* Baltimore Sun, "Will Not Call at Valencia," December 21, 1896.
139   *"trying to pick a fuss with Spain."* Columbia (SC) State, "Troubles Abroad," May 30, 1897.

Chapter 19: Publicity Agent for an Expedition

140   *its own publicity agent.* Paine, Roads of Adventure, 66.
141   *a jewel-encrusted sword.* Brown, The Correspondents' War, 63–64.
141   *pitched his case.* Paine, Roads of Adventure, 124.
141   *"nail 'em to the cross."* Smith, A Captain Unafraid, 140–41.
142   *a dark side-track.* Guerra y Sánchez, Historia de la Nación Cubana, 319; and Paine, Roads of Adventure, 66–67.
142   *the large, seagoing tug.* Paine, Roads of Adventure, 67.
142   *forced the tug to anchor.* Paine, Roads of Adventure, 80.
144   *opened his sealed orders.* Philadelphia Inquirer, "How the Three Friends Met the Dons," December 26, 1896.
144   *unlimber the twelve-pound Hotchkiss.* Paine, Roads of Adventure, 84.
144   *"full speed to sea!"* Smith, A Captain Unafraid, 145.
144   *gave a wink to Walsh.* Philadelphia Inquirer, "How the Three Friends Met the Dons," December 26, 1896.
145   *"That one was a sighting shot."* Philadelphia Inquirer, "How the Three Friends Met the Dons," December 26, 1896.
146   *They stopped on Christmas Day.* Smith, A Captain Unafraid, 151.
146   *limped into Jacksonville.* Florida Times-Union (Jacksonville), "Three Friends as a Pirate Taken," December 30, 1896.
146   *"All this pirate stuff."* Paine, Roads of Adventure, 165.
146   *from indignation to disbelief.* Philadelphia Inquirer, "Havana Newspapers Are Bitter against the United States," December 29, 1896.
146   *hatched in a Key West dive.* Paine, Roads of Adventure, 125.
147   *a white vessel came tearing up.* Smith, A Captain Unafraid, 153.
147   *put the cargo and party ashore.* Paine, Roads of Adventure, 145.
148   *the tug was stopped.* Logs of Revenue Steamer Boutwell, January 22, 1897, Records of the US Coast Guard, Revenue Cutter Service, RG 26.
148   *"send to Alaska for a jury."* Paine, Roads of Adventure, 160–61.
148   *he exploded in a turbulent rage.* Paine, Roads of Adventure, 175.

Chapter 20: "You Don't Often See a Man Like Him"

149   *a respectful advocate.* Philadelphia Inquirer, "Their Busy Term," November 3, 1896.
149   *the thrust and parry.* Philadelphia Inquirer, "Captain J. D. Hart Is Now on Trial," February 17, 1897.

252 Source Notes

150 *the naphtha launch.* Federal law, responding to frequent boiler explosions, required all steamboats to carry a licensed engineer. Small launches used mainly for personal use circumvented this law by using naphtha as an alternative power source.
150 *The government continued its case.* Philadelphia Inquirer, "Strong Testimony against Hart," February 18, 1897.
150 *$50,000 worth of arms.* Luis Espin, a former medical student, was the Junta's purchasing agent for arms, ammunition, and dynamite. Rubens, *Liberty: The Story of Cuba*, 149.
151 *an aggressive cross-examination.* Philadelphia Inquirer, "The Hart Trial Still Continues," February 19, 1897.
151 *adjourned the trial for the weekend.* Philadelphia Inquirer, "The Hart Trial," February 20, 1897.
151 *surprise visitors to the courtroom.* Philadelphia Inquirer, "Hart's Case Now with the Jurymen," February 23, 1897.
152 *one hour charging the jury.* Philadelphia Inquirer, "Hart's Case Now with the Jurymen," February 23, 1897.
153 *the Society Hermanas de Martí.* Philadelphia Inquirer, "In Cuba's Aid," November 25, 1897.
154 *protest and shouts of "Cuba Libre."* Brooklyn Daily Eagle, "Laurada's Owner Convicted," February 23, 1897; and Philadelphia Inquirer, "Hart Is Guilty, Declare the Jury," February 24, 1897.

Chapter 21: "Justly Convicted"

156 *Bulack would be a comfort.* Baltimore Sun, "News of the Shipping," February 27, 1897.
156 *"write something for me."* Hart's telegraph to President Cleveland applying for the Cuban consul position was told in the February 27, 1897, *Sun* story referenced just above. Bulack repeated the story years later in an interview with a *Sun* reporter for a story headlined "Baltimore's Part in Cuban Gun Running," which appeared on May 12, 1912.
157 *sentenced to two years in prison.* Philadelphia Inquirer, "Hart Was Sentenced," March 9, 1897; and Baltimore Sun, "Captain Hart Sentenced," March 9, 1897.
157 *further aroused a public.* Philadelphia Inquirer, "Heavy Firing at Sea and in the Senate," December 16, 1896.
157 *The most recent outrage.* Philadelphia Inquirer, "Philadelphian Slain," February 21, 1897.
157 *"a law unto themselves."* Philadelphia Inquirer, "American Citizens Must Be Released from the Cuban Prisons," February 25, 1897.
158 *the worsening Cuban situation.* Philadelphia Inquirer, "Sanguily Freed by Spain; War Talk in the Senate," February 26, 1897.
158 *McKinley took the oath of office.* John Gabriel Hunt, ed., *The Inaugural Addresses of the Presidents* (New York: Random House, 2005), 285.
158 *an old ally.* Estrada Palma to Quesada, January 20, 1897, *Correspondencia diplomática de la Delegación Cubana en Nueva York*, vol. 1, 106.
159 *reversed by the US Supreme Court.* Three Friends v. United States, US Supreme Court, 166 U.S. 1 (1897).
159 *"no basis for legal action."* Savannah (GA) Tribune, "Government Restrained," March 6, 1897.

Source Notes 253

159 *immediate repercussions.* New York Herald-Tribune, "Discussed by the Cabinet," March 20, 1897.
159 *his private office.* Gould, *The Spanish-American War*, 15.
159 *read between the lines.* Wilkes-Barre (PA) Times, March 6, 1897.
160 *the lynchpin in yet another expedition.* Smith, *A Captain Unafraid*, 167–69.
160 *anticipated piece of equipment.* Patrick McSherry, "The Navy Experimented and Gave Up on the Compressed Air 'Dynamite Gun,'" *Artilleryman Magazine* 26, no. 1 (Winter 2004): 16–21.
160 *the wealthy New York adventurer.* Rubens, *Liberty: The Story of Cuba*, 205–6.
160 *frequent visitor to Olney's office.* William Astor Chanler to Olney, November 12, 1896, Container 66, Reel 24, Olney Papers.
160 *benevolence to the Cuban cause.* Lately Thomas, *The Astor Orphans: A Pride of Lions* (New York: William Morrow, 1971).
161 *"The Open Boat."* Paine, *Roads of Adventure*, 162.
161 *spent weeks avoiding pursuit.* Baltimore Sun, "Dr. Luis Convicted," March 27, 1897.

Chapter 22: The *Laurada's* Last Expedition

162 *watching O'Brien's house.* Smith, *A Captain Unafraid*, 169–73.
163 *blowing things to smithereens.* Emory W. Fenn, "Ten Months with the Cuban Insurgents," *Century Magazine*, June 1898, 302–7.
163 *a blinding snowstorm.* New York Herald, "The Laurada Again under Suspicion," March 3, 1897.
163 *a straight face born of resentment.* Baltimore Sun, "A Mysterious Steamer," March 4, 1897.
164 *Murphy was dead drunk.* Smith, *A Captain Unafraid*, 169.
164 *waiting for a boat.* Baltimore Sun, "News of the Shipping," March 16, 1897; and Philadelphia Inquirer, "The Laurada Sighted," March 25, 1897.
165 *instruments of their survival.* New York Times, "Roloff Lands in Cuba," April 15, 1897.
165 *arriving in darkness.* Philadelphia Inquirer, "The Laurada Turns Up," March 28, 1897.
165 *They fled just in time.* Baltimore Sun, "The Laurada Is Seized," April 1, 1897; and Baltimore Sun, "Detaining the Laurada," April 3, 1897.
166 *condemned and forfeited.* Baltimore Sun, "Action against Laurada," April 14, 1897.
166 *"the Butcher" took it personally.* Smith, *A Captain Unafraid*, 181–82.
166 *the remorseful captain.* Quesada and Northrop, *The War in Cuba*, 205–6.
166 *she met three barges.* New York Tribune, "With Aid for the Cubans," April 9, 1897.

Chapter 23: Captain Dynamite's Expedition to Havana

168 *sufficient amounts of deception.* Smith, *A Captain Unafraid*, 187–95.
169 *decoy cruise fooled the feds.* New York Herald-Tribune, "Close Watch on the *Dauntless*," April 19, 1897.
170 *make good on his promise.* Philadelphia Inquirer, "Hostilities in Cuba," July 31, 1896; and Guerra y Sánchez, *Historia de la Nación Cubana*, 320.
170 *The greatest explosion.* Tampa Tribune, "Apt to Scare Weyler," June 18, 1896; and Smith, *A Captain Unafraid*, 196.

254 Source Notes

171   *Spanish atrocities.* Winfield S. Kerr, *John Sherman: His Life and Public Services* (Boston: Sherman, French and Company, 1907), 363. Sherman's Senate speeches also mentioned incidents of "butchery and rape," which he found described in a book published by the *New York Journal* that later proved to contain gross exaggerations (Offner, *An Unwanted War*, 19).

171   *more radical measures.* Philadelphia Inquirer, "Crisis Has Come in Cuba's Cause," May 14, 1897.

171   *an enthusiastic audience.* Philadelphia Inquirer, "Big Mass Meeting of Cuba's Friends," May 17, 1897.

171   *a long-debated resolution.* Philadelphia Inquirer, "Morgan and Hale Clash on Cuba," April 7, 1897.

171   *Opposing the resolution.* New York Tribune, "Fiery Cuban Eloquence," May 19, 1897.

172   *"a reflection of American sentiment."* Wisan, *The Cuban Crisis*, 299–300.

172   *political thimblerig.* Philadelphia Inquirer, "Field Day for Cuba in Both Houses," May 21, 1897.

172   *donate the steamship* Laurada. Philadelphia Inquirer, "The *Laurada* Offered," May 21, 1897.

172   *another impulsive idea.* Philadelphia Passenger Lists Index (1883–1948), courtesy of the Pennsylvania Historical Society; and Baltimore Sun, "Chased by Spanish Boats," May 24, 1897.

173   *"I obey orders."* Philadelphia Inquirer, "Arms Safely Sent to Cuban Soldiers," June 10, 1897.

173   *heading in the opposite direction.* Tampa Tribune, "Patriots Are Planning," June 6, 1897.

174   *old-fashioned bad luck.* Tampa Tribune, "Prominent Filibuster," June 11, 1897.

175   *a ship coming up from the south.* Smith, *A Captain Unafraid*, 201–7.

176   *a thunderous explosion.* New York Tribune, "The Dauntless Case Dismissed," June 10, 1897.

176   *a useful service.* Logs of Revenue Cutter *McLane*, June 20, 1897, Records of the US Coast Guard, Revenue Cutter Service, RG 26.

Chapter 24: Broke and Headed for Prison

177   *he wanted his money back.* Philadelphia Inquirer, "Hart Goes Free for a Third Time," June 19, 1897.

178   *the* Laurada *up for public sale.* Baltimore Sun, "Application for Sale of the *Laurada*," June 25, 1897.

178   *suits totaling $10,000.* Baltimore Sun, "*Laurada* Likely to Be Sold," June 29, 1897.

178   *Nuñez was forced to seek other vessels.* Philadelphia Inquirer, "Dynamite Guns for Use in Cuba," July 17, 1897.

178   *McKinley was sympathetic.* Offner, *An Unwanted War*, 54.

178   *a long and careful discussion.* New York Tribune, "A Conference in Philadelphia," May 28, 1897.

178   *"the brilliant young charge d'affaires."* Philadelphia Inquirer, "Cubans Meet Here," May 28, 1897.

179   *a more aggressive stance.* Foner, *The Spanish-Cuban-American War*, 214–15.

179   *urging McKinley to end the war.* Foner, *The Spanish-Cuban-American War*, 214–15.

179   *"cruel employment of fire and famine."* Sherman to Dupuy de Lôme, June 26, 1897, *Foreign Relations of the United States, 1897*, 507–8.

179 *the administration's new approach.* Sherman to Woodford, July 16, 1897, *Foreign Relations of the United States, 1897*, 560.
180 *the "reasonable" way of doing things.* O'Donnell to Sherman, August 4, 1897, *Spanish Diplomatic Correspondence and Documents, 1896–1900* (Washington, DC: Government Printing Office, 1905), 34–35.
180 *Hearst sent word to Estrada Palma.* Rodríguez Altunaga, *El General Emilio Nuñez*, 85.
180 *a cigar-shaped shadow.* New York Tribune, "A Novel Submarine Craft," September 17, 1896.
180 *the navy's first submarine contract.* John J. Poluhowich, *Argonaut: The Submarine Legacy of Simon Lake* (College Station: Texas A&M University Press, 1999), 18–19.
180 *built by William T. Malster.* An avid Republican, Malster would have been campaigning when Nuñez visited. In November 1897, he would be elected mayor of Baltimore.
181 *"this invention is still in diapers."* Rodríguez Altunaga, *El General Emilio Nuñez*, 85.
181 *traveled to Key West.* Nuñez to Estrada Palma, June 26, 1897, Documento no. 78, Carta no. 17-738, in Rodríguez Altunaga, *El General Emilio Nuñez*, 293.
181 *a worthy addition.* Smith, *A Captain Unafraid*, 209–13.
181 *a scathing message to Sherman.* Dupuy de Lôme to Sherman, September 28, 1897, *Foreign Relations of the United States, 1897*, 533–35.
181 *"the succor of filibusters."* Philadelphia Inquirer, "M'Kinley and Cuba," October 13, 1897.
182 *a bristling protest of Spain's complaints.* Baltimore Sun, "Will Continue the Patrol," October 23, 1897.
182 *"Everything possible has been done."* Baltimore Sun, "Neutrality Is Costly," October 22, 1897.
182 *"opposed to all acts of filibustering."* Dupuy de Lôme to Gullón, November 12, 1897, *Spanish Diplomatic Correspondence*, 39.
182 *interim governance and structure.* José M. Hernández, *Cuba and the United States: Intervention and Militarism, 1868–1933* (Austin: University of Texas Press, 1993), 65.
182 *an opportunity to vent.* Collazo, *Cuba independiente*, 73.
182 *expedition efforts had been largely bungled.* The assembly's review of Collazo's dissent can be found in *Correspondencia diplomática de la Delegación Cubana en Nueva York*, vol. 1, xv–xviii.
183 *He laid blame.* Collazo, *Cuba independiente*, 14.
183 *committee not only declined to censure.* *Correspondencia diplomática de la Delegación Cubana en Nueva York*, vol. 1, xv–xviii.
183 *Clearly chastened.* *Correspondencia diplomática de la Delegación Cubana en Nueva York*, vol. 1, xv–xviii.

Chapter 25: The King of the Gunrunners Is Affirmed

184 *legal engines were well coaled.* Baltimore Sun, "Appeal for Captain Hart," October 7, 1897.
184 *his efforts were worthwhile and appreciated.* Nuñez to Estrada Palma, October 6, 1897, Documento no. 87, Carta no. 17-747, in Rodríguez Altunaga, *El General Emilio Nuñez*, 299.
184 *evidence in the first trial was insufficient.* Baltimore Sun, "Appeal for Captain Hart," October 7, 1897.
185 *good news came two days later.* Philadelphia Inquirer, "Captain Wiborg Is Free Again," October 9, 1897.

Source Notes

185   *he was innocent.* Philadelphia Inquirer, "Wiborg's Freedom," September 9, 1897.

185   *a two-masted schooner of minor renown.* San Jose Evening News, "Deland's Flying Wedge," December 24, 1892, describes Deland's famous play, while a detailed description of the book he wrote with Walter Camp can be found in the Boston Herald, "Science of Football," November 11, 1896. Head coach at Harvard was a part-time job that Deland took as a break from his successful business ventures.

186   *Congosto's relentless Pinkertons.* Smith, A Captain Unafraid, 214.

186   *a "filibustering expedition to Cuba."* Statement of John H. McCarthy, in Re: "Silver Heels" case, Foreign Relations of the United States, 1898 (Washington, DC: Government Printing Office, 1901), 611–12.

186   *"did not figure in the matter."* Statement of Lewis L. Kennedy, in Re: "Silver Heels" case, Foreign Relations of the United States, 1898, 612–13.

187   *The bungled raid.* New York Tribune, "Filibusters Probably a Myth," October 19, 1897.

187   *investigation had unraveled.* Baltimore Sun, "A Denial that the Silver Heels Sailed on a Filibustering Expedition," October 22, 1897.

187   *winds of up to one hundred miles an hour.* National Hurricane Center, National Oceanic and Atmospheric Administration, Hurricane Tracking Chart, 1897, https://www.aoml.noaa.gov/hrd/Landsea/Partagas/1894-1897/1897.pdf

188   *A mad scramble ensued for the lifeboats.* Boston Herald, "Shrieks for Aid," October 20, 1897.

188   *orders from Washington.* Smith, A Captain Unafraid, 215–18.

188   *government eyes were watching.* Baltimore Sun, "Men-of-War on a Chase," October 28, 1897.

189   *an improvement in relations.* Gullón to Woodford, October 23, 1897, Foreign Relations of the United States, 1898, 588–89.

189   *Weyler was recalled and replaced.* Philadelphia Inquirer, "Dr. Jose Congosto Appointed Secretary-General by Spain," October 27, 1897.

189   *"the highest sense of friendly duty."* Sherman related his response to Gullón in a cable to Woodford, November 20, 1897, Foreign Relations of the United States, 1897, 610–11.

190   *"appears to be unaware or heedless."* While calculating the modern equivalent is an arbitrary exercise, a common CPI multiplier on $2 million in 1897 equates to more than $80 million today.

190   *further rebutted Spanish complaints.* New York Tribune, "Spain's Charge Refuted," December 9, 1897.

191   *awaiting disposition of his appeal.* Philadelphia Inquirer, Notes, November 7, 1897.

191   *a gang of Cubans.* Philadelphia Inquirer, "Armed Deputies on Laurada's Deck," November 21, 1897; and Baltimore Sun, "Guarding the Laurada," November 22, 1897.

191   *a dozen men on her decks.* Philadelphia Inquirer, "Crowds Stole Away," November 23, 1897.

191   *the Laurada had been sold.* Philadelphia Inquirer, "Laurada's Release," November 28, 1897.

191   *"some interesting facts."* Weinert's brief dalliance with the Laurada and her sale was reported in the December 5, 12, and 14, 1897, issues of the Philadelphia Inquirer.

191   *did not persuade the Pinkertons.* Philadelphia Inquirer, "Laurada Is Released," December 19, 1897.

192   *back behind bars.* Baltimore Sun, "Captain Hart Taken to Prison," December 22, 1897.

Chapter 26: Perceived Wrongs and Righteous Rights

193 *"uprisings usually begin at the bull ring."* O'Toole, *The Spanish War*, 111–12.
193 *who actually ruled Cuba.* New York *World*, October 4, 1897.
193 *"the hour of our liberation."* Wilkes-Barre (PA) *Times*, "Autonomy Not Wanted," October 6, 1897.
194 *Spanish troops were sapped by illness.* Lee to Day, January 25, 1898, Box 34, William R. Day Papers, Manuscript Division, Library of Congress, Washington, DC.
194 *autonomy as a surrender.* New York *Tribune*, "Crucial Days for Cuba," January 18, 1898.
194 *"the plot of a comic opera."* Philadelphia *Inquirer*, "The Outlook for Spain and Cuba," January 10, 1898; and Offner, *An Unwanted War*, 94.
194 *the first step toward American intervention.* Philadelphia *Inquirer*, "Spain Must Withdraw Autonomy; Action on Cuba Is Urged," January 18, 1898.
194 *the preestablished code.* Leech, *In the Days of McKinley*, 163.
195 *More rioting occurred.* Washington *Evening Star*, "The Siege of Havana," January 18, 1898.
195 *"loss of confidence in the future."* Dupuy de Lôme to Gullón, January 14, 1898, no. 40, *Spanish Diplomatic Correspondence*.
195 *"there is no autonomy."* Quesada to Estrada Palma, January 18, 1897, *Correspondencia diplomática de la Delegación Cubana en Nueva York*, vol. 5, 91.
195 *a personal friend of President McKinley.* O'Toole, *The Spanish War*, 113.
196 *"determined to land troops."* Dupuy de Lôme to Gullón, January 16, 1898, no. 42, *Spanish Diplomatic Correspondence*.
196 *"order is completely re-established."* Gullón to Dupuy de Lôme, January 17, 1898, no. 43, *Spanish Diplomatic Correspondence*.
196 *a "courageous act of statesmanship."* O'Toole, *The Spanish War*, 114–15.
196 *an unfriendly act.* Dupuy de Lôme to Gullón, January 20, 1898, no. 46, *Spanish Diplomatic Correspondence*.
196 *the news he had dreaded.* Hart v. United States, Circuit Court of Appeals, Third Circuit, January 18, 1898, no. 2. The third appellate judge, District Judge Andrew Kirkpatrick, did not issue a written opinion or comment.

Chapter 27: The *Maine* Explodes, and Hart Goes to Prison

199 *resume the friendly gesture.* Foner, *The Spanish-Cuban-American War*, 228.
199 *Attorney General Joseph McKenna.* McKenna was McKinley's first attorney general but would be seated on January 25 as an associate justice to the Supreme Court, replacing retiring justice Stephen J. Field.
199 *Maine to proceed from Key West.* Leech, *In the Days of McKinley*, 164.
199 *a less than genial response.* Gullón to Dupuy de Lôme, January 25, 1898, no. 50, *Spanish Diplomatic Correspondence*.
200 *"the end is approaching."* Philadelphia *Inquirer*, "*Maine* to Havana," January 27, 1898.
200 *deaths from malnourishment and disease.* Offner, *An Unwanted War*, 112–13.
201 *administration's supporters blocked a vote.* Foner, *The Spanish-Cuban-American War*, 227–28.
201 *"we must interfere."* Foner, *The Spanish-Cuban-American War*, 229.
201 *a diplomatic crisis.* Offner, *An Unwanted War*, 78.
201 *"weak and catering to the rabble."* Wisan, *The Cuban Crisis*, 380.

258   Source Notes

202   *Estrada Palma, who released it to the press.* New York Journal, "Worst Insult to the United States in Its History," February 9, 1898; and Rubens, *Liberty: The Story of Cuba*, 287–88.
202   *"I do not believe I can continue."* Dupuy de Lôme to Gullón, February 8, 1898, no. 60, and February 9, 1898, no. 61, *Spanish Diplomatic Correspondence*.
202   *a position of notorious prominence.* Wisan, *The Cuban Crisis*, 381.
203   *conditions were ripe for another expedition.* Smith, *A Captain Unafraid*, 235–37.
203   *lost in the soupy mist.* Philadelphia Inquirer, "The *Dauntless* Slips Away with *Vesuvius* in Pursuit," February 15, 1898.
203   *a quick and quiet landing.* Paine, *Roads of Adventure*, 124.
205   *"Our expeditions are ended."* Smith, *A Captain Unafraid*, 238.
205   *a feeling of calamity unmatched.* Leech, *In the Days of McKinley*, 166; and *New York World*, various stories, February 24, 1898. In 1976, Admiral Hyman G. Rickover published the results of a study he had undertaken that cast doubt the *Maine* was sunk by a deliberate act: "We have found no technical evidence in the records examined that an external explosion [such as a mine] initiated the destruction of the *Maine*." The available evidence, the report stated, "is consistent with an internal explosion alone. We therefore conclude that an internal source was the cause of the explosion." O'Toole, *The Spanish War*, 400.
206   *capitalists with business interests.* Horace Edgar Flack, *Spanish-American Diplomatic Relations Preceding the War of 1898* (Baltimore: Johns Hopkins Press, 1906), 10.
206   *summed up in a message.* John J. McCook to McKinley, March 22, 1898, William McKinley Papers, Series 1, Reel 3, Manuscript Division, Library of Congress, Washington, DC.
206   *would not send out any more expeditions.* Smith, *A Captain Unafraid*, 239.
206   *"it makes my blood boil."* New York American, "*World*'s Attack Angers Cubans," February 24, 1898.
206   *"we never faltered."* Boston Journal, "'Tis Freedom or Death, Says the Cuban Junta," March 18, 1898.

Chapter 28: A Full and Complete Pardon

207   *he was active in the interests of a cause.* Philadelphia Inquirer, "John D. Hart Dons His Prison Garb," February 24, 1898.
208   *built as a debtor's prison.* More on Thomas Ustick Walter (1804–1887), the prominent Philadelphia architect who had built the penitentiary, can be found in Ihna Thayer Frary, *They Built the Capitol* (Richmond, VA: Garrett and Massie, 1940), 201.
208   *the instrument to commit hostilities.* United States v. the Laurada, US District Court, District of Delaware, March 1, 1898; 85 Federal Reporter, 760–74.
208   *The celebrity steamer.* Philadelphia Inquirer, "Klondike, Not Cuba," March 8, 1898.
208   *he hardly recognized the steamer.* Philadelphia Inquirer, "Famous *Laurada* on a Peace Mission," March 17, 1898.
209   *last chance at freedom.* John W. Oliver, "Matthew Stanley Quay," *Western Pennsylvania Historical Magazine* 17 (March 1934): 1–12.
209   *enough support to have Hart pardoned.* Philadelphia Inquirer, "Petition for Hart's Release," March 23, 1898.
209   *efforts on Hart's behalf.* Dunlop's caricature of Charles A. Dana, the managing editor of the *New York Tribune*, hangs in the National Portrait Gallery. His pen and ink

drawing of Walt Whitman appeared in "Men of the Day" in the *Fifth Avenue Journal* and is reposited in the Library of Congress Prints and Photographs Division in Washington, DC; *Trenton (NJ) Evening Times*, "How David Plough Aided Captain Hart," November 15, 1900.

211   suggestion that Spain was to blame. Wisan, *The Cuban Crisis*, 422.
211   *The flurry of events. New York Times*, "War Department Ready," March 27, 1898; *New York Times*, "Spanish Fleet Sails," March 30, 1898; and *New York Times*, "War or Peace Monday," March 31, 1898.
211   American land and naval forces. *Philadelphia Inquirer*, "Senator Quay's Strong Words," April 12, 1898.
211   "let us give the Cubans liberty." O'Toole, *The Spanish War*, 170–73.
212   "control of the island to its people." O'Toole, *The Spanish War*, 170–73.
212   would not be recognized. Wisan, *The Cuban Crisis*, 447.
212   independence but under American guidance. Offner, *An Unwanted War*, 234–35.
212   pending indictments . . . were dropped. *Philadelphia Inquirer*, "Why Not Pardon Hart at Once?" May 13, 1898; and *Baltimore Sun*, "Filibuster Cases Ended," June 7, 1898.
212   In a delicious irony. *Tampa Times*, "The *Florida* Returns," June 2, 1898.
213   "paces a narrow cell." *Philadelphia Inquirer*, "The Filibusters Have Been Halted," April 13, 1898.
213   the petition to pardon Hart. *Philadelphia Inquirer*, "Hart May Yet Be Pardoned," April 22, 1898.
214   McKinley assured the delegation. *Philadelphia Inquirer*, "Captain Hart's Pardon," May 5, 1898; and *Philadelphia Inquirer*, "District Attorney Beck's Action," May 5, 1898.
214   A handful of newspapermen waited. *Philadelphia Inquirer*, "Hart's Pardon Expected Today," May 20, 1898.
215   he offered to turn over the *Bermuda*. *Philadelphia Inquirer*, "Hart Will Soon Have His Liberty," May 28, 1898.
215   the same logjam. Quesada to Estrada Palma, May 31, 1898, *Correspondencia diplomática de la Delegación cubana en Nueva York*, vol. 5, 136.
215   Griggs held the key. *Trenton (NJ) State Gazette*, editorial, May 31, 1898.
215   a number of other opinions. Leech, *In the Days of McKinley*, 174.
215   US warships had bombarded Caimanera. *New York Times*, "Monday's Fight at Santiago," June 9, 1898.
216   Griggs delivered to McKinley his opinion. Washington *Evening Star*, "Captain Hart Pardoned," June 9, 1898.
216   "a full and unconditional pardon." A copy of the pardon is included in the Grace Hart Holt Family Papers, courtesy of Sharon Holt Neil and Sandra Holt Luty, great-granddaughters of John D. Hart.

Chapter 29: The Importing Business Had Changed

217   the news of her husband's pardon. *New York Tribune*, "The Pen That Signed the Pardon," June 15, 1898.
217   "A *Journal Victory*." *New York Journal*, "Pardon at Last for John D. Hart, A *Journal* Victory," June 9, 1898; and *Trenton (NJ) Evening Times*, "Mrs. Hart Is Happy," June 11, 1898.
217   in typical Hearst fashion. *New York Journal*, June 10, 1898; and Grace Hart Holt Family Papers.

260 Source Notes

218 *the long ordeal of hope.* Philadelphia Inquirer, "Captain Hart Leaves the Prison Cell," June 11, 1898; and New York American, "Captain Hart, Filibuster, Is Free," June 10, 1898.
219 *"lost none of my ambition."* Philadelphia Inquirer, "Captain Hart's Future," June 14, 1898.
219 *she was headed for the Klondike.* Philadelphia Inquirer, "Laurada as a Transport," June 2, 1898.
219 *Canadian authorities.* Tacoma (WA) Daily News, "Laurada Delayed," June 15, 1898.
219 *too close to shore at low tide.* Tacoma (WA) Daily News, "The Laurada Does Damage," June 16, 1898.
219 *success as a gold transporter.* Philadelphia Inquirer, "Gold from Klondike," August 28, 1898.
219 *the "famous Laurada" in boldface.* Tacoma (WA) Daily News, "Hawaii or Siberia," October 7, 1898. Regular advertisements appeared in Seattle and Tacoma newspapers throughout November and December 1898 that announced the Laurada's runs, which took about two weeks round trip, based on the appearance of the ads and the departure dates.
220 *she was sold by the US marshal.* Baltimore Sun, "The Laurada in Trouble Again," November 29, 1898; and Tacoma (WA) Daily News, "Steamer Laurada Is Sold," December 27, 1898.
220 *from adoration to the butt of humor.* Tacoma (WA) Daily News, editorial, December 31, 1898.
220 *new owners spruced her up.* Alaska Mining Record (Juneau), "Open for Business," March 1, 1899.
220 *trouble again intruded.* Baltimore Sun, "The Laurada May Be Confiscated," April 15, 1899; and Alaska Mining Record (Juneau), "Laurada in Port," May 10, 1899.
220 *tales of deprivation and death.* New York Tribune, "Lured to Death by Gold," June 8, 1899.
220 *a "floating louse cage."* Olympia (WA) Morning Olympian, "Dawson Is Not the Place for the Working Man," August 30, 1899.
221 *out of Seattle for Cape Nome.* Olympia (WA) Morning Olympian, "The Laurada a Wreck," October 15, 1899.
221 *the distress signal flying from her mast.* New York Tribune, "Return of Revenue Cutter Bear," November 2, 1899.
221 *brought the vessel from Port Antonio.* Boston Herald, "Steamer Bermuda Freed," July 28, 1898.
221 *the centerpiece of a new empire.* Baltimore Sun, "The Bermuda at Philadelphia," October 5, 1898.
222 *such familiar captains.* Philadelphia Inquirer, "Maritime Notes," November 10, 1898; and Philadelphia Inquirer, "No Longer in Fear," January 23, 1899.
222 *no room for a struggling independent.* Adams, Conquest of the Tropics, 70–72.
222 *The future arrived.* Philadelphia Inquirer, "$20,000,000 Fruit Trust," March 31, 1899; and Philadelphia Inquirer, "A Fruit Trust? Never!," August 11, 1899.
222 *acquired by United Fruit.* Adams, Conquest of the Tropics, 72; and Lester D. Langley and Thomas Schoonover, The Banana Men: American Mercenaries and Entrepreneurs in Central America, 1880–1930 (Lexington: University Press of Kentucky, 1995), 35.
222 *as indefatigable as ever.* Baltimore Sun, "Proposed Philadelphia-Cuban Line," April 29, 1899.
223 *Hart's legal and financial problems.* Philadelphia Inquirer, "John D. Hart's Troubles," March 1, 1899.
223 *Kate Hart went to the police.* Philadelphia Inquirer, "Gracie Disappeared," July 26, 1899.

224 *business was not going any better.* Philadelphia Inquirer, "Heavy Damages Claimed," September 29, 1899; and Harrisburg (PA) *Patriot,* "Jamaica Swept by Storm," November 24, 1899.
224 *flirting with the filibustering business.* Baltimore Sun, "Volunteers for the Boers?," December 16, 1899.
224 *"a thorough American."* Philadelphia Inquirer, "Not for the Boers," December 18, 1899.
224 *defiance was not enough.* Philadelphia Inquirer, "Notes of the Courts," January 24, 1900; Philadelphia Inquirer, "Injunction Dissolved," February 9, 1900; and Philadelphia Inquirer, "Famous *Bermuda* in More Trouble," February 22, 1900.
225 *forced to sell the* Bermuda. *Trenton (NJ) Evening Times,* "Captain Hart's Failure," March 17, 1900; and Baltimore Sun, "Bermuda Sold at Auction," March 31, 1900.
225 *a new line of work.* Philadelphia Inquirer, "Howard's Music Jarred Captain Hart," October 9, 1900.

Chapter 30: He Took Up the Cause and Suffered for It

226 *resumed the runs to Jamaica.* Baltimore Sun, "The *Bermuda* Again in Service," May 11, 1900.
226 *lightning sliced down from the clouds.* Philadelphia Inquirer, "Bolt Struck *Bermuda*," June 12, 1900.
226 *collided with the three-masted schooner.* Philadelphia Inquirer, "Famed *Bermuda* Sinks a Vessel," June 12, 1900.
227 *an attachment had been issued.* Philadelphia Inquirer, "Steamer *Bermuda* Is Attached," June 13, 1900.
227 *a loud explosion.* Philadelphia Inquirer, "*Bermuda*'s Sinking Still a Mystery," August 16, 1900.
227 *multiple conspiracy theories.* Philadelphia Inquirer, "Steamer *Bermuda* Sunk by Internal Explosion," August 18, 1900.
228 *drew great attention.* Philadelphia Inquirer, "Hart's Startling Suspicion," August 17, 1900.
229 *went to an early grave.* Murphy contracted yellow fever while commanding the *Dandy*, the Associated Press's dispatch boat through the Cuban war. New York Tribune, "Death of Captain Edward Murphy," September 1, 1898.
230 *the pain grew worse.* Philadelphia Inquirer, "Death Comes to Captain Hart," November 14, 1900.
230 *Reports of Hart's death.* Philadelphia Inquirer, "Few Attended Funeral of Captain John D. Hart," November 14, 1900; and miscellaneous clippings in the Grace Hart Holt Family Papers.
230 *"He took up the cause of the Cubans."* Philadelphia Inquirer, editorial, November 14, 1900.
231 *strong affection for her late husband.* Kate Hart to Albert T. Chambers, Loudon Park Cemetery, June 7, 1920, courtesy of Loudon Park Cemetery.
231 *"(Widow of John D.)."* Polk's Baltimore City Directory of 1920 (Baltimore: R. L. Polk and Company, 1920), 1015, https://lib.guides.umd.edu/c.php?g=327119&p=2197762#10434286.
232 *a new boarding house.* Cemetery records list Kate's birthdate as April 14, 1856, which was as close to her actual birth year of 1853 as she ever admitted. Her marriage certificate in 1878 said she was born in 1858. In the 1880 census, she claimed to have been born in 1859. The 1900 census lists her birth year as 1865.

Epilogue

233 *the peace protocol of August 12.* Louis A. Pérez Jr., *Cuba between Empires, 1878–1902* (Pittsburgh: University of Pittsburgh Press, 1983), 231, quoting Emilio Nuñez: "A los jefes y oficiales del Departamento de Expediciones," *Patria*, October 15, 1898.

233 *took their places in the new order.* Tomás Estrada Palma Collection, University of Miami Libraries, Coral Gables, Florida.

233 *the American definition of Cuban independence.* Offner, *An Unwanted War*, 234–36.

234 *attention to expansionism.* Offner, *An Unwanted War*, 234–36.

BIBLIOGRAPHY

Primary Sources

Private Papers, Collections, Unpublished Sources

Broward, Napoleon B., Correspondence. Legal and Business Papers, 1879–1900. University of Florida Libraries, Gainesville, Florida.
Cleveland, Grover, Papers. Manuscript Division, Library of Congress, Washington DC.
Day, William R., Papers. Manuscript Division, Library of Congress, Washington, DC.
Estrada Palma, Tomás, Collection. University of Miami Libraries, Coral Gables, Florida.
Gray, George, Papers. Harrel-Nash Gift, Delaware Historical Society, Wilmington, Delaware.
Hart, Kate, letter to Albert T. Chambers. Loudon Park Cemetery, June 7, 1920, courtesy of Loudon Park Cemetery.
Hart Holt, Grace, Family Papers. Courtesy of Sharon Holt Neil and Sandra Holt Luty, great-granddaughters of John D. Hart.
McKinley, William, Papers. Manuscript Division, Library of Congress, Washington, DC.
Olney, Richard, Papers. Manuscript Division, Library of Congress, Washington, DC.
Preece, Carol A. "Insurgent Guests: The Cuban Revolutionary Party and Its Activities in the United States, 1892–1898." PhD diss., Georgetown University, 1976.

Public Documents

Catalogue of the Public Documents of the 53rd Congress and of All Departments for the Government of the United States, March 4, 1893, to June 30, 1895. Washington, DC: Government Printing Office, 1896.
Commercial Relations of the United States with Foreign Countries during the Years 1895 and 1896. Bureau of Statistics, Department of State. Washington, DC: Government Printing Office, 1897.
Compiled Service Records of Confederate Soldiers Who Served in Organizations from the State of Virginia. Record Group 109, Catalog ID: 586957, National Archives and Records Administration, Washington, DC, compiled 1903–1927, accessed through www.Fold3.com.
Foreign Relations of the United States, 1896. Washington, DC: Government Printing Office, 1897.

264 Bibliography

Foreign Relations of the United States, 1897. Washington, DC: Government Printing Office, 1897.
Foreign Relations of the United States, 1898. Washington, DC: Government Printing Office, 1901.
Foreign Relations of the United States, 1899. Washington, DC: Government Printing Office, 1901.
Gage, Lyman J. *Annual Report of the Secretary of the Treasury on the State of the Finances for the Year 1897, to the 55th Congress.* Washington, DC: Government Printing Office, 1897.
Hart v. United States. Circuit Court of Appeals, Third Circuit. January 18, 1898, no. 2.
Navigation of the Gulf of Mexico and Caribbean Sea. Vol. 1, 5th ed. Washington, DC: Government Printing Office, 1901.
Plessy v. Ferguson. US Supreme Court, 163 U.S. 537 (1896).
"Preventing Conveyance of Articles to Cubans." House Document 264, Serial no. 3679, 55th Congress, 2nd Session.
Record of Alien Immigrants arriving by steamship, October 2, 1894, provided by the Historical Society of Pennsylvania.
Records and Briefs of the US Supreme Court, October Term 1906. Washington, DC: Judd and Detweiler, 1907.
Records of the Customs Bureau, Special Agents Reports and Correspondence, 1865–1915. Records Group 36. National Archives, Washington, DC.
Records of the US Coast Guard, Revenue Cutter Service. Records Group 26. National Archives, Washington, DC.
Revised Statutes of the United States. First Session of the 43rd Congress, 1873–1874. Washington, DC: Government Printing Office, 1878.
Spanish Diplomatic Correspondence and Documents, 1896–1900. Washington, DC: Government Printing Office, 1905.
Three Friends v. United States. US Supreme Court, 166 U.S. 1 (1897).
United States v. the Itata. Circuit Court of Appeals, Ninth Circuit, May 8, 1893, no. 45.
United States v. the Laurada. US District Court, District of Delaware, March 1, 1898; 85 Federal Reporter.
US Census Office. Census Bulletin, 11th Census, 1890. Washington, DC: Government Printing Office, 1890.
Wiborg v. United States. US Supreme Court, 163 U.S. 632 (1896).

Secondary Sources

Articles

Auxier, George Washington. "The Propaganda Activities of the Cuban *Junta* in Precipitating the Spanish-American War, 1895–1898." *Hispanic American Historical Review* 19, no. 3 (August 1939): 286–305.
De la Cova, Antonio Rafael. "Fernandina Filibuster Fiasco: Birth of the 1895 Cuban War of Independence." *Florida Historical Quarterly* 82, no. 1 (Summer 2003): 16–42.
Fenn, Emory W. "Ten Months with the Cuban Insurgents." *Century Magazine*, June 1898, 302–7.
García Barrón, Carlos. "Enrique Dupuy de Lôme and the Spanish American War." *The Americas* 36, no. 1 (July 1979): 39–58.
Godoy, Gustavo J. "José Alejandro Huau: A Cuban Patriot in Jacksonville Politics." *Florida Historical Quarterly* 54, no. 2 (October 1975): 196–206.
Harison, William Beverley. "When the *Laurada* Appeared in Sight." *The Great Round World and What Is Going On in It*, April 22, 1897.

Lodge, Henry Cabot. "The Spanish American War." *Harper's New Monthly Magazine*, February 1899.
McSherry, Patrick. "The Navy Experimented and Gave Up on the Compressed Air 'Dynamite Gun.'" *Artilleryman Magazine* 26, no. 1 (Winter 2004): 16–21.
Oliver, John W. "Matthew Stanley Quay." *Western Pennsylvania Historical Magazine* 17 (March 1934): 1–12.
Oswald, Felix. "A Guerilla Eden." *North American Review* 162, no. 472 (March 1896): 379–81.
Portell Vilá, Herminio. "John O'Brien: Captain Dynamite of the Cuban War for Independence, 1868–1898." *Irish Migration Studies in Latin America* 7, no. 3 (March 2010): 339–48.
Poyo, Gerald E. "Key West and the Cuban Ten Years War." *Florida Historical Quarterly* 57, no. 3 (1979): 289–307.
Proctor, Samuel. "Napoleon B. Broward: The Years to the Governorship." *Florida Historical Quarterly* 26, no. 2 (October 1947): 117–34.
Public Opinion. "The Cameron Cuban Resolution." *Public Opinion* 21, no. 26 (December 24, 1896).
Public Opinion. "President Cleveland's Latest Cuban Proclamation." *Public Opinion* 21, no. 6 (August 6, 1896).
Reno, R. George. "Operating an 'Underground' Route to Cuba." *Cosmopolitan*, August 1899.
Rickenbach, Richard V. "Filibustering with the *Dauntless*." *Florida Historical Quarterly* 28, no. 4 (April 1950): 231–53.
Schellings, William J. "Florida and the Cuban Revolution, 1895–1898." *Florida Historical Quarterly* 39, no. 2 (October 1960): 175–86.

Books

Adams, Frederick Upton. *Conquest of the Tropics*. New York: Doubleday, Page and Company, 1914.
The American-Spanish War: A History by the War Leaders. Norwich, CT: Charles C. Haskell and Son, 1899.
Baltimore: Its History and People. Vol. 2, *Biography*. New York: Lewis Historical Publishing Company, 1912.
Barnes, Kenneth C. *Journey of Hope: The Back-to-Africa Movement in Arkansas in the Late 1800s*. Chapel Hill: University of North Carolina Press, 2004.
Bates, Samuel P. *History of Pennsylvania Volunteers, 1861–1865*. Vol. 2. Wilmington, NC: Broadfoot Publishing Company, 1994.
Benton, Elbert J. *International Law and Diplomacy of the Spanish-American War*. Albert Shaw Lectures on Diplomatic History. Baltimore: Johns Hopkins University Press, 1908.
Bradford, Richard H. *The Virginius Affair*. Boulder: Colorado Associated University Press, 1980.
Brown, Charles H. *Agents of Manifest Destiny: The Lives and Times of the Filibusters*. Chapel Hill: University of North Carolina Press, 1980.
Brown, Charles H. *The Correspondents' War: Journalists in the Spanish-American War*. New York: Charles Scribner's Sons, 1967.
Burnett, Gene M. *Florida's Past: People and Events that Shaped the State*. Sarasota, FL: Pineapple Press, 1988.
Carrillo Morales, Justo. *Expediciones Cubanas*. Havana: Imprenta P. Fernández, 1936.
Chadwick, French Ensor. *The Relations of the United States and Spain: Diplomacy*. New York: Charles Scribner's Sons, 1909.
Chapman, Peter. *Bananas: How the United Fruit Company Shaped the World*. Edinburgh: Canongate, 2007.

Collazo, Enrique. *Cuba independiente*. Santiago de Cuba: Editorial Oriente, 1991. First published 1900.

Cosmas, Graham A. *An Army for Empire: The United States Army in the Spanish-American War*. College Station: Texas A&M University Press, 2003.

Davis, George Breckenridge. *The Elements of International Law*. New York: Harper and Brothers, 1903.

Davis, Richard Harding. *Notes of a War Correspondent*. New York: Charles Scribner's Sons, 1912.

Davis, Richard Harding. *A Year from a Reporter's Note-Book*. New York: Harper and Brothers, 1903.

Ferrer, Ada. *Insurgent Cuba: Race, Nation, and Revolution, 1868–1898*. Chapel Hill: University of North Carolina Press, 2007.

Flack, Horace Edgar. *Spanish-American Diplomatic Relations Preceding the War of 1898*. Baltimore: Johns Hopkins Press, 1906.

Foner, Philip S. *The Spanish-Cuban-American War and the Birth of American Imperialism, 1895–1902*. Vol. 1, *1895–1898*. New York: Monthly Review Press, 1972.

Frary, Ihna Thayer. *They Built the Capitol*. Richmond, VA: Garrett and Massie, 1940.

Funston, Frederick. *Memories of Two Wars: Cuban and Philippine Experiences*. New York: Charles Scribner's Sons, 1911.

Gonzales, Narciso Gener. *In Darkest Cuba; Two Months' Service under Gomez along the Trocha from the Caribbean to the Bahama Channel*. Columbia, SC: State Company, 1922.

González Echevarría, Roberto. *The Pride of Havana: A History of Cuban Baseball*. New York: Oxford University Press, 1999.

Gould, Lewis L. *The Spanish-American War and President McKinley*. Lawrence: University Press of Kansas, 1982.

Gray, Richard Butler. *José Martí, Cuban Patriot*. Gainesville: University of Florida Press, 1962.

Guerra, Lillian. *The Myth of José Martí: Conflicting Nationalisms in Early Twentieth-Century Cuba*. Chapel Hill: University of North Carolina Press, 2005.

Guerra y Sánchez, Ramiro. *Historia de la Nación Cubana*, vol. 6, book 5. Havana: Editorial Historia de la Nación Cubana, 1952.

Halstead, Murat. *The Story of Cuba: Her Struggles for Liberty; The Cause, Crisis and Destiny of the Pearl of the Antilles*. Chicago: Franklin Square Bible House, 1898.

Hernández, José M. *Cuba and the United States: Intervention and Militarism, 1868–1933*. Austin: University of Texas Press, 1993.

Hunt, John Gabriel, ed. *The Inaugural Addresses of the Presidents*. New York: Random House, 2005.

Kemp, Peter, ed. *The Oxford Companion to Ships and the Sea*. Oxford: Oxford University Press, 1976.

Kerr, Winfield S. *John Sherman: His Life and Public Services*. Boston: Sherman, French and Company, 1907.

Knetsch, Joe, and Nick Wynne. *Florida in the Spanish-American War*. Charleston, SC: History Press, 2011.

Langley, Lester D., and Thomas Schoonover. *The Banana Men: American Mercenaries and Entrepreneurs in Central America, 1880–1930*. Lexington: University Press of Kentucky, 1995.

Lauck, William Jett. *The Causes of the Panic of 1893*. Boston: Houghton, Mifflin, 1907.

Lazo, Rodrigo. *Writing to Cuba: Filibustering and Cuban Exiles in the United States*. Chapel Hill: University of North Carolina Press, 2005.

Leech, Margaret. *In the Days of McKinley*. New York: Harper and Brothers, 1959.

Maceo, Antonio. *Papeles de Maceo*. Vol. 2. Havana: Academia de la Historia de Cuba, 1948.
Offner, John L. *An Unwanted War: The Diplomacy of the United States and Spain over Cuba, 1895–1898*. Chapel Hill: University of North Carolina Press, 1992.
O'Toole, G. J. A. *The Spanish War: An American Epic, 1898*. New York: W. W. Norton, 1984.
Paine, Ralph D. *Roads of Adventure*. Boston: Houghton, Mifflin, 1922.
Pérez, Louis A., Jr. *Cuba between Empires, 1878–1902*. Pittsburgh: University of Pittsburgh Press, 1983.
Pérez, Louis A., Jr. *The War of 1898: The United States and Cuba in History and Historiography*. Chapel Hill: University of North Carolina Press, 1998.
Poluhowich, John J. *Argonaut: The Submarine Legacy of Simon Lake*. College Station: Texas A&M University Press, 1999.
Portell Vilá, Herminio. "John O'Brien, el Capitán Dinamita." In *Vidas de la unidad americana: Veinte y cinco biografías de americanos ilustres*, 353–67. Havana: Editorial Minerva, 1944.
Post, Charles Johnson. *The Little War of Private Post: An Artist Soldier's Memoir of the Spanish-American War*. Lincoln: University of Nebraska Press, 1999.
Quesada, Gonzalo de, and Henry Davenport Northrop. *The War in Cuba; or, The Great Struggle for Freedom*. New York: Liberty Publishing Company, 1896.
Roberts, Diane. *Eight Generations of Swamp Lawyers, Conquistadors, Confederate Daughters, Banana Republicans, and Other Florida Wildlife*. New York: Free Press, 2004.
Rodríguez Altunaga, Rafael. *El General Emilio Nuñez*. Havana: Sociedad Colombista Panamericana, 1958.
Ronning, C. Neale. *José Martí and the Émigré Colony in Key West: Leadership and State Formation*. New York: Praeger, 1990.
Rubens, Horatio. *Liberty: The Story of Cuba*. New York: Brewer, Warren and Putnam, 1932.
Siringo, Charles A. *Two Evil Isms: Pinkertonism and Anarchism*. Austin, TX: Steck-Vaughn Company, 1907.
Smith, Horace. *A Captain Unafraid: The Strange Adventures of Dynamite Johnny O'Brien*. New York: Harper and Brothers, 1912.
Staudenraus, Philip J. *The African Colonization Movement, 1816–1865*. New York: Columbia University Press, 1961.
Thomas, Evan. *The War Lovers: Roosevelt, Lodge, Hearst, and the Rush to Empire, 1898*. New York: Little, Brown, 2010.
Thomas, Lately. *The Astor Orphans: A Pride of Lions*. New York: William Morrow, 1971.
Tone, John Lawrence. *War and Genocide in Cuba, 1895–1898*. Chapel Hill: University of North Carolina Press, 2006.
Underwood, Rodman L. *Waters of Discord: The Union Blockade of Texas During the Civil War*. Jefferson, NC: McFarland, 2003.
Whyte, Kenneth. *The Uncrowned King: The Sensational Rise of William Randolph Hearst*. Berkeley, CA: Counterpoint, 2009.
Williamson, Leland M., et al., eds. *Prominent and Progressive Pennsylvanians of the Nineteenth Century*. Vol. 2. Philadelphia: Record Publishing Company, 1898.
Wisan, Joseph E. *The Cuban Crisis as Reflected in the New York Press (1895–1898)*. New York: Octagon Books, 1965.
Zakaria, Fareed. *From Wealth to Power: The Unusual Origins of America's World Role*. Princeton, NJ: Princeton University Press, 1999.

Miscellaneous Sources

Biographical Directory of Federal Judges. Federal Judicial Center. https://www.fjc.gov/search/site/Biographical%20Directory%20of%20Federal%20Judges.

Broward, Napoleon B. "Autobiography, Platform, Letter and Short Story of the Steamer 'Three Friends,' and a Filibustering Trip to Cuba." Booklet, 1904. Florida Memory, State Library and Archives of Florida. http://www.floridamemory.com/items/show/346219.

Carlisle, Calderon. *Report to the Spanish Legation, with Reference to the Legal Aspect of Hostilities Committed by Vessels Specially Adapted, in Whole or in Part, within the United States to Warlike Uses* [. . .]. Washington, DC: n.p., 1896.

Civil War Index. "73rd Pennsylvania Infantry." 2010. http://www.civilwarindex.com/armypa/73rd_pa_infantry.html.

Collins Company. *A Brief Account of the Development of the Collins Company in the Manufacture of Axes, Machetes and Edge Tools*. Fitzwilliam, NH: Ken Roberts Publishing Company, 1935.

Correspondencia diplomática de la Delegación Cubana en Nueva York durante la Guerra de Independencia de 1895 a 1898. 5 vols. Havana: Archivo Nacional de Cuba, 1943–1946.

Dos Passos, John R. "In Favor of Recognition of Cuba by the United States." Pamphlet. New York, 1895.

Encyclopaedia Brittanica. "Law of Action and Reaction." http://www.britannica.com/EBchecked/topic/4447/.

Federal Judicial Center. http://www.fjc.gov.

Guiteras, John, ed. *Free Cuba: Her Oppression, Struggle for Liberty, History, and Present Condition*. Philadelphia: Publishers' Union, 1897.

Guiteras, John. "The United States and Cuba." Pamphlet. Philadelphia: Levytype Company, 1895.

Henricksen, Hendrick Christian. "Bananas in the West Indies." Pamphlet. London: Oxford House, 1909.

Latin American Studies. "Pedro E. Betancourt." http://www.latinamericanstudies.org/betancourt-bio.htm.

Lloyd's Register of British and Foreign Shipping. Vol. 2. London: Wyman and Sons, 1906.

Mills, William H. "The Purpose of the Nation in the Present War." Pamphlet. San Francisco: Murdock Press, 1898.

Morgan, John Tyler. *Belligerent Rights for Cuba: Speeches of Hon. J. T. Morgan of Alabama in the Senate of the United States*. Washington, DC, 1897.

National Hurricane Center, National Oceanic and Atmospheric Administration. Hurricane Tracking Chart, 1895. https://www.aoml.noaa.gov/hrd/Landsea/Partagas/1894-1897/1895.pdf

National Hurricane Center, National Oceanic and Atmospheric Administration. Hurricane Tracking Chart, 1897. https://www.aoml.noaa.gov/hrd/Landsea/Partagas/1894-1897/1897.pdf

Nuñez-Portuondo, Ricardo. "General Emilio Nuñez: Un Procer Cubano." Pamphlet. Coral Gables, FL: Publicaciones Cultural, 1994.

Philadelphia Passenger Lists Index (1883–1948). Courtesy of the Pennsylvania Historical Society.

Polk's Baltimore City Directory of 1920. Baltimore: R. L. Polk and Company, 1920. https://lib.guides.umd.edu/c.php?g=327119&p=2197762#10434286.

Records of Loudon Park Cemetery, 3620 Wilkens Avenue, Baltimore, Maryland.

Roberts, William K. "An African Canaan for the American Negro." Pamphlet. Birmingham, AL: International Migration Society, 1896.

Rodríguez, José Ignacio. *The Case of the Arrest, Trial and Sentence in the City of Havana, Island of Cuba, of Julio Sanguily, a Citizen of the United States of America*. Washington, DC: Press of W. F. Roberts, 1897.

Sierra, Jerry A. "The War for Cuban Independence." History of Cuba. http://www.historyofcuba
.com/history/scaw/scaw1.htm.
US Coast Guard. http://www.uscg.mil.
US Senate. "Senate Salaries (1789 to Present)." https://www.senate.gov/senators/SenateSalaries
Since1789.htm.

Newspapers

Alaska Mining Record (Juneau)
Baltimore Sun
Boston Herald
Boston Journal
Brooklyn Daily Eagle
Charlotte Observer
Charleston (SC) Evening Post
Charleston (SC) News and Courier
Chicago Inter-Ocean
Cleveland Leader
Cleveland Plain Dealer
Columbia (SC) State
Columbus (GA) Enquirer
Florida Times-Union (Jacksonville)
Harrisburg (PA) Patriot
Lexington (KY) Morning Herald
Memphis Commercial Appeal
New Haven (CT) Register
New Orleans Picayune
New York American
New York Herald
New York Herald-Tribune
New York Journal
New York Sun
New York Times
New York Tribune
New York World
Olympia (WA) Morning Olympian
Philadelphia Inquirer
Pittsburgh Press
San Jose Evening News
Savannah (GA) Tribune
Springfield (MA) Republican
Tacoma (WA) Daily News
Tampa Times
Tampa Tribune
Trenton (NJ) Evening Times
Trenton (NJ) State Gazette
Washington Bee
Washington Evening Star
Wilkes-Barre (PA) Times

INDEX

Abaco, Bahamas, 12
Abreu, Marta, 125
Academy of Music (Philadelphia), 65–66
Accomac County, VA, 4, 7
Acheson, Marcus W., 197–98, 216
Adams, John Quincy, 33
Adee, Alvey A., 51–52, 201
Agramonte, Augustin, 163
Alaska Mining Record, 219
Albany, Charles, 224
Albertini, Ricardo Diaz, 200
Alexander Jones (tugboat), 169–70
Alicia B. Crosby (schooner), 75
Allen, William V., 158
Alligator Reef Light, 176
alligators, 35, 146
Alphonse III (Spanish vessel), 76
Amadis (expedition vessel), 22–25, 124, 141, 182
American business interests in Cuba, 67–68, 179, 206
American Colonization Society (ACS), 31
Andersonville prison, 29
annexation of Cuba, 33
anti-American sentiment in Spain, 137
Antietam, Battle of, 6, 65, 111
Antigas, Juan, 57
Antoinette (schooner), 57
Ardell (schooner), 97
Argonaut (submarine), 180
Arlington, NJ, 103, 162

Arnston, Carl, 67, 69
Aspinwall, Panama, 4
Assateague Island, MD, 92
Astor House Hotel (New York), 75
Atkins, Edwin F., 67–68
Atlantic Basin (Brooklyn), 112, 163
Atlantic City (steamship), 93
autonomy for Cuba, 179, 181, 189, 193–96, 201
Autonomist Cabinet, 194

Bahama Bank, 175
Bahama Channel, 170
Bahamas, 4, 93, 96, 119, 161, 186, 188
Baire, Cuba, 26
Baker, Lorenzo D., 4
Baker & Drew, 25
Baldasano, Arturo, 60, 82, 111–12, 186
Baltimore, MD, 3, 5, 13–14, 16–17, 28, 35–36, 40, 49, 61, 74, 110, 114–15, 126, 132, 136, 139, 156, 160–65, 180, 205, 224, 229–31
Baltimore Basin, 3, 5, 50
Baltimore Fruit Company, 17
Baltimore Sun, 5, 14, 21, 49–50, 138
Baltzell, George L., 23–25, 141–42
bananas, 5, 7–8, 14–15, 17, 20–21, 39–40, 50, 53, 59, 61, 65, 68, 100, 120, 128–29, 222, 226–27, 231
Banes Bay, Cuba, 164, 190
Baracoa (expedition vessel, steamship), 23, 25, 124, 141, 182

Baracoa, Cuba, 4, 6, 12, 21, 23, 25, 28, 60, 98–99, 124, 141, 182
Barbados, 32
Barnegat Light, 67, 69, 129, 150–53, 163, 197
Barr, Robert J., 177
"Bases and Secret Statutes of the Cuban Revolutionary Party" (Martí), 18–19
Batewell, James, 23
B. A. Wagner (schooner), 12
Bayamo, Cuba, 43
Bay of Baconao, Cuba, 114
Bear (revenue cutter), 22
Beck, James M., 149–51, 214
Beckwith, J. F. B., 25
Bedia, Elias, 106
Bell, James D., 69, 102
Bell, Richard, 220
belligerency rights for Cuban rebels, 61, 66–67, 123, 171–72, 201
Bennett, James Gordon, Jr., 195
Bennett, Walsh & Co., 81
Benoit, Leon, 58
Bermuda (expedition vessel, steamship), 81–84, 87, 91–93, 99–105, 119–20, 122, 129, 161, 164, 166–67, 173, 178, 190, 213, 215, 221–22, 224–30
Bernard (steamship), 21
Berracos, Cuba, 106
Bertha Ellen (schooner), 6
Betances, R. E., 110
Birmingham, AL, 31
Bisbee, Cyrus R., 94, 104, 113, 127, 146
Bisbee, William A., 159, 173
Biscayne (steamship), 173–76
Blake, H. T., 52
Blanche (sloop), 36
Blanco y Erenas, Ramón, 189
Bluefields, Nicaragua, 14
blockades: Spanish, 9, 24, 40, 77, 151, 164, 206; Union, 89–90
Borden, Nathaniel Barnett, 22–25
Borden, Thomas J., 22
Boston, MA, 4, 19, 23, 61, 67
Boston and Alaska Trading Company, 208
Boston Fruit Company, 21, 155, 222
Boston Journal, 128
Boutwell (revenue cutter), 25, 79, 104, 113–14, 125–26, 142, 148, 166

Bowden (steamship), 164
Bowley's Wharf (Baltimore), 5, 12, 14, 231
Brabazon, Lawrence, 81–84
Bradford, Edward G., II, 191
Braganza (steamship), 21, 28, 172
Brawley, W. H., 68–69, 85–86, 102
Brewster, Benjamin H., 30
Bridgeport, CT, 46, 127, 162, 187, 203
Broad Street Station (Philadelphia), 31
Brouard, François, 95
Broward, Montcalm, 95
Broward, Napoleon Bonaparte, Jr., 94–98, 104, 113–14, 126, 140–47, 166
Brown, Addison, 102
Browne, H. P., 187
Browne, Jefferson, 188
Browne, William Henry, 171
Bru, Johannes, 21
Brucker, Ferdinand, 201
Bruff, William J., 150
Brunswick, GA, 127
Bryan, J. P. Kennedy, 68, 72–73
Bryan, William Jennings, 133
Bulack, Alexander Beauregard, 5–7, 9, 12–14, 17, 40, 156
Bulack, Jacob, 6
Bull Run, Second Battle of, 29
Burriel, Juan, 39
Butler, Matthew C., 68
Butler, William: question of a military expedition, 51–54, 66, 84, 86, 102, 117, 151–53, 157, 185, 197; trial of Hart, 134–35, 149–54, 156–57; trial of Wiborg, 85–86, 116
Byrd & Co., 4

Cabañas Fortress (Havana), 166, 170–71
Caimanera, Cuba, 215
Calhoun, William T., 171, 179
Callahan, FL, 141–42, 203
Camden, NJ, 17, 70, 92, 119–20, 208, 211
Cameron, Don, 171
Camp, Walter, 185
Canalejas, Jose, 201–2
Cánovas, Antonio del Castillo, 180
Cape Canaveral, FL, 37
Cape Cod, MA, 92, 124
Cape Cruz, Cuba, 105

Cape Hatteras, NC, 7, 92
Cape Henlopen, DE, 59, 92, 226
Cape Lucretia, Cuba, 35, 188
Cape Maysí, Cuba, 7, 93, 98–99, 114, 164, 173
Cape San Antonio, Cuba, 98, 143
Captain Dynamite. *See* O'Brien, Johnny "Captain Dynamite"
Carbó, Rafael Pérez, 142–44, 146
Cardenas, Cuba, 97–98, 102, 176, 200
Caribbean Sea, 7, 50, 172, 247, 264, 266
Carlisle, Calderon, 124
Carlisle, John G., 24–25, 56, 60
Carlist political movement (Spain), 137
Carnegie, Andrew, 56
Carrillo, Francisco, 63–65
Cartagena, Columbia, 211
Cartaya, Jose Eliseo, 174–76, 181, 188, 203, 205–6, 213
Cassidy, Butch, 160; and the Sundance Kid, 78–79
Cassidy, Michael, 218
Caughey, Charles, 139
Cervera y Topete, Pascual, 212
Ceuta, Northern Africa, 50
Cham (tugboat), 64
Champagne (steamship), 62
Chancellorsville, Battle of, 29
Chandler (revenue cutter), 82, 112, 186–87
Chandler, William, 171
Chanler, William Astor, 160–61, 164, 166, 201, 253
Chanler, Winthrop, 166
Charleston, SC, 50, 60–61, 68–69, 72, 78–79, 84, 108–9, 113, 120, 126, 213
Charles Warner Company, 51
Chesapeake House (Baltimore), 5–6, 9, 156, 231
Christiana River, DE, 126, 129
Christiansen, Ragnan, 67
Cienfuegos, Cuba, 144
cigar workers, 18
City Hotel (Baltimore), 35
City of Key West (schooner), 205
Civil War, 3, 6, 22, 28–29, 44, 57, 65, 78, 89, 108, 209
Clausen, Solomon, 23, 25
Clay, Henry, 31
Cleveland, Grover, 52, 57, 65, 67, 123, 125, 133, 158–59, 179; defends Cuba policy, 134; proclamation affirms neutrality, 34; refuses to pardon Wiborg, 118; warns citizens not to aid Cuban rebels, 124
Clipperton, Charles, 119
Colfax (revenue cutter), 79, 169
Collazo, Enrique, 23, 25–26, 58–59, 98, 102, 182–83
Collins & Company, 46
Colón, Panama, 90
Columbian Iron Works and Dry Dock (Baltimore), 180
Columbia School of Law, 20
Columbia Theatre (Washington, DC), 171
Commodore (expedition vessel, steamship), 79, 102, 108–9, 119, 126, 148, 161
Communipaw docks (New Jersey), 81
Communipaw ferry, 88
Competitor (expedition vessel, schooner), 105–7
Conception Island, 186–88
"conchs" (locals), 33, 147
Congosto, Jose, 40, 47–48, 50–52, 66–67, 78, 102, 119–20, 129–30, 186–87, 189
Conrad, Holmes, 116
Conservative Party (Spain), 41
Consumers Coal Company, 79
Cook, C. E., 119
Cornell College, 109
Corona, Patricio, 23
Cortes, the, 9, 77
Corwin (revenue cutter), 221
Costa Rica, 23, 222
Court Street Theater (Buffalo), 205
Cowley, George, 129, 130, 150–51
Cox, William H., 108–10, 114, 131
C. P. Raymond (tugboat), 112
Craig, W. W., 121–22, 154
Crane, Stephen, 161
Crooked Island Passage, Bahamas, 93
"Cuba Libre" ("Free Cuba"), 9, 40, 45, 55, 121, 154
Cuban clubs in America, 11, 18–19, 26, 42, 47, 49, 55, 106
Cuban economy, 206
Cuban Émigrés, 11, 19, 35, 39, 43, 48, 75, 87, 105, 153
Cuban military, 10, 11, 42–43, 58, 62, 66, 71, 73; fear of military state, 44

Cuban Province of Camagüey, 23, 58, 109, 113, 125, 131, 182, 203
Cuban Province of Oriente, 23, 43, 60, 165, 183
Cuban Province of Pinar del Río, 77, 105–6, 147–48
Cuban Province of Santa Clara, 11, 36, 71
Cuban Revolutionary Committee, 10, 12
Cuban Revolutionary Party, 18, 20, 22, 26, 34–35, 37, 41, 44, 57, 61, 63, 72, 74. *See also* Junta
Culmore (steamship), 172
Custom House (Charleston), 79
Custom House (Jacksonville), 113–14, 125
Custom House (New York), 60, 66, 82

Dahl, John, 23
Dallas, George M., 177, 197
"Damfoolitis," 108
Dauntless (expedition vessel, tugboat), 127–29, 146–48, 151, 153, 159, 166–68, 170, 173–76, 178, 181, 186–88, 203, 205
David I. Taylor (schooner), 4–5
Day, William R., 194, 196, 199, 201–2
de Céspedes, Carlos Manuel, 59–61, 183
DeCottes, George, 96
Deer (schooner), 89
de la Guardia, Angel, 25
Deland, Lorin and Margaret, 185–86
Delaware, 53, 84, 126, 136, 178, 190, 208, 213
Delaware Bay, 59, 101, 226
Delaware breakwater, 128, 163, 165, 221
Delaware River, 15, 50, 52, 92, 109, 120, 127–28, 165, 191, 224, 228
de Lôme, Enrique Dupuy, 33, 40, 50–51, 54, 57, 81, 104, 123, 134, 137, 182, 195–96, 199, 201; asserts Hart is behind *Laurada*'s Valencia trip, 138; claims US ignored thirteen tips on coming expeditions, 181; complains that US ignores Junta's violations of law, 124; criticizes Weyler to Madrid, 171; demands British government in Jamaica detain *Laurada*, 60; feels ignored by McKinley administration, 159; forwards intelligence on filibusters to Olney, 56; furious that *Bermuda* delivers García to Cuba, 101; insists US enforce its neutrality laws, 34; offers to expose Cuban clubs in US, 42; orders Philadelphia consul to crack down on filibusters, 47; resigns after his letter critical of McKinley is published, 202; says revolution would end if US enforces neutrality laws, 118; takes out warrant for Hart's arrest, 130
de Maritague, Henrico, 94, 104, 114, 126
Democratic Party (United States), 29–30, 55, 133
Denyse, Harry, 75
de Queralta, Fernando Lopez, 25
de Soto, Ralph, 52
Devine, James, 131–32
Diario de Marino, 76
Dickman, Charles B., 78, 109, 112–13, 120, 212, 222
Dinsmore, Hugh, 211
Dolphin (tugboat), 150, 152
Dominican Republic, 11, 26, 222
Donna T. Briggs (schooner), 163–64, 181
Dos Ríos, Cuba, 27
Dred Scott decision, 117
Dr. Esquinaldo's "infallible balm," 36
Dry Tortugas, FL, 143
Duany, Joaquin Castillo, 169, 212
Dugan, Charles, 230
Dunlop, Augustus P., 209, 217, 221
Dunn, Fat Jack, 144, 146
Duval County, FL, 94–96

Eastern Penitentiary (Philadelphia), 122, 185, 192, 198, 207–8, 213–14. *See also* Moyamensing
East River (New York), 74, 81–82, 88–89, 150, 186
Ebeneezer (schooner), 12
Echevarría, Francisco Sánchez, 50
Edmunds, Henry R., 130
Eldridge, Jeremiah L., 177, 192
Eleuthera, Bahamas, 4, 12
El Manifiesto de Montecristi, 26
Elmer, Horace, 175–76
El Yara, 47, 62
Emilio Nuñez & Co., 12
Empress (steamship), as original name of *Laurada*, 21, 28
Erie Basin (Brooklyn), 81

Escoto, Gustavo, 202
E. S. Johnson (schooner), 12
Espin, Luis, 150
Estrada Palma, Tomás, 43–46, 57, 62, 102, 105, 110–11, 119, 127–28, 171, 195, 200–203, 206, 233; cold shoulder from McKinley, 158; considers moving office from New York, 125; declines Hearst's offer, 180–81; establishes legation in Washington, 71–72; offers to resign, 74–76; Olney cuts meeting short, 67–68; resistance from the generals, 59, 182–83; supports pardon for Hart, 215
Ethelred (steamship), 172–73
expedition vessels: *Amadis*, 22–25, 124, 141, 182; *Baracoa*, 23, 25, 124, 141, 182; *Bermuda*, 81–84, 87, 91–93, 99–105, 119–20, 122, 129, 161, 164, 166–67, 173, 178, 190, 213, 215, 221–22, 224–30; *Commodore*, 79, 102, 108–9, 119, 126, 148, 161; *Competitor*, 105–7; *Dauntless*, 127–29, 146–48, 151, 153, 159, 166–68, 170, 173–76, 178, 181, 186–88, 203, 205; *George W. Childs*, 34–37, 41, 47, 105; *Horsa*, 21, 31–32, 64–67, 69, 73, 78, 85–87, 102, 116–19, 190, 213; *James W. Hawkins*, 75–76, 82, 87, 105, 112; *James Woodall*, 35–36, 41; *Lagonda*, 22–25, 124, 141, 182; *Lark*, 56–59, 182; *Leon*, 50, 61, 67, 69, 190, 213; *Silver Heels*, 185–90, 203; *Somers N. Smith*, 181; *Taurus*, 50–52, 54, 57; *Three Friends*, 96–98, 102, 113–14, 125–26, 131, 140–43, 146, 159, 166, 178, 182–83. See also *Laurada* (expedition vessel)

Fenn, Emory, 163–65
Fernandina Beach, FL, 22–26, 37, 104, 141–42, 166, 182, 203
Fiddler's Green, 90
Fifth Avenue Hotel (New York), 42–43
Figueredo, Fernando, 26, 42, 47
filibusters, 23, 33, 39, 42, 52–54, 56, 67, 117, 121, 125–26, 141, 158, 174, 181–82, 189–90, 202, 205, 212, 214, 234
Florence, SC, 169
Florida (steamship), first legal expedition to Cuba, 212
Florida Central and Peninsular Railroad, 203
Florida House Inn (Fernandina Beach), 22

Florida Keys, 40–41, 44, 123, 167, 191; Alligator, 97; Bahia Honda, 33, 57, 143, 175–76, 205; Cedar, 36, 97; Largo, 126; Marathon, 142; Matecumbe, 56; No Name, 146; Pine, 35
Florida Straits, 33, 35, 60
Florida Times-Union, 25, 106
Floyd, Jim, 175–76, 203
Flummer, Daniel J., 31, 33
Fonts y Sterling, Ernesto, 183
Fort Esperanza, Cuba, 106
Fort Lauderdale, FL, 173
Fort Sumter, SC, 60
Frank B. Hall (schooner), 226
Fred B. Dalzell (tugboat), 75, 112
Fredericksen, Emil, 66, 69
Freyre, Fernando, 183
Fritot, Alphonse, 47, 127, 141–42, 146, 169, 173–74, 203
Fritot, Henry, 47
Fruit War, 16
Fry, Joseph, 38–39
Fuller, Melville Westin, 117
Funston, Frederick, 131–32
Futuro Sociale, 136

Gage, Lyman, 159
Gamble, Charles, 300
García, Calixto, 9, 62–63, 74–76, 80–84, 87, 91–93, 99, 101–2, 112, 165, 212
García, Carlos, 74–75
Gardener's Ditch dock (New Jersey), 150
Garfield, James, 205
Gatling gun, 104
Gato, Eduardo H., 22, 56
Gaylor, Edwin S., 47, 50
George Dumois (steamship), 21
George W. Childs (expedition vessel, tugboat), 34–37, 41, 47, 105
Gettysburg, Battle of, 29
Gibraltar, *Laurada* at, 139
Gildea, William, 106
gold standard, 133
Gómez, Francisco, 134
Gómez, Máximo, 11, 23, 26–27, 44, 46, 51, 53, 58–59, 71, 77, 114–15, 131, 134, 141, 146–48, 182, 213
Gompers, Samuel, 56

Gorman, Jack, 143–44, 146–47
Governor's Island, NY, 112
Govin, Charles, 114–15
Graham, Malcolm, 46, 150
Gray, Commissioner, 112
Gray, George, 53, 129, 184, 209, 215
Gray Gables, 124
Great Britain, 67, 103, 161, 224
Great Egg Harbor Bay (New Jersey), 92
Gregorytown, Bahamas, 12
Gresham, Walter Q., 34
Griffing (captain of the *Lagonda*), 23–24
Griggs, John W., 215–17
grito, 26
Guáimaro, Cuba, 131
Guerra, Benjamin, 19, 34–35, 44, 57–58, 62, 81, 83–84
Guitéras, Juan, 47–48, 153
Gullón e Iglesias, Pio, 181–82, 189–90, 195–96, 199–200, 202
Gurly (steamship), 16, 21

Halifax, Nova Scotia, 89, 136
Hall, T. A., 23–24
Hambleton, B. E., 174–75
Hamilton (revenue cutter), 52, 165
Hampton Roads, VA, 34, 163
Harbeck's Stores, 60
Harlan, John Marshall, 117
Harlan & Hollingsworth Company, 163, 165, 178, 190
Harmon, Judson, 65–66
Harrison, Benjamin, 209
Harrity, William Francis, 30, 118
Hart, Catherine "Kate" Staylor, 6, 9, 13–17, 70, 151, 154, 156–57, 166, 214–15, 217, 219, 223–25, 230, 232
Hart, John D.: aboard the *Laurada*, 112, 127, 135, 160, 164, 172; adds Ker as business partner, 28; burial in Baltimore, 231; charters ships for Liberia settlers, 30–33, 78–79; death by apoplexy, 230; delivering García to Cuba, 79–83, 91–93, 99–100; early years in Baltimore, 3–9, 12; economic panic of 1893, 19–21; enters "Cuba trade," 39–40; financial problems, 69–70, 86–87, 118; first expeditions to Cuba, 49–51, 59; hires Captain Dynamite, 88, 91; importance to Cuban cause, 190; *Inquirer* tribute, 121, 213; marital problems, 70, 223–24; moves to Philadelphia, 14–17; new firm fails, 225; retrieves *Bermuda*, 220; sells to United Fruit, 222; visits Bulack, 155–56; volatile demeanor, 21, 61, 83–84, 102, 121–22, 130, 150, 225
Hart, John D., family: Ada Lee (daughter), 8, 15, 172–73, 231; Grace (daughter), 16, 70, 151, 154, 156, 223–24, 232; James H. (father), 3–6, 12–13, 230; Laura (daughter), 8, 9, 15, 156, 231; Levi (brother), 4; Rebecca (sister), 4; Susan Rayfield (mother), 4, 13–14, 231; Walter Jackson (son), 9, 13
Hart, John D., legal proceedings, 52–55, 66–67, 72–73, 84–87, 102; appeal denied, 196–98; appeals conviction, 184–85; arrested as flight risk, 173; begins prison term, 207–8; headed for prison, 177–78; indicted, 134–35; night in jail, 122; sentenced, 157; tried and convicted, 149–54; warrant issued, 129–30; Wiborg conviction upheld, 116–18
Hart, John D., presidential pardon, 209, 211; congressional petition, 213; full and unconditional pardon, 216; Hearst takes credit, 218; Kate campaigns for pardon, 215–16; Kate delivers pardon, 217, 219; Spanish spies and federal persecution, 59–61, 65–70, 119–20; threatens to quit Cuban trade, 119; ventures after pardon, 219
Hartley, Marcellus, 46
Hartley & Graham Company, 46, 150
Hartpence, J. W., 134
Harvard College, 45, 143, 160, 166, 185
Havana, Cuba, 12, 38, 57, 71, 77, 107, 110, 124, 146, 148, 156–58, 166, 187, 229, 233; expedition to, 168–72; *Maine* arrives in Havana harbor, 199, 200, 205; Morro Castle, 11, 47, 106, 170; new governor, 76, 78; riots over autonomy, 193, 195, 201; Rutherford B. Hayes, 85, 197; US fleet sails to, 212
Hearst, William Randolph: petitions readers for Hart's pardon, 209, 217; promotes Cuban revolution, 140–41, 147–48, 172,

180–81, 202, 210; purchases *New York Morning Journal*, 45–46; takes credit for Hart's pardon, 218
Helen H. Benedict (schooner), 75
Hell Gate, 89, 187
Henry (pilot on the *Horsa*), 38; *Madrid Heraldo*, 134, 201
Henry Brothers, 4–5, 13
Herbert, Hilary A., 34
Hernández, Charlie, 35, 37
Higginbotham, C. B., 24
Hoar, George F., 171
Holguin (steamship), 16, 21
Holttum, Charles H., 21
Hopkins Theater (Chicago), 205
Horsa (expedition vessel, steamship), 21, 31–32, 64–67, 69, 73, 78, 85–87, 102, 116–19, 190, 213
Horton, Hosea, 150
Hotchkiss cannon, 64, 75, 92, 104, 109, 127, 141, 144, 147, 160, 203, 209
Hoyo Colorado, Cuba, 78
Huau, Jose Alejandro, 47, 96, 104, 113–14, 125, 127, 140–42, 148, 167, 173
Hubbe, M., 22–23
Hudson (revenue cutter), 82–83, 112
Hudson, John F., 35–36
Hudson River, 163
Hughes, Sam, 14, 21, 50, 52, 59–61, 68–69, 72–73, 78–80, 84–85, 102, 135–36, 139, 162–66, 178, 208, 222, 224, 226–29; Margaret (wife), 135, 164, 229
H. U. Howes & Co., 15–16
hurricanes, 14, 59–60, 187, 224
Hyppolite, Louis Mondestin Florvil, 90

Inagua Island, Cuba, 98
Infanta Isabel (Spanish vessel), 33
Infanta Maria Theresa (Spanish vessel), 138
Ingham, Ellery P., 66, 69
International Migration Society, 30–31
intervention in Cuba, 135, 138–39, 179, 194, 201, 205, 208, 211–12
Itata (steamship), 73

Jackson, Andrew, 31
Jacksonville, FL, 22, 25, 37, 47, 94, 96–97, 104, 113, 121–22, 124–26, 140–42, 146, 148, 159, 168–69, 173–74, 189–90, 203, 205

Jacob's ladder, 83
Jamaica, 4, 7, 13–14, 19, 38, 52, 59–60, 65–66, 68–69, 118, 129–30, 151, 167, 173, 177–78, 215, 221–22, 224–26
James W. Hawkins (expedition vessel, steamship), 75–76, 82, 87, 105, 112
James Woodall (expedition vessel, steamship), 35–36, 41
Janney, Stuart S., 111, 114–15, 131–32, 206
Jefferson, Thomas, 52, 185, 197
Jennie Thomas (tugboat), 188
J. H. Hart & Son, 4
jingoes, 201
Johansen, Hans, 67, 69, 86, 117
John D. Long (schooner), 169
Johns Hopkins University, 111, 131
Johnston, Joseph E., 29
Jordan, Gratz C., 101, 127, 129, 150
Josephine B. (tugboat), 162–63
Jovellanos, Cuba, 78
J. S. Hoskins (schooner), 126
J. S. T. Stranahan (steam barge), 64, 69, 82, 83–84
Junta, 44, 61, 70–72, 88, 91, 110, 119, 123, 125–28, 133, 144, 159–61, 169, 182–83, 189, 193–94, 196, 200, 215; financing expeditions, 74–75, 79, 81, 83–84, 96, 125, 127, 150; generals want more support, 57–59; legal support, 53; propaganda, 10, 35, 45–46, 70–72, 98, 137, 173; relationships with McKinley cabinet, 133, 159, 178–79; rumors of leaks, 46, 57; success of expeditions, 101–2, 128, 166. *See also* Cuban Revolutionary Party; Rubens, Horatio
Juragua mines, Cuba, 27

Kane, Francis Fisher, 129–30
Kate Spencer (tugboat), 96, 104, 111, 114, 166
Keith, Minor, 222
Kemps, David, 96
Kemps, Georgiana Carolinas, 96
Kenilworth (steamship), 13–14
Ker, Herbert P., 31
Ker, Robert, 28
Ker, William W., 28–31, 39, 53–54, 66, 85, 108–9, 116, 120, 191, 207, 209, 214–15, 216, 219, 222–24, 229; as Hart's spokesman, 61, 78,

101, 107, 140, 172–73; criticizes Cleveland administration, 60, 65; defends Hart at trial, 55, 67–69, 102, 121–22, 129–30, 134–35, 149, 151–52, 154, 156, 177, 184, 197; defends Wiborg, 85–86, 116–19, 185
Kerr, John E., 61
Key West, FL, 18–20, 22–23, 26, 33–36, 47, 56, 94, 96, 98, 104, 106, 113–14, 124, 144, 146, 175–76, 188, 190, 194, 199, 205, 212
Key West *Equator-Democrat*, 114
Kilbreth, James F., 24, 112
Kilgore, W. F., 125–26
Killingsworth, Wiley Smith, 136–39
Kimball, George H., 22–23
Kingston, Jamaica, 7, 14, 59–60, 68
Klondike gold fields, 191, 208, 213, 219–20

"La Bayamesa," 144
Laborde, Alfredo, 106
Lagonda (expedition vessel), 22–25, 124, 141, 182
La Guerra Chiquita. See Little War
Lake, Simon, 180
Lannan, Hewson E., 51, 55, 129, 165
Lascelles & Co., 129
Latrobe, Ferdinand, 111
Latrobe, Osmun, Jr., 111, 114–15, 131, 206
Lark (expedition vessel, schooner), 56–59, 182
Laurada (expedition vessel), 29, 50, 52–54, 60–61, 68–69, 72–73, 78–79, 82, 84–85, 111–13, 119–22, 125–30, 135–40, 150–52, 156–57, 159–67, 172–73, 183, 190–92, 197, 208–9, 213, 221–23, 228, 230; as "a valiant ship," 136; "the famous," 219; "the gallant," 128; "the handsome," 220; "the lucky," 178
La Yaya, Cuba, 182
Leander V. Beebe (schooner), 75
Lee, Fitzhugh, 124, 156, 194
Le Havre, France, 62
Leon (expedition vessel, steamship), 50, 61, 67, 69, 190, 213
Lewis, Bill, 141–42, 144, 146
Lewis, John F., 151–52, 154
Liberal Party (Spain), 42, 189, 192
Liberia (steamship), 31
Liberia, Republic of, 30–33, 64, 78–79, 221
Liberty Island, NY, 81–82, 91, 111–12

Lillian B (tugboat), 111, 114
Lincoln, Abraham, 40, 122
Little War, 9, 62
Lizzie Henderson (steam lighter), 187
Locke, James W., 159, 168
Lodge, Henry Cabot, 178
Long, John D., 159, 199
Long Island Sound, 59, 74, 89, 187, 196
Lootz, Gjert, 23
Loudon Park Cemetery, 13, 230
Louisiana lottery, 100
Louisiana Tigers, 29
Luis, Joseph J., 35–36, 161

Macatee, C. A., 25
Maceo, Antonio, 11, 23, 26–27, 44, 50, 58, 67, 71, 77, 98, 105, 115, 125, 134, 148
Maceo, Jose, 114, 125
machetes, 36, 46, 51, 64, 97–98, 104, 106, 115, 127, 141, 158, 160, 170
Madrid, Spain, 136–38, 171, 187, 195, 200; reference to Spanish government, 10, 65, 71, 76–77, 107, 123–24, 134, 168, 179, 181, 185, 189, 194, 197, 199, 212, 215
Madrid *Imparcial*, 134
Majorca, Spain, 76
Malster, William T., 180
mambises, 11, 114
Manhattan (revenue cutter), 163
Mantell, D. E., 23
Mantilla, Manuel, 23
Marathon, FL, 142
Maria Cristina, Queen Regent, 195
Mariel, Cuba, 187
Maritime Exchange (New York), 60
Martha (tugboat), 126
Martí, Jose, 10–12, 18–26; death of, 27
Martínez Campos, Arsenio, 76–78
Mason, William, 171
Matamoros, Mexico, 89–90
Maull, Charles H., 54–55
Mauser rifle, 110, 142
Mayflower (ship), 121
Mayport, FL, 96, 126
McAleer, William, 30, 214
McCaldin Brothers (tugboat), 82
McCaldin Brothers, 82–83, 88
McCarthy, John H., 82–84, 111–12, 186, 224

McCook, John J., 206
McCready, Ernest W., 147–48
McCullough (revenue cutter), 147, 203
McKenna, Joseph, 159, 199
McKilleys, Michael J., 150
McKinley, William, 133, 158–59, 171–72, 178–79, 181, 187, 189, 195–96, 203, 233; capitalists demand war, 206; congressional petition to pardon Hart, 209, 213–14; criticized by Dupuy de Lôme, 202; dispatches *USS Maine* to Havana, 199–200; grants Hart full pardon, 216–17; joint resolution for intervention, 211–12; meets with Kate Hart, 215; meets with Spanish minister, 182; pressure from Congress, 201
McLane (revenue cutter), 33, 57, 176
Méndez, Cuban colonel, 173, 176
Menocal, Mario García, 63
Merchants Fruit Company, 16–17
Mertens, Theodore, 136–38
Mesagera (Spanish vessel), 106
Messina, Sicily, 136–37, 139
Meteor (tugboat), 51
Middlesbrough, England, 28
Miles, Nelson A., 199, 215
Milton, Owen, 106
Mobile, AL, 38
Molan, John J., 138
Monroe, James, 31
Monroe Doctrine, 66
Monrovia (steamship), 31
Montauk Point, NY, 75, 112
Montecristi, Dominican Republic, 26
Monzón, Juan, 106
Moore, Robert G., 226–27
Moore, William L., 22–24
Morales, Rafael, 142, 144–45
Morehead City, NC, 25
Morgan, John Tyler, 157, 171–72
Morrill (revenue cutter), 169
Morro Castle, Havana, 11, 47, 106, 170
Mosquito, The (Key West), 106
Mount Kilimanjaro, 160
Moyamensing, 122, 154, 198, 207, 217. *See* Eastern Penitentiary (Philadelphia)
mulatto, 9

Murphy, Edward, 91, 99, 101–2, 126, 128–30, 161, 164, 166–67, 178, 208, 213, 229
Murphy, W. P., 68, 72

Napa, CA, 42
Naples, Italy, 136
Narrows, The (New York), 83–84, 91, 112, 163
naval visits to Cuba, 199
Navassa Island, 114, 128–30, 135, 151–53
neutrality laws (United States), 24, 34, 38, 51–52, 54, 61, 66–67, 72–73, 78, 80, 84, 86, 90, 114, 116–18, 121, 123–24, 135, 140, 149, 181–82, 184, 189–90, 196–97, 208–9, 212–13, 215
New Haven, CT, 84, 113
newspaper competition, 35, 45–46, 50, 71–72, 120, 209, 217–18
New York, NY, 3, 10–11, 19–20, 22–23, 25–26, 31, 33, 35, 37, 42–43, 50, 52, 59–63, 68, 73–76, 88–89, 96, 102, 111, 118–21, 125, 128–29, 141–42, 146, 148, 160–62, 164–65, 168–69, 179, 181, 183, 186, 188–89, 191, 195, 201, 206, 212–14
New York Harbor, 62, 68, 82, 92
New York Herald, 20, 26, 34, 45, 52, 75, 107, 147–48, 195
New York Journal, 45, 77, 107, 140, 147, 172, 202, 209–10, 217
New York Sun, 45, 172
New York Times, 45, 84, 211
New York Tribune, 45
New York World, 23–24, 45–46, 107, 172, 206
Newitt, Harvey, 121
Nicaragua, 14, 24, 69, 222
Nicholson, Thomas H., 51
Nipe Bay, Cuba, 164
nolle prosequi, 212
Norfolk, VA, 14, 187
Nuevas Grandes, Cuba, 113, 203
Nuevitas, Cuba, 102, 109, 170
Nuñez, Emilio, 11–12, 20, 47, 59, 62, 102–3, 153, 229, 233; criticism from Collazo, 58; director of expeditions, 37, 44, 46, 48, 50–51, 57, 96, 110, 119, 125, 147, 166, 169, 173, 178; enlists Hart, 39–40, 184; legal problems, 121, 129, 148, 150, 175–76, 212; leaks outsmarting spies, 81, 99, 168, 203;

moves planning to Jacksonville, 140–41, 146; notable expeditions, 92–93, 99–100, 160–61, 170, 187, 205; outsmarting spies and leaks, 81, 99, 168, 203; planning expeditions with Hart, 63, 72, 76, 80, 126; scrounging for vessels, 33–34, 74–75, 105–7, 180–81, 185–87

O'Brien, Fisher, 162–63
O'Brien, Johnny "Captain Dynamite," 88–93, 98–104, 125–28, 140–42, 144–48, 161–66, 168–70, 173–76, 181, 186–89, 203, 206, 212, 229
O'Donnell, Carlos, 179–80
Ocean City, NJ, 92
Olga Steamship Company, 225, 228
Olivette (schooner), 146
Olney, Richard, 34, 40–42, 51, 54, 56–57, 60, 67–68, 81, 101, 118, 123–24, 134, 137–38, 159–60
Orange County, NY, 43
Orange Key, Bahamas, 188
Osgood, Winchester Dana, 108–10, 114, 131–33, 206
Ostend Manifesto, 33
Otto, Julius, 176

Pagliuchi, Mike, 141, 144, 205
Paine, Ralph, 141–42, 145–47
Paine, Samuel Delahaye, 141
Palermo, Sicily, 136–37, 139
Palm Beach, FL, 169
Panama, 90–91
Panic of 1893, 20
Paris, France, 43, 62–63, 110, 125
Parsons, Joe, 95
Patria, 18, 26, 45
Paul, S. W., 24
peace protocol, 233
Peanut Club, 46
Pedersen, Jens P., 67, 69, 86, 117
Peña, Braulio, 102, 109
peninsulares, 194, 212
Penns Grove, NJ, 51, 84
Pennsylvania National Guard, 108
Pennsylvania Railroad, 150, 209
Pensacola, FL, 190
Pepper, Charles M., 193, 195

Philadelphia, PA, 3, 12, 14–15, 17, 19–20, 28–31, 34–35, 40, 47–50, 52, 53, 55, 59, 61, 64–66, 69–70, 76, 78, 80, 84–85, 92, 102, 104, 109–11, 118–20, 122, 124, 126, 129, 131, 134, 138, 149, 151–53, 157, 160, 162–63, 165–66, 168, 173, 184, 186, 189, 211, 213–14, 217, 222–26, 228, 231
Philadelphia and Reading Railroad, 20, 92, 149
Philadelphia City Council, 76, 118
Philadelphia Inquirer, 16, 21, 29, 55, 84, 120, 157, 194, 207, 213–14
Philippine Islands, 189
P. H. Wise (tugboat), 187
Pier 11 (Philadelphia), 15, 31, 39, 52, 59, 61, 78, 111, 121–22, 163
Pier 19 (Philadelphia), 223–24, 227–28
Pikesville rye whiskey, 156
Pinkerton, Allan, 40
Pinkerton National Detective Agency, 40, 47, 50–51, 53, 56, 68, 78, 82, 84, 92, 101–3, 109, 129–30, 141, 151, 162, 168, 186, 191
Pirate (steamship), 13–14
Playa de Nibujón, Cuba, 50
Plessy v. Ferguson, 117–18
Plough, David, 211, 217
Poe, Edgar Allan, 208
Polk, James K., 33
Porcellian Club of Harvard, 160, 166
Port Antonio, Jamaica, 4, 7, 12, 20–21, 26, 64, 112, 119–20, 126, 128, 167, 172–73, 213, 221, 227
Porter, John Addison, 217
Port Morris, NY, 74
Portuondo, Rafael, 114, 183
Portuondo family, 12, 39, 47
Poyo, José Dolores, 47
presidential campaign of 1896, 133, 171
presidential pardons: for Hart, 172, 209, 213–19, 223; for Wiborg, 118, 135
Preston, A. W., 222
Princeton University, 109
Progreso, Mexico, 36
propaganda: Cuban, 10, 35, 45–46, 70–72, 98, 137, 173; Spanish, 71–72, 76
prostitutes, 110
public opinion: adulation of filibusters, 103, 118, 120–21, 191; favors clemency for Hart,

215; outcry over Hart conviction, 157–58, 178; outrage over sinking of the *Maine*, 205, 211; sympathy for Cuba, 120, 134, 206
Puerto Cortes, Honduras, 100, 104
Pulitzer, Joseph, 23, 46

Quaker City Fruit, 21
quarantine, 113
Quay, Matthew Stanley, 209, 211, 213–15
Quesada, Augustin, 106
Quesada y Aróstegui, Gonzalo, 19–20, 25–26, 62, 68, 125, 193, 200, 213; feuds with Guerra, 44, 57–58; impresses McKinley, 178; Junta's man in Washington, 71–72, 171, 178, 183, 195; lobbies for Hart's pardon, 209, 215; messages the press, 46, 98; supports young American volunteers, 110–11
Quinlan, Peter, 187–88

Race Street dock (Philadelphia), 15, 61, 103–4, 119–21, 129
racial divide in Cuba, 11, 18, 26, 123, 179, 201, 212
Raleigh Hotel (Washington), 71
Read, John R., 66, 73
Reconcentrado policy, 133, 200. *See also* Weyler y Nicolau, Valeriano
Reed, Thomas B., 172
Reformist Party (Spain), 76
Reick, William C., 195–96
Reilly, Edward G., 104–5, 119, 121–22
Reina Mercedes (Spanish vessel), 215
Remington Arms Company, 25, 38, 46, 49, 106
reporters, 35, 46, 52, 61, 63, 65, 75, 79, 84–86, 92, 101, 106, 120, 122, 146–48, 155, 163, 214
Republican party (United States), 55, 133, 171–72, 195, 201, 209
Republic of Cuba, 103, 212
revenue cutters: *Bear*, 221; *Boutwell*, 25, 79, 104, 113–14, 125–26, 142, 148, 166; *Chandler*, 82, 112, 186–87; *Colfax*, 79, 169; *Corwin*, 221; *Hamilton*, 52, 165; *Hudson*, 82–83, 112; *Manhattan*, 163; *McCullough*, 147, 203; *McLane*, 33, 57, 176; *Morrill*, 169; *Richard K. Fox*, 150; *USS Newark*, 142; *USS Raleigh*, 34, 142; *Winona*, 56, 175

Revenue Cutter Service, 33–34, 38, 42, 50, 60, 73, 126, 168, 190
Richard K. Fox. See revenue cutters
Río San Juan, Cuba, 146
Rockhill, W. W., 138
Rodríguez, Alejandro, 170
Rodríguez, Jose Maria, 25, 35–36
Rogers, J. H., 25
Rojas, Carlos, 203
Roloff, Carlos, 23, 25, 35–36, 44, 126, 129, 150, 152, 161, 163, 165, 181, 193, 212
Roosevelt, Theodore, 160, 178, 201
Root, Elihu, 20, 179
Rowena (schooner), 37
Rubens, Horatio, 19, 20, 26, 44, 58, 125, 127; attorney for the Junta, 53, 84, 183–84; loyal to Quesada, 57; peanut club for the press, 46; revealed Dupuy de Lôme letter, 201–2; Ricardo Ruiz, 157–58; ties to Elihu Root, 179
Ruz, Juan Fernandez, 74–75, 112–13

Sabanilla, Cuba, 78
Sagasta, Práxedes Mateo, 181, 189, 193–94, 201
Sampson, William T., 212, 215, 222
Sánchez, Serafín, 23
San Clemente Island, CA, 73
Sandy Hook, NJ, 64, 162–63, 187
San Francisco, CA, 45, 219, 222
Sanguily, Julio, 22, 213
Santa Clara, Cuba, 71
Santa Clara Mountains, 144
Santa de Argo Niaco, Cuba, 128
Santa Marta, Columbia, 82
Santana, Brig. Gen., 110
Santiago, Cuba, 23, 27, 39, 65, 105, 125, 128, 199, 215, 222, 233
Santo Domingo, Dominican Republic, 23, 35, 148
Savannah, GA, 25, 30–31, 33, 188
schooners: *Alicia B. Crosby*, 75; *Antoinette*, 57; *Ardell*, 97; *B. A. Wagner*, 12; *Bertha Ellen*, 6; *City of Key West*, 205; *City of Mexico*, 90; *Competitor*, 105–7; *David I. Taylor*, 4–5; *Deer*, 89; *Donna T. Briggs*, 163–64, 181; *Ebeneezer*, 12; *E. S. Johnson*, 12; *Frank B. Hall*, 226; *Helen H. Benedict*, 75; *Jennie Thomas*, 188; *John D. Long*,

169; *J. S. Hoskins*, 126; *Lark*, 56–59, 182; *Leander V. Beebe*, 75; *Olivette*, 146; *Rowena*, 37; *Silver Heels*, 185–90, 203; *Stephen Mallory*, 97; *Worden and Evans*, 12
Scott, William K., 208, 219
Scribner's Magazine, 218
Seattle, WA, 208–9, 219–21
Secret Service, 168, 203
Seventy-Third Regiment Pennsylvania Volunteers, 28–29
Seward, J. H. & Co., 136–39
Sherman, John, 158–59, 171, 178–81, 189–90
Sherman, William T., 29, 180
Shields, John A., 84
shipbuilding industry (New York), 3, 89
Shoreham Hotel (Atlantic City), 16, 225
Sif (steamship), 21
Sigsbee, Charles D., 194
Silva, Charlie, 174–75, 181
Silver Heels (expedition vessel, schooner), 185–90, 203
silver standard, 133
Sims-Dudley dynamite gun, 160
Smith, James, 130, 150
Smith, Joseph H., 224
Smith, S. Redmon, 129
Smith, W. H., 225
Smith, William Alden, 201
smokeless stoking, 93
snakes, 35, 146
Society Hermanas de Martí, 54, 153
Sombrero Light, 142
Somers N. Smith (expedition vessel), 181
Sooy, Nicholas J., 150
Soto, Marco Aurelio, 90
South Street Wharf (Baltimore), 3, 14
Spanish spies, 38, 40, 50, 52, 76–77, 82, 92, 102–3, 109, 114–15, 118–19, 125, 136, 166, 168, 186, 191, 203, 209, 227
Spanish treachery, 57, 99, 144, 166, 169, 206
Spanish troops, 33, 71, 76–77, 194–95, 105, 110, 128, 165, 194
Spanish vessels: *Alphonse III*, 76; *Infanta Isabel*, 33; *Infanta Maria Theresa*, 138; *Mesagera*, 106; *Reina Mercedes*, 215; *Tornado*, 38–39; *Vizcaya*, 200; *Vulcana*, 138

Stanton, Frank W., 15
starvation in Cuba, 77, 200
Staten Island, NY, 64, 186
steamships: *Atlantic City*, 93; *Baracoa*, 23, 25, 124, 141, 182; *Bermuda*, 81–84, 87, 91–93, 99–105, 119–20, 121, 122, 129, 161, 164, 166–67, 173, 178, 190, 213, 215, 221–22, 224–30; *Bernard*, 21; *Biscayne*, 173–76; *Bowden*, 164; *Braganza*, 21, 28, 172; *Champagne*, 62; *Commodore*, 79, 102, 108–9, 119, 126, 148, 161; *Culmore*, 172; *Ethelred*, 172–73; *George Dumois*, 21; *Gurly*, 16, 21; *Holguin*, 16, 21; *Horsa*, 21, 31–32, 64–67, 69, 73, 78, 85, 87, 102, 116–19, 190, 213; *Itata*, 73; *James W. Hawkins*, 75–76, 82, 87, 105, 112; *James Woodall*, 35–36, 41; *Kenilworth*, 13–14; *Leon*, 21, 50, 61, 67, 69, 190, 213; *Liberia*, 31; *Monrovia*, 31; *Pirate*, 13–14; *Sif*, 21; *Triton*, 187–88. See also *Empress* (steamship); expedition vessels; *Florida* (steamship)
Stephen Mallory (schooner), 97
Stevens House Hotel (New York), 88
St. John's River, FL, 95–97
St. Mary's River, FL, 24, 203
St. Simons Island, GA, 125
Strand, the (Jersey Shore), 48
Supreme Court (United States), 68, 86, 124, 130, 149, 153, 197; Justice Harlan dissents, 117; reverses *Three Friends* decision, 158–59; upholds Wiborg decision, 116–18
surfboats, 36, 64–65, 75, 92, 98, 104–5, 113, 130, 144
Swansea, Wales, 136
Svanoe, Frederick, 50, 67, 213
Symington, W. Stuart, Jr., 111

Tacoma (WA) Daily News, 220
Tallabacoa River, Cuba, 36
Tammany Hall, 160
Tampa, FL, 18–19, 24, 26, 33, 42, 56, 59, 97, 104, 106, 111, 146, 173, 190, 203, 212
Taurus (expedition vessel, tugboat), 50–52, 54, 57
Taylor, Hannis, 138
Teller, Henry M., 211
Ten Years' War, 9–11, 18–19, 36, 43–44, 47, 59, 63, 74, 76, 106, 142
Thompson, Peter, 185

Thom School of Navigation, 89
Thornhill, David C., 186
Three Friends (expedition vessel, tugboat), 96–98, 102, 113–14, 125–26, 131, 140–43, 146, 159, 166, 178, 182–83
Toms River, NJ, 67
Tornado (Spanish vessel), 38–39
Townsend, George F., 129–30
Travelers Hotel (Jacksonville), 25
treasury agents, 168
Trinidad, Cuba, 36
Tuckahoe, NJ, 92–93
tugboats: *Alexander Jones*, 169–70; *Cham*, 64; *C. P. Raymond*, 112; *Dauntless*, 127–29, 146–48, 151, 153, 159, 166–68, 170, 173–76, 178, 181, 186–88, 203, 205; *Dolphin*, 150, 152; *Fred B. Dalzell*, 75, 112; *George W. Childs*, 34–37, 41, 47, 105; *Josephine B.*, 162–63; *Kate Spencer*, 96, 104, 111, 114, 166; *Lillian B*, 111, 114; *Martha*, 126; *McCaldin Brothers*, 82; *Meteor*, 51; *P. H. Wise*, 187; *Taurus*, 50–52, 54, 57; *Three Friends*, 96–98, 102, 113–14, 125–26, 131, 140–43, 146, 159, 166, 178, 182–83; *W. J. McCaldin*, 82–83. *See also* expedition vessels
Twenty-Third Virginia Infantry, 6
214th Pennsylvania, 109
Tybee Island, GA, 25, 187
Tyler, John, 49, 157

Union Metallic Cartridge Company, 46
United Fruit Company, 21, 222
United States v. the Laurada, 68
University of Pennsylvania, 12, 133
US Congress, 72, 134, 171–72, 209, 214; joint resolution for intervention, 212; Quesada lobbies, 183; sentiment for intervention, 172, 201; war hawks in, 157–58, 171, 211
US Court of Appeals, 177, 184–85, 191–92, 196, 207, 216
US Department of Justice, 116, 190
US Department of the Treasury, 24, 33–34, 52, 56, 60, 111, 113, 126, 129, 146, 159, 182, 190; agents, 25, 168. *See also* Revenue Cutter Service
US Navy, 34, 78, 143, 159, 180, 182, 186, 190, 194, 199, 201, 205, 211
USS *Annapolis* (navy gunboat), 182, 188

USS *Constitution* (frigate), 120
USS *Eagle* (torpedo boat), 213
USS *Maine* (battleship), 143, 145, 182, 201, 212, 228; dispatched to Havana, 194, 199, 200; explodes in Havana Harbor, 205–7; public indignation, 209–10; report says mine triggered explosions, 211
USS *Marblehead* (cruiser), 147, 175–76, 212
USS *Montgomery* (cruiser), 180, 182, 188, 199
USS *Newark* (revenue cutter), 142
USS *Raleigh* (revenue cutter), 34, 142
US State Department, 33–34, 51–52, 107, 137–38, 189, 196, 199, 201
USS *Vesuvius* (cruiser), 166, 168, 188, 203
USS *Virginius* (steamer), 38–39
US War Department, 211

Valencia, Spain, 41, 136–39
Valera, Juan, 41
Vamoose (steam yacht), 147
Vancouver, Canada, 219
Vandegrift, Lewis C., 53, 129, 165–66, 178
Vandiver, John T., 138
Vera Cruz, Mexico, 91
Verne, Jules, 4, 180
Vidal, Leyte, 104
Vine Street wharf (New Jersey), 119
Vizcaya (Spanish vessel), 200
Vogler, John G., 224–25
von Bismarck, Otto, 41
Vuelta Abajo, Cuba, 59
Vulcana (Spanish vessel), 138

Wales, Leonard Eugene, 53–55
Walsh, Mike, 143–48
Washington Post, 72
Washington Star, 41, 72, 193, 195
Watkins universal shipbrokers code, 100
Watling's Island, 161, 164
Webster, Daniel, 31
Weed, David S., 23
Weinert, William W., 191
West India Fruit Company, 222, 227
Weyler y Nicolau, Valeriano, 76–78, 106–7, 133–34, 194–95, 206; embarrassed by O'Brien, 166, 170–71, 173; policy of *reconcentrado*, 157, 179; recalled by Madrid, 189, 193

White, Frank W., 220–21
Wiborg, Jacob Henry Jasper, 21, 31–32, 64–66, 102, 116–19, 135, 213, 222, 226, 229; appeals court upholds conviction, 118; arrested, 67; freed from prison, 185; tried and convicted, 85–86
Wiborg v. United States, 116–17, 124, 130, 149, 153–54, 190, 197
Williams, Ramon O., 106
Wilmington, DE, 50–55, 57, 68–69, 84, 129, 136, 165, 178, 190–91, 208, 213, 221
Wilmington, NC, 78–79, 168–69
Wilmington & New Bern Railway, 169
Winona (revenue cutter), 56, 175
W. J. McCaldin (tugboat), 82–83
Woodbine, Georgia, 127
Woodford, Stewart L., 179, 181, 195
Worden and Evans (schooner), 12
World's Columbian Exposition (Chicago), 42

Yara district, Cuba, 47, 62
yellow fever, 113
Yellow Press, xv, 206, 210
Yucatán Channel, 143, 146
Yukon River, 209
Yulee, FL, 142

Zafra tax, 58
Zanjón, Pact of, 9
Zapadine Bay, AK, 221

ABOUT THE AUTHOR

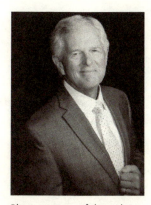

Photo courtesy of the author

James W. Miller is retired athletics director at the University of New Orleans. Prior to his tenure there, he spent eleven years as a newspaper reporter and twenty-one years in the NFL, where he worked for the New Orleans Saints, Buffalo Bills, and Chicago Bears. He is author of *Integrated: The Lincoln Institute, Basketball, and a Vanished Tradition.*